D0065733

THE KNOW-IT-ALLS

THE KNOW-IT-ALLS

The Rise of Silicon Valley as a Political Powerhouse and Social Wrecking Ball

NOAM COHEN

NEW YORK
LONDON

Published in the United States by The New Press, New York, 2017
Distributed by Perseus Distribution

ISBN 978-1-62097-210-6 (hc)
ISBN 978-1-62097-211-3 (e-book)
CIP data is available

The New Press publishes books that promote and enrich public discussion and understanding of the issues vital to our democracy and to a more equitable world. These books are made possible by the enthusiasm of our readers; the support of a committed group of donors, large and small; the collaboration of our many partners in the independent media and the not-for-profit sector; booksellers, who often hand-sell New Press books; librarians; and above all by our authors.

www.thenewpress.com

Book design and composition by Bookbright Media
This book was set in Minion and Replica Bold

Printed in the United States of America

10 9 8 7 6 5 4 3 2 1

Why, anybody can have a brain. That's a very mediocre commodity. Every pusillanimous creature that crawls on the Earth or slinks through slimy seas has a brain.

—*The Wizard of Oz*

The end of man is knowledge, but there is one thing he can't know. He can't know whether knowledge will save him or kill him. He will be killed, all right, but he can't know whether he is killed because of the knowledge which he has got or because of the knowledge which he hasn't got and which if he had it, would save him.

—*All the King's Men*

CONTENTS

THE KNOW-IT-ALLS

INTRODUCTION

"To Serve Man"

In a memorable *Twilight Zone* episode, "To Serve Man," aliens land on Earth. These aliens, the Kanamits, nine feet tall and topped with massive heads, say they've come in peace and intend to share their superior technology to benefit humanity. Immediately, they are true to their word. Barren soil in Argentina produces grain; mysterious force fields protect each nation's borders, rendering the nuclear arms race irrelevant. And when the suspicious Soviets raise concerns, the Kanamits' chief gladly takes and passes a lie detector test. A little while later, when the aliens suggest that Earthlings load up in a flying saucer to see the wonders on the Kanamits' home planet, few question it. There are lines to get a precious seat.

The story is told in flashback through the eyes of one of those passengers, Michael Chambers, an American code breaker assigned to decipher a manuscript accidentally left behind by the Kanamit leader. A member of Chambers's decryption team succeeds in piecing together the manuscript's reassuring title, "To Serve Man," and the world is confirmed in its belief that the aliens' intentions are good. Chambers rushes onto the Kanamit bandwagon as one of the last passengers aboard. Yet just as Chambers walks up the ramp of the aliens' ship, a voice below reveals the bitter truth about "To Serve Man": "It's a cookbook!" At the end, a Kanamit is heard over a loudspeaker encouraging Chambers to be sure to eat all of his supper.[1]

This story is flamboyantly absurd science fiction: How can you crack a code without a key to work off of? And would the Kanamit language really have the exact same double meaning for the phrase *to serve*? Furthermore, why would aliens come all this way to harvest people instead of something truly tasty like cattle or tuna or truffles? "To Serve Man" nonetheless manages to convey an important message: it is wise to be suspicious of those who claim to pursue selflessly the prosperity of others even as they pursue their own. Also, those dual meanings of *serve* may reveal a universal truth, in that purporting to act in service of others without their consent necessarily involves manipulation, grooming, and exploitation.

Silicon Valley surely is unrivaled in the American economy in its claims to "serve mankind." So much so, in fact, that the satirical TV show *Silicon Valley* has a running joke that whenever a start-up founder is introduced, no matter how absurdly technical his project may be, he assures the audience that he is committed to "making the world a better place." Paxos algorithms for consensus protocols . . . making the world a better place.[2] Minimal message-oriented transport layers . . . making the world a better place.[3] Yet strip away the satire, and you find that Google works from the same playbook. The company assures us that it collects and stores so much personal information about its users to better serve them. That way, Google sites can remember what language you speak, identify which of your friends are online, suggest new videos to watch, and be sure to display only the advertisements "you'll find most useful."[4] Even when Google is being paid by businesses to show you ads, it's really thinking about making your life better!

Facebook similarly insists that it acts in the best interest of humanity, no matter how its actions may be perceived. For example, there is the Free Basics project, which provides a Facebook-centric version of the Internet for cell phone users who cannot afford access to the actual Internet.[5] Critics in India objected to Facebook's apparent largesse, seeing the program as pushing a ghettoized, fake-Internet experience for poor people merely to keep its audience growing. Facebook's chief executive, Mark Zuckerberg, didn't back down, however, describing the dispute as a choice between right and wrong, between raising hundreds of millions of people out of poverty through even limited Internet access or leaving them to suffer without any access at all. He made a public appeal by video, which concluded, "History tells us that helping people is always a better path then shutting them out. We have a historic opportunity to improve the lives of billions of people. Let's take that opportunity. Let's connect them."[6]

Certainly, from time immemorial, moguls have believed that their own prosperity must be good for all of society, but only the recent batch of Silicon Valley entrepreneurs have acted as if money were an unanticipated byproduct of a life devoted to bettering mankind. Marc Andreessen, the Silicon Valley venture capitalist who serves on Facebook's board, was scathing when he learned that the Indian government had sided with the critics and blocked Free Basics. The government's decision was "morally wrong" and punishing to the world's poorest people, Andreessen wrote on Twitter, offering yet another example of how India has been on the wrong track since its people kicked out their British overlords. "Anti-colonialism has been economically catastrophic for the Indian people for decades. Why stop now?" he asked sarcastically. Andreessen quickly apologized when he saw the furious response to those comments, particularly within India,[7] but they nonetheless proved that he belonged among a tiny class of public figures who would have the self-assurance to make such a statement in the first place, to trash Indian democracy and self-determination in defense of their own belief systems and their own particular business models.

The Know-It-Alls is the story of these powerful, uber-confident men, starting with Andreessen, who helped nurture the World Wide Web to prosperity in the 1990s before switching to investing. It ends with Zuckerberg, who has the most ambitious plans for linking the world within his own commercial online platform. Along with Andreessen and Zuckerberg there's a bevy of tech Internet billionaires, including Jeff Bezos of Amazon, Sergey Brin and Larry Page of Google, Reid Hoffman of LinkedIn, and the early Facebook investor Peter Thiel. They are a motley crew—some, like Hoffman, are outwardly friendly, cuddly even, while others, like his good friend Thiel, cultivate an aura of detachment and menace. Some, like Brin and Page, one suspects would prefer to be left alone with their computers, while others, like

Bezos or Zuckerberg, seek the limelight. Some were born to program, others to make money. But they share common traits: each is convinced of his own brilliance and benevolence, as demonstrated by his wildly successful companies and investments, and lately each is looking beyond his own business plans to promote a libertarian blueprint for us all.

Collectively, these Silicon Valley leaders propose a society in which personal freedoms are near absolute and government regulations wither away, where bold entrepreneurs amass billions of dollars from their innovations and the rest of us struggle in a hypercompetitive market without unions, government regulations, or social-welfare programs to protect us. They tap into our yearning for a better life that technology can bring, a utopia made real, yet one cannot escape the suspicion that these entrepreneurs may not fully appreciate what it means to be human. That is, not just to be a human individual—the unit that libertarianism is so obsessed with—but to be part of a family, a community, a society.

The feminist political theorist Susan Moller Okin argued convincingly that libertarianism requires precisely this kind of obtuseness. In the libertarian fantasy, men magically arrive at adulthood ready to remake the world: How? Raised by whom? If advocates for extreme individualism actually had to acknowledge the work and sacrifice of women to bear and nurture children, Okin contended, as well as the assistance of society in children's upbringing, their arguments would lose all force. No one would then be able to say with a straight face that whatever he has is the product of his own hard work and should be his alone to control. "Behind the individualist façade of libertarianism," she concluded, "the family is assumed but ignored."[8]

Once women, family, and society are pushed to the side, however, individuals are free to duke it out for life's spoils unencumbered by social obligations, as Hoffman explains in his business advice book *The Start-up of You*. "For anything desirable, there's competition," he writes. "A ticket to a championship game, the arm of an attractive man or woman, admission to a good college, and every solid professional opportunity." The only sensible response, he concludes, is to labor as a high-risk, high-reward "start-up of you"[9]:

> The conditions in which entrepreneurs start and grow companies are the conditions we all now live in when fashioning a career. You never know what's going to happen next. Information is limited. Resources are tight. Competition is fierce. The world is changing. And the amount of time you spend at any one job is shrinking. This means you need to be adapting all the time. And if you fail to adapt, no one—not your employer, not the government—is going to catch you when you fall.[10]

As the harsh world dreamed up by these wealthy, powerful Silicon Valley leaders gains traction, *The Know-It-Alls* becomes the story not just of their lives but of ours, too.

Silicon Valley never would have had the wealth and power to shape America's values had there not been a World Wide Web to make computers so useful and relevant to daily life. When the British physicist Tim Berners-Lee first brought the Web into existence some twenty-five years ago at the CERN laboratory in Switzerland, he imagined he was creating a decentralized network for people to collaborate through their computers, with commerce low among his priorities.[11] Berners-Lee's original vision of a small-scale, almost anarchic Web was shed nearly immediately as Netscape, the Silicon Valley company Andreessen cofounded after graduating from college in the Midwest, took the lead in the Web's development. Netscape's early emphasis on commerce and creating a passive, user-friendly experience led the Web to where it is today—wildly popular around the world, with a few companies able to apply a chokehold on how we access and use the Internet. In search, there is Google. In commerce, Amazon. In social networking, Facebook.

Yes, despite its European parentage, the Web would be a Bay Area baby. Vital new tools for navigating within and between sites, for searching through oodles of digital information, and for sharing opinions and photos with friends and acquaintances all grew to maturity within Silicon Valley's start-up culture. Businesses based on those tools soon directed a sizable portion of the nation's wealth toward the

West Coast, as if the United States were a pool table tilted so the balls wound up in the left side-pocket. The wealth that has since accumulated around San Francisco has largely gilded over its "flower power" reputation, leaving the city inhospitable to anyone but the highest-paid programmers, who are shuttled to and from their corporate campuses on luxury buses.[12] Street protests against those buses, which serve as a private mass transit system, have helped highlight the great wealth disparity in the Bay Area, but there have been other extravagances as well. The tech investor Sean Parker staged a multimillion-dollar wedding in a redwood forest landscaped to look like Middle-earth of *The Lord of the Rings*.[13] The Silicon Valley venture capitalist Vinod Khosla caused an outcry by demanding that the state pay him $30 million before he would give the public access to Martins Beach, which sits below his property.[14] And there was the lavish, Versailles-themed fortieth-birthday party in Los Angeles for David Sacks, a former PayPal executive and successful start-up founder, who to his credit at least tried to stop his guests from sharing the gaudy details through social media.[15]

The consequences of Silicon Valley values went from classless to catastrophic, however, during the recent presidential election. A near-majority of the electorate succumbed to Donald Trump's appeal to bring back a less convulsive past, complete with its unchecked racism and misogyny, and many of us experienced for the first time the fragility of our society after so much Internet-based "disruption." America in 2016 lacked the stabilizing influences of traditional news-gathering organizations and community groups, vibrant local businesses, strong labor unions, aggressive government regulations, and engaged political parties, each of which had been undercut by Silicon Valley businesses and the libertarian principles of their founders. What remained were a few distant tech giants and a collection of angry individuals, abandoned by the global economy and lashing out at remote forces—immigrants, Wall Street bankers, trade agreements, political correctness—without serious intent. Instead, these voters empowered a cynical blowhard who promised, improbably, "I alone can fix it."

Among the circumstances for Trump supporters to rebel against were the Silicon Valley insta-billionaires themselves, who had helped bring about so much of the country's social disruption. The rapid rise of these young entrepreneurs sent an unmistakable signal that income inequality would only be getting worse. At the same time, the apparent requirement that a successful entrepreneur attend the right school and have the right backers revealed that the Silicon Valley start-up system wasn't a meritocracy, as is so often proclaimed, but was rigged, to quote the great man himself. Take the case of the photo-sharing service Instagram, which was sold for $1 billion to Facebook barely two years after being launched. One cofounder, Kevin Systrom, a twenty-eight-year-old Stanford graduate, kept 40 percent of the proceeds of the sale, with a few prominent VC firms and early investors taking big cuts as well.[16] At the time of the sale, in April 2012, Instagram employed all of thirteen workers. How any of this could help sustain a happy, productive society was a mystery.

There was a final gift from Silicon Valley during the 2016 election: the radical insistence that what was expressed on the Web should be unregulated, which allowed the hate and abuse of the Trump campaign to fester and then spread. On Twitter, Trump's followers and Trump himself were permitted to intimidate critics, particularly women and minorities.[17] This relaxed approach from Twitter was matched by Facebook and Google, which served their users made-up news about the election as long as the articles remained popular. Freedom of speech apparently trumped all other values as Google, Facebook, and Twitter encouraged the public to stew in their own hateful juices and profited handsomely in the process.

One Silicon Valley figure unafraid to explore the natural affinity between Silicon Valley values and Trump values is Thiel, who saw Trump as a Silicon Valley–style man of action and vision, a larger-than-life agent of disruption. "When Donald Trump asks us to Make America Great Again, he's not suggesting a return to the past," Thiel explained in his speech to the delegates gathered at the Republican National Convention in Cleveland. "He's running to lead us back to that bright future." That was the point, wasn't it? To apply the winning, destructive, forward-thinking vision of Silicon Valley to the rest of America. As Thiel boasted in that same address, "Where I work in Silicon Valley, it's hard to see where America has gone wrong. My industry has made a lot of progress in computers and in software, and, of course, it's made a lot of money. But Silicon Valley is a small place. Drive out to Sacramento, or even just across the bridge to Oakland,

and you won't see the same prosperity. That's just how small it is."[18] Imagine if everything in the American economy worked like Silicon Valley! This was the glorious future Thiel saw in a Trump presidency.

Thiel's high-profile endorsement of Trump certainly raised the hackles of his peers, who generally supported Hillary Clinton for president, seeing her as the continuation of the Obama administration's Silicon Valley–friendly policies on immigration and Internet regulation. But Thiel was also an outlier for being so high-profile in his support during the election, which included $1.25 million in donations to a Trump-affiliated super PAC and the Trump campaign itself.[19] The founders of Internet start-ups, like entertainers or professional athletes, aspire to be popular with all sorts of people and are quick to play down political differences. They claim to be focused on efficiency, not ideology. Elon Musk, who started as a Web entrepreneur before founding the electric car company Tesla, captured this nonpolitical political perspective in a post to Twitter in 2012: "I'm neither anti-conservative nor anti-liberal. Just don't like group think. Ideas should be considered on their own merits."[20] Even Thiel himself later sought cover from some of Trump's more extreme ideas—a wall with Mexico, mass deportations—by saying he and other supporters took Trump "seriously, but not literally."[21]

The libertarian tilt of the Know-It-Alls has been of great assistance as they pursue a version of nonpolitical politics. Libertarianism can be framed as moderate and open-minded: that is, I agree with liberals on some issues like gay rights or abortion rights, but agree with conservatives on others, like tax cuts or shrinking the social safety net. Similarly, the libertarian can say even-handedly that though the left may hate it, he believes in absolute freedom of speech, and though the right might hate it, he believes in letting people smoke marijuana if they want to. This approach fits someone like Jeff Bezos, for example, who has donated to a campaign to legalize gay marriage in Washington State as well as one to defeat a ballot initiative that would have introduced an income tax on millionaires in the state. Bezos, who now owns the *Washington Post*, has also supported the foundation that publishes the libertarian magazine *Reason*. Some observers have labeled Bezos a "liberaltarian," a liberal libertarian, which is a term that could apply to many Silicon Valley leaders, who travel in Democratic Party circles but oppose unions, hate-speech codes, or expanded income redistribution.[22]

And isn't this the rub, really, of any book trying to explain the political influence of Silicon Valley leaders? So much of what they are advocating comes at you sideways or is described not as a belief but as an inevitable turn as society matures technologically. Yet there is, of course, a distinct Silicon Valley belief system. As we've seen, it advocates for a highly individualistic society led by the smartest people, who deliver wonderful gadgets and platforms for obtaining goods, services, and information efficiently, freeing each of us to compete in the marketplace for our daily bread. There is a particular history, too, of how those values came to be, which reflects separate but intertwined influences. First, there were the original hackers of university-run computer labs, a boys' club of programming geniuses who were a source of the optimism and idealism of Silicon Valley as well as its suspicion of authority and unwelcoming attitude toward women. Later came the entrepreneurs and investors congregating around Stanford University, who were early to recognize the windfall from computers once they had been improved so that ordinary people could use them. Silicon Valley's investors and entrepreneurs taught the hackers to think of the people who used their products as assets to extract value from, rather than simple folk who through the kindness of programmers would learn about the infinite power of computers.

The hackers arrived on the scene at the Massachusetts Institute of Technology in the late 1950s, when they were first introduced to computers by a pair of junior mathematics professors, John McCarthy and Marvin Minsky. Barely in their thirties, those two had already helped chart a path toward artificial intelligence through computers, which they believed could be programmed to think as people do. McCarthy taught MIT's first freshman class in programming in 1959, and those students naturally gravitated to the computer in McCarthy and Minsky's well-funded lab, where they were granted an extraordinary level of independence, freedom, even omnipotence.

These students came to be known as "hackers" because of how much they had to figure out on their own: when problems cropped up, they had to "hack together" a solution. Surrounded by their beloved machines, which seemingly only they truly understood, the hackers were permitted by McCarthy and Minsky to live by a set of anti-authoritarian rules that made sense for a bunch of smarty-pants outsiders. The individual outranked the collective. Personal freedom was more important than empathy or compassion. Status came from programming skill, not age or grades or likability or some academic title. In sum, the hackers believed in an ethic that gave each individual the freedom to do what he wanted with his computer and to say whatever he wanted about whomever he wanted whenever he wanted. Success or failure would be based on talent alone. Still, for all the acceptance of personal eccentricity and insistence on merit, these young men reflected a uniformity that persists in Silicon Valley to this day, starting with the fact that they were all men: women weren't exactly forbidden to be hackers, they just weren't accommodated or made to feel welcome, and at times they faced harassment.[23]

The other source for Silicon Valley's values, the tech entrepreneurs, were spurred on by Stanford, which by the 1950s had turned itself into an explicitly pro-business research institution. The university was founded back in the late nineteenth century with a robber baron's multimillion-dollar bankroll, yet for much of that history it lagged behind the great institutions back east. By the mid-twentieth century, Stanford was stumbling along, known for "educating the children of the middling rich of Los Angeles."[24] During this mediocre era, the school's ambitious engineering school dean, Frederick Terman, was given broad powers as university provost and vice president to make Stanford great. A specialist in a highly practical aspect of electrical engineering, radio waves, Terman had a proven record of turning research into business opportunities, and his plan was built on that experience: he proposed that Stanford use its resources to encourage research in areas with practical applications so that students and faculty members could help industry thrive. Surely a significant share of the wealth and status they generated would find its way back to Stanford.

Under Terman's guidance, Stanford smoothed the way for researchers to partner with big business or to strike out on their own. "I used to go around and give talks to people in industry," he recalled. "My theme was always that the university is a real asset if you make use of it—industrial use. And then I would come back and beat on the backs of the professors to get out and get acquainted with those companies that were related to their research."[25] An early example of a university-brokered business success was Hewlett-Packard, which was founded in 1939 by two of his favorite electrical engineering students, William Hewlett and David Packard. Terman, who was a professor at the time, helped Hewlett and Packard obtain their first equipment, which was initially housed in a Palo Alto garage that today is listed in the national registry as the "birthplace of Silicon Valley." He then helped them land their first large order, which was to produce equipment used for the sound editing on the Walt Disney movie *Fantasia*.[26] Hewlett and Packard in turn became prominent donors to Stanford. The culmination of their generosity toward Stanford came in 1977, when they raised the funds for the $9.2 million Frederick E. Terman Engineering Building.[27]

Terman ultimately was instrumental in Stanford's decision to invest in the new field of computer science, but at first he was skeptical. The business potential wasn't obvious. In the mid-1950s, computers were just fast calculators that were helpful to applied mathematicians but to few others. The research into artificial intelligence by McCarthy, Minsky, and others, however, helped make the case for computers' broader relevance. These professors—and particularly the obsessed young hackers who worked, ate, and slept in their labs—were pushing computers to do more, creating new programming languages, devising smarter hardware designs, and proposing outlandish challenges, like playing chess against humans. Could robot butlers or robot soldiers or automated translators be far behind? Just think of the business potential then.

In 1962, Stanford successfully recruited McCarthy with an offer of full tenure and better weather. That same year, he started work on re-creating his artificial intelligence lab as SAIL (Stanford Artificial Intelligence Laboratory), and in January 1965 he was one of four founding members of the Stanford computer science department, among the first in the country.[28] McCarthy spent much of his time at SAIL increasing students' access to computers, confident that the more computers and humans interacted, brain to brain, the more each could learn from the other. His lab was a pioneer in using monitors and keyboards to allow many individuals to communicate simultaneously with a central computer, a breakthrough he called "time-sharing."

Though McCarthy never cashed in on this work—research and commerce were in conflict, he believed—his lab was the fountainhead for a wide range of Silicon Valley companies, including Sun Microsystems, Silicon Graphics, Cisco, and Yamaha's music synthesizer business.

For all that success, however, the Stanford model of integrating the hacker and the entrepreneur only fully flourished with the widespread adoption of the World Wide Web starting in the late 1990s. Richard Weyhrauch, who spent the 1970s as a researcher at the Stanford Artificial Intelligence Lab, recalled that students and faculty members back in his day would sometimes leave to start companies, but they knew that the stakes were lower. "When we were in the A.I. lab, nobody would have thought you could build a company with more than a billion customers," he said.[29] By the time the Web made such a dream of global domination plausible, a thriving venture capital industry had grown nearby, along Sand Hill Road in Menlo Park, and Stanford was reliably feeding tech entrepreneurs into the system. Thus, before the young graduate students who created the Google search engine, Sergey Brin and Larry Page, had even set up a for-profit business they were handed a $100,000 check by an interested investor. This anticipatory investment was brokered by a university computer science professor who worked down the hall from Brin and Page and was himself already a wealthy tech entrepreneur. In less than a year, Google had incorporated and concluded a $25 million investment round with two Sand Hill firms.[30]

In the subsequent two decades, Stanford has flourished, becoming arguably the most desired college in the country, granting admission to fewer than 5 percent of applicants and earning the nickname "Get Rich U." from the *New Yorker* because of the success of its students.[31] Indeed, anyone pointing out the serious flaws with the world Silicon Valley is constructing must accept its obvious successes, and not just the financial ones. People enjoy its services and clamor to use them. Amazon gains roughly half of all new online commerce in the United States.[32] Uber[33] and Airbnb[34] have quickly become indispensable to millions in their commutes and travels. Google and Facebook both now serve more than a billion people worldwide, a total that keeps growing.

So where, exactly, is the problem? Perhaps the simplest way to describe it is that the combination of a hacker's arrogance and an entrepreneur's greed has turned a collective enterprise like the Web into something proprietary, where our online profiles, our online relationships, our online posts and Web pages and photographs are routinely exploited for business reasons. Companies now regularly spy on their users as they travel across the Web, and save this information. With the help of "artificially intelligent" algorithms, these companies create profiles to place particularly effective ads before the eyes of their visitors. The public increasingly finds itself at the mercy of the choices of a few dominant tech companies, whose services have become too large and pervasive to ignore.

Facebook has been the most ambitious and most successful in expanding its audience. In 2016, more than half of the United States population visited the site at least once a month, while Facebook shot up to 500 million monthly active users worldwide in 2010, then 1 billion in 2012, with 2 billion expected in 2017.[35] The company is edging toward Zuckerberg's goal of creating "a utility—you know, something that people use in their daily lives to look people up and find information about people."[36] When Zuckerberg was asked if this global utility should be regulated by governments the same way the electric and water companies are, he replied, "In terms of regulation, I mean, we get regulated by users, right?"[37] With that answer, Facebook's chief executive revealed in equal measure the entrepreneur's impatience with regulators who would encroach on his ability to make unlimited profit and the hacker's hubris that he knows how to "regulate" his company better than any government could.

In fact, tech companies believe that through artificial intelligence tools they understand their users' state of mind in a way few other companies can, and far better than any regulator. They can track, measure, and analyze the billions of decisions their users make, and they can detect even the most minor feature that may be turning them off. And rather than wait for problems, these companies can compel their users to express a preference by staging so-called A/B testing, which involves showing groups of users slightly different versions of the site and measuring which group stays longer and is thus happier with the experience. Google famously went so far as to prepare forty-one shades of blue to test which was the best color for displaying links in its Gmail service.

When Douglas Bowman, Google's first visual designer, quit in frustration he cited the "shades of blue" episode as what happens when computer engineers run all aspects of the company, including design: "Reduce each decision to a simple logic problem. Remove all subjectivity and just look at the data. Data in your favor? O.K., launch it. Data shows negative effects? Back to the drawing board. And that data eventually becomes a crutch for every decision, paralyzing the company and preventing it from making any daring design decisions."[38] What Bowman saw as a recipe for uninspired design, Google saw as satisfying the public; after all, the highest-scoring shade of blue was the one that users clicked on the most. The company later claimed that using its superior shade of blue had generated $200 million in extra revenue because more people viewed Google's advertising.[39] As Bowman signed off with a post to his personal blog, he conceded that he had no vocabulary to make his case to Google to change its ways; his appeals to taste and judgment literally did not compute. Thus, the message coming back from Silicon Valley wasn't apologetic to the designer but was insistent that if something can't be measured then it is most likely imaginary, like religion or good design or "truth" or empathy.

With this posture, and in so many other ways, the Know-It-Alls bring to mind a precocious teenager who is sure he knows more than he does, slamming the door to his room and muttering about the "phonies" and "dummies" ruining the world. When Andreessen was well into his forties, he routinely took to Twitter to make cranky, snarky comments about idealists like the French tech minister who was quoted saying that she thought her country could take on Silicon Valley, "but without all that horrible inequality." His sarcastic putdown to her (and presumably this author as well) was, "Capitalism, without all that messy capitalism! :-)."[40] Andreessen has also been quoted in the press making misanthropic comments like "I really don't like people," or expressing a preference for lawn mowers because "your lawn mower never argues with you."[41] His venture capital partner, Ben Horowitz, is similarly bold, writing a harsh business-advice book called *The Hard Thing About Hard Things*, which is peppered with gangsta rap lyrics. Introducing a brief chapter on corporate culture, Horowitz includes a quote from the rapper Trinidad James: "This ain't for no fuck niggas, if you a real nigga then fuck with me."[42]

There are other adolescent obsessions, too, beyond the urge to shock the grownups. Peter Thiel believes that science can banish death, if only we considered it a priority. Elon Musk fears that robots will enslave humans.[43] And just about every Know-It-All holds dear the fantasy and science fiction stories that sustained them during their youth—Thiel's current company, Palantir, which uses sophisticated filtering algorithms to help companies and governments track members of the public, is named after an all-seeing stone from J.R.R. Tolkien's *Lord of the Rings* trilogy. Andreessen, who grew up unhappily in rural Wisconsin, recalled the rare joy of watching the original *Star Wars* in an unheated local theater, while Zuckerberg, who had a *Star Wars*–themed bar mitzvah, recently wrote an enthusiastic comment on the official Star Wars Facebook page about the trailer for Disney's reboot of the franchise—"This looks amazing. I love Star Wars." Disney's social media team responded immediately: "We know."[44]

As all this Star Wars talk demonstrates, the Know-It-Alls can appear to be friendly nerds, akin to the eccentric scientists on the sitcom *The Big Bang Theory*. But Andreessen, Thiel, and Zuckerberg are not scientists; they are civic and economic leaders whose ideas and wealth are too influential to trivialize. It's one thing for an awkward programmer to have a hard time speaking with women—like Raj on *Big Bang*, who in early seasons needed to be drunk to hold a conversation with a member of the opposite sex—and another for Silicon Valley companies to vastly underrepresent women, African Americans, and Hispanics. In fact, there has been remarkable demographic consistency among the employees of companies like Google, Facebook, and Uber, with a tech workforce that is anywhere from 15 percent to 20 percent women, 1 to 2 percent African American, and 2 to 3 percent Hispanic.[45]

Yet the most purely adolescent quality of the Know-It-Alls may well be their seeming glee at the destruction that can be laid at their feet. The Stanford literature professor Robert Pogue Harrison reminds us just how extraordinary such an attitude is. "Our silicon age, which sees no glory in maintenance, but only in transformation and disruption, makes it extremely difficult for us to imagine how, in past eras, those who would change the world were viewed with suspicion and dread," he writes. "If you loved the world; if you considered it your mortal home; if you were aware of how much effort and foresight it had cost your forebears to secure its foundations, build its institutions, and shape its culture; if you saw the world as the place of your secular afterlife, then you had good reasons to impute sinister tendencies to those who would tamper with its configuration or render it alien to you."[46] Instead, we have revered these social tamperers and await with interest for each new manifesto they issue with titles like "Building Global Community" or "What Happened to the Future?"

Back in 2009, Andreessen described the epic battles to come between disruptive companies and traditional businesses. The economist Joseph Schumpeter, famous proponent of creative destruction, "would be proud," Andreessen wrote, as he warned that "companies in every industry need to assume that a software revolution is coming." He rattled off a litany of the old and inefficient organizations that have been toppled or are under siege by new and nimble companies—Blockbuster video rental, Borders bookstores, Kodak film, the United States Postal Service. "Health care and education, in my view, are next up," he predicted in his piece, which is titled "Why Software Is Eating the World," or, if you prefer, "How Software Serves Man: A Cookbook."[47]

1. JOHN McCARTHY

"Solving today's problems tomorrow"

"What do judges know that we cannot eventually tell a computer?" John McCarthy asked himself with a rhetorical flourish in a debate at Stanford about the limits, if any, to artificial intelligence research. In 1973, the answer was obvious to McCarthy: "Nothing."[1] The leader of the university's highly regarded artificial intelligence lab, McCarthy appeared part mad scientist, part radical intellectual, with the horn-rimmed glasses and pocket protector of an engineer and the bushy hair and rough beard of a firebrand. McCarthy's opposite that day was Joseph Weizenbaum, a dapper, pipe-smoking MIT computer science professor, who by the 1970s had come to challenge everything McCarthy stood for. Where McCarthy believed nothing human was beyond the capability of machines when properly instructed, Weizenbaum insisted that some tasks—like sitting in judgment of the accused or giving counsel to those in distress—could only be entrusted to people. Even to consider otherwise was to commit a "monstrous obscenity."[2] A Jewish refugee from Nazi Germany at age thirteen, Weizenbaum was ever on the watch for those whom he suspected didn't believe that all human life was sacred, whether because of a commitment to racial superiority or a conviction that nothing innate separated people from machines.[3]

To Weizenbaum, McCarthy's ease in casting aside the ethical concerns of others was the clearest sign yet that elite AI scientists, whom Weizenbaum called the "artificial intelligentsia," had lost their way. They would sacrifice anything for the cause, even their own humanity. Case in point were the young computer experts—the hackers—whom McCarthy had nurtured in his labs, first at MIT and later at Stanford. "They work until they nearly drop, twenty, thirty hours at a time," Weizenbaum wrote in *Computer Power and Human Reason*, his anti-AI manifesto published in 1976. "Their food, if they arrange it, is brought to them: coffee, Cokes, sandwiches. If possible, they sleep on cots near the computer. But only for a few hours—then back to the console or the printouts. Their rumpled clothes, their unwashed and unshaven faces and their uncombed hair all testify that they are oblivious to their bodies and to the world in which they move. They exist, at least when so engaged, only through and for the computers. These are computer bums, compulsive programmers."[4]

Naturally, this assessment of the stars of his lab struck McCarthy as unfair, but that last slur—bum!—from a fellow computer scientist really stung. First, McCarthy knew that the hackers' enthusiasm, even compulsion, was crucial to running a successful lab, something Weizenbaum apparently didn't need to consider now that he was more interested in ethics than research. "We professors of computer science sometimes lose our ability to write actual computer programs through lack of practice and envy younger people who can spend full time in the laboratory," McCarthy explained to Weizenbaum in a review of *Computer Power*, which he titled "An Unreasonable Book." "The phenomenon is well known in other sciences and in other human activities."[5] But more, McCarthy saw critics like Weizenbaum as lacking the scientist's relentless drive to understand the world, no matter where that drive may take him, perhaps even to programming computers to think like judges. "The term 'appropriate science' suggests that there is 'inappropriate science,'" McCarthy said at a later debate. "If there is 'inappropriate science,' then there is 'appropriate ignorance' and I don't believe in it."[6] His young "computer bums" had nothing to apologize for.

McCarthy came easily to this take-no-prisoners debating style on behalf of science and research—ideological combat was in his blood. As a teenager, John McCarthy wasn't only a mathematics prodigy—skipping two grades at Belmont High School in Los Angeles and teaching himself advanced calculus from college textbooks he bought second-hand—he was also a young Marxist foot soldier, a full member of the Communist Party at the age of seventeen, skipping ahead there, too.[7]

John McCarthy was born back east to parents who represented two prominent streams within American radicalism—the Jewish and the Irish. His mother, Ida Glatt, was a Lithuanian Jewish immigrant who grew up in Baltimore and managed to attend the prestigious women's school Goucher College, probably with the assistance of the city's wealthier German Jewish community. His father, Jack, an Irish Catholic immigrant, hoped to avoid deportation for his political activities by claiming to be a native Californian whose birth certificate went missing in the San Francisco earthquake. Years before Ida and Jack ever met, each had already led popular protests: Ida was at the head of Goucher students marching for women's suffrage, and Jack was urging stevedores in Boston to stop loading a British ship in solidarity with a hunger strike of Terence MacSwiney, a jailed Irish Republican politician.[8]

Though Jack never made it past the fourth grade, his son John remembered his literary temperament, whether that meant quoting Browning and Kipling or reciting poems and lyrics about the Irish cause.[9] Ida was an accomplished student and an idealistic champion for the poor and oppressed. She graduated from Goucher in 1917 with a degree in political economy and went to the University of Chicago to do graduate work that quickly spilled into labor organizing. Due to her refined education and her sex, Ida was brought under the umbrella of the Women's Trade Union League, an organization identified with the wealthy progressive women who helped fund it—the so-called mink brigade. The league's motto connected workers' rights to justice for women and families: "The eight hour day, a living wage, to guard the home."[10]

A few years later, Ida and Jack were introduced in Boston—she hired him to build a set of bookshelves, according to family lore—and Ida was fully radicalized. In addition to his carpentry, Jack ran organizing drives for fishermen and dry-cleaning deliverers, trolley workers and longshoremen. Their first child, John, was born there in 1927, though soon the family moved to New York, where the couple worked for the Communist Party newspaper the *Daily Worker*; Ida was a reporter and Jack was a business manager.[11] For the sake of the health of young John, who had a life-threatening sinus condition, they relocated to Los Angeles, then known for its clean, dry air. Ida became a social worker, and Jack continued labor organizing, serving at one point as an aide to Harry Bridges, the radical San Francisco–based longshoremen's union leader who was West Coast director of the CIO during the 1930s and 1940s.

Young John regained his strength and early on showed an interest in math and science. His parents gave him a party-approved volume, the English translation of a children's science book popular in the Soviet Union, *100,000 Whys*, which ingeniously explains biology, chemistry, and physics by looking at how an ordinary household works—the stove, the faucet, the cupboard. The slim volume opens with the observation, "Every day, somebody in your house starts the fire, heats water, boils potatoes. . . ."[12] Later, he would purchase used calculus textbooks.

In an act of "extreme arrogance," John applied to a single college, the nearby California Institute of Technology. His equivalent of a college essay was a single sentence: "I intend to be a professor of mathematics." John was accepted and completed his work there in two and a half years, though graduation was delayed two years because he was suspended twice for refusing to attend mandatory gym classes. One of the suspensions led to a detour to the army, at nearby Fort MacArthur, where McCarthy and other young enlisted men were entrusted with the calculations that determined whether candidates deserved a promotion—"the opportunity for arbitrary action by just us kids was extraordinary." He harbored little anger at the delay in obtaining his diploma, noting that after World War II the army became a rather genial place. "Basic training was relaxing compared to physical education at Caltech,"[13] he recalled. After graduation in 1948, McCarthy spent a year at Caltech as a mathematics graduate student in preparation for becoming a professor. Two events that year propelled McCarthy toward what would become his lifelong quest: to create a thinking computer.

First, before ever setting eyes on a computer, McCarthy studied how to program one. He attended lectures about the Standards Western Automatic Computer, which wouldn't be completed and installed in Los Angeles until two years later. The word *computer* was being transformed during these years. Once, it had been used to describe a person, usually a woman, who carries out complicated calculations. But by 1948, *computer* could also describe a machine that in theory was able to follow instructions to perform any task, given enough time. This framework for a computer was proposed by the great British mathematician Alan Turing and called the "universal Turing machine." By breaking down any action, up to and including thought, as merely a sequence of discrete steps each of which could be achieved by a computer, Turing would give hope to dreamers like McCarthy and convince them that, in McCarthy's words, "AI was best researched by programming computers rather than by building machines."[14]

Turing was so confident that computers could be instructed how to think that he later devised a way of verifying this achievement when it inevitably arrived, through what he called "the imitation game." Turing's contention with his game, which is now more commonly called the "Turing test," was that if a computer could reliably convince a person that he was speaking with another person, whom he could not see, then it should be considered intelligent. The true potency of the test, writes the historian Paul N. Edwards, was its limited, machine friendly definition of intelligence. "Turing did not require that the computer imitate a human voice or mimic facial expressions, gestures, theatrical displays, laughter, or any of the thousands of other ways humans communicate," Edwards writes. "What might be called the intelligence of the body—dance, reflex, perception, the manipulation of objects in space as people solve problems, and so on—drops from view as irrelevant. In the same way, what might be called social intelligence—the collective construction of human realities—does not appear in the picture. Indeed, it was precisely because the body and the social world signify humanness directly that Turing proposed the connection via remote terminals."[15]

Turing's ideas were highly speculative: computers and mathematicians hardly seemed up to the task of creating an artificial intelligence, even under Turing's forgiving definition. Nonetheless, interest was building. In 1948, McCarthy attended an unprecedented conference at Caltech, "The Hixon Symposium on Cerebral Mechanisms in Behavior," which included talks like "Why the Mind Is in the Head" and "Models of the Nervous System."[16] The featured speaker was the mathematician and computer pioneer John von Neumann, who cited Turing to explain how a computer could be taught to think like a human brain. There also were lectures from psychologists who worked the other way around, finding parallels between the human brain and a computer. Within this intellectually charged atmosphere, McCarthy committed himself to studying "the use of computers to behave intelligently."[17]

When McCarthy departed Caltech, and the family home, for Princeton the next year, he was on course to earn a PhD in mathematics—there was no such field as artificial intelligence, or even computer science for that matter. By virtue of von Neumann's presence nearby at the Institute for Advanced Study, McCarthy was studying at one of the few hotbeds for these ideas. He soon met Marvin Minsky, another mathematics graduate student, who became a friend and an AI fellow traveler. McCarthy also fell in with a circle of mathematicians, including John Forbes Nash, who were devising game theory, a scheme for modeling human behavior by describing the actions of imaginary, self-interested individuals bound by clear rules meant to represent laws or social obligations.

Still on the left politically, McCarthy hadn't accepted game theory's cynical view of people and society. He recalled Nash fondly, but considered him peculiar. "I guess you could imagine him as though he were a follower of Ayn Rand," McCarthy said, "explicitly and frankly egotistical and selfish." He was there when Nash and others in their circle helped create a game of deceit and betrayal that Nash called "Fuck Your Buddy"; McCarthy said he came up with a more family-friendly name for the game, "So Long, Sucker." It stuck. The ruthless strategy needed to excel in "So Long, Sucker" offended McCarthy, and he lashed out at Nash one time as the game descended into treachery: "I remember playing—you have to form alliances and double cross at the right time. His words toward me at the end were, 'But I don't need you anymore, John.' He was right, and that was the point of the game, and I think he won."[18]

Exposed to the rationalist ideas of thinkers like von Neumann, Nash and Minsky, and others, McCarthy was becoming increasingly intellectually independent. He was finally away from his parents—even in the army he had been assigned to a nearby base—and had the freedom to drift from radical politics. McCarthy tells a story of dutifully looking up the local Communist Party cell when he arrived in Princeton and finding that the only active members were a janitor and a gardener. He passed on that opportunity and quietly quit the party a few years later. During the Red Scare led by a different McCarthy (Senator Joseph) he had to lie a couple of times about having been a Communist, "but basically the people that I knew of who were harmed were people who stuck their necks out."[19] McCarthy didn't, and thus began a steady shift to the right.

Toward the end of his life, when his political transformation from left to right was complete, McCarthy wrote an essay trying to explain why otherwise sensible people were attracted to Marxism. One of the attractions he identified—"the example of hard work and self-sacrifice by individual socialists and communists in the trade union movement"—undoubtedly sprung from the committed political lives of his parents, Ida and Jack. Nonetheless, McCarthy rates the Marxist experiment a terrible blight on human history and observes about his own radical upbringing, "An excessive acquaintance with Marxism-Leninism is a sign of a misspent youth."[20]

McCarthy's "misspent youth," however, is what gives narrative coherence to his life, even if it is the kind of narrative O. Henry liked to tell. It goes something like this: Man spends his life shedding the revolutionary ideology of his upbringing and its dream of a utopian society without poverty or oppression to commit instead to a life of scientific reason. The man becomes an internationally recognized computer genius and runs a prestigious lab. Over time, the man's scientific research fuels a new revolutionary ideology that aspires to create a utopian society without poverty or oppression. In other words, if McCarthy believed as a young man that adopting the rational values of science and mathematics would offer refuge from the emotional volatility of politics, he couldn't have been more mistaken. By the end of his life, McCarthy was more political agitator than scientist, even if he continued to see himself as the epitome of a rational being.

After McCarthy completed his PhD at Princeton in pure math, he had little direction in his academic career—mainly he was struck by what he considered the shallowness of his own mathematical research, especially when compared with the depth of the work of Nash and the others in his circle. McCarthy had original ideas he would speculate on, but he wondered if that was enough for the highest levels of mathematics. McCarthy was hired by Stanford as an assistant professor and then quickly let go—"Stanford decided they'd keep two out of their three acting assistant professors, and I was the third."[21]

McCarthy continued his academic career at Dartmouth, where in 1955 he began planning a summer workshop on thinking computers. There wasn't yet a term describing this type of research. "I had to call it something, so I called it 'artificial intelligence,'" he recalled. An earlier name for the topic, *automata studies*, came from the word for self-operating machines, but didn't describe the goal nearly as breathlessly as *artificial intelligence* did.[22] The Dartmouth summer workshop matched up McCarthy and Minsky with famous names in computing, the information theorist Claude Shannon, who had left Bell Labs for MIT, and Nathaniel Rochester, an IBM researcher, though perhaps the most famous name of them all, von Neumann, would not be there: by the summer of 1956, he was too sick to attend. The youthful arrogance of Minsky and McCarthy was on bright display throughout the proposal to the Rockefeller Foundation asking for $13,500 to cover stipends, travel expenses, and the like, including this succinct description of their core belief: "Every aspect of learning or any other feature of intelligence can in principle be so precisely described that a machine can be made to simulate it."[23]

Buoyed by the success of the conference, which now has its own commemorative plaque on the Dartmouth campus, McCarthy maneuvered himself to MIT. First, he persuaded the head of the mathematics department at Dartmouth, John Kemeny, to arrange a fellowship, which McCarthy elected to take at MIT, and then, "I double-crossed him by not returning to Dartmouth, but staying at MIT," he recalled. By 1958, Minsky had arrived at MIT, too; the next year, the two were running the artificial intelligence project there. MIT was so flush with government money in those years that administrators offered the newly arrived junior professors the funds to support six mathematics graduate students, no questions asked.[24]

McCarthy and Minsky's graduate students were put to work applying their training in mathematical logic to computers; they were asked to find ways to represent the outside environment, as well as a brain's stored knowledge and thought processes, by means of a series of clearly defined statements. In this sense, the early AI project was conceived as a reverse-engineering problem. How to build an intelligent computer? Well, first you "open up" a person and study in detail what makes him tick. For example, Minsky and his graduate students would ask probing questions of children—so probing that Margaret Hamilton, an MIT graduate student at the time and later a famous software engineer, recalls Minsky's team making her three-year-old daughter cry during an experiment that had a researcher read a computer's critical comments back to her. "That's how they talked back then; they thought computers were going to take over the world then," Hamilton said.[25] In one unpublished paper, called "The Well-Designed Child," McCarthy tried to detail what we know and don't know about the tools for reasoning that are born to human babies. A short section, titled "Unethical Experiment," shows just how curious he was: "Imagine arranging that all a baby ever sees is a plan of a two-dimensional room and all his actions move around in the room. Maybe the experiment can be modified to be safe and still be informative."[26]

From what AI researchers deduced about people, by experiment or intuiting, they devised computer code to imitate the process step by step, algorithm by algorithm. In an essay for *Scientific American* in 1966, McCarthy made the same confident assertion he had first expressed as part of the Dartmouth conference, that nothing, in theory, separated a computer from a person. "The computer accepts information from its environment through its input devices; it combines this information, according to the rules of the program stored in its memory, with information that is also stored in its memory, and it sends information back to its environment through its output devices," he wrote, which was just the same as people. "The human brain also accepts inputs of information, combines it with information stored somehow within and returns outputs of information to its environment."[27] McCarthy's every instinct was to demystify the process of human thinking and intelligence. Behavior could be explained by "the principle of rationality"—setting a goal (not necessarily a rational goal) and then coming up with a plan to achieve it.[28]

The tricky thing for a computer to replicate was ordinary common sense, not differential calculus, McCarthy concluded. By 1968, a robot in McCarthy's lab had an arm with refined touch, yet it still could not tie a pair of shoes. Maddening. "I have observed two small children learn how to do this, and I don't understand how they learn how to do it," he said. "The difficulty in this case is not so much in getting the sense itself but programming what to do with it."[29] Thus, McCarthy spent a lot of time trying to understand precisely how people got through daily life. He was forever challenging his intelligent machines with "mundane and seemingly trivial tasks, such as constructing a plan to get to the airport," or reading and comprehending a brief crime report in the *New York Times*.[30]

In his pursuit of a thinking machine, McCarthy was making a bunch of dubious leaps, as he later came to acknowledge. To deconstruct a human being necessarily meant considering him in isolation, just as the designers of an intelligent machine would be considering it in isolation. Under this approach to intelligence there would be no pausing to consider the relevance of factors external to the brain, such as the body, social ties, family ties, or companionship. When people spoke about the mystery of the human mind, McCarthy would scoff. Could a machine have "free will"? A colleague recalled his answer, which sought to remove the sanctity of the term: "According to McCarthy, free will involves considering different courses of action and having the ability to choose among them. He summarized his position about human free will by quoting his daughter, Sarah, who said at age four, 'I can, but I won't.'"[31]

In the spring of 1959, four years after he finally learned to program properly, McCarthy taught the first freshman class in computers at MIT, turning on a generation of aspiring programmers who followed him to the artificial intelligence lab.[32] The curriculum was brand-new, and the term *computer science* had only just surfaced. One of its first uses was in a report commissioned by Stanford around 1956 as it considered whether the study of computers could be an academic discipline. Stanford's provost, Frederick Terman, was always thinking of ways to raise the university's profile and add to its resources, and there was a tempting offer from IBM that it would donate state-of-the-art equipment, including its pathbreaking 650 mainframe, to any university that offered classes on scientific and business computing. Stanford asked a local computer expert, Louis Fein, to study the topic and propose an academically rigorous curriculum in the "science" of computers.

The university's mathematics faculty was skeptical. One professor told Fein that he thought computing was like plumbing, a useful tool to be applied to other projects. "We don't have plumbers studying within the university," he told Fein. "What does computing have to do with intellect?" But Fein was inclined to flip the question around in his head. "Why is it that economics and geology is in a university," he'd ask himself, "and why is it that plumbing isn't?"[33] For his report, "The Role of the University in Computers, Data Processing, and Related Fields,"[34] Fein interviewed the nation's computer experts—a total in the "tens" at the time, he recalled—including McCarthy, when he was still at Dartmouth, and Weizenbaum, when he was a researcher at Wayne State University. Fein recommended that Stanford move forward in creating a separate department for computer science, and the university, as a first step, introduced a division within the mathematics department.

Stanford's administrators ignored an unstated conclusion in the report: namely, that Fein should be brought in to lead Stanford's new computer science department. Terman's deputy made it clear to Fein that Stanford would only be recruiting big names—"what we need is to get a von Neumann out here and then things will go well," he was told.[35] McCarthy might fit the bill, however. In 1962, Stanford offered him a big promotion—immediate tenure as a full professor in mathematics—as a prelude to joining a newly minted computer science department. Yet the quick return and advancement of McCarthy at Stanford after initial failure would give ammunition to those mathematicians who argued that computer work must not be rigorous. Wasn't this big shot McCarthy only just passed over as a junior professor?

Intelligence was the coin of the realm in those years in a preview of how Silicon Valley would operate—that is, everyone was intent on identifying who was most brilliant and rewarding him, all the while looking for the magic formula to mass-produce intelligence in the computer lab. Not even McCarthy was above reproach. No one ever is, really. In 2014, the Web site Quora began a discussion, "How did Mark Zuckerberg become a programming prodigy?" Coders were eager to burst that bubble and explain that Zuckerberg, despite his success, was no prodigy. "The application he wrote was not unique, and not all that well-made," one Quora contributor explained.[36]

Any doubts about McCarthy's brilliance, based on his early failure as a mathematics professor, weren't fair, of course. McCarthy had found his academic purpose within computer science. While at MIT, he had invented a powerful programming language called Lisp, which allowed complicated instructions to be given to the computer with relatively simple commands and is still used today. Paul Graham, the cofounder of the company Y Combinator, which encourages and invests in start-ups, considers McCarthy a hero programmer. "In 1958 there seem to have been two ways of thinking about programming. Some people thought of it as math . . . others thought of it as a way to get things done, and designed languages all too influenced by the technology of the day. McCarthy alone bridged the gap. He designed a language that was math. But designed is not really the word; discovered is more like it," Graham writes in appreciation.[37] Another academic achievement of McCarthy's at MIT was the AI lab itself, which was filling up with eager young programmers who lived and breathed computers.

McCarthy had recognized early on that for the lab to hum with breakthroughs—and for such breakthroughs to build on each other—there had to be more computer time to spread around. The old system had been too limiting and too forbidding: hulking IBM mainframes guarded by specially trained operators who behaved as priests at the ancient temple. Students and the staff skirmished frequently as the hackers tried to trick the IBM guardians into leaving their post.[38] The balance of power began to shift toward the hackers by the end of the 1950s with the arrival of the TX-0, a hand-me-down computer from a military electronics laboratory affiliated with MIT. The TX-0 did not need special operators. In 1961, it was joined by a donated prototype of the PDP-1, the first minicomputer from Digital Equipment Corporation, a Boston-area start-up founded by former MIT scientists who had worked on the TX-0. McCarthy proposed "time-sharing"[39] as a way of replicating the flexibility of these new computers on the IBM mainframe while removing the bottleneck for computer time by replacing one-at-a-time use of a computer with a system that allowed as many as twenty-four people to connect individually with a computer; eventually each person would have his own monitor and keyboard.[40]

Indeed, once the students interacted with a computer directly the seduction was complete. Young people camped out at McCarthy and Minsky's lab, waiting often into the wee hours of the night for a time slot to open up. When they were dissatisfied with the performance of a vital piece of code that came with the PDP-1, the assembler, they asked the lab for the assignment of writing a better one and were given a weekend to do it. The technology writer Steven Levy recounts the "programming orgy" that ensued: "Six hackers worked around 250 man-hours that weekend, writing code, debugging and washing down take-out Chinese food with massive quantities of Coca-Cola." Digital asked the hackers for a copy of the new assembler to offer to other owners of the PDP-1. They eagerly complied, Levy writes, and "the question of royalties never came up. . . . Wasn't software more like a gift to the world, something that was reward in itself?"[41]

The ecstasy from directly interacting with the computer—not the chance for profits—was the basis of what became the Hacker Ethic, a set of principles these young programmers lived by as they pursued a personal relationship with computing. This first principle was called the "hands-on imperative," the belief that there could be no substitute for direct control over a computer, its inner workings, its operating system, its software. The deeper you went, the better—whether that meant manipulating the so-called machine language that the computer used at its core, or opening up the box to solder new pathways in the hardware that constituted the computer's brain. The access not only had to be direct, but casual, too. "What the user wants," McCarthy wrote at the time, "is a computer that he can have continuously at his beck and call for long periods of time."[42]

If this all sounds sort of sexual—or like an old-fashioned marriage—well, you aren't the first to notice. McCarthy's lab may as well have had a No Girls sign outside. Levy described this first generation of hackers at MIT as being locked in "bachelor mode," with hacking replacing romantic relationships: "It was easy to fall into—for one thing, many of the hackers were loners to begin with, socially uncomfortable. It was the predictability and controllability of a computer system—as opposed to the hopelessly random problems in a human relationship—which made hacking particularly attractive."[43] Margaret Hamilton, the MIT graduate student who later led the software team for the Apollo space mission, would occasionally visit the AI lab and clearly had the chops to be one of the "hackers." She says she had a similar mischievous approach to computing and "understood these kids and their excitement." Even so, she kept a healthy distance. The age gap may have been small, but Hamilton must have seemed a generation older. In her early twenties, she was already married with a child; her computer talents were focused on a practical problem, helping to interpret research within MIT's meteorology department. Hamilton remembers wondering how it was that the AI lab could always be filled with undergraduates. When she was studying math as an undergraduate at Earlham College, she didn't remember having so much free time: "These kids weren't worried about bad marks and satisfying their professors?"[44]

Of course, hackers didn't care about grades. Computers had changed everything. There were other principles to the Hacker Ethic, as explicated by Levy—including "mistrust authority," "all information should be free," and "hackers should be judged by their hacking, not bogus criteria such as degrees, age, race, or position"—but each was really a reframing of the hands-on imperative. The goal was to get close to a computer, and anyone or anything that stood in your way was the enemy. In the competition for computer time, for example, the higher up the academic ladder you were, the greater access you had, whether you were adept or not. That isn't right. Programming skill, not age or academic degrees, is all that should matter in deciding who gets his hands on a computer. Later, there were the businesses that insisted on charging for the programs necessary for you to operate your computer. No way. Information should be free and lack of financial resources shouldn't be an impediment to programming.

These young men were fanatically devoted to computers, which they valued for being more reliable, helpful, and amusing than people. The hackers dreamed of spreading their joy. "If *everyone* could interact with computers with the same innocent, productive, creative impulse that hackers did, the Hacker Ethic might spread through society like a benevolent ripple," Levy wrote in 1984, "and computers would, indeed, change the world for the better."[45]

By 1962, the thirty-five-year-old McCarthy had already made a series of important professional contributions, arguably the most important of his career: the Lisp programming language, time-sharing, an early framework for instructing a computer to play chess, a quintessentially intellectual activity once considered safely beyond machines. Nonetheless, as Stanford quickly became aware, McCarthy was ripe for the picking. He was annoyed that MIT was dragging its feet in implementing his beloved time-sharing idea; an offer of full tenure there would be a few years off, if it came at all. The cold Cambridge winters weren't helping matters, either. McCarthy accepted Stanford's offer.

McCarthy was a big get for Stanford, and not just because he was coming from the pinnacle, MIT. McCarthy was an academic rock star, the kind of professor students wanted to work with. He was indulgent of his students; his field, artificial intelligence, was on the cutting edge. By contrast, George Forsythe, the first computer science professor at Stanford and the first chairman of the department, had a wonky specialty, numerical analysis. At least he had a sense of humor about it. "In the past 15 years," he wrote in 1967, "many numerical analysts have progressed from being queer people in mathematics departments to being queer people in computer science departments!"[46] AI research and programming languages and systems, on the other hand, would be where the growth in computer science would occur because they "seem more exciting, important and solvable at this particular stage of computer science."[47] McCarthy was set up in a remote building that had been abandoned by a utility company, where he went to work re-creating the MIT lab as the Stanford Artificial Intelligence Lab (SAIL).

"What you get when you come out to Stanford is a hunting license as far as money is concerned," McCarthy recalled, and he already had well-established, MIT-based connections to DARPA, the defense department's research group. "I am not a money raiser," McCarthy said. "I'm not the sort of person who calls somebody in Washington and makes an appointment to see him and says, look here, look at these great things, why don't you support it? As long as you could get money by so to speak just sending away for it, I was O.K., but when it took salesmanship and so forth then I was out of it."[48] These government funds came with barely any strings attached, and no supervision to speak of: "I was the only investigator with a perfect record," he liked to say. "I never handed in a quarterly progress report."[49] Because of this benign neglect, McCarthy was able to use money assigned to artificial intelligence research to support a series of important improvements in how computers worked, including individual display terminals on every desk, computer typesetting and publishing, speech recognition software, music synthesizers, and self-driving cars. By 1971, SAIL had seventy-five staff members, including twenty-seven graduate students pursuing an advanced degree, who represented a range of fields: mathematics, computer science, music, medicine, engineering, and psychiatry.[50]

The transfer from MIT to Stanford led to some California-esque adjustments. To start, there was a sauna and a volleyball court.[51] And while still members of a boys' club, SAIL's hackers were more likely to take notice of the opposite sex. A *Life* magazine profile from 1970 helped establish Stanford's reputation as the home of a bunch of horny young scientists, so different from asexual MIT. The article quoted an unnamed member of the team programming a computer psychiatrist and "patient" as saying they were expanding the range of possible reactions a computer can experience: "So far, we have not achieved complete orgasm."[52] The lab's administrators insisted to the student newspaper that the quote was made up, but a reputation was taking shape.[53] In one notorious episode a year later, some computer science students shot a pornographic film in the lab for their abnormal psychology class, recruiting the actress through an ad in the student newspaper seeking an "uninhibited girl."[54] The film was about a woman with a sexual attraction to a computer—for these purposes, one of the experimental fingers attached to a computer used in robotics research proved an especially useful prop. The entire lab was able to watch the seduction scene through an in-house camera system connected to the time-sharing terminals dispersed throughout the building.[55]

At this point in the history of AI, researchers were intrigued by the idea of a computer having sex with a woman, which was central to the plot of *Demon Seed*, a 1970s horror film. Makes sense: there was still confidence (or fear) that AI researchers would succeed in making independent thinking machines to rival or surpass humans. The male scientists identified with the powerful computer they were bringing to life. When the goals for AI had diminished, and computers would only imitate thought rather than embody it, the computers became feminized, sex toys for men in movies like *Weird Science*, *Ex Machina*, and *Her*.

Despite the sexual hijinks and the California sun, the Stanford lab was otherwise quite similar to the MIT lab in its isolation and inward-looking perspective. Located five miles outside of campus, SAIL provided built-in sleeping quarters in the attic for those hackers who wouldn't or couldn't leave; the signs on the doors were written in the elvish script invented for *The Lord of the Rings*. One visitor from *Rolling Stone* described the scene in 1972: "Long hallways and cubicles and large windowless rooms, brutal fluorescent light, enormous machines humming and clattering, robots on wheels, scurrying arcane technicians. And, also, posters and announcements against the Vietnam War and Richard Nixon, computer print-out photos of girlfriends, a hallway-long banner SOLVING TODAY'S PROBLEMS TOMORROW."[56]

During these rocking, carefree years, McCarthy and his team were forced to recognize just how flawed the original artificial intelligence project was. They were stuck in a research quagmire, as McCarthy freely admitted to a reporter for the student newspaper: "There is no basis for a statement that we will have machines as intelligent as people in 3 years, or 15 years, or 50 years, or any definite time. Fundamental questions have yet to be solved, and even to be formulated. Once this is done—and it might happen quickly or not for a long time—it might be possible to predict a schedule of development."[57] By accepting this new reality, McCarthy freed himself to write a series of far-sighted papers on how computers could improve life without achieving true artificial intelligence.

In one such paper, from 1970, McCarthy laid out a vision of Americans' accessing powerful central computers using "home information terminals"—the time-sharing model of computer access brought to the general public.[58] The paper describes quite accurately the typical

American's networked life to come, with email, texting, blogs, phone service, TV, and books all digitally available through what is the equivalent of the digital "cloud" we rely on today. He was so proud of that paper that he republished it with footnotes in 2000, assessing his predictions. Over and over, the footnote is nothing more than: "All this has happened." He allowed, however, "there were several ways things happened differently."[59] For example, his interests were plainly more intellectual than most people's, so while he emphasized how the public would be able to access vast digital libraries, "I didn't mention games—it wasn't part of my grand vision, so to speak."[60]

McCarthy's grand vision for domestic computing was notable for being anti-commercial. He predicted that greater access to information would promote intellectual competition, while "advertising, in the sense of something that can force itself on the attention of a reader, will disappear because it will be too easy to read via a program that screens out undesirable material." With such low entry costs for publishing, "Even a high school student could compete with the *New Yorker* if he could write well enough and if word of mouth and mention by reviewers brought him to public attention." The only threat McCarthy could see to the beautiful system he was conjuring were monopolists, who would try to control access to the network, the material available, and the programs that ran there. McCarthy suspected that the ability of any individual programmer to create a new service would be a check on the concentration of digital power, but he agreed, "One can worry that the system might develop commercially in some way that would prevent that."[61] As, indeed, it has.

Just as AI research was on the wane, McCarthy's lab became a target of radical students, who cited SAIL's reliance on defense department funds to link the work there, however indirectly, to the war in Vietnam. In 1970, a protester threw an improvised bomb into the lab's building—fortunately, it landed in an empty room and was quickly doused by sprinklers. Lab members briefly set up a patrol system to protect their building, while McCarthy responded by taking the fight to the enemy.[62] When anti-war protestors interrupted a Stanford faculty meeting in 1972 and wouldn't leave, the university president adjourned the meeting. McCarthy remained, however, telling the protestors, "The majority of the university takes our position, so go to hell." When they responded by accusing him and his lab of helping carry out genocide in Vietnam, McCarthy responded: "We are not involved in genocide. It is people like you who start genocide."[63] Six years later, McCarthy debated, and had to be physically separated from, the popular Stanford biology professor Paul Ehrlich, who warned that humanity was destroying the environment through overpopulation.[64] McCarthy's disdain for Ehrlich could be summarized in his observation that "doomsaying is popular and wins prizes regardless of how wrong its prophecies turn out to be."[65]

In Joseph Weizenbaum, however, McCarthy found a more persistent and formidable critic, one who spoke the same technical language. The two wrote stinging reviews of each other's work: McCarthy would berate Weizenbaum for foggy thinking that paved the way for authoritarian control of science; Weizenbaum, the AI apostate, insisted on bringing morality into the equation. Weizenbaum also questioned the self-proclaimed brilliance of his peers. He, for one, chose to study mathematics because, "Of all the things that one could study, mathematics seemed by far the easiest. Mathematics is a game. It is entirely abstract. Hidden behind that recognition that mathematics is the easiest is the corresponding recognition that real life is the hardest."[66]

Weizenbaum was born in Berlin in 1923, the second son of a furrier, Jechiel, and his wife, Henrietta. After the anti-Semitic laws of 1935, Weizenbaum's family made their way to the United States by way of Bremen. His studies were interrupted by service in the U.S. Army Air Corps during World War II,[67] but by the early 1950s, he was a graduate student in mathematics at Wayne State University, where a professor had decided to build a computer from scratch. Weizenbaum was part of the group that assembled and programmed that computer, even soldering the components. Based on that experience, Weizenbaum in 1952 was asked to join the team that produced the huge check-processing computer for Bank of America, the first for any bank.[68]

All that mattered to Weizenbaum at the time were the technical challenges that lay ahead—how to teach a computer to read checks that were crumpled, or of different sizes. "It was a whale of a lot of fun attacking those hard problems, and it never occurred to me at the time that I was cooperating in a technological venture which had certain social side effects which I might come to regret," he said. "I was totally wrapped up in my identity as a professional, and besides, it was just too much fun."[69] In other words, when Weizenbaum, in *Computer Power and Human Reason*, described the intoxication that comes from being a compulsive programmer he was sharing firsthand experiences. "The computer programmer," he wrote, "is a creator of universes for which he alone is the lawgiver. . . . No playwright, no stage director, no emperor, however powerful, has ever exercised such absolute authority to arrange a stage or a field of battle and to command such unswervingly dutiful actors or troops."[70]

After Weizenbaum arrived at MIT in 1963 as an associate professor in electrical engineering, his familiarity with computers led him toward artificial intelligence and an intriguing project he called Eliza (named for Eliza Doolittle of *Pygmalion*). Eliza was programmed to ask a user probing, if vague, questions in the manner of a therapist. A sample conversation between a "patient," played by Weizenbaum, and Eliza, circa 1966, is quite revealing, proving how adept Eliza was at pushing all the right (human) buttons.[71]

PATIENT. Men are all alike.

ELIZA. In what way?

PATIENT. They're always bugging us about something or other.

ELIZA. Can you think of a specific example?

PATIENT. Well, my boyfriend made me come here.

ELIZA. Your boyfriend made you come here?

PATIENT. He says I'm depressed much of the time.

ELIZA. I am sorry to hear you are depressed.

PATIENT. It's true. I am unhappy.

ELIZA. Do you think coming here will help you not to be unhappy?

PATIENT. I need some help, that much seems certain.

ELIZA. What would it mean to you if you got some help?

PATIENT. Perhaps I could learn to get along with my mother.

ELIZA. Tell me more about your family.

PATIENT. My mother takes care of me.

ELIZA. Who else in your family takes care of you?

PATIENT. My father.

ELIZA. Your father.

PATIENT. You are like my father in some ways.

ELIZA. What resemblance do you see?

PATIENT. You are not very aggressive but I think you don't want me to notice that.

ELIZA. What makes you think I am not very aggressive?

PATIENT. You don't argue with me.

ELIZA. Why do you think I don't argue with you?

PATIENT. You are afraid of me.

ELIZA. Does it please you to believe I am afraid of you?

Eliza was meant to explore an obscure concept, "knowledge representation," but became a turning point for Weizenbaum's career; he and his software were a media phenomenon. TV cameras arrived at the lab. In 1968, the *New York Times* headlined a report on Eliza, "Computer Is Being Taught to Understand English." The *Times* reported that Weizenbaum's secretary apparently felt so connected to Eliza that she was offended when he casually presumed he could eavesdrop on her conversation. After typing a few sentences, she turned to him to say, "Would you mind leaving the room, please?" Weizenbaum was taken aback.[72]

When confronted with his power to manipulate people with relatively simple coding, and then to have access to their most personal thoughts, Weizenbaum retreated in horror. He began to ask hard questions of himself and colleagues. The artificial intelligence project, he concluded, was a fraud that played on the trusting instincts of people. Weizenbaum took language quite seriously, informed in part by how the Nazis had abused it, and in that light he concluded that Eliza was lying and misleading the very people it was supposed to be helping. A comment like "I am sorry to hear you are depressed" wasn't true and should appall anyone who hears it. A computer can't feel and Eliza isn't "sorry" about anything a patient said.

As we'll see in the pages that follow, the Know-It-Alls have moved boldly ahead where Weizenbaum retreated, eager to wield the almost hypnotic power computers have over their users. Facebook and Google don't flinch when their users unthinkingly reveal so much about themselves. Instead, they embrace the new reality, applying programming power to do amazing—and amazingly profitable—things with all the information they collect. If anything, they study how to make their users comfortable with sharing even more with the computer. Weizenbaum becomes an example of the path not taken in the development of computers, similar, as we'll see, to Tim Berners-Lee, the inventor of the World Wide Web. Weizenbaum and Berners-Lee each advocated stepping back from what was possible for moral reasons. And each was swept away by the potent combination of the hacker's arrogance and the entrepreneur's greed.

Weizenbaum kept up the fight, however, spending the remainder of his life trying to police the boundary between humans and machines, challenging the belief, so central to AI, that people themselves were nothing more than glorified computers and "all human knowledge is reducible to computable form."[73] This denial of what is special about being human was the great sin of the "artificial intelligentsia," according to Weizenbaum. In later debates with AI theorists, he was accused of being prejudiced in favor of living creatures, of being "a carbon-based chauvinist."

One bizarre manifestation of this charge that Weizenbaum favored "life" over thinking machines (should any arrive) came during a discussion with Daniel Dennett and Marvin Minsky at Harvard University. Weizenbaum recalled that "Dennett pointed out to me in just so many words: 'If someone said the things that you say about life about the white race in your presence, you would accuse him of being a racist. Don't you see that you are a kind of racist?'"[74] Weizenbaum couldn't help but consider this accusation as the abdication of being "part of the human family," even if he suspected that the drive behind artificial intelligence researchers like McCarthy, almost all of whom are men, was all too human. "Women are said to have a penis envy, but we are discovering that men have a uterus envy: there is something very creative that women can do and men cannot, that is, give birth to new life," he told an interviewer. "We now see evidence that men are striving to do that. They want to create not only new life but better life, with fewer imperfections. Furthermore, given that it is digital and so on, it will be immortal so they are even better than women."[75]

Weizenbaum never could have imagined how the Know-It-Alls, beginning in the 1990s, managed to amass real-world wealth and power from the imaginary worlds on their screens and the submerged urge to be the bestower of life. His later years were spent in Germany, far removed from the events in Silicon Valley.[76] However, in 2008, a few months before he died in his Berlin apartment at age eighty-five, Weizenbaum did share the stage at the Davos World Economic Forum with Reid Hoffman, the billionaire founder of LinkedIn, and Philip Rosedale, the chief executive of the pathbreaking virtual reality site Second Life. Hoffman explained why LinkedIn was such an important example of "social software": "What happens is this is my expression of myself, and part of what makes it social is it is me establishing my identity. It's me interacting with other people." Weizenbaum shakes his head in disbelief. People were misleading each other about their "identities" via computers much the way his Eliza program misled the people who communicated with it. Speaking in German, which was simultaneously translated, Weizenbaum tried and failed to rouse the crowd. "Nonsense is being spouted. Dangerous nonsenses. . . . You've already said twice, 'it's happening and it will continue'—as if technological progress has become autonomous. As if it weren't created by human beings. Or that people are doing it for all sorts of intentions. The audience is just sitting here, and no one is afraid, or reacting. Things are just happening."[77]

As the 1970s ended, so, too, did McCarthy's independent laboratory. By 1979, DARPA's funding was largely eliminated, and SAIL merged with the Stanford Computer Science Department and relocated on campus. McCarthy the scientist was already in recess, but McCarthy the polemicist had one last great success: he led the fight against censorship of the Internet, and arguably we are still dealing with its consequences today.

The World Wide Web wasn't up and running in early 1989, but computers at universities like Stanford were already connected to each other via the Internet. People would publish, argue, and comment on Usenet "newsgroups"—conversations organized around particular subjects—which were accessible through computers connected to the university's network. The newsgroups reflected the interests of computer users at the time, so if you think today's Internet is skewed toward young men obsessed with science fiction and video games, just imagine what the Internet was like then. Some newsgroups were moderated, but frequently they were open to all; send a message and anyone could read it and write a response. At the time, Stanford's electronic bulletin board system hosted roughly five hundred newsgroups with topics ranging from recipes to computer languages to sexual practices.

The controversy began with a dumb joke about a cheap Jew and a cheap Scotsman on the newsgroup rec.humor.funny.[78] The joke was older than dirt and not very funny: "A Jew and a Scotsman have dinner. At the end of the dinner the Scotsman is heard to say, 'I'll pay.' The newspaper headline next morning says, 'Jewish ventriloquist found dead in alley.'" But it landed at an awkward time. Stanford in the late 1980s was consumed by the identity politics ferment. The university was slowly becoming more diverse, which led the administration to replace required courses on Western civilization with a more inclusive curriculum featuring texts by women and people of color. Similarly, there were demonstrations demanding that Stanford offer greater protection to minorities and women on campus who didn't feel fully welcome.[79] These changes brought a backlash as well, leading Peter Thiel and another undergraduate at the time to start the conservative magazine *Stanford Review* to fight the move toward "multiculturalism," which, Thiel later said, "caused Stanford to resemble less a great university than a Third World country."[80]

With these charged events in the background, Stanford administrators decided to block the rec.humor.funny newsgroup, which included a range of offensive humor, from appearing on the university's computers. As McCarthy never tired of pointing out, no one at Stanford had ever complained about the joke. An MIT graduate student was first to object by contacting the Canadian university that hosted the newsgroup. The university cut its ties, but the man who ran the newsgroup found a new host and wouldn't take down the joke. Stanford administrators learned of the controversy in the winter of 1989 and directed a computer science graduate student to block the entire newsgroup. The administrators, for once, were trying to get ahead of events, but they were also presuming to get between the university's hackers and their computers. The graduate student whose expertise was needed to carry out the online censorship immediately informed McCarthy.[81]

McCarthy, the computer visionary, saw this seemingly trivial act as a threat to our networked future. "Newsgroups are a new communication medium just as printed books were in the 15th century," he wrote. "I believe they are one step towards universal access through everyone's computer terminal to the whole of world literature." The psychological ease in deleting or blocking controversial material risked making censorship easy to carry out. No book need be taken off the shelves and thrown out, or, god forbid, burned. Would the public even recognize that "setting up an index of prohibited newsgroups is in the same tradition as the Pope's 15th century Index Liber Prohibitorum"?[82] He rallied his peers in the computer science department to fight for a censorship-free Internet.

Throughout this campaign, McCarthy barely acknowledged the racial tensions that had so clearly influenced the university's actions. He once discussed what he saw as the hypersensitivity of minority groups with a professor who approved of the censorship and was amazed to learn that this professor believed that a minority student might not object to a racist joke because of "internalized oppression." McCarthy was suspicious of this appeal to a force that was seemingly beyond an individual's control.[83] The question of racism finally managed to intrude in the internal discussions of the computer science department through William Augustus Brown Jr., an African American medical student at Stanford who was also studying the use of artificial intelligence in treating patients.

Brown was the lone voice among his fellow computer scientists to say he was glad that "For once the university acted with some modicum of maturity."[84] Drawing from his personal experience, Brown described the issue quite differently than McCarthy and the overwhelmingly white male members of the computer science department had. "Whether disguised as free speech or simply stated as racism or sexism, such humor IS hurtful," he wrote to the bulletin board. "It is a University's right and RESPONSIBILITY to minimize such inflammatory correspondence in PUBLIC telecommunications." He saw what was at stake very differently, too. "This is not an issue of free speech; this is an issue of the social responsibility of a University. The University has never proposed that rec.humor's production be halted—it has simply cancelled its subscription to this sometimes offensive service. It obviously does NOT have to cater to every news service, as anyone who tries to find a Black magazine on campus will readily discover."[85]

McCarthy never responded directly, or even indirectly, to Brown, but others in his lab did, offering an early glimpse at how alternative opinions would be shouted down or patronized online. These responses from the Stanford computer science department today might collectively be called "whitesplaining." One graduate student responded to Brown, "I am a white male, and I have never been offended by white male jokes. Either they are so off-base that they are meaningless, or, by having some basis in fact (but being highly exaggerated) they are quite funny. I feel that the ability to laugh at oneself is part of being a mature, comfortable human being."[86] Others suggested that Brown didn't understand his own best interests. "The problem is that censorship costs more than the disease you're trying to cure. If you really believe in the conspiracy, I'm surprised that you want to give 'them' tools to implement their goals," a graduate student wrote.[87]

The reactions against him were so critical that Brown chose a different tack in reply. He opened up to his fellow students about his struggles at Stanford as a black man. "Having received most of my pre-professional training in the Black American educational system, I have a different outlook than most students," Brown wrote. "I certainly didn't expect the kind of close, warm relationships I developed at Hampton University, but I was not prepared for the antagonism. I don't quite know if it's California, or just Stanford, but . . . I don't know how many times I have had the most pompous questions asked of me; how many times a secretary has gone out of her way to make my day miserable. I sincerely doubt any of my instructors even know my name, although I am in the most difficult program in the medical center. Even my colleagues in my lab waited until last month to get the courage to include me in a casual conversation for the first time, although I have been working there five months." He continued: "I don't really mind the isolation—I can still deal, and it gives me PLENTY of time to study. But I really don't like the cruel humor. Once you come down from the high-flying ideals, it boils down to someone insisting on his right to be cruel to someone. That is a right he/she has, but NOT in ALL media."[88]

Needless to say, such displays of raw emotion were not typical of the communication on the computer science department's bulletin board. No one responded directly to what Brown had shared about his struggles as an African American medical student and computer scientist at Stanford; they continued to mock his ideas as poorly thought out and self-defeating. The closest there was to a defense of Brown was the comment of one graduate student who said he didn't agree with the censorship but worried that many of his peers believed that "minority groups complain so much really because they like the attention they get in the media. People rarely consider the complaints and try to understand the complaints from the minority point of view." He ended his email asking, "Do people feel that the environment at Stanford has improved for minority students? Worsened? Who cares?" Based on the lack of response, Who Cares carried the day.

The twenty-five years since haven't eased the pain for Brown, who left Stanford for Howard University Medical School and today is head of vascular surgery at the Naval Medical Center in Portsmouth, Virginia. The attitude at Stanford, he recalled, was elitist and entitled: "If you came from a refined enough background you could say whatever you wanted. Somehow the First Amendment was unlimited and there was no accountability. Any time you wanted to hold anyone accountable it was un-American. But those comments are neither American nor respectful." The lack of engagement from his peers was "very typical," he said. "It was isolationist there, almost hostile. Hostile in a refined way toward anyone who was different. Dismissive. That's my experience. Unfortunately, I see that attitude today, it doesn't matter whether it's Stanford or the alt-right."

What was particularly painful for Brown was that, other than for his skin color, this was his tribe—he was a hacker, too, who taught himself how to manipulate phone tones, who could discuss the elements in the blood of the Vulcans on *Star Trek*. Yet, he recalled, "As a minority, you are in the circle and not in the circle." He never felt comfortable retreating from society and going so deep into computers. The AI movement, he said, was based on the idea that "I'll be a great person because I will have created something better than me. But that misses the whole point of life—the compassion for humanity. That has nothing to do with how you do in school, whether you can program in seven different languages. Compassion for others, that is the most complex problem humanity has ever faced and it is not addressed with technology or science."[89]

No personal testimony posted to the Stanford bulletin board, no matter how gripping, would ever persuade McCarthy to see the issue of censorship as a matter of empathy for the targets of hate speech. To his mind, there was no such thing as inappropriate science or inappropriate speech. Others may disagree, he allowed. "Stanford has a legal right to do what its administration pleases, just as it has a legal right to purge the library or fire tenured faculty for their opinions," he wrote in an email to the computer science department. But he predicted the university would pay a price in loss of respect in the academic world if the authorities were given control over the Internet. McCarthy's hackers didn't respect authority for its own sake, and he was no different—letting the administrators responsible for information technology at the university decide what could be read on the computers there, he contended, was like giving janitors at the library the right to pick the books.[90]

McCarthy's colleagues in computer science innately shared his perspective; the department unanimously opposed removing the rec.humor.funny newsgroup from university computers. The computer science students overwhelmingly backed McCarthy as well, voting in a confidential email poll, 128 to 4.[91] McCarthy was able to win over the entire university by enlisting a powerful metaphor for the digital age. Removing a newsgroup, he explained to those who may not be familiar with them, was like removing a book from the library system because it was offensive. Since *Mein Kampf* was still on the shelves, it was hard to imagine how the decision to remove an anti-Semitic, anti-Scottish joke would make the cut. Either you accepted offensive speech online or you were in favor of burning books. There would be no middle ground permitted, and thus no opportunity to introduce reasonable regulations to ensure civility online, which is our predicament today.

The newsgroup and the dumb joke were restored in a great victory for McCarthy, which took on greater meaning in the years that followed, when the Web brought the Internet to even more parts of the university. Stanford had agreed that "a faculty member or student Web page was his own property, as it were, and not the property of the university," McCarthy told a crowd gathered for the fortieth anniversary of the Stanford Computer Science Department in 2006.[92]

This achievement represented McCarthy's final act in support of the hackers he had helped introduce to the world. He had ensured that their individualistic, anti-authoritarian ideas would be enshrined at Stanford and later spread across the globe, becoming half of what we know as Silicon Valley values. Only half because McCarthy had no role in that other aspect of Silicon Valley values—the belief that hackers' ideas are best spread through the marketplace. McCarthy was no entrepreneur, and periodically he felt compelled to explain himself. That same fortieth-anniversary celebration featured a panel of fabulously wealthy entrepreneurs who studied computer science at Stanford (and often didn't graduate). McCarthy took exception to the idea that "somehow, the essence of a computer science faculty was starting companies, or at least that that was very important." How could this be true, he asked the audience, since he himself hadn't started any companies? "It's my opinion that there's considerable competition between doing research, doing basic research and running a company," he said, adding grumpily, "I don't expect to convince anybody because things have gone differently from that."[93] To understand why things have gone so differently, we must look elsewhere on the Stanford campus.

2. FREDERICK TERMAN

"Stanford can be a dominating factor in the West"

When McCarthy arrived in 1962, Stanford was fully in the thrall of Frederick Terman, an engineering professor who had been given broad powers as provost to take the university to new heights in higher education. To MIT heights. To Harvard heights. Dragged by the scruff of the neck, if need be. The stakes had always been quite clear to Terman. Two decades earlier, in a letter to a prominent Stanford fund-raiser, he wrote with an engineer's precision: "We will either . . . create a foundation for a position in the West somewhat analogous to that of Harvard in the East, or we will drop to a level somewhat similar to that of Dartmouth, a well-thought-of institution having about 2 percent as much influence on national life as Harvard. Stanford can be a dominating factor in the West, but it will take years of planning to achieve this."[1]

Terman's strategy for Stanford's ascent can be summed up by a single word: entrepreneurism. He wanted the university's faculty and students to think creatively about how to bring in money to the university. When Stanford was flush with cash, there would be scholarships to attract the best students, higher salaries to poach star faculty members from other schools, investments in top-flight facilities befitting such talented students and faculty members. With enough money, Terman concluded, Stanford could overcome its less-than-elite reputation and become the Harvard of the West. Naturally, the number-crunching engineer had a plan to speed things along. Terman identified the various sources for Stanford to tap—primarily government scientific agencies and private businesses—and then made sure that the university pointed its students and faculty members in the right direction with their research.

The way Terman saw it, the benefits to Stanford could flow in any number of ways. There were the significant payments from the government to cover overhead costs at the research labs; the expensive equipment donated by companies eager to encourage research related to their specific technologies; the experts from industry who, for similar reasons, became visiting professors in Stanford's science departments, their salaries paid for in part by their employers; and, more broadly, there was the goodwill Stanford earned from alumni and faculty members who had achieved business success and would give back to the school with hefty donations. The happy coalition of academia, government, and private industry that Terman proposed has been called "the military-industrial-academic complex"; he preferred to call it "win-win-win."[2]

No doubt, the government held the largest pot of money for a university eager to grow. World War II had demonstrated over and over the importance of scientific research: the early computers helped crack the German codes; radar bolstered the Allies' air defenses, while radar-jamming devices thwarted the Germans'; the proximity fuse made bombs more accurate and thus more destructive. Above all else was the atomic bomb, which brought the war to a hasty conclusion, saving the lives of hundreds of thousands of American soldiers, many of whom later became members of Congress. Scientific research would evermore be at the heart of America's defenses, organized around university laboratories, and Terman made sure that Stanford was included among the universities destined to receive those grants. During the 1950s, government-sponsored academic research had more than tripled, reaching nearly $1 billion by the end of the decade—more than three-quarters of those funds went to just twenty elite universities, which thanks to Terman now included Stanford. By 1960, 39 percent of Stanford's operating budget came from federal support, the overwhelming majority directed at physics and engineering.[3]

But Terman's innovation was in converting Stanford research into business opportunities for students and faculty members. The marketplace represented a pot of money for Stanford to tap, too, and Terman wasn't about to ignore it. These ideas first occurred to him in the 1930s in his own engineering lab on campus. Terman's electronics research had practical applications for devices like radio-wave amplifiers and bomb fuses, and he eagerly worked with businesses—established ones as well as start-ups—to bring these products to market. Famously, in 1939 he helped stake two promising former students, William Hewlett and David Packard, in a start-up run out of a Palo Alto garage. In part, Terman was responding to the Great Depression, when even his best students were having a hard time finding steady work. Being in partnership with businesses, or starting your own, was an excellent way to ensure employment immediately after graduation. But he was also thinking of Stanford. Hewlett, who along with Packard became a lifelong Stanford donor, recalled a long-ago conversation: "We were walking out of the old engineering building, and Terman said he was looking forward to the day when I gave my first million dollars to this laboratory. I remember this, because at the time I thought it was so incredible."[4]

Later, when Terman became university-wide provost in 1955, he applied this same strategy to build up Stanford's status through efforts like the Stanford Industrial Park, which brought dozens of new and established high-tech companies into the bosom of the university.[5] He consciously, and unapologetically, steered Stanford toward academic disciplines like biochemistry, statistics, and aeronautics, which were likely to generate business opportunities or government grants, and away from dead-end fields like taxonomy or geography or classics. A later Stanford president, Richard W. Lyman, marveled at how Terman could display such cool confidence while "downplaying or even eliminating established programs or academic emphases that lacked promise for the future."[6] Terman did, however, shed his calm demeanor when challenged over his plans for reinventing Stanford's academic priorities. His typical response to those who stood in the way was to question their competence, motives, or intelligence.

For example, there was a prominent Stanford naturalist, George Myers, who criticized Terman for shifting the biology department away from its strength in zoology and the environment toward research done in laboratories, which was more likely to be marketable. Myers went over Terman's head to complain to the university president, J. Wallace Sterling, about his provost's obvious disdain for scientists "who operate in muddy boots." Despite Terman's insinuations, the nature sciences were eminently practical fields, Myers wrote, addressing humanity's most pressing concern: "The destruction and poisoning of man's complex biological and physical environment by man himself."[7] Sterling backed up Terman, as he always did. Terman never directly engaged with Myers but did privately dismiss his complaints as coming from "a hardworking but not particularly bright biologist . . . who specializes in fish."[8]

Seemingly less controversial was Terman's decision to shrink the classics department at Stanford by failing to replace two professors who had retired. Who could dispute that the department failed to pull its weight financially? Not that Terman was blaming the faculty members for their lack of entrepreneurial zeal: business opportunities from the study of Latin and Greek were painfully small. Still, facts are facts. Why would Stanford direct its limited resources toward a field with such a small potential payoff? When the senior member of the department, Hazel Hansen, a specialist in ancient Greek pottery, wrote to object to the unfilled vacancies, Terman was dismissive. He didn't reply, but again disparaged privately: Hansen, a 1920 Stanford graduate who had risen from lecturer to full professor, was a "single woman—lonely—frustrated."[9]

Opponents of Terman's plans never managed to gain any traction. They were isolated, and he had the numbers on his side. He knew more about most departments than the chairmen did, and he proved it with detailed spreadsheets and charts that tracked, say, the number of graduate students supervised per faculty member, or the average number of years a graduate student spent to complete a PhD. Collecting the relevant data became his personal obsession. Faculty members recall graduation ceremonies attended by Terman: there he'd be, sitting quietly on this day of celebration, with a mechanical pencil in hand, "carefully using his program to calculate and compare doctoral production statistics."[10] His policy was to insist that budget requests arrive on Christmas Eve, "so that while others were celebrating he could get a head start on the next year's work."[11]

For our story, Terman's role was vital. He laid the groundwork for a new relationship between a university and business, which proved particularly relevant when computer science was later shown to have the potential to extract fortunes from the American economy. Because of Terman's ideas, improved techniques for indexing the Web (Yahoo), or searching the Web (Google), or sharing photos online (Instagram)—three among thousands of business-ready ideas developed on the Stanford campus—didn't remain there as part of some free, public trust. (Google, in particular, seemed well on its way to a noncommercial future if not for the pull of Stanford's entrepreneurism.) Instead, all of these start-ups were aggressively brought to market, where they have become central to our lives and hugely valuable assets.

Fittingly, Stanford itself was an ambitious start-up backed by a wealthy couple, Leland and Jane Stanford. The Stanfords planned to reinvent higher education by investing the millions of dollars they had made by connecting Americans through the new transcontinental railroad. As Leland Stanford explained: "If I thought that the university at Palo Alto was going to be only like the others in our country, I should think I had made a mistake to establish a new one, and that I had better have given the money to some existing institutions."[12]

The creation of Leland Stanford Jr. University represents the triumph of hope over overwhelming grief. The Stanfords' son, Leland Jr., was nearly sixteen in March 1884 when he died of typhoid fever during a European tour. The story goes that the father was in such despair at the bedside of his dying boy that he questioned whether he should go on living, and his son appeared in a dream to say: "Father, do not say you have nothing to live for. You have a great deal to live for. Live for humanity." When Leland Sr. awoke, the boy had passed away, and the Stanfords had a new purpose in life.[13] They considered building a combined museum and lecture hall in San Francisco, but concluded that their idealistic son who loved learning would have wanted them to create a university to make higher education accessible to the masses, men and women, rich and poor.

Back east, they sought an audience with the formidable president of

Harvard University, Charles William Eliot. How much money, they asked, would it take to create a world-class university? Eliot's response was that they should be prepared to spend at least $5 million, a sum that was significantly more than Harvard's endowment at the time and perhaps was meant to put a scare into his visitors. Eliot recounted what happened next: "A silence followed, and Mrs. Stanford looked grave; but after an appreciable interval, Mr. Stanford said with a smile, 'Well, Jane, we could manage that, couldn't we?' And Mrs. Stanford nodded."[14] Clearly Eliot hadn't a clue about the kinds of fortunes there were out west even then.

Leland Stanford was worth tens of millions of dollars when he met with Eliot. Though the loss of his son changed his perspective radically, Stanford continued robber baron–ing, simultaneously running the Central Pacific Railroad, the western end of the transcontinental railroad, while also holding political office. Decades earlier, Stanford had been California's governor; during the years the university was being built he was a U.S. senator. Much of Stanford's fortune was in the form of vast tracts of land he had acquired in the course of expanding his railroads; they were among his first gifts to the university. An 8,180-acre parcel in the Santa Clara Valley, the so-called Farm where Leland Sr. would graze his horses, and where Leland Jr. would take his lunches, was set aside for the campus and according to the founding grant could never be sold.[15]

The Stanfords' plans for a university "created something of a sensation in the insular world of American higher education" when they became public in 1885, both for the huge sums of money involved and the new approach—there would be equality between the sexes, a nondenominational religious life, and free tuition.[16] Stanford University's pledge in its founding document to provide an education that led to "personal success and direct usefulness in life" was a head-on critique of East Coast schools whose students "acquire a university degree or fashionable educational veneer for the mere ornamentation of idle and purposeless lives."[17] Leland Stanford promised he would spare no expense to remake education in this way. Pocketbook out, he first searched for a suitable university president. "The man I want is hard to find," he said. "I want a man of good business and executive ability as well as a scholar. The scholars are plentiful enough, but the executive ability is scarce."[18]

In what would become a familiar pattern, Leland set his eyes on the president of MIT (then known as Boston Technical Institute), Francis A. Walker, a Civil War hero and economist. During visits east, Stanford wooed Walker and promised to increase his salary several times over, but never could persuade him to relocate from Cambridge to the frontiers of California.[19] The Stanfords instead settled on David Starr Jordan, a young nature scientist who was president of Indiana University. Jordan was educated at Cornell, something of a model for the Stanfords in that it was cofounded in 1865 by a successful businessman, Ezra Cornell, with the purpose of expanding access to higher education. Up to that point, there hadn't been universities supported by a single wealthy patron. The largest donation to an American college was $50,000 given to Harvard by Abbott Lawrence in 1847 to create an engineering school. In rapid succession after Cornell came multimillion-dollar donations to Johns Hopkins, Stanford, the University of Chicago, and Duke, among others.[20]

"Inevitably, the increase in the size of gifts changed the relations of donor to recipient," wrote the historians Richard Hofstadter and Walter P. Metzger. "Borrowing a term from economic history, one may say that the givers became entrepreneurs in the field of higher education. They took the initiative in providing funds and in deciding their general purposes."[21] Even more than other founding donors, the Stanfords made clear that their grant to the university came with strings attached. The authority one would expect to reside in a board of trustees or president would reside in them, including the power to hire and fire faculty members and to make strategic plans. Jordan was expected to go along with this new way of doing business and in return he was promised that the faculty he recruited would have "at least a little more than is paid by any other university in America."[22]

When Stanford opened its doors in 1891, after six years of planning, many feared that no students would show up, even if the tuition was free. Instead, Stanford enrolled 555 men and women, who were taught by a faculty of fifteen that grew to forty-nine by the second year.[23] Among the members of that pioneering class was the future U.S. president, Herbert Hoover. But despite this fast start and fabulously wealthy patron, Stanford endured a hard few years: "That the infant university survived was something of a miracle," one university historian concluded.[24] In 1893, before the first class had graduated, Leland Stanford died, depriving the university of a powerful protector. His estate was tied up in court while the federal government pursued millions of dollars of what it said were unpaid loans. There was an economic panic that year as well, which threatened the economic growth in the west and made the fight over Leland Stanford's estate even more hard-fought.

Jane Stanford stepped up to keep the school afloat during this period of economic uncertainty, ignoring business managers who recommended that she allow the school to shutter until she could regain her financial footing.[25] Instead, she convinced the judge presiding over the claims against her husband's estate to allow her to maintain the usual household expenses—$10,000 a month to operate three large homes with seventeen servants. She then petitioned the court to consider the Stanford faculty as her "servants." By reducing her household staff to three, and expenses to just $350 a month, she was then able to direct $9,650 a month toward university salaries. In letters to President Jordan, Stanford made clear the depths of her suffering: "I have curtailed all expenses in the way of household affairs and personal indulgencies. Have given up all luxuries and confined myself to actual necessities." Her visits to New York City, where the Stanford estate was being litigated, were an ordeal as well: "It is no pleasure to be on the fifth floor of the Fifth Avenue Hotel in a small bedroom opening on a court, economizing almost to meanness, when I have a sweet beautiful home to go to."[26]

In 1898, when Leland's estate was freed from its entanglements, Jane Stanford transferred $11 million in assets to the university, out of what would be a total of $20 million in gifts.[27] After making such deliberate sacrifices on behalf of her school, which began as a surrogate for her lost only child, Jane Stanford expected unquestioning loyalty from Jordan and the administration. Thus the university was transformed, in the words of Hofstadter and Metzger, from "this unusual oligarchy into a still more unusual matriarchate."[28]

Intriguingly, this matriarch's greatest influence on Stanford came through her insistence that the university cap the number of women who could attend. The trend line quickly grew worrisome to Mrs. Stanford: 25 percent women in the student body when the school opened its doors in 1891, 33 percent four years later, when the first class graduated, and 40 percent in 1898. There were other troubling indicators that year too. Stanford was routed in athletics by its rival, Berkeley, and the student yearbook, weekly newspaper, and debating team were all led by women. Mrs. Stanford asked openly the question that weighed on her mind: How could such a feminine institution, the soon-to-be Vassar of the West, be a fitting final tribute to her son?[29]

The next year, Jane Stanford decreed that the university could never have more than five hundred women enrolled. It was a draconian step, taking no account of how Stanford's enrollment might grow, and entirely out of keeping with the progressive founding mission.[30] Back in 1885, at the first meeting of the university's board of trustees, Leland Stanford said an education "equally full and complete" was of the highest importance. In a newspaper interview four years later he went one step beyond equality between the sexes and said, "I am inclined to think that if the education of either is neglected, it had better be that of the man than the woman, because if the mother is well educated she insensibly imports it to the child."[31]

President Jordan was sympathetic to Mrs. Stanford's concerns in this matter, particularly the noticeable decline in Stanford's sporting prowess. "The university must have more men if we expect to make a better showing in athletics," he said, but he asked that Jane Stanford be reasonable and impose a percentage cap, instead of a fixed number. Mrs. Stanford's response was clipped and impatient: "To carry out this idea would be violating my instructions and very disappointing to me."[32] In later years, administrators employed various work-arounds to keep talented women in the fold, such as letting them audit classes while they waited for one of the five hundred slots to become available, but only after more than thirty years did the board of trustees relax the limit on women to 40 percent of total enrollment. Not until the 1970s was any limit on women's enrollment removed from Stanford's rules.

There were other interventions by Mrs. Stanford. For example, because of her disapproval of automobiles, aka "devil wagons," there would be no cars on campus during her lifetime.[33] She pushed Jordan to use the university's funds to complete construction of the campus, rather than add more professors, as he preferred. The most controversial action by Mrs. Stanford in her day was to demand that a radical economics professor and friend of President Jordan, Edward Ross, be fired for extreme anti-immigrant comments he made during the 1900 election. She got her wish, but it came at cost. In 1903, in the wake of the "Ross Affair," Jane Stanford agreed to give up personal control of the university, allowing the board of trustees to run it. It's true that she simultaneously joined the board of trustees and was elected its president, but, still, the devolution of power had begun. Jane Stanford was dead within two years, under mysterious circumstances.

Today, historians are confident in saying that Mrs. Stanford was poisoned, the victim, in fact, of two separate attacks barely a month apart, the first in San Francisco, the second in Hawaii, where she traveled to recover from the first poisoning. But because Jordan acted quickly, immediately traveling to Hawaii when he learned she had succumbed there, he convinced the national press that the cause of death was heart failure. Jordan disparaged the Hawaiian doctor who treated Mrs. Stanford as she was dying, Francis Howard Humphris, as "a man without professional or personal standing," in order to cast doubt on his conclusion that her death was a homicide.[34] However, an investigation of the death a century later by a Stanford medical professor, Robert W.P. Cutler, concluded that Humphris offered excellent medical care: he did all he could to save Mrs. Stanford's life, and his judgment that she was poisoned was spot on too.

Jordan managed to avoid a public relations nightmare, but whose reputation was he protecting, the university's or his own? "The question need not be skirted," writes another Stanford professor who has studied the case, W.B. Carnochan, about whether Jordan killed Jane Stanford to free himself from her meddling. "He had the motive . . . but could he have brought it off without help from a pharmacist and a household servant? Even the most vivid conjecture resists the notion of Jordan slipping into Mrs. Stanford's San Francisco pantry, bath, or bedroom to spike her mineral water or lace her bicarbonate of soda with strychnine."[35] Mrs. Stanford's personal secretary, Bertha Berner, a beloved long-term employee, "seems to have had ample opportunity but no obvious motive," Cutler concludes. "Jordan seems to have had motive but no obvious opportunity."[36] There simply isn't enough evidence, both scholars say, to reach a conclusion.

After Mrs. Stanford's death, Jordan remained president of Stanford for eight years, free of her second-guessing. He expanded the faculty by recruiting scholars in his mold—young ambitious midwesterners willing to help build up a school that was new on the scene. Among that wave was Lewis Terman, a junior professor of educational psychology born to a large family on a rural Indiana farm and educated at Indiana University. Terman arrived in 1910 to a campus that was still repairing the damage from the earthquake four years earlier; he was joined by his wife, Anna; ten-year-old son, Frederick; and seven-year-old daughter, Helen. As a Stanford professor, Terman planned on continuing his studies of human intelligence: What is it? How do we measure it?

Terman's friend and colleague, Edwin G. Boring, offered a facetious definition: intelligence was the ability to do well on intelligence tests.[37] Obviously, Terman believed a well-constructed test was more significant than that. Building on the work of the French education reformer Alfred Binet, Terman devised the first popular intelligence test in America, what came to be known as the Stanford-Binet IQ Test, a standard tool in education, government, and industry.[38] Once he had IQ scores that he believed reflected innate intelligence, Terman could then test his theories. He could, for example, compare fathers to their sons, to study whether intelligence was inherited, or compare members of one race to those of another to determine if one was superior. He could correlate intelligence to other measurable qualities to explore a theory like the smarter you are the more money you earn, or the better grades you get, or the fewer years in prison you serve.

In his long Stanford career, Terman researched every one of these questions, concluding, among other things, that intelligence indeed was inherited and that the white race had more of it than the black race. But it was that last question—what benefits accrue from being intelligent?—that most preoccupied Terman. He wanted his research to reverse the public's perception of geniuses (male geniuses, actually) as peculiar, even deviant, weak, feminine, socially awkward. He wanted to prove what he knew firsthand, that brilliant children grow up to be highly productive, brilliant adults, if only they are recognized and given opportunities. Clearly, Terman's own life was a motivation.

Despite his evident talents, Lewis Terman had seemed destined for a life on the farm. Through exceptional hard work, however, and a powerful drive to escape rural life, Terman arrived at a bare-bones teacher's school before transferring to Indiana University to complete his undergraduate education and then a master's degree in education. He later earned a doctorate at Clark University in Massachusetts, which had built a reputation as a leader in the relatively new field of psychology. Terman's feeling of intellectual inadequacy never quite left, and he devoted his professional life to finding all the little Lewis Termans out there and encouraging society to support them while they were still young. Smart kids shouldn't have it as hard as he did.[39]

At Clark, Terman first experimented with ways of testing for intelligence, recruiting seven "stupid" children and seven "bright" children as his subjects.[40] When he arrived at Stanford, he learned of Binet's intelligence test and realized that he didn't need to start at the beginning. He paid a token fee of a dollar to the uninterested Binet for the rights to publish a revision, Stanford-Binet.[41] The purpose of Binet's test, which was created at the behest of the French government, was to identify children who were falling behind so they could receive specialized instruction. Terman in his research projects pointed the test in the other direction, using it to identify brilliant young people, "It is to the highest 25 percent of our population and more especially the top 5 percent that we must look for the production of leaders who will advance science, art, government, education and social welfare generally."[42] Terman also saw the business potential in IQ tests, which were sold to schools, governments, and businesses. According to estimates based on sales of the test record forms, about 150,000 persons a year took the Stanford-Binet test from 1916 to 1937, which increased to about 500,000 persons a year from 1937 to 1960.[43]

Though Binet never spoke up during his lifetime, he apparently disapproved of Terman's amended test and how it was applied. According to Binet's close collaborator in France, Theodore Simon, Binet considered attempts like Terman's to render a verdict on someone's potential based on a test score to be a betrayal of its purpose. More important than intelligence was judgment, Binet and Simon had written a few years earlier, a quality otherwise known as "good sense, practical sense, initiative, the faculty of adapting one's self to circumstances." They concluded: "A person may be a moron or an imbecile if he is lacking in judgment; but with good judgment he can never be either. Indeed the rest of the intellectual faculties seem of little importance in comparison with judgment."[44]

Terman defended his obsession with intelligence in an essay that appeared in 1922 in a popular magazine of the time, *World's Work*. "When our intelligence scales have become more accurate and the laws governing IQ changes have been more definitively established," he wrote, "it will then be possible to say that there is nothing about an individual as important as his IQ, except possibly his morals."[45] The year before, Terman began work on his ambitious research project, "Genetic Studies of Genius." His assistants ultimately found more than 1,500 young people in California who scored at least 135 on Terman's IQ test, where a score of 100 is defined as normal, making them the top 1 percent of the population.[46] He matched the students, who typically were born in 1910, with a similar number of ordinary young people as a control group; Terman's team would check in periodically—the first time was five years later—to see how the geniuses were faring as compared to young people of average intelligence.[47] This research, he suspected, would demonstrate the general superiority of the smartest, not just intellectually, but physically, morally, socially. Terman wanted to reassure the public that the geniuses his test identified were just like them, only more so. And thus most fit to lead.[48]

The years Terman was starting his research were the high-water mark in the United States for eugenics, the movement that applied Darwin's ideas about inherited traits and "survival of the fittest" to humanity. The elites who promoted eugenics, including President Jordan of Stanford, were reacting to the influx of poor European and Asian immigrants and an inarticulate sense that, as a result, the population was becoming less intelligent and less moral. In crude terms, eugenics was a plan to ensure that the "right" people were reproducing and that the "wrong" people were not. Most eugenicists focused on the "wrong" side of the equation, so-called negative eugenics, and used the IQ test to identify the "feeble-minded" who needed to be prevented from having children for the sake of the human gene pool, through increased use of birth control, and, in the most extreme cases, forced sterilization, a practice that was endorsed by the Supreme Court in 1927.[49]

Terman's research emerged from his belief in "positive" eugenics: if he could prove the overall superiority of brilliant men, they would find it easier to attract the best women and hand down superior genetic material to the next generation. Almost from the start, however, Terman's methods were controversial. The critic Walter Lippmann, writing in the *New Republic* in the early 1920s, took aim at a key vulnerability in Terman's project, his IQ test. "It is not possible, I think, to imagine a more contemptible proceeding than to confront a child with a set of puzzles, and after an hour's monkeying with them, proclaim to the child, or to his parents that here is a C- individual," Lippmann wrote. "It would not only be a contemptible thing to do. It would be a crazy thing to do, because there is nothing in these tests to warrant a judgment of this kind."[50]

In a familiar pattern for the Terman family, Lewis responded harshly and dismissively when crossed. His reply, also in the *New Republic*, ridiculed Lippmann's lack of scientific rigor in suggesting that high-quality childcare was the best way to produce smarter and healthier children. If how we raise children really made them smarter, Terman replied, then Lippmann had to immediately share what he knew, for the sake of the nation. "If there is any possibility of identifying, weighing and bringing under control these IQ stimulants and depressors we can well afford to throw up every other kind of scientific research until the job is accomplished," he wrote less than a month later, imagining how "the rest of the mysteries of the universe would fall easy prey before our made-to-order IQ of 180 to 200." In a sense, Terman was mocking Lippmann for claiming he could produce an "artificial intelligence."

Terman couldn't resist continuing his mockery: think of the entrepreneurial opportunities from a Lippmann-licensed childcare system for improving children's IQs. "If he could guarantee to raise certified 100s to certified 140s, or even certified 80s to certified 100s, nothing but premature death or the discovery and publication of his secret would keep him out of the Rockefeller-Ford class if he cared to achieve it," Terman writes, adding cruelly that he knows a rich father who would gladly pay Lippmann "10 or 20 million if he could only raise one particular little girl from about 60 or 70 to a paltry 100 or so."[51]

Terman was much more kindly disposed toward his young

geniuses—"my gifted children," he called them, a phrase he coined. He tracked the young people with high IQs in his study through adolescence into adulthood and beyond, producing four separate volumes during his lifetime. Upon being enrolled in the genius study, the children, who were kept anonymous, provided a raft of information about themselves and their upbringing—their health, family background, family income, home life. This was the data Terman used to demonstrate how well his geniuses fared in life. Indeed, he found that two-thirds of the "Term-ites" earned bachelor's degrees, ten times the national rate, as well as an unusually high number of doctorates and medical and law degrees. The geniuses' earning power was higher too: while the median salary for white-collar jobs in 1954 was $5,800, the equivalent in Terman's group was $10,556.[52]

The study's usefulness, it should be said, was quite limited. There were the flaws with the test itself, and how it was applied: the geniuses discovered by the test were a bit more likely to be male than female, but that was less jarring than near total absence of blacks, Japanese Americans, or American Indians. Also, incredibly, Terman's team individually tested two California boys who grew up to win Nobel Prizes in physics and neither scored high enough to be included in the study. One of those boys who was particularly stung by being passed over was young Billy Shockley of Palo Alto, whose Nobel Prize recognized his role in producing the first transistor; alongside Lewis Terman's son, Frederick, Shockley would become a central figure in the growth of Silicon Valley.

Beyond the test's dubious accuracy, there was a flaw in how the study itself was conducted over the years: Terman repeatedly intervened in the lives of his high-IQ subjects, often without their knowledge. He couldn't help himself. He wrote them recommendations for admission to Stanford, gave small sums of money during tough times, and, in one case, helped a fourteen-year-old be placed in a good foster home rather than returned to his abusive father. (To be clear, Terman didn't intervene to help any in the control group.) These intrusions by Terman made the study's conclusions scientifically unreliable, to say the least: readers could rightly question if the geniuses outshone the control group because of their talents or because they had an influential guardian angel. For all its statistical charts and plots of standards of deviation, his work wasn't science—it was advocacy. His dream was a society led by a hereditary class of super-intelligent beings. A beehive run by a few king bees.

In summing up Lewis Terman's life, his friend Edwin Boring tried to explain his commitment to the talented 1 percent. "Some persons . . . wonder how such an undemocratic view could be held by this tender-minded, sensitive, ambitious person, but the fact is that Terman thought of the intellectually elite as those who would save civilization for democracy," Boring wrote in a biography of Terman for the National Academy of Sciences in 1959. "The gifted were given. You do not choose to have them, for there they are, whether you will or no. You can, however, choose to use them, to separate them from the crowd so that they may be trained to devote their special talents to benefit the crowd from which they have been taken."[53] Lewis Terman, patron saint of the Know-It-Alls.

Frederick Terman grew up on the Stanford campus idolizing his father, who in time became the chairman of the psychology department. The feelings between Lewis and Fred were no doubt mutual—the son had pleased his father with his overall academic success. A classmate's caricature, which appeared in the 1916 Palo Alto High School yearbook, showed Fred in academic dress with a book planted right in front of his face. He had other interests as well. He ran track in high school and at Stanford, and was obsessed with ham radio—the personal computer of its day. When Fred graduated from Stanford, first with a bachelor's degree in chemistry, then an advanced engineer's degree in 1922, he had nearly perfect grades. Despite the family's deep Stanford loyalty, both father and son agreed that Fred should head east for the sake of his career. He was accepted at MIT, where he earned a PhD in electrical engineering under the tutelage of influential professor Vannevar Bush. After completing his PhD, Terman was offered a teaching position at MIT and was tempted to stay. A bout of tuberculosis, best treated in the climate back home, was enough to end that flirtation.[54]

With a year of recuperation behind him, Fred Terman accepted a full-time appointment at Stanford, where he taught the science of radio broadcasting. Terman negotiated for the big radio companies to donate equipment to his lab so students could carry out practical scientific work. "Even Terman's textbook, *Radio Engineering*, reflected this strong commercial bent," one historian of the Cold War university wrote, noting, "It became an immediate bestseller because, like his courses, it placed real-world problems at the center with an elegance and simplicity that especially appealed to working engineers."[55] Around this time, Terman began courting Sibyl Walcutt, who was a graduate student in Lewis Terman's psychology lab, where she naturally would have been expected to take an IQ test. Son was no different than father when it came to valuing intelligence. "The young professor went over to the Psychology Department and looked up her IQ scores," Terman's biographer writes, "then, according to Sibyl, things heated up."[56]

During World War II, Fred Terman again traveled east, this time with his family, wife, son, and daughter. He was sent to Harvard by Professor Bush, who supervised the government's wartime research as the chairman of the Office of Scientific Research and Development. Terman's mission there, as head of the Radio Research Laboratory, was to find countermeasures to Axis radar systems. By 1943, the lab had a staff of more than eight hundred and a budget bigger than all of Stanford University. Terman made sure to include Stanford scientists in his plans—more than thirty graduate students and faculty members crossed the country to work at the lab, learning firsthand the kind of research being conducted back east.[57]

When Terman returned to Stanford for good, as new dean of the engineering school, he was ready to lead, confident in his managerial skills and his ability to bring lucrative military research grants westward.[58] At the same time, Terman continued the business-friendly policies he began before the war. The success of Hewlett-Packard had great personal meaning for Terman, but more importantly it was proof of concept. In the 1950s, Stanford began a series of programs to formalize the strong ties between businesses and the university. One idea was to recruit visiting professors from the labs of private companies, so that Stanford faculty and students could learn about the latest trends in industrial research, while the university paid at most half the salary. Another, the Industrial Affiliates Program, made sure that the university's ideas flowed in the other direction by granting prepublication access to Stanford research in exchange for substantial fees.

Each policy gave Stanford the resources to keep growing, as Terman insisted, while creating the mutual dependence between the university and nearby companies that he craved.[59]

The construction of an industrial park on university land in the mid-1950s gave these relationships a sense of permanence. Stanford labs and industrial labs would be cheek-by-jowl. Many of the firms at the industrial park had explicit Stanford ties—Varian Associates, Hewlett-Packard, Shockley Semiconductors. Others were branches of industry leaders like Lockheed and General Electric. Truth be told, the industrial park wasn't devised by Terman, or run by him. Other administrators had promoted an industrial park as a way of extracting revenues from the prized land, the Farm, which couldn't be sold. The combination of the industrial park and a shopping center with half a million square feet of retail space, both of which operated under ninety-nine-year leases, brought in nearly $1 million a year in revenue to the university.[60]

Stanford's tight embrace of individual businesses, even as it was subsisting on government research grants, perhaps should have raised more concerns. Tax money was enriching investors, but these were different times. "Cold war rhetoric," writes the historian Rebecca Lowen, "linked economic prosperity and military might as the two pillars of America's defense against the Soviet threat. Framed in this way, with the emphasis on the 'national good,' the fact that private companies were profiting from the expenditure of public funds could go unremarked."[61] Thriving industry meant thriving country. And thriving industry required well-trained experts, which is how universities made their contribution to industry, with the help of the federal government. When Fred Terman praised this system for bringing technical skill to big business in a 1956 address to engineers there were clear echoes of Lewis Terman's ideas about ensuring that the smartest are in charge. "The idealists, the social planners, the do-gooders, the socialists and others of their ilk . . . called for better distribution of wealth," Frederick Terman said, while engineers, working within the system of free enterprise, simply got it done, "making possible the creation of so much new wealth that redistribution was unnecessary."[62]

In 1955, Terman was promoted to university provost by President Sterling and three years later added the title of vice president of academic affairs after the consulting firm McKinsey and Company recommended a reorganization of Stanford's administration that gave Terman "responsibility for the affairs of each of the university's schools, libraries and eventually all institutes."[63] The brains of the operation. The engineering school was making gains under Terman, but the university as a whole was in decline. The war years had been harder for Stanford than other universities because of the vestiges of Mrs. Stanford's quota on women. In 1933, the board of trustees had relaxed Jane Stanford's strict limit of five hundred women to a 40 percent cap on women, but when war came Stanford was stifled from admitting enough women to fill its classrooms. As a result, Stanford's salaries were not keeping up with the competition back east—in 1954, 75 percent of full professors there made less than the minimum salary at Princeton.[64]

Terman had a mandate to apply his engineering school ideas more broadly. Not only would Terman pour resources into lucrative research areas, but he would recruit only the top men in those fields. He called this strategy "steeples of excellence." The same efficiency argument for academic departments—ecology bad, biochemistry good—would apply to individuals. What made this strategy even more compelling was the decision by Vannevar Bush, as the government's civilian science chief, to automatically include within research grants a percentage to cover "indirect" costs, the university's overhead.[65] Professors who could win large research grants weren't just helping themselves, they were helping Stanford compete with other big-name schools. As to complaints that Stanford was abandoning huge swaths of knowledge under this scheme, Terman replied that such a responsibility fell on schools like Harvard and Yale, which could afford it.[66]

The main challenge for Terman under "steeples of excellence" was how to locate and lure these star professors. First, he evaluated the talent. No matter what the field was, Terman felt empowered to ask, "Is this person smart enough to be a Stanford professor?" In several cases, he discovered that candidates already approved by departmental hiring committees had received poor grades in calculus while in college and declared them unfit. When a candidate had been agreed upon, Terman would look for a way in—whether through a steep raise or speeded-up tenure or by exploiting the internal politics at the candidate's school. Planning trips to Stanford in the winter for candidates from the Northeast was another tactic.

The hiring of John McCarthy is a case in point. As we've seen, McCarthy had reasons to leave MIT, but he was still raw over the earlier rejection by Stanford as a junior mathematics professor, so much so that when the university's only computer science professor, William Forsythe, first called McCarthy about joining him, McCarthy was dismissive. "I thought to turn him off by saying, 'I'd been to Stanford before. I'd only come as a full professor,' and he said, 'I think I can arrange that,' which surprised me very much, since MIT had just made me an associate professor."[67] Computer science had become important to Terman, as he told his top aide: "We got to do this. I see a field coming up and Stanford's got to be in that."[68]

Indeed, in the decades that followed, microprocessing chip makers like Fairchild and later Intel flourished in Silicon Valley, right on Stanford's doorstep. A thriving community of venture capitalists grew there too, along Sand Hill Road. Thanks to Terman, Stanford would be poised to take advantage of the computer revolution. His market-obsessed thinking is now standard at Stanford: the outgoing president, John Hennessy, was a professor of electrical engineering and computer science who spent a sabbatical year launching a successful chip-manufacturing start-up. Hennessy's successor, Marc Tessier-Lavigne, is a neuroscientist who had been an executive at the biotechnology firm Genentech.[69] Since 1970, Stanford has licensed 3,500 inventions, across a range of fields, generating about $1.5 billion in revenue.[70] A large chunk of that total came in 2004, when the university pocketed $336 million for the stake in Google it was given in return for a license of the underlying search technology Sergey Brin and Larry Page developed there.[71]

This wealth has flowed back to Stanford in other ways, as Terman predicted, including a crown jewel engineering center built in 1977, which was named in Terman's honor and funded by Hewlett and Packard at a cost of $9.2 million. In 1982, at age eighty-two, Terman died in campus housing after witnessing this fitting campus tribute, embodying all he preached about Stanford's path to success. But what came nearly thirty years later, in 2010, was perhaps the truest vindication of Terman's ideas. In that year, Stanford built a new science and engineering quad, which included a new engineering center, named in honor of a different Stanford figure, Jen-Hsun Huang, who has a master's degree in electrical engineering and cofounded the tech company Nvidia. Huang and his wife donated $30 million to the project.[72]

The next year, the Terman engineering center was demolished, with as much as 99 percent of the building material recycled: Spanish clay roof tiles were carefully removed and incorporated in a new outdoor education and recreation center; the cedar planks in the roof were sold to Stanford students and faculty members for use in school projects.[73] Terman is not entirely forgotten: inside the Huang center, on the second floor, is where you'll find the Frederick Emmons Terman Engineering Library.[74]

3. BILL GATES

"Most of you steal your software"

If the Know-It-Alls' values represent a merger of a hacker's radical individualism and an entrepreneur's greed, then only one man can be considered their forefather: Bill Gates. Before he arrived on the scene, the hackers were largely unchallenged in their instinct for sharing what they had learned and general disdain for making money from the computers they loved. Certainly, their pied piper, John McCarthy, shared this inclination. Gates, however, was prepared to call his fellow hackers out—call them thieves, even—as he built the first great software empire and became the prototypical hacker-entrepreneur.

The story begins one winter day more than forty years ago, as Gates and his high school friend, Paul Allen, were walking in Harvard Square. They spotted at a newsstand the cover of the January 1975 issue of *Popular Electronics*, which featured the Altair, the first build-it-yourself computer, under the banner headline, "Project Breakthrough!" The news was simultaneously inspiring and troubling to Gates and Allen.[1] The arrival of Altair's relatively inexpensive "kit computer" vindicated their shared conviction that a computing revolution was soon to come. Intel had just introduced a microchip so dense with circuits that it could contain the brains of an entire computer, a breakthrough with the potential to allow computers to piggyback on the advances in microchips and become smaller, faster, cheaper. Soon enough, personal, too. All very exciting. The worrisome part came from the recognition that others had the same intuition about personal computers and, what's more, some had already acted. What if Gates and Allen were too late to the party?[2]

Gates was unusual among his hacker peers: he cared deeply about being a business success. His interest in making money could be traced to early childhood, when he pored over issues of *Fortune* magazine, and became evident after he transferred to Lakeside, a private boys' school outside Seattle, as a junior high school student. At Lakeside, Gates was introduced to Allen, who was two years older; they both excelled at computers and learned to program in the BASIC language. In 1968, the school could communicate via teletype with a remote computer owned by General Electric, using a version of McCarthy's time-sharing system. Access fees approached $10 an hour, however, and paying for computer time became a problem almost immediately. Gates and the others quickly convinced the Lakeside Mothers' Group to contribute some of the proceeds of an annual rummage sale to their new computer club. Those funds, too, were used up almost immediately.[3]

Feeding their computer habit would be an obsession of Gates and Allen throughout their teenage years. One way of ensuring access to a computer, the two discovered, would be to go into business. They started a company that used computers to manage a corporate payroll and later were hired by Lakeside to produce new class schedules when it merged with a nearby girls' school. They also created a business that analyzed traffic patterns for the government.[4] "We were kind of desperate to get free computer time one way or another," Gates recalled of his coming of age.[5] A new business in town, the Computer Center Corporation, which was created by University of Washington professors, relieved some of that pressure.

The CCC hoped to expand the market for time-sharing by selling programming time to small businesses. The company, which was housed in a converted car dealership in downtown Seattle, rented a Digital PDP-10, a minicomputer beloved by hackers, and recruited three of the top programmers from John McCarthy's artificial intelligence lab at Stanford. Even so, the time-sharing system was buggy and paying customers certainly weren't as understanding as students when the system crashed and all their work was lost. Too many crashes and the CCC couldn't continue as a credible business. That's where Gates and Allen fit in. They were among a crew of young hackers invited to discover flaws in the time-sharing system. "Having a few of the students, including me, bang on it and try to find bugs seemed like a good idea," Gates explained. "And particularly, let us do that mostly at night. . . . So, for a few years that is where I spent my time. I'd skip out on athletics and go down to this computer center."[6] The students got free computer time, and CCC got an energetic debugging team.[7]

A couple of years later, Gates was a Harvard undergraduate majoring in applied mathematics, playing in a regular dorm poker game, when the Altair news lit a fire under him. Allen, who had dropped out of college and moved to Boston as a programmer for Honeywell, stoked Gates with the cry, "It's going to be too late. We'll miss it."[8] The Altair was already prospering among a core audience of "hobbyists" who were so committed to the idea of owning a personal computer that they didn't mind that they had to assemble the machine themselves.[9] Incredibly, the hobbyists also apparently didn't mind that, at first, "there was really nothing you could do with it," Gates recalled. "There was no teletype hook-up in the early days, there was no software for it. All you could do was use these switches, key things in into this front panel and maybe do a little program that does things in the lights. . . . People just bought it thinking that it would be neat to build a computer."[10]

Gates and Allen recognized that software would be the way to make these computers both more user-friendly and more engaging. This would be the sea change: up until that point computers were expensive, and mainly used by programmers themselves. Sometimes hackers would write useful software and share it with the computer manufacturer, who in turn would share it with other customers. Mostly, though, the manufacturer would just include whatever software it had produced for its expensive machine and a talented programmer would improvise what he needed. With Micro-Soft, Gates and Allen proposed a different model: users would pay for software that was written to a professional standard by paid programmers.

The first program their company produced for the Altair was one they knew well, BASIC. As the name suggested, BASIC (Beginner's All-Purpose Symbolic Instruction Code) was intended to allow a user to perform tasks on a computer without deep programming experience. Its creators, two Dartmouth mathematicians, John Kemeny and Thomas Kurtz, devised BASIC in 1964 while working under a National Science Foundation grant to make computing more accessible to undergraduates.[11] Like most software of that era, BASIC was freely distributed. The challenge for Gates and Allen was to create their own version of BASIC that fit the constraints of the new Intel microchip. As hard as the programming might be, the greater hurdle would be gaining access to a computer. This time Harvard University would be the main supplier.

While programming BASIC, Gates camped out in the university computer lab. He shared his access with Allen, who lived nearby. The two, with some hired help, quickly produced a working version of BASIC, which was such a hit that every computer owner had to get their hands on it.[12] Gates recalled, "Before we even shipped BASIC, somebody stole the demo copy out of the van and started copying it around and sending it to different computer clubs. There was a real phenomenon taking place there, right around this Altair computer."[13] Seeing the enthusiasm for BASIC, Gates eventually took a leave to focus on Micro-Soft and never returned. He ultimately obtained a Harvard diploma, however, when the university awarded him an honorary law degree in 2007.[14]

The timing of Gates's leave could appear suspect since it came on the heels of a disciplinary hearing with college administrators. An auditor from the Defense Department discovered how much time Gates had spent programming on the PDP-10 computer, which was provided by the U.S. government, and began to ask questions. Gates's explanations were flimsy: first, he was doing work for his own company, and, second, some of that outside work was carried out by Allen, who wasn't a student. The records of the Gates disciplinary hearing are sealed, but accounts say that the punishment fell short of his being asked to leave.

Undoubtedly, however, the time was ripe for Gates to see how far software could take him. An early problem, as we've seen, was how to manage the enthusiasm for Micro-Soft BASIC. If the plan was to get paid to write the software that all computer owners used, the hackers' insistence on sharing software was an obvious impediment. Events were moving fast: only a year after first seeing the Altair on a magazine cover, Gates already had a business that he believed was under attack. He directed his fire at the most influential group of Altair hobbyists of the time, the Homebrew Computer Club, which met every two weeks on the Stanford campus to trade stories about their personal computers and, at times, trade software.

The existence of such a club showed the potential of the Altair—and its inevitable imitators—to disrupt computing, which up to that point had been limited to people who worked at universities, the government, or corporations, or had managed to connect to a remote computer through an expensive time-sharing system. These "homebrewers," however, were the vanguard of what would become the personal computer movement; early members included Steve Wozniak, who would go on to design the first Apple personal computer. As little as these primitive Altair computers could do at first, their owners still enjoyed possessing them, controlling them. After barely a year, the Homebrew club regularly had three hundred members at its meetings on the Stanford campus; six hundred people subscribed to its newsletter.

Gates, who was nineteen years old at the time, made his case in the club's newsletter, which published his "Open Letter to Hobbyists" in the January–February 1976 issue. He didn't mince words. "As the majority of hobbyists must be aware, most of you steal your software," he wrote. "Hardware must be paid for, but software is something to share. Who cares if the people who worked on it get paid?" He then framed the issue in familiar terms of market incentives. That is, if software producers don't get paid, then vital software won't be written: "Who can afford to do professional work for nothing?" Furthermore, there was the computer time, whose "value" exceeded $40,000, Gates informed the hobbyists. This odd phrasing jumped out to some readers, even before people learned of Gates's reliance on Harvard's computers. Gates wasn't claiming that Micro-Soft had spent $40,000 for the computer time, which it needed to recoup; rather, it had obtained that time somehow.[15]

Young Gates certainly had chutzpah. He was writing to a bunch of excited young computer enthusiasts to object to the "theft" of a version of a program that was, to start, based on software created by academic researchers working on a federal grant and was created using "borrowed" time on a university computer that was also paid for by the federal government. The facts may not have been ideal, but Gates nonetheless succeeded in defining the question in a way that played to his advantage. He was insisting that programmers be paid and that computer owners recognize that professional software would make their machines ever more useful.

In computer history, 1976 marks the end of an innocent time. The Homebrew hobbyists had started as a group of barely thirty hackers, yet in no time they had made a sworn enemy, an innocent-looking teenager who was committed to challenging their way of life.[16] While most hackers viewed computers as a great gift to the world that mustn't be sullied by commerce, Gates had seen them only through the lens of business. A fascination with computers frequently had cost Gates money, while at other, magical times, it had sent money his way. When Stanford and the Silicon Valley venture capitalists later insisted that computer innovation should spread through the market and reward entrepreneurs with enormous fortunes, they had to look no further than Gates and Microsoft.

Microsoft's software empire would prove instructive to Mark Zuckerberg as he went about building his social-networking empire, Facebook. Microsoft offered an early example of the potency of the network effect in computing, teaching that if you become the most popular software, new users will sign up just to fit in. The dominant Microsoft operating systems were a source of fascination too. "I thought, you know, building this ecosystem was really neat, and that kind of inspired me. Right?" Zuckerberg said in an interview. "And the way that they built a platform, I kind of thought, 'Okay. Well, maybe one day, you know, the tools that I'm building can be part of a broader ecosystem as well.'"[17]

Under Gates's leadership, Microsoft reached unprecedented levels of profitability for a company its size. Yet Gates didn't allow himself to become quite as utopian about computers as the Know-It-Alls who followed. Unlike the founders of Google, Facebook, Amazon, Uber, and dozens of other Silicon Valley start-ups, Gates never shouted to the world that his company would make the world a better place, in addition to making huge profits. Only after Gates had amassed a fortune did he begin to think in terms of "saving the world," and it wasn't by recommitting himself to Microsoft's success. Beginning in 2006, he shed day-to-day responsibility of the company to focus on the Bill and Melinda Gates Foundation, whose mission is "to help all people lead healthy, productive lives." He recently wrote on Twitter that his nineteen-year-old self's view of humanity was far too limited: "When I left college, there are some things I wish I had known, e.g., intelligence takes many different forms. It is not one-dimensional. And not as important as I used to think. I also have one big regret: When I left school, I knew little about the world's worst inequities. Took me decades to learn."[18]

4. MARC ANDREESSEN

"By the power vested in me by no one in particular"

As Bill Gates and others had shown, there were fortunes to be made by an enterprising hacker willing to sell his computer expertise to the general public. But there still was a wide gulf that cut off the tech leaders of this era from social and political power. On one side of the gulf were the leaders themselves, engineers and coders obsessed with computers; on the other were their customers, members of the public or businesses who relied on computers to carry out important tasks but nonetheless thought that having a deep, personal connection with a machine was a bit strange, perhaps even perverse.[1] Tech businesses like Microsoft, IBM, and Hewlett-Packard were already driving the economy, but until this gap was bridged—until regular folks shared a hacker's delight in having a machine fulfill their every whim—these leaders would lack the influence to reshape society according to their values.

This observation may seem, in part, obvious: until computers were intertwined with people's daily lives, improvements in software or hardware wouldn't matter much. But there was another aspect as well. Before there could be a generation of Know-It-Alls to bring Silicon Valley–style disruption to America and the planet, the public's view of hackers needed to radically change. Instead of being feared or pitied, they had to be respected. Their fixation on teaching a machine how to act human—an outgrowth of John McCarthy's original computer-based artificial intelligence project—had to seem benevolent, not menacing or peculiar. In fact, a comprehensive recalibration was about to begin. Not only would hackers soon be admired for their great wealth and ingenuity, but a different class of people—the Luddites who saw computers as a threat to civic life—would take the hackers' place as the new obsessives who lacked basic social skills.

A key marker in the public's changing attitude toward computers—and the young men who loved them—was the arrival of the World Wide Web in the early 1990s. Each of us would grow to love our computers, too. And why not? A computer with access to the Web was nothing less than a revelation, taking you free and easily from essays to stock quotes to pornography to an old forgotten friend to new music to classical literature to video games and back again. A network of clickable hyperlinks propelled a "surfer" along on the Web, an intuitive mechanism for navigating online, especially when compared with the arcane commands and long strings of numbers hackers had used to access the Internet. By this time, there already were paid-subscription services like Prodigy, CompuServe, and America Online, which offered customers a few online tools like email and chatrooms, but the Web was different, promising more and free. Unlike the people who signed up to a subscription service and contributed only to that service or its affiliates, everyone on the Web was pulling together. The collective potential of the Internet, which had largely been hidden from the public since its creation as Arpanet in 1969, would be made plain through the Web.[2]

The first plans for how the Web might work were sketched out in 1989 by Tim Berners-Lee, a consultant at CERN, the European particle-physics research center located in Switzerland. A circumspect, thirty-five-year-old physicist born in Britain, Berners-Lee fit a very different profile than the one we have grown accustomed to among our brash tech leaders. He stumbled on the idea of the World Wide Web, he says, while building a computer database to keep track of the many scientists and support staff members who shuffled in and out of CERN's laboratories. Over time, Berners-Lee discovered that he was more fascinated by the links between individuals than by the individuals themselves. His project, which came to life the following year, was meant to highlight and strengthen the ties among the CERN staff, like a shared language or similar research specialty. "The philosophy was: what matters is in the connections," he recalled. "It isn't in the letters, it's the way they're strung together into words. It isn't the words, it's the way they're strung together into phrases. It isn't the phrases, it's the way they are strung together into a document."[3]

There was a power in this simple philosophy, for it meant that the Web grew thicker and more interconnected every time someone or some group created a new page or simply added a link to a related page. A decentralized network of users, including many not so adept at computers, were creating what was already an unprecedented digital resource. "The Web made the Net useful because people are really interested in information (not to mention knowledge and wisdom!) and don't really want to have to know about computers and cables," Berners-Lee explained.[4] Regular folk, not programmers, were steering this ambitious computer project along, and its designer was fine with that.

In fact, so much about the birth of the Web came, as soccer fans might say, against the run of play in computer innovation. A template had emerged from Silicon Valley: young programmers and engineers, nurtured in the windowless computer labs of America's great universities, came up with projects that they were encouraged to take to market with the backing of venture capitalists. Instead, this most recent breakthrough had bubbled up from a physics lab in the middle of Europe, under the direction of an anti-hacker of sorts who apparently made no effort to profit personally from his discovery!

These developments led to more than a little consternation back in the States, mixed with a determination to get in the game. After all, the hackers were all about how computers, in the right hands, could change the world. A civilization-bending project like the Web was simply too attractive—too potentially profitable—to be ignored and left to its own devices. Users would demand a better system, and Silicon Valley would give it to them. In short order, the Web was pulled toward America, where Berners-Lee's decentralized, noncommercial vision succumbed to the innovative powers of a new generation of hackers-turned-entrepreneurs. First among this generation was Marc

Andreessen, the influential Silicon Valley venture capitalist who at the time was an ambitious twenty-one-year-old computer science major at the University of Illinois, Urbana-Champaign. He was quick to recognize the business potential of a global network like the Web and nearly as quick to act.

Born in 1971, Marc Andreessen grew up unhappily in New Lisbon, Wisconsin, about eighty miles north of the liberal college town of Madison and a world apart. During his childhood in the 1970s and '80s, New Lisbon had a population of about fourteen hundred and was more than 97 percent white. Marc's father, Lowell, was a sales manager for a company that sold genetically modified corn seeds, and his mother, Pat, worked in customer service at, among other places, Land's End. Marc Andreessen describes a life of relative privation—a shared "party" telephone line at home; relatives who had an outhouse; a winter of "chopping fucking wood" when his father decided to stop paying for gas.[5] (His friend and business partner, Ben Horowitz, is genuinely nonplussed by the thought of Andreessen, a large man who stands six foot five, wielding an axe: "It is still hard for me to really visualize Marc chopping wood. It's like asking Einstein to mine coal. How crazy that must have been.")[6]

Andreessen displayed classic "compulsive programmer" characteristics as a child, to use Joseph Weizenbaum's resonant phrase. To start, there was his preteen fascination with the TRS-80 personal computer, which he bought with money saved from mowing lawns, supplemented by a contribution from his parents. Andreessen also had the requisite anti-authoritarian streak. Like John McCarthy at a similar age decades earlier, Andreessen fought a losing battle to be excused from gym class.[7] He thought his public high school was an embarrassment, and didn't hide that opinion. The school had a blandly religious culture, which opposed science, Andreessen recalled, while one history class was "taught out of our teacher's unpublished 800-page manuscript on the JFK assassination conspiracy."[8] There was a computer lab in high school, but it lacked a modem to connect to the wider world of Internet bulletin boards and university computer centers. Young Marc Andreessen was trapped in rural Wisconsin and, alas, even computers offered little help in making an escape.[9]

Yet escaping was precisely what Andreessen's neighbors remembered was on his mind. "I got the feeling that New Lisbon wouldn't keep him," said Paul Barnes, the manager of the local supermarket where Andreessen worked as a bagger and stocker, who recalled being impressed by his employee's large vocabulary and big ideas.[10] Andreessen can rattle off the deprivations of being raised in New Lisbon: the cold weather; the poor diet; the ignorant, superstitious farmers; the husbands waking up early to go ice fishing to avoid their wives; the barren intellectual landscape.[11] In a profile that appeared in the *New Yorker*, Andreessen complained of driving an hour to the west to La Crosse, where all you could find was a Waldenbooks with nothing but cookbooks and cat calendars. "Screw the independent bookstores," Andreessen said in praising the disruption later brought by Amazon .com, which began its march through e-commerce by selling books. "There weren't any near where I grew up. There were only ones in college towns. The rest of us could go pound sand."[12]

Notwithstanding Andreessen's especially dim view of rural life, he still acts as the protector of his former townsfolk, who, as he once expressed in a post to Twitter, are "well aware that the left, intellectuals, politicians, et al look down on them."[13] The chip that Andreessen carries about his rural upbringing—expressed today from the comfort of the Bay Area—raises questions about what drives his enthusiasm for Internet-based social disruptions. Is it faith in the wonderful new world to come, or anger at the hurdles, real and imagined, that he faced as a super-smart teenager growing up so far from the action? If we as a society are going to accept so much disruption and destruction, the assurances that it will be worth all the suffering should come from a place of compassion, not resentment.

Andreessen's first steps toward leaving New Lisbon and finding that action included winning a Merit Scholarship in high school and enrolling at the University of Illinois, where he planned to study electrical engineering. There was nothing romantic or idealistic about these choices, he insists. They were purely mercenary. While in high school, Andreessen read an issue of *U.S. News & World Report* from 1986, which ranked undergraduate majors based on whose graduates earned the highest starting salary; electrical engineering was at the top of the list. The same issue ranked the University of Illinois among the top three schools in electrical engineering, and in short order his college decision was made as well.[14] As to why someone fleeing rural Wisconsin would choose a school in nearby rural Illinois, Andreessen says he thought he was heading to a city of sorts, and then discovered that in Urbana-Champaign, "they had a cow with a hole in its gut so you could see it digesting its food. It was that kind of school."[15]

Soon after arriving at the university, Andreessen concluded that electrical engineering was too demanding and switched to computer science, still something of an obscure discipline in the late 1980s. "Sometimes I just made things up, but then the field was so new, my professors were making things up, too," he recalled.[16] Andreessen found a purpose in programming and was good at it, to boot. He was chosen for a coveted part-time job on campus at the National Center for Supercomputing Applications (NCSA), one of five such centers created in the 1980s by the National Science Foundation.[17] At the center, Andreessen made just $6.85 an hour, but on the bright side he had a desk and an expensive Indigo computer, which he managed to connect to the cable TV box so he could have CNN playing in the background. Around the lab, Andreessen was known as a generally grumpy figure apt to reject tasks as boring or beneath him . . . until that time when a project worthy of his ambitions appeared.[18]

In 1992, the World Wide Web was up and running but was still lacking a browser that worked on all computers, not just the NeXT computer that Berners-Lee first programmed with. A proper browser, which was highly compatible . . . now that was a worthy project! After all, the Web was the new, new thing on the Internet and a browser was the crucial program for the Web—your transportation, your translator, your window, your pad and pencil, your safety blanket. Later, the Web browser would take on more sinister responsibilities—ankle bracelet, chaperone, corporate listening device. But let's not get ahead of ourselves. In that ancient year, 1992, the NCSA was among a number of computer labs quick to take up the challenge of producing a browser that was easy to install, could work on different operating systems, and would improve on the intuitive navigation of the Web.

Andreessen lobbied hard to land the assignment and in the fall he was paired with an experienced staff programmer, Eric Bina, who took on the difficult coding, freeing up young Andreessen to keep his eye on the big picture. "Marc is a strong driving force for changing the world. He is clearly driven to do that," Bina said. He added, by way of contrast, "I don't feel driven to change anything but my own situation."[19] Bina and Andreessen and their growing team of coders worked out of the dark basement offices of the old Oil Chemistry building, offices that soon filled up with piles of pizza boxes, stray cookie packages, empty soda cans, and Skittles wrappers.[20] In a matter of months, they had created a working version of the browser. Significantly, their browser, which was given the name Mosaic, could embed images directly on the page rather than clumsily requiring images to pop up in a new browser window. On January 23, 1993, Andreessen posted a file containing a first working version of Mosaic, under the words, "By the power vested in me by no one in particular, X-Mosaic is hereby released."[21]

Andreessen expected there to be immediate demand for what was, by all accounts, a vastly superior browser. "We just tried to hurry and get it out there, initially to a limited group of 10 or 12 alpha and beta testers," he said. "Of course, the Internet is a great way to distribute viruses, too; put a virus out and then it propagates."[22] Born on a university campus, Mosaic had additional advantages in quickly finding an audience. To start, the campus itself was filled with young people with computers and unusually fast Internet connections who were eager to try something new. When the public did in fact quickly engage with Mosaic—and the original twelve downloads grew to several hundred thousand by December—the team could depend on the university's infrastructure to keep up with demand.[23] No surprise, then, that the most prominent Web browser (Mosaic/Netscape), portal (Yahoo), search engine (Google), and social network (Facebook) all germinated at universities, whether Illinois, Stanford, or Harvard.

The immediate popularity of Mosaic meant that there would be two very different guardians of the nascent Web: Berners-Lee, the scientist who conceived it, and Andreessen, the Midwest-born college student who helped it to catch on quickly. Both men were obviously transfixed by the Web's potential, but if anything, Andreessen was the one more enthralled: great idea, Tim, now let's get on with it. There had never been anything like the Web before; who knew if it would even be popular? Thus the Mosaic team focused on making the Web experience simple, intuitive, and eye-pleasing, starting with the browser's newfound compatibility with images. Andreessen acted more like the leader of a hungry start-up than a member of a university research team. Berners-Lee noticed that after the first version of Mosaic was released, Andreessen maintained "a near-constant presence on the newsgroups discussing the Web, listening for features people were asking for, what would make browsers easier to use . . . almost as if he were attending to 'customer relations.'"[24]

Berners-Lee, by contrast, made a priority of promoting the values of individual autonomy and collaboration on the Web. He insisted that a browser should be a text editor as well, so that Web surfers would be encouraged to add to the interconnections, not just surf across them. Users would have handy tools to create and publish a page on their own or cooperate with friends to write, edit, and publish together. Think of Wikipedia, the online encyclopedia where thousands of contributors create articles individually, but usually improve them collectively, or a shared Google document, which similarly grows as more people are invited to contribute. Berners-Lee wanted these experiences to be the norm. Not just a part of the Web experience, but central to it. This was the democratic instinct as applied to the Internet, with the general public driving the development of the Web, rather than programmers, with all the inefficiency and lack of professionalism that implies, as well as the unpredictability and personal control.[25]

When Andreessen and Berners-Lee finally met face-to-face in 1993 in Illinois, there already was a "strange tension," Berners-Lee reported.[26] The Mosaic team exuded a confidence that they represented the future of Web development, which rankled Berners-Lee. They described material online as being "on Mosaic," rather than "on the Web," another annoying trait.[27] More significant, the Mosaic developers early on dropped the collaborative, text-heavy tools that Berners-Lee championed as empowering the public, seeing them as inefficient and a distraction from the central mission of creating a compelling, entertaining Web experience. With a better browser and faster Internet connections, the Web could become more like the television that Andreessen had already wired into his computer—passive and commercially friendly. But with a crucial difference: a television signal that could reach the entire world at once!

From a Silicon Valley perspective, the Mosaic team was strategically "pivoting" the Web browser toward Andreessen's commercial friendly vision and away from Berners-Lee's, which wasn't. The timing couldn't have been better. By the early 1990s, the last official barriers to business and commerce on the Internet were torn down through a combination of congressional legislation and new rules from the National Science Foundation, the organization that supported the Internet.[28] The noncommercial status of the Internet was rooted in its history as a government-funded project operating mainly through universities and government agencies, but businesses were persistent in arguing that they belonged online as well. In 1993, the Internet became fully open for business with the passage of the National Information Infrastructure Act, which "clearly took the development of the Internet out of the hands of the government and placed it into the hands of the competitive marketplace."[29] This shift didn't necessarily mean that the young programmers like Andreessen who built Mosaic would benefit from its success. They were merely salaried employees at a lab; the University of Illinois retained the rights to Mosaic.[30]

Years later, those early design choices by the Mosaic programming team still made Berners-Lee cringe. "The Web, which I designed to be a medium of all sorts of information, from the very local to the very global, grew decidedly in the direction of the very global, and as a publication medium but less of a collaboration medium," he said in dismay.[31] The experience was a useful harbinger, however. Going forward, the Web experience would largely be in the hands of hacker-entrepreneurs committed above all else to bringing in the most users to the Web, at first to make sure the project would survive, later, to reach profitability. If gaining a huge global audience was your primary goal, even Berners-Lee had to concede, why would you fight for tools to encourage collaborative editing, which "didn't seem to promise that millionfold multiplier"?[32]

Andreessen certainly pled guilty to wanting to please the largest possible audience. "I'm a Midwestern tinkerer type," Andreessen says. "If people want images, they get images. Bring it on."[33] In response to Berners-Lee's other concern, that Andreessen was hijacking control of the Web, the young hacker would turn the question back on him. Andreessen's goal was to share the Web with the world and give users a chance to shape its development by carefully watching which features were popular and which were not, and revising accordingly. He would later press for changes to the browser that helped businesses operate online and, in the process, usher even more users to the Web. Berners-Lee, by insisting that the Web be collaborative and less flashy whether the public wanted these features or not, was the better example of a programmer trying to impose his will on the public. "The Web had already become a brush fire, and he was uncomfortable that he was no longer controlling it," Andreessen said about Berners-Lee in those early days.[34]

Brush fire indeed. Aided by the steady adoption of the Mosaic browser, the amount of information being conveyed by the Web grew more than two thousand times from January 1993 to January 1994, a figure that caught the attention of people attuned to how the economy might be changing, including a young investment banker, Jeff Bezos, considering whether to leave finance to start his own business. "Things just don't grow that fast," he observed.[35]

In December 1993, Andreessen left the University of Illinois to head to Silicon Valley to start earning the high salary promised in that issue of *U.S. News & World Report*. He had just graduated, so this was a natural time to be departing, but he would also be leaving behind Mosaic, the project that had defined his time there. Andreessen's frustration with the Mosaic team had been growing, as the success of the browser outside the lab had caused administrators to take notice.[36] They began to schedule regular meetings to review progress and kept adding members to the programming team. Meanwhile, the university was weighing proposals to license the Mosaic code. The terms of participation were now very different for Andreessen. He had been running the equivalent of a lean, fast-moving Web start-up. Great fun. Going forward, he would be navigating academic turf wars as a recent graduate. Not so much fun. "There was no reason to stay there," Andreessen explained. "The environment was falling to pieces compared to what it had been, simply because there was this influx of money. The project grew from 2 people to 20. It was completely different."[37]

Just before Andreessen left the lab, however, he was given a bloody flag to wave to unite his fellow hackers at the lab. That December, John Markoff wrote a prescient article in the *New York Times* about Mosaic, calling it "a map to the buried treasures of the Information

Age." The big photo accompanying the article featured Larry Smarr, the director of the NCSA, and Larry Hardin, who directly supervised the Mosaic project, but no one else. Neither Andreessen nor Bina, nor any of the other programmers, was mentioned by name.[38] This was the traditional academic model in a nutshell: the students do the work, the professors get their names first on the journal article and in the news media. This public diss would prove quite helpful in the months that followed, as Andreessen tried to lure members of his old team to a new commercial project.

When Andreessen first headed to Silicon Valley in the winter of 1994, however, he had no intention of resuming work on a browser. He joined a small company, Enterprise Integration Technologies, and lasted three months before being recruited by Jim Clark, a former Stanford electrical engineering professor turned entrepreneur. They were to work together on the hot business idea of the time, interactive television. Only when the plan for interactive TV fell through, and Andreessen and Clark were brainstorming ideas, did Andreessen bring up the idea of creating a commercial browser to compete with Mosaic.[39] Clark and Andreessen began hiring as many of the disgruntled NCSA programmers to their new company as possible; they would be joined by a few other early Web programmers as well as some more seasoned hands Clark knew from his previous company, Silicon Graphics. Smarr, who considered Clark a friend, at the time felt betrayed by the "raiding" of the talent at his lab.[40]

Clark, an engineer himself, believed that hiring the best technical talent would be the key to the success of his and Andreessen's new company, Mosaic Communications, MCom for short. Clark flew out to Illinois to close the deals personally. Bina, for example, only signed on after Clark personally agreed to let him work from Illinois so he could stay with his wife, who was a professor.[41] Another important hire, Lou Montulli, a recent graduate from the University of Kansas who had created Lynx, a text-based Web browser, recalled being summoned to Champaign and flying with a last-minute ticket that was so expensive that he wanted to be assured he would be reimbursed for its cost.[42] Nothing to worry about, he was told. Clark's new company would make sure the programmers were appropriately compensated, starting with Andreessen, but extending to the entire programming team. Clark had learned a painful lesson from Silicon Graphics, which grew out of his research at Stanford and was founded with a team of departing Stanford graduate students: over time, the financiers had profited much more from the company's initial success than the engineers, including Clark, even, who at the start sold a 40 percent stake in the company to an investor for $800,000.[43] Ultimately, the investors took over the board and made business decisions that forced Clark to leave.

The MCom team set to work on creating a new browser from scratch, Mosaic Netscape. Clark had raised the idea of paying the University of Illinois a fee to license the Mosaic code, as other companies were doing, but Andreessen said no. Alma mater wouldn't see a penny of MCom money if he had anything to do with it.[44] The programming team would construct a better browser, which would be designed for the slow 14.4 kb modems of the real world, not the fast cables of well-financed universities. What came next was a programming binge straight out of the hacker annals—Montulli, who had extensive responsibilities for coding the browser, painted a picture of programming life at MCom: "Essentially 10 Mountain Dews (full strength, no diet), horrible food and I think my regular schedule back then was to come in, work for 20 hours straight, we had a futon room, which is a little disturbing to think about now, it was a mattress in a conference room that was dark, I would catch 4 or 5 hours of sleep at the office, wake up, do another 20 hours, and then go home and sleep for 12 or 15 hours and start the whole cycle again."[45]

Everything about the MCom work environment resembled the hacking days at MIT, not just the working hours and the bathing habits, but also the near-complete absence of women in any meaningful role. A 1994 Web page presents the team at the time, a total of twenty-three members, some with short descriptions like "Marc Andreessen—the Hayseed with the Know-How" or "Jim Clark—Uncle Jim's Money Store." Seemingly, not a woman among them. The motto of the group, taken from Sartre's *Being and Nothingness*, is filled with collegiate angst: "All human actions are equivalent . . . and . . . all are on principle doomed to failure."[46] The Web, however, seemed to defy gravity or entropy, growing frantically—roughly 600 Web sites at the beginning of 1994, became 10,000 at the end of the year, became about 100,000 by the end of 1995.[47] By late 1994, the original Mosaic browser had an estimated 3 million users. In the next year, 1995, about 18 million American homes had a computer with a modem for connecting to the Internet, an increase of more than 60 percent from the year before, and, for the first time, a majority of Americans used a computer either at home, at work, or at school.[48]

In the fall of 1994, Andreessen was invited to explain the burgeoning online ecosystem to a San Francisco conference for entrepreneurs eager to learn about Web commerce. He was twenty-three and still relatively new to Silicon Valley. His company's built-from-scratch Mosaic Netscape browser had just been released. Working with an overhead projector and a bunch of transparencies, as one did at the time, Andreessen began his self-deprecating talk: "We tried really hard not to invent anything new or solve any hard problems, which makes it easier to get something done." He then listed some of the obvious challenges his team happily ignored: "How do you search across the entire information space? I don't know. How do you know where you are going? Beats me." He then tried to describe to the audience the larger purpose of the Web, saying it is "fundamentally about communication. The applications that are going to be successful are the ones that tie together people."[49] It was a bravura performance that in a few words, we can now see, sketched out the commercial history of the Web, identifying niches in the ecosystem that would feed tech titans like Yahoo, Google, and Facebook.

Soon after he flicked off the projector, however, came the inevitable audience question: "What is the Mosaic Communications business model?" Without missing a beat, Andreessen answered: "Making money."[50] Another jokey comment, certainly, but perhaps the only one that could capture what he and Clark were thinking. Making money was the plan and, to that end, MCom would need the Web to be entertaining and useful. If no one wanted to use the Web then no one would need whatever MCom planned on selling. However, if the Web proved useful and entertaining, then businesses might pay MCom for servers to host their websites or for help running their online business. Or maybe MCom's Web site would become a valuable portal in its own right, as people new to the Web inevitably visited there to learn more about the browser that opened up the Web.

Microsoft had already demonstrated that there was money to be made from becoming the standard software for operating your computer. In Gates's days, you wanted to enforce your dominant position by preventing any copying or sharing—you withheld the program or operating system until the public came crawling, dollar bills in hand. In the two decades that separated Gates from Andreessen, however, the Web changed what qualified as an astute business strategy. A company like MCom didn't need to wield its power quite so heavy-handedly. Why send interested users away if acquiring a large audience was how a Web business ultimately hoped to make its money? In that sense, Andreessen the professional programmer had very similar priorities to Andreessen the undergraduate programmer. They both pursued the "shareware model of free distribution. . . . Get it out there and into people's hands."[51] The browser initially wasn't free, but was free on a trial basis, and the company didn't object if a user began a new trial over and over again. Gaining a large audience was so important that Andreessen was happy to suggest opportunities for entrepreneurs to explore, knowing that the browser maker should come out fine in the process as the proverbial store that sells pick axes during the gold rush.

Weeks after the San Francisco talk, MCom changed its name to Netscape Communications, and the browser's name to Navigator, in response to a complaint from the University of Illinois that it could be confused with the original Mosaic browser. The university also claimed that despite a thorough rewrite, the Navigator browser still contained code from the original version of the program that Andreessen and Bina first put together at the NCSA.[52] Andreessen is still angry about the experience, which he recounted on Twitter: "Netscape never got rights to Mosaic. We rewrote code base from scratch," he wrote. "Univ Illinois then threatened to sue us and tried to kill our business. So we sued them to stop harassment. . . . Univ of Illinois got small-$ cash payoff. Refused stock."[53] Andreessen enjoys reminding the world that had the university wisely taken stock instead of the $2.7 million Netscape paid in compensation it could have netted $5 million more.[54]

For all of his foresight in that early talk about the way the Web would grow and organize itself for commerce, Andreessen never mentioned advertising, which would become the predominant economic engine of the Internet. For the time being, Netscape's path to profitability would center on promoting online commerce. The company would sell businesses powerful servers and other tools to reach their customers, while the Netscape browser would be made commerce friendly, with new features to allow secure financial transactions. "Our goal is to get millions of copies in use quickly to really start enabling the market for lots of commercial services to come online," Andreessen said in the San Francisco talk.[55]

Despite Andreessen's initial omission, the Netscape browser would ultimately prove crucial to introducing the advertising-centric, data-collecting Web we have today. Not that this was Netscape's intention. The change in the browser that would have such long-term implications for the Web was a new snippet of code created by Montulli, who called it a "cookie." This new code was meant to fix what was seen as a flaw in Berners-Lee's original design for the Web, namely users traveled anonymously "from server to server afresh, with no reference to any previous transactions."[56] This lack of "memory" on the Web—that your past wouldn't, couldn't, accumulate—posed problems. Encounters with Web sites became "a bit like talking to someone with Alzheimer's disease," Montulli wrote.[57] You may have visited a site ten times a day, every day, but you were nonetheless considered a stranger. Unless you registered at a site, sales would have to be conducted along the time-consuming "vending machine" model[58]: You want six different candy bars? Put in the money six times and pull the lever six times. The inability to retain even the most basic information about users could have been fatal to online commerce, and Montulli devised cookies as a way for Web sites to keep tabs on their regular visitors the better to sell them things.

Montulli recalls coming up with the idea in July 1994, after meeting with an in-house team focused on supporting e-commerce. The team was planning an online shopping cart system, but the browser seemingly wouldn't allow it, since there was no way for a shopper to pick something to buy, leave it in a cart, keep shopping, add something else to the cart, and again return to shopping. Montulli wrestled with a solution for days, proudly holding the line against a proposal to give each browser a unique ID as it traveled across the Web. Such a solution was antithetical to how Montulli understood the Web—yes, a browser ID would help a Web site keep track of its customers, but it would turn every visitor into an open book, as businesses could easily pool their knowledge to create an online portrait.[59] Instead, Netscape's cookies would be built around each visit, or "session," between a particular Web site and a browser. This bit of memory would be enough to speed commerce by allowing a business to recall its customer's past preferences, credit card number, earlier selections, and the like, though that information wouldn't be carried to other Web sites.

Netscape's business customers were told of this new powerful tool for commerce in fall 1994, with the release of the first browser, and advised how best to employ it. The ordinary users of that browser—who typically were not paying customers, after all—were never told.[60] Here was a vivid example of the truth in the adage, "If you are not paying for it, you're not the customer; you're the product being sold," which was coined in 2010 by a commenter to the Web site MetaFilter.[61] Nonetheless, Montulli and the others felt good about what they had accomplished, confident that they had the interests of users—not just businesses—at heart. Yet, in one of those painful ironies that illustrate the importance of early design decisions, the user protections that Montulli cared so much about ultimately wouldn't make a difference. Web businesses found a work-around and managed to create the kind of "cross-site tracking" he dreaded from the start.

The weakness these businesses exploited, as Montulli was forced to admit later, was that Web pages typically included embedded content from a variety of outside sources, "third parties," each of whom was able to install a cookie on a visitor's browser and keep track of where she had been and what she had done. Each visit to a Web site in actuality represented many simultaneous "sessions." Certain third parties, particularly the companies that placed digital advertisements across the Web, were ubiquitous online; an ordinary Web user could cross paths with the same "third party" site after site. Thus, it might seem that the user of a Web browser was starting a new "session" with a site, even as she was continuing a session with an advertising company that began many Web sites earlier. A business like DoubleClick, which was acquired for $3.1 billion by Google in 2008, could therefore stitch together a detailed profile of a Web surfer's online life on its own, exactly what Montulli had tried to avoid.

When, in 1996, journalists in Britain[62] and the United States informed Web surfers of the surprising news that "the Web sites you're visiting may be spying on you," there were protests over cookies and calls for the government to step in.[63] Netscape was concerned enough to ask Montulli to think of a coding change to thwart third parties. "Tracking across Web sites was certainly not what cookies were designed to do, they were designed with the opposite intention," he wrote in 2013 on his blog, explaining the predicament, "but what could be done at that point to fix the problem?" He agonized for weeks and then opted to do nothing, convinced that at this point businesses trying to profile Web users couldn't be stopped: "If third-party cookies were disabled, ad companies would use another mechanism to accomplish the same thing, and that mechanism would not have the same level of visibility and control as cookies."[64]

When Microsoft introduced a browser to compete with Netscape, there never was a question about whether it would have cookies too. The gains from cookies were tangible, the loss of privacy less so. Montulli's warning about how the tracking would only get worse without cookies proved correct. Two decades later, Facebook, for example, has access to so much more information about its users than mere browsing history—what they like and dislike, whom they communicate with, their relationship status, what articles they click on, what articles they read to the end, even—and the mechanism to limit what it retains is much less visible.

Despite the many improvements Netscape introduced to assist in Web commerce, the company itself hadn't achieved commercial success. Past practice on Wall Street was for a company to hold off on an initial public offering of stock until there had been at least three consecutive profitable quarters; in the summer of 1995, Netscape was still waiting for its first. But Clark argued that Netscape should play by its own rules—after all, no other company had experienced the kind of viral growth that Netscape had, approaching 90 percent of the browser market. If Clark's experience in Silicon Valley had taught him anything it was to take the money when it's sitting there. "I wanted us to go public, because I thought it'd be good for us from a P.R. standpoint, and I did go into this thing to make money, so I was looking for a reward as well," he said.[65]

The day of the IPO, August 9, 1995, appeared to be perfectly timed, producing a mania that surprised even Clark. Shares spiked to nearly three times the opening price, from $28 to $75, before settling at $58. By the end of that day's trading, Clark's stake in Netscape was worth $663 million, a fact he recalled a little later when he needed to come up with a tail number for an airplane he bought. "I told them to use 663, because that meant something to me."[66] Andreessen clocked in with around $60 million. Jimmy Wales, the cofounder of Wikipedia, is one of a number of aspiring Internet entrepreneurs who consider 8/9/95 a life-changing date. Wales had already dropped out of graduate school to become a futures and options trader in Chicago, but "when Netscape went public and it was worth more than $2 billion on the first day," he recalled, "it clicked in my mind that something big was happening on the Internet."[67]

Shares of Netscape stock never eclipsed their peak of $171 in December, and from such heights, seemingly the company had only one direction to go. The frenzy leading to the IPO made Microsoft finally take notice of the Web, after Bill Gates had dismissed it as so much hype.[68] In a bit of painful payback for Andreessen, a version of Mosaic licensed by the University of Illinois to a local software company, Spyglass, helped Microsoft quickly challenge the Netscape browser. Working from Spyglass's browser, Microsoft released its first version of Internet Explorer the same month as the Netscape IPO, followed in October 1995 by the release of the beta version of the much-improved Internet Explorer 2.0, which was available free for surfers and businesses alike. New versions quickly followed, and Microsoft aggressively promoted them. A turning point came two years later, in October 1997, when the company released Internet Explorer 4.0, which was tightly bundled with the Windows operating system. At that point, Netscape was still roughly twice as popular—65 percent of the market versus 32 for Internet Explorer.[69] In November 1998, however, the tide was turning, and a declining Netscape was bought by AOL in a stock swap valued at the time at $4.2 billion.[70]

Andreessen's wild run from Mosaic to Netscape to AOL thoroughly transformed the computing world. Microsoft may have succeeded in taking down Netscape—with Internet Explorer, for example, reaching a peak market share well above 90 percent—but that success took a toll. The company's win-at-all-cost approach to "the browser wars" produced important evidence when the U.S. government filed an antitrust lawsuit against Microsoft in 1998, particularly testimony alleging that Microsoft had conspired to cut off Netscape's "air supply." After Microsoft settled that lawsuit in 2001, Microsoft didn't have the same strut or chokehold on how the public used computers. In a fitting final twist to the Netscape-Microsoft fight, the code for Netscape Navigator was released as free software—that is, free to be shared and improved upon by whoever acquired a copy. That code became the basis of the Firefox browser (original name Phoenix because it rose from Navigator's ashes), which helped chip away at Internet Explorer's dominant market share. Today, Firefox lives on as part of a nonprofit project supported by a community of programmers who were motivated to push back against Microsoft.

Andreessen is a dual figure, the hacker-entrepreneur. At the same time that the Netscape team helped make the Web commerce friendly, it also helped install anarchic hacker values onto the Web. For example, on the Web, as in the artificial intelligence lab, little deference would be given to authority: anyone can publish online no matter his age or experience. Your work speaks for itself. The Web also adopted the hackers' belief that information should be free to circulate: music files, newspaper articles, movies, and software all bouncing from computer to computer, unrestrained by duplication costs and seemingly one step ahead of the authorities. There was also a similar consensus that freedom of speech should trump all other concerns: the Web would be beyond the reach of "politically correct" censors declaring some comments as too hateful or cruel or obscene to appear. A more society-focused vision of the Web lost out, although it has been kept alive on the margins, often by European governments who try to prop up traditional newspapers as a stabilizing force and where some topics, like far-right political parties, are barred from appearing online. Some European governments have gone so far as to resist computers' unrivaled memory skills, promoting a right to be forgotten so that an individual can insist that material be taken off the Web if it is old and embarrassing.

In the early 1990s, administrators at the NCSA had briefly suggested that the Mosaic browser warn users if a Web site might not be suitable for children. The problem arose from a link on the What's New page Andreessen maintained for the Mosaic homepage, back when a single person could actually try to keep up with what was new on the Web! A child of a lab employee had clicked on the link and was sent to an arts site with a prominent display of a nude sculpture. Administrators asked Andreessen to come up with a fix. It was the Stanford censorship case all over again, and the hackers' loyalties hadn't shifted. They knew that censorship was stupid and antithetical to the Web, and Andreessen offered a suitably stupid proposal. Let's have a box appear before a user reaches any new Web site, he suggested, with the following warning: "ARE YOU SURE YOU WANT TO TAKE THIS CRAZY STEP AND KEEP SURFING?" The administrators decided to pass.[71]

One clear articulation of how hackers' anti-authoritarian views were shaping the Web appeared in 1996 as "A Declaration of the Independence of Cyberspace," written by John Perry Barlow, the libertarian cofounder of the influential digital rights group the Electronic Frontier Foundation. No government, Barlow declared, had the authority to limit the freedoms inherent to cyberspace. "Governments derive their just powers from the consent of the governed," he announced. "You have neither solicited nor received ours. We did not invite you. You do not know us, nor do you know our world. Cyberspace does not lie within your borders." More broadly, Barlow was arguing that nothing from the offline world—traditional rules, institutions, and codes of behavior, even history itself—carried any weight in cyberspace, which was "a world that all may enter without privilege or prejudice accorded by race, economic power, military force, or station of birth." Having ditched America's living history of racism in less than a sentence, and ignored the misogyny outright, Barlow was then free to demand the familiar absolutist line about online speech. "Anyone, anywhere," he wrote, "may express his or her beliefs, no matter how singular, without fear of being coerced into silence or conformity."[72]

The declaration is a political statement about as nuanced and considered as the hand-scrawled "Keep Out" sign that a teenager tapes on his door. Nonetheless, it accurately describes much of the Web today—the hostility to authority and rules or regulations of any kind; the privileging of freedom over empathy; the fantasy that the Internet is immune to the pull of history. Barlow certainly drew inspiration from the early hackers as he wrote his declaration, but the radical ideology promoted by the Know-It-Alls over the last twenty years involves so much more than the hackers' desire to be left alone. Other troubling aspects of Silicon Valley values described in this book—blind faith in the power of markets to do good all the time, trafficking in people's private information as a commodity, acquiring obscene personal wealth and pursuing economic and social disruption for their own sake with no thought to the human cost—have nothing to do with the hacker ethic. In fact, McCarthy and the other early hackers were critical of those who saw the computer revolution as a path to personal wealth or its close cousin, personal power. Even Lou Montulli recalls being taken aback by the promise of a quick fortune from Jim Clark. "He filled our heads with giant numbers of how we were going to make riches and be the most important people on the planet," Montulli recalled,[73] which conflicted with his own "sort of Marxist" belief that "you couldn't make more than a million dollars honestly."[74]

After a decade of trying to replicate the success of Netscape at other ventures, Andreessen in 2009 found his calling as a Silicon Valley venture capitalist. He promotes disruptive capitalism among a new generation of hacker-entrepreneurs who, as he memorably put it in the title of a *Wall Street Journal* op-ed, create software that "is eating the world."[75] Certainly he was better suited to be an investor than to run a company of his own. To start, his misanthropic personality, a liability in a manager, is seen as an asset in an investor.[76] His partner, Ben Horowitz, explains: "If you say to Marc, 'Don't bite somebody's fucking head off!,' that would be wrong. Because a lot of his value, when you're making giant decisions for huge amounts of money, is saying, 'Why aren't you fucking considering *this* and *this* and *this*?'"[77]

Think back, too, to Andreessen's 1994 talk to aspiring online entrepreneurs: when it came to how the Web would adapt to become more business friendly he was brimming with ideas, but as to the details of the business plan for his own company, he offered the generic "make money." In his role as a VC, he is expected to survey the economy, weighing in as a public intellectual and pointing to broad trends. Back in 2003, when Andreessen was still an entrepreneur, he scoffed at a reporter who wondered if he kept a personal blog. "No," he responded,

"I have a day job. I don't have the time or ego need."[78] More recently, however, he has been inclined to marvel at the influence of his Twitter feed, where he had posted more than 100,000 times and acquired an audience of half a million followers. "Reporters are obsessed with it," he bragged to a reporter. "It's like a tube and I have loudspeakers installed in every reporting cubicle around the world." Andreessen was using Twitter as a Trumpian bullhorn for his ideas of software-led disruption before Donald Trump was a serious enough figure to communicate effectively in 140-character bursts.

On Twitter, Andreessen's praise of disruption has been exclusively economic, not political or social. For example, in a Twitter "essay" from 2014, Andreessen praised the slow and deliberate steps America has made in opening up its political system to all citizens. Don't dwell on all the improvements yet to be enacted, he advised, but instead think about how far we've come. "Common thing one hears in US is 'Political system broken; Founding Fathers never intended politics to be dominated by moneyed interests.' But in 1776, voting 'restricted to property owners--most of whom are white male Protestants over the age of 21.' In 1789, George Washington was elected president. 'Only 6% of the population can vote,'" he wrote, adding, "We have far broader-based voting and political participation today than ever before, due to hard work by many activists over 200 years. And we're still by no means perfect; lots of progress yet to be made. But we're leaps and bounds ahead of 50-100-150-200 years ago."[79]

Imagine Andreessen's reaction to someone who made a similar argument concerning the economic disruption caused by Internet companies—you know, think how far we have already come, let's not act too hastily. Well, we don't have to imagine, actually. In another Twitter essay, Andreessen argued that technological progress has benefited the poor much more than the rich—an observation he insists "flows from basic economics." Therefore, he writes, "Opposing tech innovation is punishing the poor by slowing the process by which they get things previously only affordable to the rich."[80] To recommend patience in implementing technical changes is simply immoral. What's the difference? Well, one difference is the power relationship. In the case of the disruptive democratic politics that Andreessen appears leery of, members of the public are being given greater control over their lives at the expense of an elite; in the case of disruptive technologies, an elite is driving the change.

In September 2016, just when Trump was deploying Twitter to strike out at his foes and communicate without speaking to the press, Andreessen stopped posting to Twitter, not long after having to apologize for posts that praised British colonialism in India as superior to democracy in providing for the poor.[81] In a clever work-around, however, Andreessen has remained active on Twitter by "liking" as many as forty posts a day written by others. That way he seemingly expresses his opinion—and continues tangling with Web idealists—without bearing ultimate authorial responsibility for what has been said.

The first idealist Andreessen ever tangled with, of course, was Berners-Lee. In his memoir, Berners-Lee is quick to reject the anticapitalist label, denying that he thinks the Web should be treated as some hallowed space, "where we must remove our shoes, eat only fallen fruit and eschew commercialization."[82] But he also clearly isn't comfortable with how it has been twisted to generate runaway profits. At one point in this same memoir, Berners-Lee pauses to answer why he never tried to amass a fortune from his ideas, even as so many other key figures in the Web's development did. "What is maddening is the terrible notion that a person's value depends on how important and financially successful they are, and that that is measured in terms of money," he writes. "To use net worth as a criterion by which to judge people is to set our children's sights on cash rather than on things that will actually make them happy."[83]

Berners-Lee tells a story about a technical breakthrough in the development of the Web that occurred on Christmas 1990. That day, his computer at CERN for the first time used a primitive browser/editor to communicate with a server hosting the Web's first URL, info.cern.ch. The Web worked! Even so, Berners-Lee writes that he "wasn't that keyed up about it," because he and his wife were expecting their first child and, "As amazing as it would be to see the Web develop, it would never compare to seeing the development of our child."[84] Even at this late date, we would do well to try to restore the human-scale perspective and idealism Berners-Lee brought to the Internet project from the start. The lesson the Know-It-Alls took from those early years, however, was to grow big and grow fast.

5. JEFF BEZOS

"When it's tough, will you give up, or will you be relentless?"

In his talk in 1994 to wannabe Web entrepreneurs, Marc Andreessen imagined a system of e-commerce that resembled small-town life. "The corner pizza store in a box" is how Andreessen pitched Netscape's product that included a server and software. "You put up your corner pizza store, your flower shop, your bookstore. I really believe that this is where things are heading. It is going to be interesting when it arrives."[1] This system wouldn't be quite as decentralized as it looked, however. Netscape, as the provider of the browser, server, and related software, would become the beneficiary of the network effect that comes from holding the dominant position online. Netscape products would be what everyone used, and therefore what millions of new arrivals would choose to use when they joined the Internet party. This was the dream, at any rate, albeit a short-lived one. The next year, 1995, the Web took a sharp turn toward centralized online marketplaces as Craigslist, eBay, and most notably Amazon got their first taste of how being popular online only made you more popular.[2]

Craigslist and eBay both grew organically, almost by accident. Craig Newmark, a former IBM programmer living in the Bay Area, began maintaining and distributing his "list" of local events and job openings in early 1995. He sent the listings as a mass email to friends, at first just ten to twelve people. Word spread quickly, and to meet the growing demand Newmark soon professionalized his system for sending the emails. In early 1996, Craigslist—its nickname from the start—migrated to the Web. By the end of 1997, Craigslist was getting about a million page views a month and Microsoft approached him about running banner ads on the site. Newmark recalls turning down the offer, knowing in doing so he had "stepped away from a huge amount of money."[3] Though Craigslist was a for-profit enterprise (except for a short stint when it switched to nonprofit status), Newmark wasn't in a particular hurry to grow Craigslist or to cash in. He was making a good living as a programming contractor and his priority was Craigslist's users, not making a bunch of money.

To this day, the site has been slow to assess fees of any kind, limiting them to certain job and real estate listings as it has steadily added cities and countries to its service. In 2000, Craigslist expanded from San Francisco to nine other United States cities, including Boston, New York, and Chicago; the next year, Vancouver became the first city outside of the United States. In 2003, the London site launched, the first outside of the Americas.[4] "Remember," Newmark said, "in the conventional sense, we were never a startup. In the conventional sense, a startup is a company, maybe with great ideas, that becomes a serious corporation. It usually takes serious investment, has a strategy, and they want to make a lot of money. We've done something very different."[5] As Craigslist's chief executive, Jim Buckmaster, once explained to a room full of equity analysts and fund managers, Craigslist has no business development team and politely declines any offer that shows up in its inbox.[6] Newmark describes himself as the company's founder and customer service representative.

EBay was born a bit later in 1995 as AuctionWeb, the project of another programmer in the Bay Area, Pierre Omidyar, who at first hosted the online marketplace on his personal Web site.[7] His plan for publicizing AuctionWeb included posting notices on Usenet groups and getting listed on the What's New page at the supercomputing center at the University of Illinois, which was created by Marc Andreessen when he was still an undergraduate. Through such informal channels, Omidyar reached enough Web users to have hosted thousands of free auctions with tens of thousands of bids by the end of 1995. Word of mouth did the rest. His personal Internet service provider noticed the spike in activity and raised his monthly fee from $30 a month to $250—the business rate—even though the site wasn't yet operating as a business. "That's when I said, 'You know, this is kind of a fun hobby, but $250 a month is a lot of money,'" Omidyar recalled.[8]

Omidyar started charging a fee that was a percent of the final sale price, a system well designed for ensuring that you had the resources to grow as fast as your audience would take you. The project's first employee and first president came the following year; in June 1997, a Silicon Valley firm, Benchmark Capital, invested $6.7 million for what became approximately a quarter of the company. Omidyar deposited the check, but didn't touch the money, he said. More than its capital, Benchmark was providing prestige, connections in hiring, branding, and marketing advice[9]; in September, AuctionWeb was officially renamed eBay.[10] After eBay had its successful IPO in 1998,[11] many called the Benchmark deal "the best-performing Silicon Valley investment ever."[12]

Amazon.com offers a stark contrast to these hacker-founded marketplaces, which bloomed naturally, one as a popular, profit-agnostic Web site, the other as a Silicon Valley–endorsed tech titan. Amazon, too, started small in July 1995 as an eager-beaver online bookseller, but the intention was always to become the one-stop shop for all online commerce. Nothing accidental about its path to greatness. First books, then everything else. The plan was hatched by a young Wall Street analyst, Jeff Bezos, while he worked for D. E. Shaw & Co., an elite "quantitative" hedge fund founded by David E. Shaw, who was a veteran of McCarthy's artificial intelligence lab at Stanford in the 1970s. "The idea," which Shaw says occurred to him and Bezos, "was always that someone would be allowed to make a profit as an intermediary. The key question is, 'Who will get to be that middleman?'"[13]

At Stanford, Shaw had researched how to improve the underlying architecture of thinking computers, periodically leaving the lab to start high-tech ventures. He earned his computer science PhD in 1980 after he "was eventually coerced into going out of business by his thesis supervisor."[14] Shaw's years at the lab were spent "living in the future," he recalled, with robots wandering the grounds and music streaming from the lab's PDP-10 computer. The future appeared well confined within those walls, however. In a message to his former colleagues, Shaw wrote: "Although I'm sure that some of you foresaw more than I did, I can't remember sharing a collective vision, for example, of how the Arpanet we took for granted then might someday turn into anything remotely resembling the Internet we take for granted now."[15] For all its obvious innovation, the Stanford lab of that era was inward looking, skeptical of entrepreneurism, and proudly peculiar, like its leader, John McCarthy. The message was clear: to make a mark in society and put some cash in one's pocket, best to leave the lab and its quixotic pursuit of artificial intelligence and look for a market to disrupt.

After earning his degree, Shaw initially continued his computer science research at Columbia, constructing the supercomputers that he had designed while a Stanford graduate student. In time, he drew up a business plan based on that research, which is how Shaw first crossed paths with Morgan Stanley investment bankers. Shaw's start-up idea fell through, but the bankers' pitch to him to bring his computer skills to investing found a receptive audience. "I couldn't help wondering whether state of the art methods that were being explored in academia could be used to discover the other investment opportunities that weren't visible to the human eye," he recalled.[16] In 1986, Shaw joined Morgan Stanley, where he applied his high-speed computers and sophisticated algorithms to financial markets, earning six times his assistant professor's salary.[17] When things were going well, Shaw's computers and algorithms could find assets that hadn't reached a stable, global price, allowing Morgan Stanley to buy that asset where it was undervalued and sell it where it was overvalued. In other words, artificial intelligence could discover a sure thing, the dream of everyone who plays the horses or the stock market.

Though Shaw's computers and accompanying algorithms produced a handsome return on investment, they didn't represent an important breakthrough about the nature of intelligence. Like the machines of that era that ran chess programs that could beat even elite players, Shaw's investing algorithms may have been much smarter than their predecessors, and more capable than people, but not because they were better at independent thought. They benefited from faster computers that could process more information, combined with the fact that there was so much more financial information to be processed from an increasingly global economy. However, there was one obvious difference between chess and investing—the extent of the prize money. After a couple of years' success at Morgan Stanley, Shaw decided to strike out on his own and was able to attract $28 million in capital.

D. E. Shaw & Co., which began trading in 1989, moved into offices in Manhattan's Flatiron district, above a famous Marxist bookstore.[18] The dress code was straight out of the computer lab, and even in those pre-Web days the firm's employees were equipped like the members of a lab—Sun SPARCstations with Internet access, which could be used for email and analysis.[19] At this computer lab/investment firm, however, there was a single, overarching research goal: "To look at the intersection of computers and capital and find as many interesting and profitable things to do in that intersection as we can."[20]

Hiring at the firm was treated with academic rigor, focused exclusively on finding the biggest brains with the best degrees. Shaw didn't wait to hear from interested candidates and instead sent unsolicited letters to top students that explained, "We approach our recruiting in unapologetically elitist fashion."[21] The interviews at Shaw were grueling and meant to explore how a candidate thinks by asking gnarly questions like, How many gas stations are there in the United States? This method of detecting genius by posing riddles has been popular in Silicon Valley at least since the 1950s when the transistor pioneer William Shockley began hiring for his influential start-up, Shockley Semiconductors. Shockley grew up in Palo Alto, where he knew the Termans. To his lifelong shame, Shockley was tested for Lewis Terman's study of gifted children and came up short. Shockley nonetheless relied on tests of all kind—personality, intelligence, lie detector—to assess job candidates as well as to keep tabs on current employees. The more about a person that could be converted into a number, from Shockley's perspective, the better.

For Shockley, however, part of the point was that no candidate should score higher than he did. One time, a young physicist, Jim Gibbons, was asked during his interview to figure out how many tennis matches were required to settle a singles elimination tournament with 127 players. Shockley started his stopwatch, expecting to see a bunch of calculations, but in a barely a moment, Gibbons gave his answer: 126. The candidate explained his logic: there is only one winner, with 126 others eliminated; a match is needed to eliminate a player; therefore, 126 matches to eliminate 126 players. Shockley replied in fury, "That's how I'd do it!" He wanted to know if Gibbons had been tipped off. Only when the next question stumped Gibbons was peace restored to the hiring process, though in truth, Shockley never found peace from tests.[22] He spent his later years in the 1970s and 1980s as a reviled figure, an emeritus professor of engineering at Stanford who would travel the country to promote his claims that blacks were intellectually inferior and advocating voluntary sterilization programs for mothers with low IQs.[23] Without any personal sense of irony, the Nobel prize–winning Shockley would cite results from a test that found him not-quite-genius material to make his case for group differences in intelligence.[24]

When Jeff Bezos arrived for his interview at the Shaw offices, he was already prepared to leave Wall Street to somehow start his own business, but he discovered a soul mate in David Shaw.[25] Shaw soon promoted Bezos to cover the Internet for the firm. In no time, Bezos and Shaw became convinced of the Web's nearly boundless commercial potential, which was reflected in the unprecedented burst in traffic in 1993 as the Mosaic browser was quickly being adopted. The question for Bezos became whether to start a Web commerce site as part of Shaw's company or to begin his own. In the spring of 1994, Bezos scheduled a heart-to-heart with his mentor, who "took me on a long walk in Central Park, listened carefully to me, and finally said, 'That sounds like a really good idea, but it would be an even better idea for someone who didn't already have a good job.'" Bezos considered the point for forty-eight hours, and decided to leave Shaw and his 1994 bonus. Looking back on that crucial meeting as part of a speech to Princeton graduates, Bezos concluded that life was best considered as a series of choices: "Will you follow dogma, or will you be original? . . . Will you play it safe, or will you be a little bit swashbuckling? When it's tough, will you give up, or will you be relentless? Will you be a cynic, or will you be a builder?"[26]

Bezos was a builder, clearly, and was prepared to play the long game with his Web site, which wouldn't appear online for nearly a year. At thirty years old and after nearly a decade on Wall Street, Bezos wasn't some young hacker who stumbled on a great Web idea and then would shyly go about inquiring how to produce a business plan. He was a young investor who enlisted hackers to carry out the business plan he had mapped out with spreadsheet projections and a general's sweep. Books were the perfect beachhead for an aspiring e-commerce giant trying to build a loyal customer base, he concluded. A book, unlike a razor, a pizza, or a blender, could inspire. People loved books. People gave books as presents. "We've all had books that have changed our lives," Bezos said early on, "and part of what we're doing at Amazon .com is trying to help you find and discover that next one."[27]

In the year between deciding to start his own e-commerce Web site and when that site would go live, Bezos raised capital from friends and family, hired employees, and prepped and tested the Web site. Bezos was proficient enough technically to know that he needed to hire professionals to design a site that could win an audience and accommodate rapid growth. His favorite to do that initial build would have been Jeff Holden, who had recently graduated with undergraduate and master's degrees in computer science from the University of Illinois, Urbana-Champaign. An alumni newsletter traced Holden's path out of Illinois: "As a good, hard-working student, Holden caught the attention of a recruiter for D. E. Shaw, the investment powerhouse. Holden had never given investment banking a thought, but not one to say no to something he didn't understand, he decided to check out the company. Mesmerized by New York City, the amazing people at Shaw, and the physical presence of Shaw's corporate headquarters, which he described as 'a super sexy, totally artistic view of the office space,' he took the job." At D. E. Shaw, Holden and Bezos worked together, and when Holden heard his colleague would be starting an e-commerce site he was eager to join. Unfortunately, Bezos couldn't act until two years had passed as part of a nonpoaching agreement with Shaw.[28]

Holden would join Bezos "two years and four seconds" later, but in the interim Bezos signed up a West Coast hacker named Shel Kaphan, who built the first version of the Amazon Web site. Kaphan came with less pedigree and was older—he was self-taught and had been hacking since the 1970s.[29] Kaphan felt he had missed out on the earlier computer revolution, in part because he lacked a strong business sense. Seemingly, nothing had changed. Even before speaking with Bezos,

Kaphan was thinking about how the Web could help people find the books they were interested in. But his idea was to hack the clunky notecard system used in libraries by creating a clickable digital version of *Books in Print*. "I wasn't thinking about it in the context of selling books," he explained, "but I was thinking, 'Man, I hate going to the library and ruffling through those card catalogues and trying to find that thing that I'm looking for.'"[30]

Bezos, however, was only thinking of selling books. Creating an online index along the lines Kaphan described was crucial to Amazon.com's impressive claim to give its customers access to "a million titles." As a Web start-up, the company wouldn't actually stock copies of those million titles, but neither did the biggest bookstore, for that matter. Book buyers were accustomed to learning that a book they wanted wasn't in stock and would be delivered later. Bezos was introduced to Kaphan through a friend of a friend who worked with Bezos at D. E. Shaw. After a few meetings in Santa Cruz, California, Kaphan agreed to build the Web site for a company then still known as Cadabra, as in the magical abracadabra. The meetings were in late spring 1994, and Kaphan's participation was contingent on where Bezos decided to put down roots. At the time, the choice was between Seattle and somewhere in Nevada, with California out of the picture, Kaphan recalled, because of its sales tax. When Bezos chose Seattle over Nevada, Kaphan was in—employee No. 1. He arrived in October 1994 and went about acquiring the computers, software, and expertise to build the site.[31]

In a month, Kaphan was joined by another programmer and in spring 1995, Amazon had a "friends and family" soft launch. In July, the site had its hard launch as Amazon.com. Among the many attributes Bezos liked about the new name—besides conveying the size and breadth of the world's largest river—was that it began with an *A*, and would be at the top of the What's Cool, What's New pages on the Netscape home page, the heir to that first list on the Mosaic home page. Barely a week after launching, Yahoo, an up-and-coming Web index created on the Stanford campus by two engineering graduate students, offered to feature Amazon.com on the site. Kaphan worried if Amazon.com could handle the surge in traffic, but Bezos said yes, setting the stage for a turbo-charged start.

Within its first month, Amazon.com had sold books to residents of all fifty states and of forty-five countries.[32] Even so, the book distribution system posed an early challenge because distributors had a rule that they had to ship a minimum of ten copies at a time. At the start, Amazon may only have needed a single book from a certain distributor. Bezos discovered a hack: the distributors required that ten books be *ordered* at a time, not that ten books be *delivered* to a client. "So we found an obscure book about lichens that they had in their system but was out of stock," he explained. "We began ordering the one book we wanted and nine copies of the lichen book. They would ship out the book we needed and a note that said, 'Sorry, but we're out of the lichen book.'"[33] That would not be a lingering problem. The site's traffic was doubling every quarter as Amazon expanded its purview, first by adding music and videos, which necessitated changing its motto from "Earth's Biggest Bookstore" to "Books, Music and More."

After two years, Bezos was free to hire D. E. Shaw employees, and Kaphan found himself being pushed aside. "The company started growing and we started attracting zillions of MBAs," he recalled. "It just stopped being fun."[34] He remained at the company for five years, so that all his stock could vest, but he was well out of the loop. Kaphan bears a grudge toward Bezos about how he was treated, even if that intense period of work left him very wealthy. He wonders if his work benefited society. "At this point, I don't know," he told an interviewer. "When I look at technology these days, I see that it's either doing something to connect people or it's doing something that isolates people." Amazon, in particular, he says, "is more on the isolating people side. Everything caters to convenience so much that you don't even have to get out of bed to take care of your day-to-day business. To me, that's a step too far."[35]

In early 1999, Amazon bought a controlling share in Drugstore.com and began a service called "Shop the Web," which added still more products for online purchase. Bezos was frequently raising money, which allowed Amazon to propose "megadeals" with the largest Web portals like AOL, Yahoo, MSN, and Excite; Amazon would pay tens of millions of dollars to be the exclusive bookseller and to have its results show up on searches. This was inorganic growth, to be sure, but Bezos considered growth too important to leave to chance. Around the time of the Drugstore.com acquisition, a journalist tried to explain Bezos's drive to expand before even returning a profit. "While his beleaguered physical rivals are mired in the present, where they have to attend to sticky details like making money, the specifics of Amazon.com's ultimate form remain forever elusive, a lovely shimmering at the edge of the horizon," he wrote. "In this way Amazon.com truly is a virtual company, existing only in the imagination."[36]

Amazon has continued to expand to encompass all aspects of commerce, including an increasingly lucrative business selling cloud-based computing. The company now has a dominant share of online retail sales and has become for all intents and purposes the "middleman" for online commerce that Bezos and Shaw imagined, shaping our economy and our lives. In 2015, Amazon surpassed $100 billion in sales and registered 300 million customers; analysts estimate that more than half of any growth in e-commerce will go directly to Amazon.[37] Upon achieving that $100 billion milestone, Bezos was prompted to look back twenty years to when he was "driving the packages to the post office myself and hoping we might one day afford a forklift." Even as he celebrated how far Amazon had come, he noted that, "measured by the dynamism we see everywhere in the marketplace and by the ever-expanding opportunities we see to invent on behalf of customers, it feels every bit like Day 1."[38]

There is something rejuvenating about approaching every day as if it were your first. But something unnatural, too. The workplace pressure never ceases—each day you must return to the marketplace to have the public render its verdict. Again. Again. And again. The Web-based marketplace keeps everybody productive and on their toes by instantaneously shuttling information between customers and businesses. If Amazon somehow isn't attentive to its customers, the dollars quickly go elsewhere. The tricky issue for Bezos has been to look beyond how this system serves customers to consider how the system serves Amazon's workers.

In 2015, the *New York Times* published a detailed report that portrayed Amazon as a ruthless employer on behalf of its customers the company's white-collar workers were crying at their desk from the stress and pressure.[39] And this account didn't begin to address the treatment of blue-collar workers in Amazon's warehouses around the world, which, depending on where on the globe they are and depending on the season, can be unbearably cold or unbearably hot.[40] Bezos expressed disbelief at the *Times* account—he was confident, he wrote in a note to employees, that he would never, could never, lead the kind of "soulless, dystopian workplace where no fun is had and no laughter heard," as described in the *Times*.

The market simply wouldn't allow it, he explained to his employees. "I don't think any company adopting the approach portrayed could survive, much less thrive, in today's highly competitive tech hiring market," he wrote. "The people we hire here are the best of the best. You are recruited every day by other world-class companies, and you can work anywhere you want."[41] This response appeared to be willfully ignorant of the pressures on employees to fight through unpleasant work experiences, to resist switching jobs. But more so, Bezos's response revealed his unalloyed libertarian faith in markets as the path to a moral workplace and a moral society. He had convinced himself that the market would somehow protect workers.

6. SERGEY BRIN AND LARRY PAGE

"It was like, wow, maybe we really should start a company now"

In a matter of a couple of years, the anarchic Web of Tim Berners-Lee was downright business friendly as Web sites took advantage of tools to keep tabs on their visitors and accept secure payments. These were important first steps in imposing some order, but they didn't begin to address the fact that the Web itself was a shambles . . . by design. A growing, decentralized, seemingly chaotic mess, the Web had resisted attempts to be thoroughly mapped, either by people or by computers. By November 1997, there were an estimated hundreds of millions of Web pages,[1] yet as Marc Andreessen observed early on, the Netscape development team simply skipped the hard navigation problems in order to get a browser to market quickly. "How do you search across the entire information space?" Andreessen asked rhetorically. "I don't know. How do you know where you are going? Beats me. The sort of surprising thing is we ended up with something useful anyway."[2] To Sergey Brin and Larry Page, Stanford PhD candidates in computer science who met in 1995, such questions weren't so disposable. If users didn't have the means to discover what was on the Web, then it may as well not be there. How, Brin and Page asked, could the Web ever meet its potential as a vital new public resource?

At its start, the Web was just small enough to be approached on a personal level. Its contents could be organized by indexers, modern-day equivalent of librarians, who kept up with what new sites had arrived on the scene and discovered interesting themes and connections among sites. There were potential flaws with this system, which would be particularly obvious to computer scientists like Brin and Page. "Human maintained lists cover popular topics effectively," they wrote, "but are subjective, expensive to build and maintain, slow to improve, and cannot cover all esoteric topics."[3] In Silicon Valley jargon, the problem with human indexers was that they couldn't "scale" along with the Web. People were too expensive for the task, especially considering how little processing power they came with.

In a biting account of her time as an English major working at Facebook, Katherine Losse explained the importance of scalability to Silicon Valley. "Things were either scalable, which meant they could help the site grow fast indefinitely, or unscalable, which meant that the offending feature had to be quickly excised or cancelled, because it would not lead to great, automated speed and size," she wrote. "Unscalable usually meant something, like personal contact with customers, that couldn't be automated, a dim reminder of the pre-industrial era, of human labor that couldn't be programmed away."[4] The answer to meaningful Web search would have to come through computers, Brin and Page were convinced, not squads of librarians. Up to that point, however, computers had been found deficient, too.

One notable attempt to search the Web with computers was AltaVista from the Digital Equipment Corporation. AltaVista began December 15, 1995, with an impressive 16 million Web pages indexed by its computers, which could be searched through to answer a query.[5] AltaVista wasn't very intelligent, however. It focused on keywords in Web pages, seeing how often and with what prominence those words appeared when deciding what results to return for a query. What keyword-based searches typically produced, in Brin and Page's professional opinion, were "junk results" that "wash out any results that a user is interested in."[6] Not only was the technique unsophisticated, it was ripe for manipulation by unscrupulous Web sites, which added potential keywords to their text willy-nilly. If one mention of the word *car* on a page helped it show up in the results for a search about automobiles, the thinking went, then surely twenty *cars* would be even better.

Seeing a computer act so stupidly was an affront to Brin and Page. The tools of artificial intelligence, they believed, would allow a computer to understand what was on the Web and help guide users to exactly what they were searching for. Their insight was to use the clickable links between Web pages, rather than keywords. Links, it turned out, conveyed much more information about a site than parsing which words appeared most frequently. Each link announced, in essence, I've been to this other Web site and found something helpful there. In addition, the text underlined by the link explained what in particular was so helpful—one person's attempt to map what she had discovered about the Web. Perhaps those millions of Web links and descriptions, interpreted by a clever algorithm, were all that was needed to produce an effective, automated online catalog. The best part was that those millions of links were just sitting there for the taking. Thanks to the Web's open design, Brin and Page, or anyone for that matter, in most cases could freely collect as much of the material on the Web as they wanted, whether individual links or copies of entire Web sites.

Brin and Page viewed this project in strictly academic, philanthropic terms at the start. They were computer scientists planning to follow in the footsteps of artificial intelligence pioneers like John McCarthy, who was a living legend to Brin and Page, walking the same halls of the Stanford computer science department. Their search engine would be tackling familiar AI questions—how does a computer receive information about the world and can it be trained to interrogate the information it receives to make real-world judgments? Had all gone according to plan, the two young academics would have created their uncannily accurate search engine, published the results in an important academic paper, earned their PhDs, and become professors. At the same time, the search engine they developed—at first called BackRub and later Google, in reference to the absurdly large number called a googol—would remain noncommercial and freely available to the public through Stanford.

When Brin and Page reversed course, however, and reluctantly dropped out of graduate school to run Google as a business, they would be sharing with the world a different discovery—an important new technique for profiting from the Web. By this time, there were companies like Netscape and Microsoft, among others, that profited from creating the software used online. There also were companies like Amazon and eBay, soon to be joined by PayPal, which intended to take a cut from online commerce. Google, however, would pave the way as a big business that extracted value from the ordinary material folks posted online while they were going about their digital lives.

Executing Brin and Page's innovative ideas for building a high-functioning search engine posed a number of challenges to surmount. The computers that "crawled" the Web, making copies of pages and collecting the links, were expensive, but Brin and Page were not above cadging what they needed by hanging out on the loading docks to learn who in the computer science department might be getting free equipment he didn't need.[7] Brin and Page then had to devise efficient methods for searching through the oodles of information they were collecting to isolate Web links. The last challenge: how exactly should the algorithm interpret those links?

Page and Brin, the sons of professors, used a technique that was similar to how the academic world evaluates a scholar's reputation. Say there were two scholars you wanted to compare; each has articles you haven't read or that were beyond your understanding. A natural approach would be to seek the opinions of experts in the field. You might even automate the process by sending out a survey to many scholars and then counting how often they had cited each candidate's research in their own. The higher the total, the more important the scholar, you might conclude. If you wanted to get fancy you might devise some formula—an algorithm—that didn't merely count the number of citations but somehow simultaneously factored in the importance of the scholars whose citations you were using. After all, if you were trying to assess the quality of somebody's work, you would do well to assess the quality of the assessors, too.[8] Think back to Frederick Terman's time as Stanford's provost, when he was determined to raise the university's stature in comparison to the top schools back east. Armed with a slide rule and similar kinds of formulas, Terman had no qualms about determining the precise numerical value of scholars far from his area of expertise—say, a proposed new English professor or the entire history department faculty. With these tabulations at the ready, Terman would then confidently rank the hiring of this person compared to the hiring of that one.

In many ways, a search engine faced a similar predicament to Provost Terman's. It, too, was trying to assess the quality of something it didn't or couldn't personally "understand"—in the search engine's case, a random Web page written by a human being. Still, Page and Brin figured that with the proper algorithm a computer could rank the importance of Web pages and their relevance to any particular query. The algorithm treated links like academic citations: a page that was referred to by many different sites must be pretty important, especially if the sites doing the linking had themselves been judged important. Likewise, a page that was frequently described with the word *baseball* most likely had something to do with the sport. The algorithm for ranking Web pages' relevance was given the name PageRank in a nod to co-creator, Larry Page.

PageRank didn't just produce results far superior to other search engines', the two wrote in an academic paper about their project, but it produced results that agreed with "people's subjective idea of importance."[9] That is, the algorithm's recommendations appeared to jibe with what you yourself would have come up with if you were a search engine. This was true even though Google was giving generically useful answers. The search engine didn't necessarily know you from Adam, but imagine if it did? The more Google knew about the person searching—where she lived, what she liked to do—the better its search engine would perform when trying to answer user queries. No matter how intelligent an algorithm is, if it doesn't know if you live near Berlin, Germany, or Berlin, Ohio, it's not likely to give the most useful answer to the search "bookstore in Berlin."

Google would become aggressive in compiling digital dossiers about its users to keep perfecting search, remembering each query and which results were deemed relevant. But even before such tracking became regular practice, Page and Brin used John McCarthy's sprawling Stanford Web site to run an experiment on personalization. McCarthy was freely sharing his papers and reviews, and links to other Web sites, as well as his short, biting opinions about current events. Using all this material, the two created a filter personalized to McCarthy; not surprisingly, when PageRank applied that filter to search results they were likely to be much more relevant to McCarthy than those produced by the generic algorithm. Personalized search engines, the two wrote in a paper coauthored with their academic advisors, "could save users a great deal of trouble by efficiently guessing a large part of their interests given simple input such as their bookmarks or home page." For example, "while there are many people on the Web named Mitchell, the No. 1 result is the home page of a colleague of John McCarthy named John Mitchell."[10] McCarthy had collected an unlikely honor: he was perhaps the first of a billion or more people to be profiled by Google so that it could generate personalized search results.

Page and Brin indeed are direct descendants of McCarthy and his artificial-intelligence-inflected computer science, although when the two were getting started in the mid-1990s, the field's ambitions had been severely clipped and McCarthy was known as a legend rather than a cutting-edge researcher. Like David Shaw's gifted investing computers, PageRank was a highly practical use of artificial intelligence techniques based on faster calculating and access to more data rather than a breakthrough in independent thinking. The computers running PageRank appeared to think like a person by working efficiently and incessantly as only a silicon-based machine can. "We don't always produce what people want," Page said early on. "It's really difficult. To do that you have to be smart—you have to understand everything in the world. In computer science, we call that artificial intelligence."[11]

Again, this application of AI may have fallen short of the high ambitions of those who believed they were on the verge of creating a new form of intelligence, but in terms of how we live the impact of the uncanny Google search engine was immense. The forty years between 1956, when McCarthy came up with the term *artificial intelligence*, and 1996, when Google arrived on the scene, encompassed a digital revolution. The pioneers of AI began their work on huge, expensive, memory-deprived mainframe computers. Only a select group of experts in business, academia, and government were capable of programming these colossuses, and only a minuscule group of MIT undergraduates—the hackers—particularly wanted to. The general public experienced computers from afar, and were quite suspicious. IBM was well aware of this suspicion, McCarthy recalled with regret, and didn't conduct any AI research from 1959 to 1983. Their slogan attempted to lower the stakes: "data processing, not computing."[12]

By the time Google was invented, however, computers had become epically faster and cheaper; memory was becoming manageable as well. The PC had inserted itself into daily lives. Under those conditions—let alone today's world of pocket-size devices—AI research oozed with real-world implications. Anything that made computers act more "human" was of immediate interest either to regular folks in their daily lives or the elites in finance, as well as the military and government, which had highly specialized tasks for computers to perform. There was abundant enthusiasm for Shaw's computer algorithms, which discovered and exploited minor inefficiencies in the stock market to make billions of dollars, as well as for PageRank, which for the first time allowed hundreds of millions of Web users to go exactly where they wanted online.

When Page and Brin started asking hard questions about search, seemingly everything online was taking a turn toward the crass commercialism best exemplified by the blinking banner ads that had multiplied across the Web. In 1993, barely 1 percent of servers belonged to a .com domain, meaning commercial; by 1997, that share was 60 percent.[13] Web search was no different, filling up with opportunists looking to make a quick buck. Many of the leading companies preferred to manipulate results on behalf of advertisers rather than improve the underlying technology. In their paper introducing the ideas behind the Google search engine, Brin and Page express dismay that these companies wouldn't share their raw data so that the two researchers could test their ideas. Not surprisingly, the companies that had the information considered it too valuable to part with and weren't necessarily interested in what a couple of up-and-coming researchers might have to contribute.[14] Google would be different, they promised, with its data organized so that "researchers can come in quickly, process large chunks of the web, and produce interesting results that would have been very difficult to produce otherwise."

Entrepreneurs may have been content to treat search like just another service ripe for pillaging, but Page and Brin saw the stakes as so much higher. A search engine, more than other Web tools, only worked if it had a user's trust, which required transparency. Too much of what a search engine did occurred out of sight. If it steered you away from a certain site to please an advertiser, how, precisely, would you know? Even computer experts were hard-pressed to determine if the commercial search engine they were using was playing fair when it published its results. Again, Google would be different, a project run by academics who were committed to improving search for its own sake, not to make a quick buck. There would be no ads. In a paper the two delivered to a conference in Australia in 1998, Brin and Page took pains to explain why advertising inevitably corrupted search technology and had to be kept out. They offered both ethical and practical arguments.

The ethical obligation to run a Web search engine without advertising reflected an academic's belief in the importance of public access to information, which could be a matter of life and death. In a remarkable appendix to that 1998 paper, "The Anatomy of a Large-Scale Hypertextual Web Search Engine," Brin and Page offered an example of the danger to the public from search results that were tainted by advertising. As a test, they typed in the query "cellular phone" at all the prominent search sites. Only the Google prototype, they reported, returned a top result that was critical of cell phones, specifically a cautionary study about speaking on the phone while driving. PageRank didn't return the link in order to do the right thing, the two explained; it was simply conveying to its users what the Web thought were the most relevant links to someone interested in cell phones. The better question to ask was, Why didn't the other sites link to that study? Page and Brin's answer: "It is clear that a search engine which was taking money for showing cellular phone ads would have difficulty justifying the page that our system returned to its paying advertisers."[15]

Practically speaking, as well, advertising led to an inferior product. Brin and Page didn't point to obvious examples of manipulation like a search engine that promoted an advertiser's business undeservedly to the top of results, or, as in the cell phone example, buried results that might offend. Instead, they were struck by the opposite effect: that a search engine might tamper with useful results to punish an advertiser. There was the case of one prominent search site that appeared to intentionally ignore an airline in the results of a search of the airline's name. The airline had paid to have a prominent advertisement linked to such a query, and the owner of the search site must have feared that if the airline discovered that its name already appeared in front of users who were looking for it, then it might not bother to advertise at all. This meant, incredibly, that under certain conditions, more relevant search results were actually bad for business. What could be more offensive to a pair of artificial intelligence researchers than a system with a feedback loop that made things worse?

Brin and Page had put their finger on the Catch-22 of the search business: if results improved so much that they became uncannily accurate and precise—like a chess computer arriving at the single best move for a certain position—then advertising will have lost much of its purpose. You would be shown where to go based on the consensus "best result," and thus should have little interest in hearing what an advertiser wanted to tell you. OK, there might be a few ads to introduce a new product, or to try to persuade you to switch between brands, but this wasn't the basis of growing business. A search engine needed to sell something valuable—like reaching customers in a way competitors couldn't—if it wanted to make a lot of money. The bad incentives were clear: search companies would stop trying to improve their services for business reasons, which is why Page and Brin toward the end of their paper made the following assertion: "We believe the issue of advertising causes enough mixed incentives that it is crucial to have a competitive search engine that is transparent and in the academic realm."[16]

The Google search engine from the start was a monumental improvement on the other search engines and the good news spread across the Web purely by word of mouth, just as was the case with the Mosaic browser a few years earlier. Traffic to Google grew 50 percent a month, month after month.[17] Here was another Internet-defining creation from students barely in their twenties, who were working out of a university computer lab and reaching a worldwide audience through the university's wires and cables. Google was operating with a nest of different computers housed in cooling cabinets made out of Legos and through an Internet connection at the Bill Gates Computer Science building, a $38 million complex that opened in 1996 spurred by a donation of $6 million from Gates.[18] When Google's Internet connection appeared to reach its breaking point, a member of the team suggested switching a toggle so its computers could tap into the T3 line serving the entire university, which relieved the pressure for a time.[19]

A Web phenomenon like Google didn't remain a secret for long to the university (with that toggle flip, the search engine grew to use as much as half of Stanford's total bandwidth) or the news media or potential investors. What would the young computer scientists say to those who wanted to commercialize their magnificent new Web tool? Histories of Google tend to rush past what was an epic decision to abandon their conviction that advertising corrupted Web search. One account of these events put it this way: "Soon, the temptation to spin it off as a business was too great for the twenty-something cofounders to bear."[20] In his insider account of Google's history, *In the Plex*, the writer Steven Levy doesn't even credit the pull of temptation. "Page and Brin had launched their project as a stepping-stone to possible dissertations, but it was inevitable that they began to eye their creation as something that could make them money."[21] Inevitable.

Brin and Page have come to terms with their change in priorities by concluding that ordinary rules don't apply to brilliant engineers like themselves: Google would somehow remain a research project with noble aims even as it transformed itself into a business with a duty to make money. One explanation for how they managed this particular form of cognitive dissonance can be found in Page's obsession with Nikola Tesla, the brilliant Serbian-American inventor who died in relative obscurity. Tesla's superior ideas in electricity and other fields lost out to Thomas Edison and others, who had a superior business sense. Tesla's life became a cautionary tale. "I feel like he could've accomplished much more had he had more resources," Page said. "I think that was a good lesson. I didn't want to just invent things, I also wanted to make the world better, and in order to do that, you need to do more than just invent things."[22] A great scientist needed to tend to business, if only to be sure his ideas had a chance to take hold. Placating your investors—in Google's case by accepting advertising tied to search results—wasn't ethical compromise but a way to make the world a better place.

There is another way of explaining why Brin and Page reversed course. They were students at Stanford, after all, and at Stanford, you don't look for investors, investors look for you. Marc Andreessen cited his own experience at the University of Illinois working on the Mosaic browser to describe what was so different about Stanford. "Had we been at Stanford," he said, "of course we would have started a company. In the Midwest, no way. Not a chance."[23] As discussed earlier, Only when Andreessen flew to Silicon Valley did his entrepreneurial horizons broaden. There, under the guidance of a former Stanford engineering professor, Jim Clark, was he educated in the ways of investment and entrepreneurism. Together, they built a browser business, Netscape, which got the dot-com era started with a bang.

Stanford meant something very different to Brin and Page, who first met there in 1995, a year after Andreessen arrived. After impressive academic careers at the state universities of Maryland and Michigan, Brin and Page were joining the academically prestigious Stanford computer science department to complete PhDs. They had committed themselves to an academic life. They weren't blind, however, to the entrepreneurial legacy of Frederick Terman, what Brin called Stanford's "big history of company building."[24] Even before they became fast friends and research partners, there was an example of a wildly successful Web start-up on the Stanford campus, Yahoo, which was built by a pair of electrical engineering graduate students, Jerry Yang and David Filo, working in their spare time.

Yang and Filo created their first Web index in January 1994, which quickly became "Jerry and David's Guide to the World Wide Web" and then Yahoo, to keep track of the technical papers online related to their PhD research. Other electrical engineers found the index helpful and sent suggestions of cool things on the Web; the mission and the audience kept expanding. "All of a sudden both of them went from doing their graduate work to adding Web sites to their list for eight hours a day," Tim Brady, Yang's college roommate at Stanford, recalled. "As chance would have it, their thesis advisor was on sabbatical, so there was really no one looking after them, so it all worked. Had their advisor been there, it might not have happened."[25]

On the face of it, Yahoo, which incorporated in 1995, was a very different project from the expensive engineering projects that Terman had encouraged Stanford graduate students and faculty members to pursue at first within the university lab and later in the private sector. Those projects typically earned government research grants, which included overhead payments to Stanford, before being brought to market in partnership with large multinational corporations. In the case of Yahoo, Stanford graduate students were working on a marketable project that had nothing to do what they were researching—actually took time away from what they were researching. This development path raised an interesting question: would Stanford claim to own the index, since it was created on university equipment, even if it wasn't related to university research?

Brady, a recent Harvard Business School graduate and the first outside employee at Yahoo, recalled being nervous about this central, even existential, question for the company. But Yang and Filo reassured him. "Stanford is very progressive in that," Brady said. "Yahoo is far from the first startup that originated there and will be far from the last one. It was new enough, and it wasn't a specific technology; it was a brand."[26] Unlike the University of Illinois, which didn't bend to the will of its students, Stanford as designed by Terman was content to bet on its students, even when they were playing academic hooky. Brady explained the Stanford philosophy, as it applied to Yahoo. "They were smart enough to know that anything they would do to stifle it would kill it," he said of the university's administrators, "so their best hope was to just let it go and hope that Jerry and Dave gave money back later, which they did. They optimized their outcome, trust me."[27]

Indeed, after getting the go-ahead from the university, as Yang and Filo had predicted, Yahoo grew through an early investment by venture capitalists on Sand Hill Road. In April 1996, when Yahoo had its IPO, it reached a valuation of more than $700 million.[28] The next year, Yang and Filo each donated $1 million to Stanford to endow a professorship at the engineering school—at ages twenty-eight and thirty, they were the youngest donors to make such a significant donation since the school kept records.[29] And today, Yang is on the Stanford board of trustees; he and his wife, Akiko Yamazaki, have pledged $75 million to the university to expand interdisciplinary studies.[30] All was going according to Terman's plan. Stanford was encouraging its entrepreneurially minded students to start a business—playing the role, one might say, of the canny initial investor, providing crucial start-up equipment, overhead, and technical assistance. Instead of shares in Yahoo, the university produced goodwill that translated into donations, almost immediately. Stanford's reputation was soaring, right along with its endowment.

Brin and Page were a different case, however. Their idea for how to navigate the Web wasn't meant to assist their PhD research—it was their PhD research. They hadn't stumbled on a business idea, they were methodically wrestling with difficult questions involving data storage, data retrieval, and artificial intelligence. Their initial discomfort in starting a business from their research reflected how seriously they took these profound questions. There had been a countervailing belief system within the Stanford computer science department, represented by John McCarthy, among others, that considered commercial success inappropriate for a serious academic. A deep thinker, a true scientist, should stay at the lab and try to change the world from there. Only the short-term students—dropouts, even—were focused on making a fortune from the ideas they had picked up at school.

Google, like Yahoo, required substantial Internet bandwidth, especially as it became more popular, but the PageRank algorithm was PhD-level research being conducted at a world-class university. It could hardly have been the most ambitious or costly research project operating there; consider the massive particle accelerator that Terman had helped land for the university in the early 1960s. Couldn't support for Google be just another case of the university backing its scientists wherever their research took them, money be damned? Wasn't studying the burgeoning World Wide Web a subject worthy of academic research and university investment?

From that perspective, Stanford's backing of Google shouldn't be seen as acting as a venture capitalist but rather as a nonprofit institution committed to supporting cutting-edge research. In fact, what turned Brin and Page into entrepreneurs wasn't Stanford's early "investment" in their research project, but rather its decision to *stop* supporting the fast-growing Google project. The withdrawal of support in the summer of 1998 meant that Brin and Page would have to fend for themselves. "The resources just weren't there in the academic environment," Brin recalled. "We decided, 'Hey, there's a lot of commercial interest here. People will give us a lot of money to solve this problem of search. Why don't we go and do it commercially?'"[31] Hector Garcia-Molina,

Brin's advisor at Stanford, has a slightly different view of the events of this period, seeing the Google founders as being pulled toward the market rather than being pushed there by Stanford. "It wasn't like our lights were dimming when they would run the crawler," he said of Google's supposed overreliance on the university's equipment. "I think it would have made a great thesis. I think their families were behind them to get PhDs, too. But doing a company became too much of an attraction."[32]

In August 1998, when Brin and Page were exploring how to keep Google going, they sought the advice of David Cheriton, a professor wise in the ways of start-ups, who worked a few doors down on the fourth floor of Margaret Jacks Hall. Cheriton had made a small fortune a couple of years earlier when Cisco paid $220 million for a company he created with Andy Bechtolsheim, a former Stanford computer science graduate student who had dropped out to help start Sun Microsystems. Cheriton encouraged Brin and Page to seek funding for Google, looping in Bechtolsheim. "If you have a baby, you need to raise it," the professor told the students.[33] The next morning, Brin and Page took a meeting with Bechtolsheim at Cheriton's house.

Brin and Page demonstrated Google on a laptop, and, as Brin recalled, Bechtolsheim interrupted to say, "Oh, we could go on talking, but why don't I just write you a check?" He ran to his Porsche, cut a $100,000 check made out to Google Inc., and handed it to Brin and Page. They explained to him that there was no Google Inc., and therefore no account in which to deposit the funds. No matter, Bechtolsheim replied, "Well, when you do, stick it in there."[34] No terms were discussed. It was unclear what exactly he was buying with his money, or if it was only a loan. But just like that, Bechtolsheim had turned two graduate students' curiosity about starting a business into something tangible and real. "It was like, wow, maybe we really should start a company now," Brin said. "The check sat in my desktop drawer for a month. I was afraid I'd lose it. But until it really happened, until then, it had sort of been this intermediate state. Things hadn't really happened yet. But when he wrote the check—well, it certainly does speed things up."[35]

Google incorporated on September 7, 1998, and Cheriton would become one of four early investors in the company, each said to have written checks for $250,000. In addition to Bechtolsheim, who supplemented his initial investment, and Cheriton, there was Ram Shriram, an angel investor who was introduced to Brin and Page through a different Stanford computer science professor, Jeffrey Ullman, who also encouraged the two graduate students to go into business. You can always come back and complete your degree, Ullman assured them. Shriram signed up the fourth investor, Jeff Bezos.[36] The seduction of Brin and Page wasn't simply about greed, or having the resources necessary to "raise their baby" and thus avoid becoming modern-day Teslas, whose best ideas never reached maturity. There also was the thrill for these star students of getting A's in real life, not just in the classroom. Cheriton, Bechtolsheim, Shriram, and Bezos were talented, wealthy men who were clearly impressed by the business potential of PageRank. The multimillion-dollar investment round that Brin and Page pursued next would be another big fat gold star right on top of their business plan, one that everyone could see.

While making the rounds to pitch the Google search engine to eager Sand Hill Road firms nearby, Brin and Page were impressed both by John Doerr of Kleiner Perkins, which had invested in Netscape and Amazon, and Mike Moritz of Sequoia Capital, which had backed Yahoo. What to do? Why not work with both? Bechtolsheim told them there was a "zero percent possibility" that this would happen: hypercompetitive, hypercapitalist investors, he explained, don't like to share their quarry.[37] Those words were all the motivation Page and Brin needed. When the road show was over, the two firms agreed to split a $25 million investment at a valuation of $100 million. Making the sale wasn't exactly easy, Page said, but he and Brin had the advantage of "being at Stanford and having a product that was really good. . . . It was much better than anything else, and so we would show them and say, 'Hey we've got this great thing. It works better than anything out there. What do we do?'"[38]

As these events illustrate, Google's founders displayed a particular mix of iconoclasm and respect for status. They clearly didn't care for the rules for how VC funding was done, but that rebellion was in pursuit of being the rare start-up that could win over two competing firms. Page and Brin set an idealistic goal for the company—"To organize the world's information, making it universally accessible and useful"—and because of the difficulty of that task, they insisted on hiring applicants from a narrow range of top-tier universities who met the rigorous academic standards common to Silicon Valley. Google intended to measure the "pure" intelligence of the candidates for its jobs and liked to deploy riddles on the spot as a way of detecting genius.

It's hard to know exactly where the attraction lay for the Termans or David Shaw or Jeff Bezos or the Google founders in trying to measure intelligence so exactly. That is to say, did they want to assign numbers to intelligence because they liked the efficiency of using an algorithm to make judgments about hiring and promotion, or did they sincerely think intelligence was best rendered as a number, the way a computer's processor could be assigned a speed? Whatever the motivation, they were all sticklers about getting as much relevant data as possible about a job applicant's brain power and acting on that information. Thus Terman would routinely step in to reject a candidate for a professorship in a field like biology based on his undergraduate grades in calculus. Similarly, Page and Brin would insist on reviewing the standardized test scores of each Google applicant. A candidate with low test scores could be instantly disqualified. As recently as 2010, Page had the ability to examine the dossier of grades and test scores for every Google applicant. Occasionally, he did a spot check on a candidate's credentials, "to ask what is the real quality of person we're hiring." Google wallowed in grades and scores, whether ancient or newly manufactured. For example, each answer during the hiring interview was rated on 4.0 scale—just like college—and scoring an average below 3.0 meant you didn't pass.

Again, the values of the computer lab were imported into a company. "We just hired people like us," Page explained. There were classes, cafeterias, esteemed visitors like McCarthy, who showed up early on to talk to employees. Sometimes programmers would take the final leap and sleep at work. "The fact of the matter is that for some people living here makes sense," says Eric Schmidt, the older computer science PhD who was brought in to run Google in 2001. "Their friends are here, it's what they're familiar with, and the things they do here are very similar to what they did in college."[39]

In the year before the dot-com crash, there was a broad acceptance of and patience for the strategy of putting together the best computer lab, giving it a goal, and then figuring out how to turn a profit. The $25 million investment in Google Inc. came in June 1999, and at the sparsely attended press conference in the Gates computer building on the Stanford campus, Brin was asked how Google intended to make money. He replied, "Our goal is to maximize the search experience, not to maximize the revenues from search."[40] The next month Google made a grudging acknowledgment of those newly arrived investors by assigning its first staffer to study how to bring advertising to the site. Generally speaking, however, the company's brilliant founders felt free to focus on making the search engine better and adding more users—as if nothing had changed from their university days. When the subject of advertising came up, Brin and Page insisted that it wouldn't be allowed to threaten the integrity of PageRank, which was sacrosanct. Licensing the company's search technology seemed like the better business. The purer business. Advertising remained an ethically suspect backwater.

In late 2000, however, after the dot-com bubble burst, Google was under real pressure to perform—the company still hadn't registered a profit despite 70 million daily visitors. Cheriton, among others, made his disappointment known, joking that all he would have to show for his investment was Google swag, including what he called "the world's most expensive T-shirt."[41] Some investors started to suggest that they might withdraw their money if others could be found to step in—the specter of failure for the first time hung over Google's founders. Doerr and Moritz used this stressful time to again insist that Google have an outside chief executive, something Page and Brin had agreed to but pushed off at the start. This time, however, they had to accept, and after many interviews arrived at Schmidt, a forty-five-year-old engineer who had already led a large tech company.[42]

With investors suddenly skeptical of how Google was operating as a business, advertising became a higher priority and Page and Brin assigned a number of talented executives to come up with an answer. After a series of small failures, Google in 2002 developed AdWords Select, an improved system for delivering ads next to search results that seemed to have solved a multidimensional puzzle. The ads ran well to the side so no one would confuse ads for search results, a taboo for Brin and Page. Under Page's prodding, AdWords Select embraced an automated sales procedure that could scale easily, stepping in for the company's human sales team. Anyone with a credit card could use the system and advertisers were only charged by Google for a click-through, that is, when someone left the search results page for their landing page, as opposed to being charged based on how many people were shown the ad. The system tapped into all Google knew about Web pages and its users to guide a customer to the strategy that would work best. The auction system for deciding which ads would appear next to certain searches relied on feedback loops that produced better outcomes for everyone involved. Winning bidders were refunded the difference between their bids and the runner-up and, by treating bidders fairly in this way, Google gave them the confidence to be bold with their bids, spending as much as they could afford. Likewise, Google ranked ads in part based on how effective they were, not simply rewarding the highest bid. This encouraged advertisers to make ads more useful, thus pleasing Google's users.

In each case, the ethical system proved the most effective. Google's first profitable year was 2001: $10 million. The next year, when AdWords Select arrived, profits were $185 million. Revenue was growing fast, too. The next year, Google introduced another advertising system, AdSense, which allowed small-scale Web sites to carry AdWords-style ads based on the kind of material they published, guided by the data Google had collected about who clicked on which ads. Google took roughly a third of what the advertising brought in, with the rest going to Web site publishers, many of whom otherwise never would have had the wherewithal to run ads.[43] In 2004, when Google went public and had to show its books, investors could see exactly how profitable the company was, even in what clearly were lean years for dot-com companies. With the company on firmer footing, Brin and Page's iconoclasm returned during the IPO, which was designed to work around investment banks by selling shares directly to individuals through an auction. (The original filing sought to raise $2,718,281,828, an allusion to the mathematic constant e, 2.718281828. . . .)[44]

The two founders were confident they had threaded the needle, finding a way to bring in lots of revenue with ads that were distinct from the search engine proper, thus avoiding the harm they had so carefully documented in other commercial search engines that accepted advertising. The ads displayed next to Google search results were so well targeted that users didn't even know the ads were there unless they were looking for them, Brin said. "Do you know the most common feedback, honestly?" he asked. "It's 'What ads'? People either haven't done searches that bring them up or haven't noticed them. Or the third possibility is that they brought up the ads and they did notice them and they forgot about them, which I think is the most likely scenario." Google ran an A/B test to learn more, displaying an ad-free experience for some users, while others saw ads. The visitors who were shown ads, the test revealed, used Google more than those in the ad-free group, leading to the happy conclusion that people liked Google's ads.

However, Brin and Page's critique of advertising relied on some clear guideposts for judging if search was being harmed by advertising and the search for profits and whether someone who stayed on the site longer wasn't one of them. One issue to investigate, according to the two when they were in graduate school, was whether advertising stifled innovation. In terms of queries about people, places, and things (that have nothing to do with commerce), Google has undoubtedly been improving, approaching the kind of uncanny results that the founders originally envisioned. Google effectively anticipates what you are typing and usually can provide a précis on any topic of your choosing, relying on Wikipedia and other deep online resources as well as the information the search engine has collected itself.

In today's version of Google, however, ads are no longer automatically segregated from results; they frequently appear directly above them. Enter an open-ended search term like "bicycles" and Google will direct you to some neutral sites that provide some perspective on the subject, but there may also be ads, and above those ads may be a row of shopping opportunities. The effect can feel highly commercialized. Here is the explanation Google offers for the sponsored shopping deals that frequently appear: "Based on your search query, we think you are trying to find a product. Clicking in this box will show you results from providers who can fulfill your request. Google may be compensated by some of these providers." There is a bit of a chicken-egg aspect to that explanation. Is Google merely reflecting the Web by focusing on commerce and assuming that someone who makes a generic search must be "trying to find a product"? Or is it helping to shape this reality through its decisions about how to organize information? A search engine was supposed to be an honest, disinterested broker between a seeker and what is available on the Web, according to Brin and Page. Google obviously isn't that anymore.

Another point that Brin and Page warned against as graduate-student foes of commercial search was the lack of transparency. Research at a university is typically published so that it can be reproduced and scrutinized and improved, while research done for a business is done in secret. The latter leads to what the two back in 1998 called "a black art," which can be used for good or ill depending on who knows the magic formula.[45] Today, Google Inc. jealously guards its secrets, PageRank first among them, and has offered a couple of justifications. To start, there are competitive reasons. Schmidt had battled with Microsoft in his previous job at Novell, and thus advised Page and Brin to keep as much secret as possible to avoid giving a competitor any angle to exploit. Netscape had experienced how Microsoft could quickly take over a market—like browsers—by applying its tremendous resources to reverse engineer a problem. Even revenue breakdowns, by Schmidt's lights, could offer clues as to how Google works. There were the practical arguments, too, for practicing secrecy as it related to search. If the public knew even in broad strokes how PageRank made its calculations some enterprising souls would be able to game it and search results would suffer. Without giving opportunists that advantage, Google still battles against companies and individuals who practice what is called "search engine optimization."

Page and Brin have done a true 180 on the topic—transparency was once the path to the best results, and now they view it as an obstacle. Moving from a research lab to a start-up obviously has changed their perspective. If Google still operated transparently and noncommercially in a university setting, then when some companies tried to trick the search engine the consequences wouldn't be so dire. An open system would be self-correcting: anyone keeping up with the project could spot the dirty tactics and propose a solution. Wikipedia, for example, has created a system that relies on human volunteers as well as "bots" to control vandalism or self-motivated editing. It tolerates some slip-ups but generally has succeeded in sapping the will of troublemakers.

Such deception is much more threatening to a commercial entity like

Google, however. It goes right to the heart of the company's pitch to advertisers and Web site owners alike that it runs a closed system that is beyond significant manipulation. Beyond outside comprehension, really. The algorithm does its job secretly and fairly—that is Google's promise. Its results are above reproach and the only way to deviate from this preordained "correct" outcome—to make an extraordinary impact for your business in search results—is to pay for a reasonably priced, demonstrably effective ad. This is good for search, which is in the trusted hands of the experts who work for Google. And good for Google.

In this way, Google tries to cultivate in the public the same cognitive dissonance it displays about whether it is a high-minded research lab or a profit-minded business. The entity that collects all that information, Google assures you, isn't some company spying on your behavior to sell ads, but a research lab trying to improve your search experience and only show you ads that you'll want to see. The same goes for the broad definition of "fair use" that Google favors, which would permit it to collect all manner of copyrighted material—movies, music, books—in its computer storage to be included in its search results. This is not because it wants to profit from others' work, but because of its high-minded purpose of organizing the world's information and making it accessible. Same goes for its opposition to the European "right to be forgotten," which requires that someone mentioned in an old news article be able to demand that that article be excluded from search results.

There was a final experiment that Brin and Page proposed twenty years earlier to gauge the influence of advertising on search: type in the query "cellular phone," they suggested, and see what results appear. Running that search on Google (today *cell phone* is the preferred term) produces what the two predicted would be the case for any search engine dependent on advertising. You do not find a negative Web page anywhere near the top of the results. First, there is a banner of links to buy cell phones, with the label "sponsored." Then there are two ads, clearly labeled as such, and then a map showing you a few places to buy phones. Then the proper listings begin—Wikipedia's article, Walmart's article. Then cell phones in the news. Then, about a dozen or so items down is a *Scientific American* article from 2008,

"Mind Control by Cell Phone," that is mildly cautionary. Brin and Page's paper didn't claim that the absence of critical links about cell phones directly proved corruption in the search process. They offered a rational explanation: "A search engine which was taking money for showing cellular phone ads would have difficulty justifying the page that our system returned to its paying advertisers." This subtle point, coming from would-be academics, recognized that you can produce bad outcomes without having that intention. You may just be doing what it takes to make your business run and "being evil" in the process, without even noticing.

All of which raises some intriguing alternative history: Would Brin and Page have remained true to noncommercial search had they met at a top-class school with a less go-go culture, like, say, MIT? Could they and we have avoided this reimagining of Google's relationship with its users? Or would we instead be talking about a different pair of brilliant Stanford graduate students who researched how to improve Web search and inevitably found their way to Sand Hill Road, while our alternative-universe Brin and Page would be obscure but distinguished computer science professors?

Looking back two decades, Google's rise from research project to Google Inc. may represent the last gasp of the Terman model at Stanford. Certainly innumerable start-ups have their roots in Stanford, including Instagram, but the university's resources aren't nearly as significant. Less than a decade from Google's founding, an ambitious hacker could make his mark from his dorm room, using just the money in his pocket. Mark Zuckerberg was a twenty-one-year-old chief executive of Facebook when he returned to his old Harvard computer science class to tell the students how lucky he was to have started his company in the era he did. "The fact that we could sort of rent machines for, you know, like $100 a month and use that to scale up to a point where we had 300,000 users is, is pretty cool and it's a pretty unique thing . . . that's going on in technology right now." A decade earlier, he said, eBay had to run off of two $25,000 machines from the start. Google was somewhere in the middle of these two poles and had some serious bills to pay.[46]

If Google was a last gasp for Stanford, what a last gasp it was.

Because PageRank was developed at Stanford, the technology behind Google is owned by Stanford, which exclusively licensed it to Brin and Page for a portion of Google stock, the last of which Stanford sold in 2005 for a total payout of $336 million.[47] The Google-Stanford connections are many and varied, as Terman imagined—students, faculty, alumni, and the university all helping each other make a fortune. Google has returned those good turns from Stanford in so many ways, from $1 million a year directly donated to the computer science department, to money donated to honor the memory of an inspiring computer science professor, to hiring Stanford graduates, and on and on. The recently departed president of Stanford, John Hennessy, is on Google's board.

But, just as the building named after Terman was torn down to make way for an entrepreneur donor, this Stanford model for success ended up being replaced by other systems offering financial and social support, whether that meant informal networks of already successful entrepreneurs or specialized tech incubators like Y Combinator and Tech Stars. One Stanford graduate, Peter Thiel, proposed cutting through the pretense. Why pay tuition if you weren't there to study? "College can be good for learning about what's been done before, but it can also discourage you from doing something new," his organization, the Thiel Fellowship, explains on its Web site. "The hardest thing about being a young entrepreneur is that you haven't met everyone you'll need to know to make your venture succeed. We can help connect you—to investors, partners, prospective customers—in Silicon Valley and beyond."[48]

This was Thielism in its raw form—no half measures or false solicitousness. Stanford already was breaking down the purpose of academia by being so eager to turn research into profits, which it would share indirectly or directly. Why keep up the charade about university life? Why not go all the way and accept that market success was all that really mattered?

7. PETER THIEL

"Monopolists lie to protect themselves"

If moguls like Gates, Andreessen, and Zuckerberg started as ambitious young hackers who discovered that their obsession with computers could lead to great wealth and power, Peter Thiel was something like the opposite—an ambitious young man who discovered that his obsession with great wealth and power would lead to computers. After graduating Stanford with both a B.A. in philosophy and a law degree in the early 1990s, Thiel pursued a conventional career in finance, briefly working for a blue-chip corporate law firm and then shifting to become a Wall Street banker. By 1998, however, Thiel was running his own small investment firm back in the Bay Area, where the dot-com gold rush was in full effect.[1] He had already helped friends with start-ups that had "sort of blown up in catastrophic ways" and was determined that, the next time, he would be involved from the beginning and do things differently.[2] Later that year, Thiel returned to the Stanford campus to give a guest lecture—fittingly, his talk was held in a small room in the not-yet-torn-down Frederick Terman Engineering Center. It was there he would find the ambitious hacker to help him on his way.[3]

The subject of Thiel's talk was currency trading, his investment specialty, but inevitably he touched on a broader political point—

how market globalization would lead to political freedom. "It was a topic dear to his heart. . . . Peter's philosophical underpinnings were influenced by accounts of totalitarian oppression such as the works of Aleksandr Solzhenitsyn," writes Eric Jackson, who had just graduated from Stanford and knew Thiel as the founder of the conservative campus magazine, *Stanford Review*, where he had been on the staff.[4] Among the small handful in the audience was Max Levchin, an intense, libertarian-leaning Soviet Jewish émigré who had recently graduated with a computer science degree from the University of Illinois at Urbana-Champaign.

Levchin had arrived on the Illinois campus in 1993, just as Marc Andreessen was leaving, declaring the Midwest an entrepreneur-free zone and taking the best programmers with him to Silicon Valley. Levchin was among the undergraduates hired as their replacements at the supercomputing lab where the Mosaic Web browser was developed, but he wouldn't be as naive about business opportunities. He started companies while still in school, and was clamoring to head to Palo Alto as soon as he could convince his immigrant parents that he wouldn't be pursuing a higher degree. Levchin's life goals had been fundamentally transformed by Andreessen's example from "somebody who thought of myself first and foremost as a scientist/future academic to someone who thought there's no better way to be than to create businesses. Be an entrepreneur, that's what it's all about."[5]

Upon graduation, Levchin was invited by a friend from the computer lab to stay on the floor in his small Palo Alto apartment, which lacked air-conditioning. To say cool in the hot summer of 1998, Levchin snuck into talks on the Stanford campus, which is how he says he found himself listening to Thiel discuss financial markets and political freedom. "I went to see this random lecture at Stanford—given by a guy named Peter, who I had heard about but never met before," he recalls. Because there were so few people in the audience, Levchin was able to buttonhole Thiel afterward. What do you do? Thiel asked. I start companies, Levchin replied. That's great, I invest in companies, Thiel answered. The two committed to working together on a start-up. "We hit it off really quickly—I have this IQ bias—anybody really smart I will figure out a way to deal with," Levchin says. "When we met, we sort of hung out socially, and then one night we had this showdown where we sat around in this café for like eight hours and traded puzzles to see who could solve puzzles faster—just this nonstop mental beating up on each other. I think after that we realized that we each couldn't be total idiots since we could solve puzzles pretty quickly."[6] It was a match made in heaven, or in Terman's Stanford, at least. Two young strivers—one proficient in the ways of computers, the other in the ways of law and finance—but each eager to promote radical change in a society they barely understood.

After some fumbling with other ideas, Thiel and Levchin came up with PayPal, which would create "a new Internet currency to replace the U.S. dollar." Thiel pitched the idea as fulfilling his anti-government dream of a global market that protects the welfare of the public by empowering them as consumers: "What we're calling 'convenient' for American users will be revolutionary for the developing world. Many of these countries' governments play fast and loose with their currencies. . . . Most of the ordinary people there never have an opportunity to open an offshore account or to get their hands on more than a few bills of a stable currency like U.S. dollars."[7] But there was that other thing, too, the chance to make a fortune. If you happened to create and own a new digital currency, you could collect a cut from each online transaction. You would become the middleman of e-commerce, as David Shaw and Jeff Bezos had sketched out, without incurring a retailer's burden of keeping track of orders, maintaining warehouses, and making deliveries.

There, in microcosm, were the two sides of Thiel, and two sides of disruptive Silicon Valley values: the self-proclaimed advocate for personal liberation who dreams of overthrowing the current order, as well as the ruthless entrepreneur dreaming of making a large fortune at Internet speed. Rather than those two identities' being in conflict, Thiel discovered, each can bolster the other. An appetite for the utopian social destruction represents a higher purpose than pure greed as your employees sacrifice to build your business. On the flip side, business success becomes vindication of all that destruction and proof that the right man is in charge.

Thiel was born in Frankfurt-am-Main in 1967, to German parents. His peripatetic father was an engineer who traveled around the world, briefly settling in, among other places, Cleveland, Ohio, where he studied at Case Western Reserve University and where Peter first arrived in the United States as a one-year-old and became an American citizen.[8] At age six, he spent two years and a half years in apartheid South Africa and South West Africa (current-day Namibia), where his father worked for a uranium mining company. When Peter was ten, the family settled down in Foster City, outside San Francisco.[9] By Thiel's account, his was a conventional, if overachieving, upbringing: "My path was so tracked that in my eighth-grade yearbook, one of my friends predicted—accurately—that four years later I would enter Stanford as a sophomore."[10]

At Stanford, Thiel studied philosophy and began to separate even further from the pack. In June 1987, he started the right-wing publication *Stanford Review*, which Thiel reckons was his first entrepreneurial venture, and a successful one at that. He introduced the *Review* to give voice to young conservatives, who he felt were not being heard during the divisive debates of the day, like whether to allow military recruiters on the Stanford campus, or in the highly publicized fiasco over whether Stanford should agree to house the Ronald Reagan presidential library. Thiel put together the first issues of the *Review* in his dorm room with the help of a high school friend, but in barely a year, there were forty staffers who distributed twelve thousand copies of each issue.[11] Three decades later, the magazine still flourishes, with ample financial support from former editors, many of whom have reached the heights of Silicon Valley by following in Thiel's footsteps.

The topic that sustained the *Review* from the early days was the fight against "multiculturalism," the movement to make higher education more inclusive and welcoming to women, gays, blacks, and Latinos. Multiculturalism championed two main causes at Stanford in the late 1980s. The first was to overthrow a curriculum of "dead white males"—otherwise known as the Western canon—by insisting that Stanford's required courses on literature, philosophy, and art include more racial and gender diversity among the writers and artists being taught. The second was to demand that the university admit more women and minorities and protect them on campus by, among other things, aggressively punishing hate-filled student behavior.

The *Review* saw these efforts as trampling on university traditions, whether that be the tradition that students can say whatever they want on campus, including something hateful, or the merit-based system whereby the academy anoints the Great Writers and selects who can study at Stanford. When these two causes were taken together, it appeared to Thiel and his comrades, multiculturalism had the single, overarching purpose of coddling the weak. Stanford students, some of the most talented young people of their generation, shouldn't need to be shielded from occasional strong language or from the uncomfortable fact that the world's best thinkers were not neatly divided among various racial, sexual, ethnic, and social groups.

In *The Diversity Myth*, Thiel's look back at those times written with his friend David O. Sacks, a former editor of the *Review*, Thiel and Sacks describe a campus that has lost its grip on reality.[12] For example, they describe how women on campus didn't have it any harder than men, and mock a professor who argued that "women are so oppressed that we don't even know how oppressed we are—there are layers upon layers of institutionalized oppression." Not very intellectually rigorous, they write, since under this argument, "oppression was both pervasive and undetectable. Once again, sexism . . . had been defined as to be nonfalsifiable."[13] The same sleight of hand occurred on behalf of racial minorities. "The primary problem for multiculturalists is that there are almost no real racists at Stanford or, for that matter, in America's younger generation," the two wrote back in 1995. "The few exceptions, like the 'skinheads,' are highly visible (precisely because they are so few) and are not often spotted at elite schools like Stanford."[14] Ditto for gays and Latinos. All were being conned by their leaders to think that they were oppressed in order to avoid the burden of personal responsibility. There was class envy, too: "In the multicultural allegory, the wealthy are per se oppressive, because their success creates misfortunes for others. The other two possible causes of poverty—bad fortune or bad choices—are rejected a priori. Quite naturally, multiculturalists conveniently overlook the fact that without productive people paying taxes, there could be no welfare for the poor."[15]

Interestingly, the root conflicts of Stanford's culture wars—"merit" versus diversity (or lack thereof), and "freedom" versus tolerance (or lack thereof)—are precisely the ones that weigh so heavily on Silicon Valley today. Questions like: How do we bring more women and racial minorities into the tech world? Should we even try? And do we need limits on speech to make the Internet more welcoming to women and minorities who are frequently threatened online by hate-filled comments? Thiel and Sacks then, and now, resist official interventions on behalf of tolerance and diversity. Their vision at the time was of a campus of strong individuals who navigate their way in the world, judged by their deeds and their deeds alone, not asking for help nor wasting any time to take offense. That's pretty much the vision Silicon Valley is selling now, too.

An early incident involving graffiti on a picture of Beethoven became a cause for the *Review*. Two white students, Gus and Ben, had a heated discussion with a black student at Ujamaa House, Stanford's African American–themed dormitory, that culminated in the black student, B.J., claiming that Beethoven was African.[16] Thiel and Sacks pick up the story in *The Diversity Myth*: "The following evening, Ben noticed a Stanford Symphony recruiting poster featuring a picture of none other than Beethoven himself (in the poster, Beethoven appeared white). Inebriated, Gus and Ben used crayons to color in the Beethoven flier with the stereotypical features of a black man—brown face, curly black hair, enlarged lips—and posted the flyer on a 'food for thought' bulletin board adjacent to B.J.'s door."[17]

Thiel and Sacks agreed that the drawing was "certainly in bad taste," and that, undoubtedly, "the black residents did not consider the satire amusing," but they also detected hypocrisy in the reaction: "Overnight, with the most minute shift in inflection, the symbolic significance of the claim that Beethoven was black had changed 180 degrees—from a source of multicultural pride to a point of multicultural derision." The importance of context—who says what when—appeared to mystify Thiel and Sacks. "B.J.'s words and the two white students' drawing had said precisely the same thing. Nevertheless, the fact that these students were of different races made B.J.'s expression legitimate and the white students' something of a crime."[18] Is their description of these events another provocation? That is, are they "trolling" minority students, to use the popular term for online harassment, or did Thiel and Sacks sincerely think there was no difference in how a black student might say he believes that Beethoven was black, and how a drunk white student might? In a sense, the answer doesn't matter. The message is clear either way—we are tired of all this complaining from women and minorities and don't dare tell me what I can say.

The two freshmen who defaced the Beethoven poster were kicked out of student housing for the fall and winter quarters, but avoided any additional punishment when the university's top lawyer concluded that the racist graffiti was protected speech.[19] This solution left neither side happy: people sympathetic to the black student in the case were angry that the university ultimately concluded that painting stereotypical big lips, big nose, and an afro on a poster left next to a black student's room was permissible speech on the Stanford campus. People more sympathetic to the white students, including the *Review* editorial team, were angered that the stakes had become so high that a pair of freshmen were in danger of being expelled from Stanford over what they saw as at worst a joke in poor taste, which was made while intoxicated.

The university itself was left flailing, unable to find a workable middle path. During these tense events, tetchy Stanford administrators, as we've seen, removed a joke about a cheap Jew and a cheap Scotsman on an Internet Usenet group, which led John McCarthy to rally his computer science peers to fight for an uncensored Internet. Their victory in that fight, McCarthy says, laid the groundwork for the anything-goes Internet we live with today, which he considered one of his greatest accomplishments. Though the *Review* crowd didn't advocate for an unfettered Internet from a hacker's perspective, they shared the view that the Internet—and offline life, too—should be beyond the reach of meddling authorities. They, like the hackers, insisted they were living in a world where the effects of racism and sexism could be willed away, if they even existed in the first place.

There were other free-speech martyrs championed by Thiel and the *Review*, including Keith Rabois, a former editor at the *Review* who attended Stanford Law School with Thiel. Walking by a dorm that was led by a resident fellow the *Review* editors considered overly politically correct, Rabois yelled toward the home of the resident fellow there, "Faggot! Faggot! Hope you die of AIDS!" The hateful words were intended to educate the students who witnessed them about the extent of free speech protections on campus, Rabois explained.[20] "The entire point was to expose these freshman ears to very offensive speech," he wrote in a column for the *Stanford Daily* defending his actions. "Admittedly, the comments made were not very articulate, not very intellectual, nor profound. The intention was for the speech to be outrageous enough to provoke a thought of 'Wow, if he can say that, I guess I can say a little more than I thought.'"[21]

When administrators wanted to talk with Rabois about the incident, he told them he wasn't interested, confident he was beyond their discipline. "My time's too valuable," he told them. "Whatever was said was certainly legitimate criticism. I'm a first-year law student. I know exactly what you can say and what you can't."[22] Later, Rabois was hounded out of Stanford Law School by his peers, rather than school administrators, and transferred to the University of Chicago. "For all practical purposes, he was expelled," Thiel and Sacks write.[23] He reunited with Thiel at PayPal, one of at least ten former *Stanford Review* editors who "had played a vital role in shaping the direction of the company."[24]

There was a complicating factor about this particular campus incident, however: Rabois and Thiel were themselves gay, though both were still well in the closet. Homophobia was prevalent on college campuses throughout those years, and not just among conservative students, but especially among them. No doubt, the pressure of hiding who they were played out in bizarre tales like the "faggot, die" episode and in the *Review*'s criticism of an openly gay lecturer in computer science, Stuart Reges, who now teaches at the University of Washington. The *Review* took Reges to task for a comment he posted to a bulletin board at Stanford calling on gay students to be more vocal on campus to show administrators the hostility they faced. He proposed staging a kiss-in outside a gym known for homophobic incidents, or having gay couples attend fraternity parties to "find out just how open they are." This fit the pattern Thiel and Sacks observed among women and minority groups on campus—"the need to manufacture incidents indicates that there is not much of a problem."[25] How else could a libertarian-leaning publication like the *Review* oppose individual sexual freedom? Gay rights had to be seen as yet another minority group's attempt at special treatment.

Thiel was publicly outed as gay in 2007 by the Silicon Valley–based Web site ValleyWag, one of the Gawker family of Web sites that revel in making public the private lives of celebrities, or the sort of well known.[26] The headline was an exuberant "Peter Thiel is totally gay, people." Thiel has described the experience as like facing a terrorist attack: "I don't understand the psychology of people who would kill themselves and blow up buildings, and I don't understand people who would spend their lives being angry; it just seems unhealthy. . . . Terrorism is obviously a charged analogy, but it's like terrorism in that you're trying to be gratuitously meaner and more sensational than the next person, like a terrorist who is trying to stand out and shock people. It becomes this unhealthy dynamic where it just becomes about shocking people."[27]

Already a wealthy investor at that point, Thiel began a long-term strategy to turn the tables, helping to bankrupt Gawker Media by spending what he said was as much as $10 million to sponsor lawsuits against the online publisher. Nearly a decade after the ValleyWag item appeared, Thiel drew blood with a particularly potent grievance from the professional wrestler known as Hulk Hogan. Hogan, whose given name is Terry Bolea, sued Gawker over the publication of a tape showing him having sex with his friend's wife. When a Florida jury awarded Hogan $140 million in damages, Gawker had suffered a mortal blow.[28] Thiel says he didn't sponsor the lawsuits to exact revenge against an institution that did him wrong but, rather, to make the world a better place. His sub rosa campaign against Gawker, he said, was "one of my greater philanthropic things that I've done. I think of it in those terms."[29]

During the 2016 presidential campaign, Thiel was forced to confront some of the more extreme arguments in *The Diversity Myth*—like its description of date rape as sometimes masking "seductions that are later regretted" by the women making the accusations.[30] Thiel apologized for those comments, which he said have been taken, incorrectly, to mean he didn't think rape in all forms is a crime.[31] But he didn't renounce the book in its entirety, which is filled with small cruelties that don't lend themselves to headlines. As *The Diversity Myth* recounts in detail, the *Review* was always trying to get under the skin of its political opponents. If there weren't any wrenching disputes over race, gender, and class on the Stanford campus, the magazine would concoct them. There usually was some issue at stake—a professor's alleged abuse of power; conservative students' being denied a chance to get their views across—but take a step back and these provocations appear to be little more than an excuse to be mean.

There was the time that the *Review* identified an undergraduate class, Drama 113 (Group Communications), that seemed to lack the intellectual rigor befitting Stanford. Incredibly, to the *Review* editors, the instructor told her students at the start: "I am not interested in facts—I care about how you feel."[32] Sacks and other *Review* editors decided to infiltrate the class and start taking notes. One day in class, they reported, a Latina student became emotional while describing her working-class upbringing. "Trying to be helpful, an upper-middle-class person asked whether Tamara wanted her children to be members of the upper-middle class," Thiel and Sacks write. "Without a moment's hesitation, Tamara replied: 'absolutely not'; her children would grow up in a lower economic class as well. Several students responded: Then how could she be sorry for her own childhood?" They never did get an answer, Thiel and Sacks write matter-of-factly, "because the distraught young woman promptly ran out of class," adding that "those who are taught to run away from hard questions will not even make it past their first job interview."[33]

In addition to his studies and his right-wing agitation, Thiel was elected to the student government both as an undergraduate and as a law student. In his first campaign statement, as a junior, he promised to bring the disruption of an "outsider" to the organization, known as the Associated Students of Stanford University: "I have no experience in the ASSU Senate. I have no experience wasting $86,000 of student money on ASSU office renovations, helping friends pack resumes with positions in the ASSU bureaucracy, and giving them disproportionate salaries on top. As an outsider looking at the current student government, I am disgusted."[34] Thiel rose to become the chairman of the appropriations committee, where he was a stickler about the rules for disbursing money collected from student dues. At one point, Thiel tried to exclude a women's group that failed to set up a meeting with him, telling the *Stanford Daily*, "People have got to understand that they have to arrange for an interview."[35] He was overruled. In another case, he stepped in to ensure that the *Review* received student support after a different committee had voted against it. Thiel's decision to give the *Review* nearly a fifth of all the money assigned to student publications was challenged as a conflict of interest, since, of course, he had helped create the *Review*. But Thiel noted that, according to the bylaws, a conflict would only kick in if he were an officer at the *Review*, and by that time he was simply a contributor.[36]

After graduation, Thiel not surprisingly gravitated to a life in law and high finance. His career arc, which began with so much promise, met with an early failure—being passed over for a prestigious Supreme Court clerkship by two conservative justices, Antonin Scalia and Anthony Kennedy. Had he secured this ultimate distinction, Thiel reckoned, he would have had an express route to the top of the conservative legal movement. "But I didn't. At the time, I was devastated," he writes. Looking back, though, he smiles: "Had I actually clerked on the Supreme Court, I probably would have spent my entire career taking depositions or drafting other people's business deals instead of creating anything new."[37]

Even after missing out on the Supreme Court clerkship, Thiel was still heavily recruited by top corporate law firms, and he joined a prominent one in New York, Sullivan & Cromwell, as an associate. But the spell was broken. He only lasted seven months and three days, he recalls with uncanny exactitude. When he left the firm, the other young lawyers were astounded, he says, overcome by the same thought: "I had no idea it was possible to escape from Alcatraz."[38] There was another relatively brief stint, as a trader at Credit Suisse First Boston, before he started his own small fund back in California.

Then Thiel met Levchin. Though Thiel wasn't a hacker, he was an expert chess player and had reason to think a bit about computers. When he was on the Stanford chess team in the late 1980s, computers were raising their game to compete with the best. In an interview with a student reporter, Thiel was complimentary, to a point. "Although some of the computer chess programs are very impressive, they are still far from perfect," he told the reporter. "Chess computers tend to go through all of the possible moves from a given position, which makes it hard for them to look very far ahead, since the possibilities grow exponentially. Human players, on the other hand, focus on specific goals in a given position. Until the computers become goal-oriented as well, they will probably continue to lose."[39] Thiel wasn't correct about how computers would need to improve before they could beat the best human players—they succeeded through brute-force calculation—but he wasn't exactly wrong, either. For all their success in competition against the top chess masters, computers still want for the deeper intelligence that can plan and scheme in pursuit of a goal. This is the type of intelligence reserved to humans. Thiel, the nonhacker, has persisted in this view of computers as "complements for humans, not substitutes," which pretty much describes the current approach to artificial intelligence in Silicon Valley.[40]

Thiel and Levchin made a nice match, with Thiel thinking about how to harness computers to assist people and Levchin finding the most efficient ways to get computers to do what you wanted. "I'd much rather focus on building than running," Levchin said.[41] The founders shared a hiring philosophy, too. They brought in people who were comfortable with each other and saw the world in the same way. Levchin assembled his technical staff by leaning on the friends he made at the University of Illinois, while Thiel looked for employees who shared his political views by using the *Stanford Review* as a feeder organization. If D. E. Shaw & Co. was run like a computer lab focused on understanding finance, PayPal was a computer lab whose administrators happened to come from a right-wing think tank.

These two distinct pools of candidates for PayPal resulted in an initial staff that was nearly all white and nearly all male. Of the six original founders, the one nonwhite person was an immigrant from China. All were men. All but Thiel were twenty-three or younger. Four had built bombs in high school.[42] A picture of the staff six months later shows that it had grown to thirteen and included one woman, an office assistant.[43] "The early PayPal team worked well together because we were all the same kind of nerd," Thiel recalled. "We all loved science fiction: 'Cryptonomicon' [by Neal Stephenson] was required reading, and we preferred the capitalist Star Wars to the communist Star Trek."[44]

PayPal began as a company named Confinity, a combination of "confidence" and "infinity." The name was meant to convey the reliability of its initial business, which was transmitting money wirelessly between Palm Pilots, though Thiel and Levchin settled on a more promising business plan of transferring money via email and renamed the company PayPal. Only then did the libertarian rhetoric flow, with the promise of giving "citizens worldwide more direct control over their currencies than they ever had before."[45] In practice, however, PayPal never managed to escape the reach of governments, particularly the U.S. government. The company remained tightly moored by state and national regulators who, depending on the jurisdiction, might apply to PayPal the rules for banks or money transmitters.[46] No revolution was launched; no business was ever done outside of the government's watchful eyes.

What PayPal offered was an easy, secure way of transferring money via email, a convenience that could become the basis of a powerhouse company once you added a little shrewd thinking about people and markets. The key to success, Thiel and Levchin quickly concluded, was to get enough users of PayPal to convince businesses and individuals that they had to accept its payments. This was the same "network effect" sermon that Andreessen had given before there even was a Web economy. Keep adding users by any means necessary and suddenly people will be begging to join. To start, however, you must do the begging, while also employing some basic Psych 101 techniques to win over the public.

"PayPal was a very friendly name," Thiel explained. "It was the friend that helps you pay."[47] No doubt even more compelling was PayPal's plan to give users $10 for joining and another $10 for referring someone. The idea of potentially handing over $20 to whoever came knocking wasn't considered particularly radical at the time. During the dot-com boom, Levchin recalled, "the classic insanity of Silicon Valley was basically selling dollar bills for 85 cents."[48] It's hard not to compare Thiel and Levchin to scientists teaching rats how to complete a maze. Thanks to the immediate connection with its customers through the Web, PayPal could closely monitor how incentives influenced behavior, tinkering with the size of payouts for referring new customers and raising the fees charged for using a credit card to fund a PayPal account to discourage the practice.

Still, growth was slow until PayPal identified a flaw in the growing Web economy: eBay, already a hugely successful commerce site, never created an effective way for customers to transfer money electronically. Most sellers were too small to accept credit cards on their own, and, incredibly, were content to conduct business via snail mail with checks or money orders. "It was a clumsy process for an Internet service, one that PayPal could clearly improve," writes Jackson, the *Stanford Review* editor who was brought in as a PayPal executive and describes stumbling on the untapped eBay market.[49] PayPal focused laser-like on signing up the eBay clientele, knowing that each "power seller," for example, who signed on to PayPal represented a network in her own right, the center of orbit for buyers.

One tactic was to create "bots," simple computer scripts programmed by Levchin, which imitated human bidders on eBay. With these bidders, however, there would be a catch, which they explained via email. They could only complete their purchase through a new service called PayPal—maybe you want to join me there? The mysterious arrival of these eager new bidders ought to have been enough reason for sellers to sign up for PayPal, since more bidders at an auction site meant higher prices. But PayPal executives thought of yet another inducement: What if the bots told sellers that the purchases would be donated to charity? Will you sign up for PayPal now?

Pulling off this plan required more than programming skills, however; PayPal had to find a charity willing to accept sight unseen the random knickknacks the bots had bought. Jackson was given this assignment and discovered that many large charities didn't want to be part of this unusual scheme. Ultimately he found a local branch of the Red Cross that agreed to accept whatever PayPal sent them and the new charitably minded bot was then released into the eBay ecosystem.[50] With the eBay strategy in place in early 2000, PayPal began a growth spurt. The total number of users increased by more than 5 percent a day, from 100,000 in February to 1 million in mid-April; among the eBay subset, the growth rate was almost twice as fast.[51]

EBay initially didn't take these incursions by PayPal very seriously. Periodically, executives would question why they were allowing another company to build a business off of their own. They would either come up with a plan for an eBay online payment system or choose a finance company to partner with. The efforts were at best half-hearted, while PayPal, as we've seen, was always full steam ahead. Later, when eBay executives decided to drop the hammer and try to chase away PayPal by exploiting its obvious advantages with its own customers—say, by adding extra hurdles for users of PayPal—the libertarian-leaning company didn't hesitate to threaten to enlist U.S. regulators to restrain what they argued was eBay's anti-competitive behavior. Reid Hoffman, a Stanford friend of Thiel's who became PayPal's executive vice president, for a time managed to keep the path clear at eBay by merely raising the specter of government intervention.

At this point, PayPal was committed to losing millions of dollars a month to build up its audience quickly and was succeeding on both fronts. Adding to PayPal's financial challenges—beyond, ironically, its growing popularity—was an aggressive, direct competitor, x.com, which was four blocks down the road and led by another young, ambitious entrepreneur, Elon Musk. Rather than destroy themselves in competition, the two companies merged after intense negotiations. The combined company kept the PayPal service, renamed X-PayPal, as part of x.com's suite of online financial services. The company managed to raise $100 million in investment capital just days before the dot-com bubble burst in April 2000. Initially, Musk was the top dog in the merger and Thiel was pushed to the sidelines, so much so that he resigned from the company. Six months later, an executive-led coup brought Thiel back as well as the PayPal identity; Musk left day-to-day operations, but remained the largest single shareholder of the combined company with a stake of more than 10 percent.[52]

Despite the wreckage all around from the expanding dot-com collapse, PayPal appeared to be in good shape. Growth continued to be frantic and the competition had been kept at bay, either through merger or threat of government regulation. There was money in reserve. Yet PayPal still faced an existential threat in the form of consumer fraud. Solving this problem would be crucial. So crucial, in fact, that Levchin says he prefers to think of PayPal as "a security company that pretends to be a financial services company."[53]

PayPal was vulnerable to fraud by customers who, among other things, would use the service to purchase a product and then ask their credit-card company to perform a "chargeback," claiming something was amiss in the transaction. Levchin jokes about how ill prepared he and Thiel were to deal with scams like that: "Somebody told us, 'You're going to be drowned in chargebacks. You're going to die under all this massive pressure of all these people who are going to be out there just to take your money.' Peter and I were going, 'What's a chargeback? We never heard of this. OK, well, we don't have to worry about stuff we don't know.' So we just went right along. And six months into it, we still had no chargebacks. So we figured that people are actually fundamentally good. 'It's all right. No one is going to charge money back.'" Levchin then learned that six and a half months typically pass before the first chargebacks begin to appear, and sure enough, two weeks later PayPal was fast being overrun by fraud, to the tune of $12 million a month in June 2000.[54]

One response by PayPal was to become an early innovator in CAPTCHAs, tests meant to screen out malevolent bots that help in chargeback fraud. The tests involved completing a task—like copying the letters shown in an image—explicitly designed for people. In a bit of AI humor, Levchin called the technique a "reverse Turing test"; that is, instead of trying to welcome machines by offering a broad definition of intelligence, as Turing's test does, CAPTCHAs were meant to identify and keep out computers by focusing on particularly human qualities. The tests were effective in keeping out conniving computers but were useless in separating honest people from dishonest. To achieve this vital screening, Levchin would apply artificial intelligence to the information PayPal already collected about its users.[55]

The right algorithm, Levchin believed, could search through "immense quantities of behavioral data captured in processing millions of transactions per day" to detect patterns revealing fraud.[56] Think of all that PayPal knew about its customers—what kinds of items they bought, when they bought them, whom they bought them from, how they paid for their accounts. Levchin named his security program Igor in sarcastic tribute to Russian mobsters who were masters at Internet scams. Igor would have the power to freeze accounts that raised flags. Invariably, there would be "false positives," innocent people who were denied access to their own money for weeks until a human investigator could follow up, but PayPal forged ahead. A class-action lawsuit over PayPal's lack of response to consumer complaints, including over frozen accounts, was eventually settled for $9.25 million, part of the expense of creating a security system that could scale, which was a requirement because fevered, automated growth was the priority.[57]

By September 2001, PayPal had 10 million registered users.[58] The fraud rate, which at its worst amounted to well above 1 percent of the total money being exchanged in the system, was reduced by more than two-thirds because of Igor and other methods. The way was paved for PayPal's profitability and inevitable IPO. The company went public in February 2002, the first offering after the 9/11 attacks, making the founders and early employees millionaires many times over. The company hosted a party with kegs of beer and a piñata in the shape of a dollar sign, while Thiel chose to celebrate in his own special way. He played chess simultaneously against the rest of the executive staff. Only one opponent of the ten managed to beat him: Sacks, his good friend and the company's chief operating officer.[59]

Even after the IPO, PayPal was feeling the pressure. EBay again focused on controlling the online payments on its site, and PayPal responded by filing a formal complaint with the justice department and Federal Trade Commission accusing eBay of anti-competitive acts. This was an uncomfortable step for Thiel, Jackson writes: "While philosophically reluctant to get the government involved, Peter recognized that the company's increasingly unstable competitive situation, coupled with its legal and stock market woes, posed a risk too great to be ignored and consented to filing the complaint."[60] That complaint would have an unfortunate blowback not long thereafter, when PayPal agreed to be bought by eBay for $1.5 billion in August 2002.[61] If eBay could exploit anti-competitive advantages in online finance when it had a relatively strong rival like PayPal, how fair and open would the market be once it had absorbed PayPal? PayPal's own accusations against eBay should have been compelling evidence that one acquiring the other would be anti-competitive. The legal teams for both companies certainly were concerned. But the justice department under George W. Bush chose to keep its hands off.[62]

The PayPal experience was an intense, three-year ride for a relatively small team that ended in a significant cash payout: Thiel made about $55 million, while Musk left with three times as much.[63] But those events from the turn of the millennium remain influential for a number of reasons, not least for releasing into the wild a wealthy, self-satisfied Peter Thiel, a one-man wrecking crew who has been sowing chaos through American society up to this very day.

After PayPal, Thiel created a company, Palantir, that built on

Levchin's algorithms for analyzing and making judgments based on an individual's highly personal digital records. Named after magical stones in *The Lord of the Rings*, Palantir helps governments and private companies make judgments from online and offline records based on patterns recognized by algorithms. For example, the company produces software that in seconds can scan through hundreds of millions of pictures of license plates collected by the Northern California Regional Intelligence Center, pieces of information that can be interpreted with the help of other large data sets. Palantir's chief executive, Alex Karp, a law school friend recruited by Thiel, defends his company's role in sifting through this material, which was collected by the government, after all. "If we as a democratic society believe that license plates in public trigger Fourth Amendment protections, our product can make sure you can't cross that line," Karp said, adding: "In the real world where we work—which is never perfect—you have to have trade-offs."[64]

For someone identified as a "libertarian," Thiel has been comfortable operating businesses that relied on analyzing the personal information of its customers or the general public. Just as profiling by PayPal kept it afloat by excluding potential fraudsters, well-conceived government investigations, Thiel contends, keep America safe. After revelations by Edward Snowden about the government's surveillance capabilities, Thiel was asked if he thought the National Security Agency collected too much information about United States citizens. Thiel didn't object to those practices from a libertarian perspective but, rather, said he was offended by the agency's stupidity. "The NSA has been hoovering up all the data in the world, because it has no clue what it is doing. 'Big data' really means 'dumb data,'" he told readers of Reddit who asked him questions. "BTW, I don't agree with the libertarian description of the NSA as 'big brother.' I think Snowden revealed something that looks more like the Keystone Kops and very little like James Bond."[65]

Similar to Andreessen, Thiel lately has combined the roles of investor and public intellectual. Of Thiel's many successful investments—LinkedIn, YouTube, and Facebook come to mind—perhaps his most far-sighted has been the decision to publicly back Donald Trump for president, which required Thiel to break ranks with his Silicon Valley peers. In return for his prime-time endorsement on the final night of the Republican National Convention in Cleveland, as well as $1.25 million in contributions to Trump's campaign through affiliated super PACs and direct contributions, Thiel was rewarded with a place of privilege when president-elect Trump met with tech leaders during the transition, and an important advisory role in the next administration. Who knows what dividends are yet to be collected?[66]

The Trump endorsement reestablished Thiel's reputation as a uniquely polarizing Silicon Valley figure, a Trumpian character, you might say. Indeed, Thiel has become an almost toxic spokesman for the tech world, so much so that his close friends and business partners, like Zuckerberg and Hoffman, have felt obligated to defend their relationships publicly. During the presidential election, Zuckerberg was confronted by Facebook employees who objected to Thiel's continued role on the company's board of directors because of his support for Trump. In a fine example of rhetorical jujitsu, Zuckerberg referred to Facebook's commitment to diversity to answer those who were appalled by Trump's disparagement of Mexicans, Muslims, and women, among others, and the idea that a board member could be supporting his candidacy. "We care deeply about diversity," Zuckerberg wrote in defense of Thiel. "That's easy to say when it means standing up for ideas you agree with. It's a lot harder when it means standing up for the rights of people with different viewpoints to say what they care about. That's even more important."[67]

No doubt Thiel is an odd bird with a penchant for fringe ideas. In his pursuit of limited government, he has given substantial financial support to seasteading, which encourages political experimentation through the development of floating communities in international waters, presumably outside the reach of governments. He is unusually obsessed with his own death and sickness, a condition he traces back to the disturbing day when he was three and learned from his father that all things die, starting with the cow who gave his life for the family's leather rug.[68] Thiel supports a range of potential life-extending innovations, including cryogenics, which involves keeping a body alive by cooling it; genetic research to fight diseases; and, most resonantly, a treatment based on cycling through blood transfusions from young people in the belief that the vigor therein can be transferred to the older recipient. Thiel says he is surprised that his obsession with death is considered weird—for what it's worth, he considers those complacent about death to be psychologically troubled. "We accept that we're all going to die, and so we don't do anything, and we think we're not going to die anytime soon, so we don't really need to worry about it," he told an interviewer. "We have this sort of schizophrenic combination of acceptance and denial . . . it converges to doing nothing."[69]

Yet, cut through Thiel's eccentricities and harsh language and you discover that Thiel is simply articulating the Know-It-All worldview as best he knows how. In Thiel's ideas one finds Terman's insistence that the smartest should lead, as well as his belief in using entrepreneurism and the market to introduce new technologies to the people. There is the hackers' confidence that technology will improve society, as well as their suspicion of ignorant authorities who would try to rein in or regulate the best and brightest. There is the successful entrepreneur's belief that the disruption that has made him fabulously wealthy must be good for everyone. The main difference between Thiel and his peers is that he acts forcefully and openly in support of his ideas, while they are inclined to be more cautious and circumspect.

As we noted above, Stanford may embrace the idea that its students should become entrepreneurs, but only Thiel pays students to drop out and start a business. Larry Page of Google may propose the creation of "some safe places where we can try out some new things and figure out what's the effect on society, what's the effect on people, without having to deploy it into the normal world," but only Thiel backs floating sea-based states.[70] Those peers may privately worry that democracy isn't the ideal way to choose our leaders, but Thiel will write straightforwardly in a 2009 essay for the libertarian think tank the Cato Institute that "the vast increase in welfare beneficiaries and the extension of the franchise to women—two constituencies that are notoriously tough for libertarians—have rendered the notion of 'capitalist democracy' into an oxymoron." For these reasons, Thiel names the 1920s as "the last decade in American history during which one could be genuinely optimistic about politics," though presumably 2016 restored his faith in the electoral process.[71]

PayPal only managed to become a valuable company under Thiel's watch because eBay never could squash its tiny rival, thanks in part to the protection of the U.S. government. The decision of PayPal to complain that eBay was anti-competitive can appear hypocritical in light of Thiel's anti-government views or even in light of the company's decision to turn around and be acquired by eBay only months later. Yet when you get to brass tacks, Thiel's complaint against eBay wasn't so much about its monopoly powers, but that it was becoming a monopoly in online payments instead of PayPal. According to Thiel, a truly free market, with perfect knowledge and perfect competition, leads to failure for everyone. "Under perfect competition, in the long run *no company makes an economic profit*," he writes, adding the emphasis. "The opposite of perfect competition is monopoly." Thus, the goal of any sane start-up should be to create a monopoly.[72]

When Thiel uses the term *monopoly*, he hastens to add, he does not mean one based on illegal bullying or government favoritism. "By 'monopoly,' we mean the kind of company that's so good at what it does that no other firm can offer a close substitute," he writes in *Zero to One*, his business-advice book.[73] Yet for a company involved in online payments or for a social network like Facebook, being good at what one does is directly tied to the network effect—that is, becoming and remaining the service that is so dominant you *must* belong. Ensuring that your business has no viable competitors is at the heart of monopolistic success in social networks, a lesson that Thiel has drilled into his protégé, Marc Zuckerberg. Under Zuckerberg's leadership, Facebook has managed to keep growing and growing, spending billions to buy out any rival social networks, like Instagram and WhatsApp, before they could grow to challenge Facebook, with one notable exception—Snapchat. Founded by a pair of Stanford fraternity brothers in 2011, Snapchat rejected a reported multi-billion-dollar offer from Facebook in 2013 and has watched as Facebook aggressively copied its most popular features for sharing photographs.[74]

For Thiel, monopoly businesses like Google, Facebook, and Amazon serve as a welcome replacement for government. Freed from the unrelenting competition of the market, these businesses can afford to have enlightened values, like investing in the future or treating their employees well. They can actually think about society as a whole. Google, he writes, represents "a kind of business that's successful enough to take ethics seriously without jeopardizing its own existence. In business, money is either an important thing or it is everything." Dominant tech businesses like Google are "creative monopolies" as well, which means that they won't sit on their profits in the manner of so-called rent collectors but will push new ideas. "Creative monopolists give customers more choices by adding entirely new categories of abundance to the world," he writes. "Creative monopolies aren't just good for the rest of society; they're powerful engines for making it better."[75]

Under this theory of benevolent monopolies, government regulations and laws are unnecessary. Taxes are in effect replaced by monopoly profits—everyone pays their share to Google, Facebook, Amazon, PayPal. And in contrast to the government, these profits are allocated intelligently into research and services by brilliant, incorruptible tech leaders instead of being squandered by foolish, charismatic politicians. Levchin, during an appearance on *The Charlie Rose Show*, was asked about the libertarian cast to Silicon Valley leaders. He said he personally was OK with taxes being used to build and maintain roads, for well-functioning law enforcement and national security. For helping those less fortunate, too. But, he added, "I have relatively low trust in some of my local politicians . . . to spend my taxes on things that really do matter. And so this lack of inherent trust of the local or broader political establishment is probably the most defining, most common feature of Silicon Valley 'libertarians.'"[76]

In Thiel's version of this anti-democratic fantasy, where tech businesses set policy priorities rather than elected officials, the public need never learn the truth, that they are in essence paying "taxes" to companies while government can be belittled and whittled away. "Monopolists lie to protect themselves," Thiel writes. "They know that bragging about their great monopoly invites being audited, scrutinized, and attacked. Since they very much want their monopoly profits to continue unmolested, they tend to do whatever they can to conceal their monopoly usually by exaggerating the power of their (nonexistent) competition."[77] And the transfer is complete, from democracy to technocracy, through monopolistic tech companies that are so indispensable they impose a tax on the economy and no one complains.

This surely represents a scary political future, but it bears repeating that Thiel is no marginal character in Silicon Valley. Not only are his views surprisingly mainstream, but he operates at the very heart of the tech world as an investor and a trusted advisor to a new generation of leaders, who first spread his influence in the Valley through a network of former PayPal employees. They provided each other with cash, counsel, and contacts and called themselves, a bit facetiously, "the PayPal mafia." Their offspring include YouTube, Yelp, LinkedIn, Tesla, and, by extension, Facebook, whose first outside investment opportunity was passed from one PayPal veteran, Reid Hoffman, to another, Thiel, once Hoffman concluded that his new company, LinkedIn, could pose a conflict of interest.

In 2007, a crew of a dozen or so of these "made men" went so far as to pose for a group photo at Tosca, a San Francisco café, garbed in cliché Italian mafia outfits. That photograph, for an article in *Fortune* magazine, quickly joined the annals of over-the-top Silicon Valley images, right up there with the *Time* cover a decade earlier that featured a barefoot twenty-four-year-old Marc Andreessen sitting on a throne next to the headline, "The Golden Geeks."[78] Levchin is in the front, wearing a black leather jacket; Hoffman sports an open-collared silk shirt revealing a gold chain; others donned track suits. Front and center is Thiel in a dark, pinstriped suit, purple shirt and tie, and pinky ring.[79]

8. REID HOFFMAN ET AL.

"My membership in a notable corporate alumni group in Silicon Valley has opened the door . . ."

The Silicon Valley era that produced the PayPal mafia companies—the years immediately following the tech stock market crash of 2000—couldn't have been more different from Andreessen's golden age. This bleak time, which was exacerbated by the 9/11 attacks, has been called the valley's "nuclear winter" when high-profile dot-coms disappeared and weren't replaced. Over a period of three years, venture capitalists cut their investments by 80 percent.[1] The events called to mind nothing so much as when a massive meteor collided into the Earth eons ago, casting a pall that wiped out the large, lumbering dinosaurs. We would do well to recall how that ancient calamity provided a great opportunity to the early mammals, our ancient ancestors. Once a minor class of animals on the fringe, the mammals were finally out of the dinosaurs' shadow and could use their bigger brains and more advanced social skills to take charge of a relatively barren ecosystem. In due course, their descendants—us, of course—reached the top of the food chain. In much the same way, Silicon Valley's nuclear winter provided a clear path to dominance for a group of clever, well-connected, already wealthy entrepreneurs.

Tough times do have a way of clarifying things for wannabe entrepreneurs. Remember, it was only during the tech world's nuclear winter that Google's investors put their feet down and insisted that the company's founders, Sergey Brin and Larry Page, find a way to turn their happy, re-created computer lab into a profitable business. By 2001, barely a year later, Google was profitable; by 2004, it was a runaway success. PayPal, too, had been forced by the tough economic conditions to focus on a winning strategy; using venture capital to purchase an audience $20 at a time was no longer an option. Strange to say, but this actually was an extraordinary time to start a tech business, assuming you had the resources to get off the ground. Was the Web any less useful after the bubble in tech stocks burst? Of course not. The Internet was still going strong, even if many Internet companies weren't.

In that fateful year, 2000, about 120 million Americans had access to the Internet in their homes; by 2003, the total had grown by nearly 60 million, to 179 million.[2] The global growth in Internet users over that same period was even more impressive: roughly 415 million users in 2000 became more than 781 million by the end of 2003.[3] Online commerce kept growing during these dark days as well. Total e-commerce in the United States in 2000, according to Census data, was $27.6 billion. That total doubled by 2003, to $57.6 billion.[4] As far as anyone could tell, the winning Web strategy remained largely the same, too: be quick to market and ruthlessly exploit the network effect, the virtuous loop that drives people to join a service because others have already joined.

Start-ups of this era would need to run on lean budgets, but then again, conditions had never been better for pulling that off. To begin with, there was the relative lack of competition, which meant that a new company could build an audience without fear of being undercut by a well-financed rival. Another advantage was that expenses were falling across the board—computer hardware was getting faster and less expensive, while free software was becoming more reliable and pervasive. Perhaps the greatest advantage of that era was the spread of faster broadband Internet connections, which enabled enthusiastic Web users to post online all manner of creative work and personal information—essays, recommendations, technical advice, photos, videos.

The tools for collaboration and direct publishing that Tim Berners-Lee had argued for at the start were introduced to the mainstream during these years as Web 2.0. This phrase immediately stuck in his craw, however. What exactly was new—2.0-ish, that is—about these companies built around user contributions? They were simply fulfilling the original vision for the Web, where "interaction between people is really what the Web is."[5] There was one vital difference, however. In Web 2.0, the tools for sharing and publishing were part of a social network or service that profited off of what you created there. You weren't publishing a video to the Web, you were publishing a YouTube video; you weren't writing a restaurant review on the Web, you were posting a Yelp review. The truly new idea expressed by Web 2.0 was a commercial one, and perhaps that is why Berners-Lee couldn't recognize it.

Directly profiting from what the public posted online certainly was a much better deal for tech businesses. While Google had proven that there was a business to be made by treating everything freely published on the Web as a collection of "user-generated content," think how hard the task was: Google had to collect and store enormous quantities of data and then build a complicated algorithm to extract value from it. By contrast, a Web 2.0 company could find itself flooded with valuable contributions from its own users, which it could exploit. The method for profiting might have been the same—publishing compelling material that would appear next to relevant advertisements—but a Web 1.0 company had the enormous challenge of sifting a fast-changing river of information for gold powder, while the others were, in effect, melting down gold jewelry that had arrived as a package left on the porch. Google eventually understood this distinction, too, and began collecting troves of user-generated content that it could exploit, whether through homegrown services like Gmail or Google+ or through its acquisition of businesses like YouTube or its ambitious scanning of the world's libraries.

A trailblazer of Web 2.0 strategy was HotorNot.com, which was founded in 2000 and immediately became an online sensation by allowing a user to upload a photo and receive a snap judgment on "hotness" from the site's visitors, who voted on a scale of 1 to 10. When three PayPal veterans—two programmers, Jawed Karim and Steve Chen and a designer, Chad Hurley—created YouTube, they were intending to bring the hot-or-not idea to video. In an interview, Karim said he was impressed by HotorNot because "it was the first time that someone had designed a Web site where anyone could upload content that everyone else could view. That was a new concept because, up until that point, it was always the people who owned the Web site who would provide the content." After a few months, YouTube broadened its mission by allowing all manner of online videos and was acquired by Google in 2006 for $1.65 billion.[6]

This openness to user contributions on the part of Web 2.0 companies easily blended into a laid-back approach to potential copyright violations, in that much of what users wanted to "share" was material others had made or owned. This was the hacker ethic from the computer labs, which insisted that a frictionless system for passing along material meant that anyone should be allowed to do so. Copyright owners in the music, film, news, and TV industries, however, quickly recognized that these sites could threaten their businesses. Silicon Valley would have to fight in federal and state courthouses for greater tolerance for posting copyrighted material.

Google's YouTube division, among others, came to rely on the "safe harbor" provision of the 1998 Digital Millennium Copyright Act to be spared liability for hosting illegal copies of copyrighted material. As long as they promptly removed material when notified by the copyright holders, these services wouldn't be liable for what might otherwise be infringing behavior. YouTube benefited from being a comprehensive video-sharing network with many uses beyond transmitting copyrighted material. Courts treated it differently from, say, Napster, the peer-to-peer music sharing site that was seen by friends and foes alike as principally a means of acquiring copies of copyrighted music; Napster was shut down by a judge's order in July 2001.[7] YouTube thrives to this day. The safe harbor provision proved crucial to the acceptance of Web 2.0 sites, helping to mainstream the practice of copying and posting clips of copyrighted material, even as these services created automated systems for identifying and removing material once copyright owners complained.[8]

Thus the Web, even through 2.0, made another detour from the Berners-Lee model of personal and direct online collaboration. Instead, collaboration continued to be centralized and commercialized, as Andreessen had conceived from the start, like a global TV network. YouTube and Facebook and Amazon became the way people accessed news and entertainment. The single-minded pursuit of large online audiences by tech companies threatened the financial underpinning of traditional news outlets and cultural businesses and organizations, in yet another example of how the combination of hacker freedoms and entrepreneurial greed produced the social disruption we are experiencing today.[9]

The formula for Web 2.0 success at the dawn of the new millennium was ideally suited to members of the PayPal mafia: there was a chance for great success quickly, provided that you arrived on the scene with a new service that was interesting, reliable, and scalable. During the nuclear winter in Silicon Valley, when outside investor money had largely disappeared, the PayPal mafia had each other—millionaires who either were talented programmers or knew how to run a start-up. They established the kind of business-friendly support system that Terman perfected at Stanford in the 1950s and '60s: there were early investments that acted like government grants; access to well-trained former colleagues, who were the equivalent of graduate students or research assistants; and there often was spare office space to borrow, so a team could move in immediately.

In addition to YouTube there was Slide, a photo-sharing service from Max Levchin, which was quickly snapped up by Google for $200 million; Yammer, cofounded by David Sacks, which produced an internal communication tool and was bought by Microsoft for $1.2 billion in 2012; and Yelp, the publicly traded company cofounded by two former PayPal programmers, which harnesses user responses to create reviews of a restaurant or even of a local doctor. Facebook, which launched in 2004, joined the PayPal mafia's orbit when its founder, Mark Zuckerberg, moved to Silicon Valley and needed an infusion of cash.

To see how the PayPal mafia worked in practice, consider how Reid Hoffman used the connections he made at PayPal to build his start-up, LinkedIn.[10] In 1997, Hoffman cofounded the Web site SocialNet, which tried to turn online connections into offline relationships, romantic and otherwise. Looking back, you could say that SocialNet was too early to social networking, and consequently never managed to build a large audience or figure out how to profit from the small one it had. When Hoffman sold the company, he had a mere $40,000 to show for his efforts.[11] After giving up on SocialNet, however, Hoffman was invited by Thiel, his close college friend, to join PayPal, first as a board member and later as a top executive.[12] At PayPal, as we've seen, Hoffman was front and center in maintaining the company's access to eBay's customers one way or another; at times, he would cajole eBay's lawyers into playing nice, at others he would encourage the Department of Justice to investigate eBay for anti-competitive behavior.

Once eBay decided to buy its pesky rival for $1.5 billion, Hoffman's profile in Silicon Valley changed radically. "They tracked SocialNet as modestly interesting," Hoffman said of his fellow entrepreneurs and investors, but, he added, "PayPal was my induction into the circuit. It pegged me as legit; it pegged me as a player."[13] And, indeed, when Hoffman proposed a new company called LinkedIn for building professional networks, he was able to get started quickly because of his enhanced reputation and personal wealth, as well as a network of friends who served as cofounders, early employees, and investors. Financing for the company came from, among others, Thiel and Keith Rabois and other multimillionaires created by PayPal's sale to eBay; the company's first office space was provided by a former PayPal colleague. Later, once LinkedIn was a viable company, Hoffman was able to pay it forward, giving office space to the former PayPal employees who created YouTube and joining them as an early investor.[14]

There is something jarring about a group of self-styled survival-of-the-fittest free-marketeers committing to a strategy of collective risk and mutual support. At least one pillar of the Silicon Valley ideology was toppled by this arrangement: that success was handed out to an entrepreneur strictly according to ability and hard work, no matter his station in life or place of origin. Marc Andreessen once expressed this faith in individual merit in an interview with the *New York Times* journalist Tom Friedman, offering another example of how the world is flat: "The most profound thing to me is the fact that a 14-year-old in Romania or Bangalore or the Soviet Union or Vietnam has all the information, all the tools, all the software easily available to apply knowledge however they want. That is, I am sure the next Napster is going to come out of left field."[15] Somehow, things haven't quite worked out that way. Instead, a collection of male executives from a single company, a few of whom were hired as much for their right-wing political beliefs as for any latent computer or business talent, managed to create a roster of successful companies. A kid in Romania, it seems, no matter how talented, didn't stand a chance against these guys.

Considering their origin in university friendships and earlier start-ups, networks like the PayPal mafia tended to be nearly uniform when it came to sex, race, and educational background: white, male, elite. Somehow, though, the experience of profiting from connections and college friendship hasn't diminished the lecturing from Silicon Valley about how other institutions—typically highly unionized ones like the public school system or the automobile industry—are rife with favoritism. Here is Hoffman explaining Detroit's decline in *The Start-Up of You*, his business-advice book: "The overriding problem was this: The auto industry got too comfortable. . . . Instead of rewarding the best people in the organization and firing the worst, they promoted on the basis of longevity and nepotism."[16] Hoffman makes no mention of any similarity to the PayPal mafia, which he describes this way: "My membership in a notable corporate alumni group in Silicon Valley has opened the door to a number of breakout opportunities."[17]

Though considered a liberal in Silicon Valley, Hoffman adheres to the consensus view there that society is organized around unbridled competition within a market. "Keep in mind," he writes, "that the 'market' is not an abstract thing. It consists of the people who make decisions that affect you and whose needs you must serve: your boss, your coworkers, your clients, your direct reports and others. How badly do they need what you have to offer, and if they need it, do you offer value that's better than the competition?"[18] And you had better please this market, he continues, because the social safety net is an illusion. In a footnote, Hoffman counsels his readers to "consider the Social Security tax that comes out of your paycheck like you would a loan to a second cousin who has a drug problem. You might get paid back, but don't count on it."[19]

Thiel and Hoffman say they became friends through dorm-room political arguments including one over Thiel's agreement with Margaret Thatcher's statement that "There is no such thing as society. There are individual men and women and there are families." Hoffman considers himself on the left, and vehemently disagreed with Thiel over this harsh view of humanity.[20] But if the society that Hoffman advocates for is little more than a marketplace where individuals must slug it out, then the gap between the two isn't so significant. Hoffman's society—Silicon Valley's, really—ain't much of a society.

For instance, knowing how unforgiving the market is, why would Hoffman begrudge workers the right to form a union as a way of ensuring some stability and protection? Hoffman prefers that each of us build "a network of alliances to help you with intelligence, resources and collective action."[21] A wealthy Stanford graduate, Hoffman has undoubtedly benefited greatly from his "mafia" of similarly situated peers. However, an economy based on personal networks undoubtedly disadvantages nearly everyone else, even ambitious, well-educated entrepreneurs like Jimmy Wales, born in Huntsville, Alabama, and eager to cash in on the Web craze.

9. JIMMY WALES

"Wikipedia is something special"

In the mid-1990s, Jimmy Wales had a lot in common with Jeff Bezos and Peter Thiel—an early career in finance, libertarian-leaning politics, youthful fascination with science and computers, and a determination to make it rich from the Web. What he lacked, however, was their elite educational pedigree and Wall Street experience. And that would make all the difference for Wikipedia, the brilliant project Wales has shepherded since its inception in 2001.

The encyclopedia anyone can edit, Wikipedia appeared to offer a golden ticket to a Web 2.0 entrepreneur like Wales with its oodles of user-generated content. But Wikipedia has taken a different path: no advertising appears next to the articles its editors have written or the photos they have posted; there are no suggestions of products to buy based on your search; the project doesn't track its visitors, and hasn't once thought to acquire a rival online encyclopedia. Wikipedia is a shining outlier in the commercialized Web, a site that has benefited enormously from the network effect but has never sought to profit from it. And Wales, the Web entrepreneur, has watched it all happen.

Jimmy Wales was a precocious kid, born in Huntsville, Alabama, in 1966. His early education came at a small school started by his mother and grandmother, though he later attended a private high school.

Huntsville was a scientific hub, the home to a space research center led by the infamous Wernher von Braun, who had masterminded the Nazis' rocket program. In high school, Wales learned to program a PDP-11 minicomputer, one of the Digital machines that were beloved by the early hackers. Wales kept up his interest in computers and programming as a side hobby while he studied finance at Auburn and the University of Alabama, getting bachelor's and master's degrees. He left a PhD program in finance at Indiana University to become a futures and options trader in Chicago.[1]

The Netscape IPO in late 1995 caught Wales's attention, and he made another career change: Web entrepreneur. The next year, Wales started his own online business called Bomis, which included a simple search engine and an index of Web sites assembled by registered users, who were called "ringmasters." What these human indexers produced were "rings" about a specific topic, one site joining the next. In classic Web 2.0 fashion, Bomis was planning to profit from the indexes it solicited by surrounding them with advertisements. The company made an appeal to ego and self-interest to spur contributions. "If your ring is really good, we may choose to include it in our search engine and tree structure," the Web site said. "This is a great honor because it means that we think you've gotten at the essentials of some topic, and that we think you have been reasonably fair and unbiased in your selection and descriptions. (Of course, putting your own page first in the ring is PERFECTLY fine with us!)"[2] This was not an ideal situation for runaway growth, however; Bomis was highly dependent on the work of humans, either its small group of contributors or its even smaller staff. There was little artificially intelligent about the company, and thus little chance of its scaling.

Wales was open to any new idea for encouraging users to produce material that he could then sell ads against; like many sites of this era, Bomis wasn't shy about helping its users find porn.[3] In January 2000, when the company had about a dozen employees and tech stocks were at their peak, Wales proposed that Bomis publish an online encyclopedia created by users, which he called Nupedia. For the first editor of Nupedia, Wales hired Larry Sanger, a technically proficient philosophy PhD, whom Wales had met through an online discussion group about Ayn Rand, the "virtue of selfishness" philosopher.[4] As any sensible encyclopedia operators would do at that time, Sanger and Wales established a thorough review system for articles, one so thorough that after a year barely twenty articles had been given the green light to be published. At that rate, Nupedia would challenge the *Encyclopedia Britannica* in a few thousand years.[5]

This system obviously couldn't last, and the dot-com crash, again, had a way of bringing clarity to the situation. Bomis hadn't discovered an automated way to unlock profits from the Web, as Google or PayPal or Amazon had. Wales and his partners had no rich friends to lean on in tough times, either. His company, which was based in San Diego and then Florida, was "on the periphery of the Internet," recalled Terry Foote, an old friend of Wales's who was Bomis's advertising director. "Jimmy and I, each in our own different ways, pounded on the metaphorical doors of all the Silicon Valley big shots, and mostly what we got was a solid wall of silence."[6] Under pressure to rethink Nupedia, Sanger recalled proposing a way to speed up the review process, but "everything required extra programming," he said. "By then, Jimmy Wales was worried about keeping costs low, the dot-com boom was turning to bust, and so whatever we did to solve the problem had to involve no more programming." That's where "wikis" came in. A friend told Sanger about the free wiki software that allowed users to collaborate online on a single article, roughly along the lines that Berners-Lee had planned for the original Web browser.[7]

The Web site Wikipedia.com began operating on January 15, 2001, and, like Mosaic and Google before it, found an audience almost immediately. With its software innovation, Wikipedia had six thousand entries after six months. By the end of the year, there were twenty thousand articles, most in English but hundreds of others in more than a dozen languages, including German, Spanish, Polish, and the artificial tongue Esperanto.[8] When the original wiki software was unable to handle this growth, a German volunteer created the more capable version that is still used today.

In addition to its enthusiastic volunteers, many of whom were originally drawn to Nupedia, the Wikipedia project found crucial assistance from the new Google search engine, whose algorithm didn't care a whit about offline reputation. Google knew only what could be conveyed through Web links, and according to that calculus Wikipedia could have a loftier reputation than the *Encyclopedia Britannica*, whose articles didn't freely circulate online. Speaking to a Stanford class almost exactly a year after Wikipedia was created, Sanger described the positive feedback loop his project was experiencing through Google. "We write a thousand articles; Google spiders them and sends some traffic to those pages," he said. "Some small percentage of that traffic becomes Wikipedia contributors, increasing our contributor base. The enlarged contributor base then writes another two thousand articles, which Google dutifully spiders, and then we receive an even larger influx of traffic. All the while, no doubt in part due to links to our articles from Google, an increasing number of other websites link to Wikipedia, increasing the standing of Wikipedia pages in Google results."[9]

Those first twelve months, shattered by the 9/11 attacks, included the absolute trough of the dot-com collapse. Under those conditions, Bomis had yet to make money from its runaway hit, Wikipedia. The company laid off half of the staff, including Sanger in February 2002.[10] Without Sanger's salary, the costs of running Wikipedia were surprisingly low—by 2004, total expenses for a significantly larger Wikipedia were still less than $25,000[11]—but even those sums were a drain on Bomis when it could least afford one. Sanger understandably agitated for Bomis to raise some money to restore his salary as the editor in chief of Nupedia and "chief organizer" of Wikipedia, jobs he described as the best he'd ever had. In a letter to the Wikipedia community explaining that he would have to reduce his involvement in the projects while he looked for full-time employment, Sanger opened Pandora's box, writing hopefully that "Bomis might well start selling ads on Wikipedia sometime within the next few months, and revenue from those ads might make it possible for me to come back to my old job."[12]

The mere mention of advertising was so disturbing to the volunteers who were building Wikipedia that the project was nearly destroyed by the backlash. Why this group of content generators—as opposed to people listing their résumés or reviewing restaurants—would be particularly offended by advertising is hard to explain. Was their anger based on the fact that writing an encyclopedia article is fundamentally altruistic and thus shouldn't be exploited for profit? Maybe it was Wales's laid-back posture toward the project that gave them such self-confidence? He didn't come off as a typical Silicon Valley entrepreneur, convinced how brilliant he was, treating users like idiots to be exploited. Bomis knew it was bringing very little to the table when it came to Wikipedia—the inmates were running the asylum, and that seemed to be working out fine. Perhaps the best explanation is that Wikipedia didn't begin with ads, which meant that they would have to be introduced, which gave the opposition something to fight against.

There was a final factor: Wikipedia was created under a so-called "free" software license, and those terms applied not only to the software but to the articles as well. While there certainly was no rule against running advertising next to material made under a free license—free software's most prominent activist, Richard Stallman, is fond of saying, "free as in free speech, not free beer"—this license gave anyone the right to copy all the material that appeared on Wikipedia and begin his own project, a process known as "forking." An exact duplicate of Wikipedia—a fork—could appear under a new name at a new Web address; the only condition was that the new project operate under the same free license. Immediately after Sanger made his idle suggestion about advertising, a group of contributors to the Spanish version of Wikipedia forked the encyclopedia. The articles were copied and stored on servers at the University of Seville, where the project was renamed Enciclopedia Libre Universal en Español.

The Spanish contributors were on the left politically and already annoyed to be part of a for-profit business. Furthermore, Edgar Enyedy, one of the leaders of the Spanish fork, resented having to go through Bomis to make improvements to his own community's Wikipedia. "We were all working for free in a dot-com with no access to the servers, no mirrors, no software updates, no downloadable database, and no way to set up the wiki itself," he said. "Finally, came the possibility of incorporating advertising, so we left. It couldn't be any other way." The threat that other foreign-language Wikipedias might fork if there were ads—or potentially that the English Wikipedia itself would—was enough to get Wales to take notice and say no to advertising.[13]

With the best opportunity for profiting from an online encyclopedia cut off, Wales in 2003 shifted ownership of Wikipedia to a charitable foundation; at least the project wouldn't be a financial drain anymore. A few prominent articles in the tech press spread the word about the new Wikimedia Foundation and donations from individuals and institutions almost immediately managed to cover whatever expenses were connected to running the site. In 2004, when English Wikipedia had 150,000 articles, the foundation raised more than $80,000 to cover $23,000 in expenses.[14]

Late in that year, Wales channeled his thwarted entrepreneurial energy into Wikia, a for-profit venture built on wiki principles. The articles on the Wikia site are like Wikipedia articles, created and edited by visitors, but they reflect the enthusiasm of a 'zine rather than the neutral view of an encyclopedist, which is why the San Francisco–based company recently renamed its Web site "Fandom powered by Wikia." The company has followed a traditional strategy for a Web 2.0 company, running targeted advertisements on article pages and seeking investments from venture capital firms, as well as Amazon.[15]

To this day, the Wikimedia Foundation is never short of funds, even as the size of its staff and the number of articles within its dozen or so wiki projects has grown substantially. Wikipedia alone has 40 million articles, which can appear in any of 290 different languages. In the 2016 fiscal year, expenses at the foundation were $65 million, including paying for a staff of more than 280 people. In that period, total revenue at the foundation was more than $80 million, with $77.7 million coming from donations and contributions.[16]

The unconventional development of Wikipedia presents an interesting contrast to how Google grew. Google's founders, as we've seen, were academics fundamentally opposed to advertising, who eventually succumbed to the start-up-friendly vortex surrounding Stanford. As a result, Larry Page and Sergey Brin had the resources to continue operating during dark times until they discovered a way to make advertising work. Jimmy Wales, on the other hand, was committed to Web advertising from the start and would have loved nothing better than to bring advertising to Nupedia and its new incarnation, Wikipedia. He has spent his entire entrepreneurial life trying to create user-generated content to place ads against, yet when he finally hit a gusher he was unable to capitalize.

Had Wales not stumbled on the idea of Wikipedia in absolutely the worst time for dot-coms—or if he had a network of Stanford friends like the PayPal mafia to call upon—perhaps he could have pushed through and operated Wikipedia as a business. He could have ignored the Spanish fork and introduced advertising. With the appropriate resources, he then could have hired programmers to add artificially intelligent features to make the Bomis version of Wikipedia—ads and all—such a superior experience to a forked, ad-free version that few would turn away.

Wales would occasionally return to the idea that the site might accept ads, if not for company profits, then to benefit a charity. "That money could be used to fund books and media centers in the developing world," he said in 2004. "Some of it could be used to purchase additional hardware, some could be used to support the development of free software that we use in our mission. The question that we may have to ask ourselves, from the comfort of our relatively wealthy Internet-connected world, is whether our discomfort and distaste for advertising intruding on the purity of Wikipedia is more important than that mission."[17] After the community again objected to such a flirtation with advertising, Wales gave up on the idea forever. Not that advertising is evil, he wrote later: "But it doesn't belong here. Not in Wikipedia. Wikipedia is something special. It is like a library or a public park. It is like a temple for the mind. It is a place we can all go to think, to learn, to share our knowledge with others."

In that same statement, he glosses over the early, contentious history of the project, declaring, "When I founded Wikipedia, I could have made it into a for-profit company with advertising banners, but I decided to do something different."[18] The narrative that Wales offers in regard to Wikipedia, of being tempted by, and rejecting, a lucrative opportunity to run advertisements is actually closer to what happened at Craigslist. In late 1997, you will recall, the site's founder, Craig Newmark, was approached about accepting banner ads for a Microsoft service on his site, which had already gone through a growth spurt. He turned the offer down, knowing he had "stepped away from a huge amount of money," because it wasn't in the best interest of Craigslist's users.

Wikipedia and Craigslist are indeed the exceptions that help define what is standard Silicon Valley behavior. They both have scaled to become worldwide phenomena, but not by automating every experience through artificial intelligence. Newmark welcomes personal interactions with his users and proudly describes himself as a customer service representative for the site, albeit one who also relies on automated tools.[19] Wikipedia likewise has teams of volunteers who help new users and watch out for vandalism, also aided by automated tools. Truly, they are what Berners-Lee expected the Web to be from its inception, before it took a sharp turn toward commerce. They are decentralized and collaborative; regular folks are given an important voice. Doubtful we will see their like again.

Starting in the 2000s, Thiel, Hoffman, Andreessen, and their ilk shifted from cashing checks to writing them. In their role as investors and mentors, they made sure that the next generation wouldn't make the same mistakes they had. They warned founders to keep control, pushing back meddling VCs by being sure to retain a majority of voting shares. And they advised start-ups to be ruthless in acquiring market share and then protecting that share—Thiel's stealth monopolist strategy. When Mark Zuckerberg visited the Bay Area the summer after his sophomore year at Harvard, this crew found their prodigy, like the weathered boxing trainer Cus D'Amato being introduced to the thirteen-year-old Mike Tyson, whom he would shape into a fearsome champion. Zuckerberg was a talented programmer with both a hacker's belief that computers could save the world and a Thielian ruthlessness about using the network effect to replace the Web with his own service, which would soon be renamed Facebook.

10. MARK ZUCKERBERG

"Nerds win"

The first significant computer program young Mark Zuckerberg wrote was a version of the board game Risk set in the Roman Empire. "You played against Julius Caesar. He was good, and I was never able to win," Zuckerberg recalled with a twinge of pride.[1] That's the thing about playing a video game of your own creation while barely a teenager: even if the character you control loses, you've still won. Caesar's victories, the computer's victories, were Zuckerberg's, too. This veneer of ultimate control, according to the computer science pioneer Joseph Weizenbaum, was the best explanation of what motivated the young hackers he found toiling away at all hours of the night at MIT. "No playwright, no stage director, no emperor, however powerful, has ever exercised such absolute authority to arrange a stage or a field of battle and to command such unswervingly dutiful actors or troops," he wrote back in the 1970s. "The computer programmer is a creator of universes for which he alone is the lawgiver."[2]

Zuckerberg was given the chance to build his own universes beginning in the sixth grade. This was the mid-1990s, the World Wide Web was catching fire, and PCs were well within reach for a well-to-do family like the Zuckerbergs. Young Mark wouldn't need to hustle for computer time the way young Bill (Gates) did twenty-five years earlier, proposing school rummage sales and then creating businesses just to get his hands on a minicomputer for a few hours. Mark's parents were enthusiastic partners in his youthful computer obsession, buying him a first personal computer when he was eleven; and after their son was initially stumped by a programming book "for dummies," they provided him with a tutor, as well.[3] Mark was hooked. "I'd go to school and I'd go to class and come home and the way I'd think about it would be, 'I have, you know, five whole hours to just sit and play on my computer and write software,'" he recalled about his time growing up in Dobbs Ferry, a suburb just outside New York City. "And then Friday afternoon would come along and it would be like, 'Okay, now I have two whole days to sit and write software.' This is amazing."[4]

Even as a youngster, Zuckerberg planned on shaking up the world with his brilliant programs in a way the original hackers never could have imagined. The hackers of earlier generations were basically coding to impress their computers and themselves, while Zuckerberg was coding to impress his classmates. Video games of all stripes sprang from young Mark's fingers, often based on drawings from friends who would sketch while he was programming. In 1996, he hacked together a messaging system for his dad's dental office to announce that a patient had arrived. Later, while away in prep school, Zuckerberg and a classmate, Adam D'Angelo, created an "artificial intelligence" program called Synapse that studied your music listening habits to suggest the next track to play. The program was powered by an algorithm they named "the brain," whose accuracy in assessing your musical preferences, Zuckerberg and D'Angelo insisted, was within a hundredth of a percent, whatever that means.[5]

Throughout these experiences, Zuckerberg wasn't just coding, but "building things," as his older self likes to say. Synapse gave Zuckerberg his first taste of the rewards to come; the program received a positive mention on the influential Web site Slashdot and drew the interest of a number of big companies, including Microsoft and AOL.[6] Initially, Zuckerberg and D'Angelo were reluctant to sell their program, but by the time they had a change of heart the offers (said to be in the $1 million to $2 million range) were gone. All that remained for Zuckerberg, who attended Harvard, and D'Angelo, the more talented programmer who went to Caltech, was a memorable lesson about striking while the iron is hot.[7]

Zuckerberg, with intense eyes and an easy grin, long resisted being defined by the traits of a traditional hacker, even if he put in similarly obsessive hours in front of his computer and was known to indulge in the same silly programmer jokes, like how to instruct a computer to get drunk. The hackers were antisocial and anarchic, their vision shrunken to fit the dimensions of a metal box; Zuckerberg was worldly, as proud of his broader interests—whether in human psychology or fencing or ancient history—as of his programming skills. The hackers were inward looking; Zuckerberg was constantly taking stock of his environment. The hackers considered Microsoft the Evil Empire; Zuckerberg was in awe.

The hackers loathed Microsoft not only for its opposition to the free software movement but also for what one might call aesthetic reasons. Microsoft software was plain and uninspired, as if the company wouldn't waste the effort on elegant programming since whatever it produced was destined to become the standard anyway. To hackers, the only reason to program was to do it elegantly. Zuckerberg, by contrast, told the world how impressed he was by Microsoft's commercially dominant operating systems. "I mean, I grew up using Windows 3.1 and then Windows 95, and I just thought that those were, like, the most unbelievable things," he said in a talk with Paul Graham, a self-proclaimed hacker and important investor in start-ups through Y Combinator. Graham appears taken aback by this praise of Microsoft products and replies cryptically, "In a sense, they are [unbelievable]." Zuckerberg carries on: "Yeah, they were. They really were awesome. Right?" The crowd chuckles, assuming Zuckerberg is being sarcastic. "Well, I don't know if you meant that positively, but I did. And I thought, you know, building this ecosystem was really neat, and that kind of inspired me."[8]

Yes, the hackers may have correctly observed that Microsoft products impose a dull uniformity, but Zuckerberg was willing to let that pass. He was focused on what that simplicity and uniformity provided in return: millions of people using the same operating system and software as they composed their letters or balanced their financial books or played their video games. Here was the age-old tension between indulging individuality (hackers) and imposing order so things could run smoothly (builders). Monty Python's *Life of Brian* captured it well when Reg, the ornery leader of a small sect of Judean rebels resisting Roman occupation, tries to rally his followers by asking, "What have the Romans ever done for us?" Annoyingly, they offer example after example, until Reg shouts in frustration: "All right, but apart from the sanitation, the medicine, education, wine, public order, irrigation, roads, the fresh-water system, and public health, what have the Romans ever done for us?"

Zuckerberg found a role model in Gates, the Harvard dropout who became a tech billionaire. Gates, like Zuckerberg, was a computer obsessive intent on building things—a company, operating systems, suites of software, an entire computer ecosystem. Gates, like Zuckerberg, was out of step with his fellow hackers, which became apparent when Gates, at age nineteen, accused a group of Bay Area hackers of stealing the software his company, Micro-Soft, had produced. In 2004, Gates was invited to speak to Zuckerberg's computer class, where he encouraged students to take time off to start a new project. As Zuckerberg recalled it, Gates said, "You know, one of the things about Harvard is they let you take off as much time as you want and then you can always come back, so you know if Microsoft ever falls through, I'm going back to Harvard."[9] The class chuckled. Turns out, that would be Zuckerberg's last semester before relocating to the Bay Area and (so far) never returning.

Zuckerberg is Gatesian in seeing how computing might prosper under one company's Roman-like system for connecting people across the globe. The hacker types, like Reg, would hate that rules were being imposed from above, but the public would love the ease of use that such uniformity would deliver. When Zuckerberg was still in college, he allowed his mind to wander. "I was working on this Facebook thing and I thought it would be cool for Harvard and . . . I thought that over time someone would definitely go build this version of this for the world but it wasn't going to be us." The job of creating a platform to connect the world seemed too monumental for a bunch of undergraduates to pull off. "It was going to be you know, Microsoft or you know someone who builds software for hundreds of millions of people."[10] To Zuckerberg's eternal surprise, or so he says, the task of creating a global social network fell to a bunch of kids barely out of their teens. They would be the new Microsoft and so much more.

While at Harvard, even more than in prep school or back in Dobbs Ferry, Zuckerberg had the freedom to program all the time. He routinely skipped classes and ignored study periods to tinker on his computer. Yet in college there was an opposite pull, too—opportunities seemed to be opening up before his eyes, and Zuckerberg was naturally curious about how he would fit in. Would he be liked? Would he have friends? Would he be successful? What would he make of himself? In the span of a year, Zuckerberg built a series of campus-wide Web sites, one more famous than the next, that were fundamentally social in nature. Zuckerberg was keenly aware of belonging to a community, which by turns he wanted to impress, intimidate, imitate, get to know.

First, he created a Web site called CourseMatch, which allowed students to share what classes they were taking. He was planning his schedule and wondered what students he knew from computer science classes would be studying. Was he looking for new areas of study or wanting to keep tabs on what everyone else was doing? A bit of both? In a matter of weeks, two thousand Harvard undergraduates had joined CourseMatch, which Zuckerberg ran from a laptop in his dorm room. He wasn't expecting this level of interest and his laptop was fried in the process. Zuckerberg quickly abandoned CourseMatch, after gaining valuable experience in how to create a campus-wide Web site that spread virally, and perhaps how to keep one running in the future, as well.[11]

In that same vein, Zuckerberg in the fall of 2003, his sophomore year, built the infamous Facemash, which was an even quicker hit on campus. The idea was to let students compare the attractiveness of their classmates head-to-head, the tried-and-true hot-or-not method for reaching an online audience with advertising. But Zuckerberg at this point wasn't an entrepreneur on the make. He says he wasn't planning to turn Facemash into a business and he wasn't trying to persuade students to upload personal material Web 2.0 style. In fact, much of the fun for Zuckerberg was "liberating" photos of Harvard students by hacking the university's servers. In a digital journal that appeared on the Facemash site, Zuckerberg detailed how he obtained the pictures the site used. It's a brief glimpse into his puzzle-solving mind, as each dorm on campus offered its own obstacles: for some, Zuckerberg had to deduce the student passwords before accessing a photo file, in others he only had to run a computer script that could copy photos twenty at a time. When one cache of photos proved particularly hard to hack, he writes, he took a break and opened another Beck's.[12]

After he had collected the photos and completed the programming during a couple of all-nighters, Zuckerberg published the site, which randomly matched two photos to be compared by a visitor to the site. His slogan: "Were we let in for our looks? No. Will we be judged on them? Yes." Word spread over a single weekend and there were already 450 visitors who voted at least 22,000 times. Student organizations complained, and Zuckerberg quickly shuttered the site. He wrote to apologize to two campus women's groups, Fuerza Latina and the Association of Black Harvard Women, saying he didn't anticipate how quickly interest would spread and that he hadn't really thought the idea through. "I definitely see how my intentions could be seen in the wrong light," Zuckerberg wrote in his apology. In a student newspaper article on the controversy, he portrayed himself as little more than a junior computer scientist: "I'm a programmer and I'm interested in the algorithms and math behind it."[13]

The fallout from Facemash was intense, and Zuckerberg was brought before Harvard's disciplinary board, providing yet another parallel with Gates, who faced the same board back in the 1970s over his use of a university computer for company business. Zuckerberg says he and his friends were convinced he would be expelled. Not only could the project be seen as bullying in its premise, but Zuckerberg had trampled over students' privacy by copying and then publishing their photos without permission. The Harvard College Administration Board found Zuckerberg guilty of "improper social behavior" and placed him on probation.[14] One good thing to come from the whole experience, he says looking back, was that he met his future wife, Priscilla Chan, at what was supposed to be his farewell party.[15]

Yet there were other benefits, too, important lessons about building online networks. First, he saw how being part of a relatively small community like Harvard made a social Web site take off—even something as tangential as a hot-or-not site blew up because of the likelihood that a user knew at least one of the participants. Clearly there was an urgent need (call it prurient, call it social, call it mean, call it supportive) to engage online with the people you were living next to. Second, he now grasped what would be the primary challenge in running a successful social site: enticing people to share their personal information online. Hacking that information wasn't a practical solution, of course, but neither was limiting oneself to what was already available.

Zuckerberg took heart from an editorial in the student newspaper, the *Harvard Crimson*, which accepted Facemash for the mischievous idea that it was and just wished that he had limited himself to students who agreed to participate. "Such a site," the *Crimson* wrote, "would have brought joy to attention-seekers and voyeurs alike."[16] Zuckerberg said at one point that this editorial gave him the idea of building Facebook with voluntary participants and built-in privacy restrictions. But within that praise from his fellow students was that fundamental misperception—Zuckerberg's next project couldn't simply appeal to attention-seekers and voyeurs. It had to appeal to everyone or, alternatively, bring out the attention seeker/voyeur in all of us.

During what turned out to be his two years at Harvard, Zuckerberg seemed to be pursuing a curriculum designed for operating a technical/social project like Facebook. He planned to major in psychology—his mother is a licensed psychiatrist[17]—where he could study what made people tick, while taking the most classes in computer science to learn what made machines tick. There would be a dash of Roman history thrown in as well. Not surprisingly, Zuckerberg homed in on the central question in computer science and psychology—namely, can a computer be programmed to think like a human? And if not, why not? His reading in psychology, he said, taught him to be wary of the idea. "The biggest thing that I took away from the psychology classes that I took were how little we know about how the human brain works," Zuckerberg says. "I think that our understanding of the brain is kind of like if you opened up a computer and were like, 'Oh, when you're typing this command this part gets warm.'"[18]

Zuckerberg's views on the potential for artificial intelligence typified the shift in computer science over its fifty-year history. What began as an esoteric discipline largely fueled by the ambitious search for the essence of thought and intelligence, today is a highly practical subject pursued at some level by nearly all undergraduates at a school like

Stanford.[19] Computers haven't proved as profound as John McCarthy and others hoped, but they are certainly quite capable. Computer science has become content to design computers that simulate people well enough that people will acknowledge them, play with them, take their suggestions. In either approach, computer scientists relied on psychology: the early researchers studied the human brain to build thinking machines that worked along the same lines, as hubristic as that may have sounded; the Zuckerbergian social-network operators studied the brain to understand why people do what they do, the better to influence them. As Joseph Weizenbaum's experiment with the computer therapist Eliza showed back in the 1960s, people didn't need much cajoling to open up about themselves to computers—it seemed to come naturally. Weizenbaum was horrified at this misplaced trust by the public and ran away from AI, while Zuckerberg has tried to capitalize on it at Facebook.

Zuckerberg's primary lesson from psychology classes is that people need people and are driven to satisfy this need. We notice and appreciate minute differences in each other's faces and recognize that slight shifts in expression can convey a profound change in mood. "I think that that's something that we often overlook in designing products," he said. "And that's one of the things that I'm just really interested in—and with Facebook—is [that] people are still interesting to other people." People generally want to be with other people and do what other people, particularly their friends, are doing—the network effect, in other words. This interest in both hacking and psychology has allowed Zuckerberg to recognize that a social Web site could become the mechanism for connecting the world, as opposed to, say, a site about money or shopping, entertainment or information: "If you can build a product where people can go and learn about the people around them and share information and stay connected with people then that's something that's super important to people."[20]

However, the Facemash experience chastened Zuckerberg, at least momentarily. He was very nearly kicked out of school in disgrace. He had some serious explaining to do to his parents. And for what? Just to build something? Anything? Yet all the controversy served as great advertising for his programming skills and skills at promotion. In the immediate aftermath of Facemash, a pair of entrepreneurially minded

Harvard undergraduates, the twins Cameron and Tyler Winklevoss, and a friend who had recently graduated, Divya Narendra, sought Zuckerberg's help in completing a student social-networking site they planned to call HarvardConnection and then rename ConnectU once it invariably spread to other schools.[21] None of these three was a hacker, however, a fact that became apparent once Zuckerberg discovered that they had spent almost a year on their idea and had nothing to show for it. Over that same period, Zuckerberg must have created and ditched a dozen projects, including a computer application that would synch up music players so he could try to persuade everyone at Harvard to play the same song at the same time. Why? Because it would be really funny.[22]

This restless energy was what the HarvardConnection team hoped to enlist from Zuckerberg, and they were prepared to name him a partner in the business and give him a share of the company in return for getting the Web site working. But, in truth, no offer from the HarvardConnection team, other than complete surrender, could fix what was a profoundly unequal relationship. Zuckerberg, the programmer, held all the cards. One day, he emailed to say that he had completed most of the coding and that the site could launch soon, and then he ghosted the team for the next two months. When they managed to get a reply, Narenda says, Zuckerberg would invariably write back to ask for a little more time. After this sputtering couple of months, Zuckerberg broke off the arrangement entirely and informed the HarvardConnection team that he was working on a different project. On January 11, 2004, Zuckerberg registered the domain name, thefacebook.com, his next social-networking Web site for the Harvard campus. On February 4, the site went live, though the Winklevosses learned about it only from an article in the *Crimson* almost a week later.[23] Their first thought, "Well, that sounds like our idea."[24]

The drama that followed from this college breakup has been described in magazine articles, books, and even a movie, *The Social Network*. There was a court case, too, during which Zuckerberg had to submit to a long, contentious deposition and texts were made public in which he mocked his three wannabe partners. The case settled in 2008 with a payment of money and Facebook stock worth tens of millions of dollars to the Winklevosses and Narenda.[25] The central question raised by the court case and the media coverage was: did Zuckerberg steal the idea for Facebook or was an idea like Facebook too obvious for any individual or individuals to own?

One of Zuckerberg's computer science professors, Matt Welsh, defended his former student in a blog post by observing, "Ideas are cheap and don't mean squat if you don't know how to execute on them. To have an impact you need both the vision and the technical chops, as well as the tenacity to make something real. Mark was able to do all of those things, and I think he deserves every bit of success that comes his way." The lesson to Welsh, who left academia to become an engineering manager at Google: "Nerds win."[26] Think about it: Zuckerberg needed nothing that the rich and connected Winklevosses could offer, while they needed everything he had to contribute. For better or worse, these young computer experts now had the power to promote their own big ideas . . . not only about computers, but about everything.

As Zuckerberg anticipated, thefacebook.com filled a vital need on campus, providing a directory for all Harvard students and some basic ways to share information like what courses you were taking and your phone number. It was introduced in early February, and by the end of the month three-quarters of all undergraduates had signed up.[27] Zuckerberg couldn't help taking a shot at the IT team at Harvard, whom he considered cautious bureaucrats in need of student-led disruption. "Everyone's been talking a lot about a universal face book within Harvard," he said in the days after launching his site. "I think it's kind of silly that it would take the university a couple of years to get around to it. I can do it better than they can, and I can do it in a week." Never mind that the Harvard team was delayed in releasing its official online facebook in part because it had to remove the kind of security flaws that allowed a hacker like Zuckerberg to create Facemash. From his nineteen-year-old hacker's perspective, it was clowns to the left of me, jokers to the right.[28]

Initially, what proved fascinating to Zuckerberg about thefacebook was that it provided a platform for social networking that was tied to a particular place, a campus, and a particular group of people, the students there. In this way, the Internet was supplementing offline relationships, not replacing them. The goal of thefacebook "wasn't to make an online community, but sort of like a mirror for the real community that existed in real life."[29] At times, 10 or 20 percent of all Harvard students were logged in at the same time. How could you not belong if all your neighbors did? Thefacebook.com ran as a self-sufficient operation almost from the start, relying on the revenue from a few ads on the site to pay the modest $85-a-month server fees.[30]

This brief time of happy camaraderie lasted the better part of a month. Soon Zuckerberg was, as Professor Welsh describes, "swept up by forces that were bigger and more powerful than anyone could have expected when thefacebook was first launched."[31] Take the central question of whether thefacebook should become a full-fledged business. Zuckerberg was confident that it would not. Though Zuckerberg was never a serious computer science researcher like Brin and Page, who possessed an engineer's commitment to running an ethical, efficient search engine, he shared their instinct that vital Web services like online directories were too important to sully with commerce. A few months into the project, Zuckerberg told a student reporter: "I mean, yeah, we can make a bunch of money—that's not the goal . . . I mean, like, anyone from Harvard can get a job and make a bunch of money. Not everyone at Harvard can have a social network. I value that more as a resource more than, like, any money." He said he had rejected a number of early money-making ideas for his project, like selling email addresses or allowing students to upload résumés and charging companies to search through them. Zuckerberg reassured the student reporter that he would be all right: "I assume eventually I'll make something that is profitable."[32]

Yet Zuckerberg was almost immediately forced to consider whether thefacebook had to grow. For example, what should happen to Harvard students when they graduate? Should they be abandoned? What about students at other colleges who were clamoring for a similar service on their campus? And what about friends on different campuses who wanted to keep up with each other? How about expanding internationally? When thefacebook on March 1 decided to move beyond the Harvard campus, it had a unique advantage at its disposal: status envy. Which schools would be deemed worthy to follow Harvard? As it happens, the next schools thefacebook chose were also elite—Yale, Columbia, Stanford—which stoked a frenzy at the 99.9 percent of American schools that were still excluded. This was a nice twist on the network effect: not only did people want to join thefacebook because others had already joined, but they wanted to join because they suspected they had been deemed unworthy of joining. Studio 54 meets the viral Web.[33]

Growth soon turned into a necessity for thefacebook, however, and the velvet rope was replaced by an open door. In the better part of a year, thefacebook was on nearly every campus in America, and dozens in Europe as well. Turns out that the network effect could be as much of a threat as a benefit. If thefacebook didn't keep growing, another service presumably would spread across the country and what would become of this little, Harvard-only project? Even loyal users would leave in order to have access to all their friends at other schools. Standing still simply was not an option. In fact, Zuckerberg says that the schools where Facebook first expanded may have been elite, but they were in fact chosen because his small team had heard that they were closest to having their own student-run Facebook-type services that could potentially leap to other schools.[34]

Growth and fighting off competitors became the order of the day. Zuckerberg recalled that about a year into the project a rival emerged that called itself College Facebook, which appeared to be a clone of thefacebook, right down to the name. Its plan, he said, was to sign up schools on the West Coast where Facebook hadn't arrived. The response from Zuckerberg's team was to immediately engage the battle under a practice called "lockdown," which meant "we literally did not leave the house until we had addressed the problem," Zuckerberg said. He added that "now it's a little looser of an interpretation inside the company. We don't literally lock everyone inside the office but about as close to that as we can legally get."[35] Once Zuckerberg changed his view on expanding thefacebook to other campuses, rampant growth became the highest priority. His identity as a genius would now be linked to the vibrancy of his project.

Unlike the Google guys, however, Zuckerberg was under little pressure to turn his baby into a business. Even as it grew, thefacebook was able to keep the servers running with little difficulty. And because he was at Harvard, not Stanford, there was no gateway professor to make an introduction leading to an investment offer that he couldn't refuse. The move from cool project to lucrative business seemed to run in relative slow-motion for thefacebook: after his sophomore year, Zuckerberg relocated for the summer to Silicon Valley—he's not exactly sure why, except that it somehow made sense: "Originally when we went out there, we weren't expecting to move out there, we wanted to go out there for the summer because we had this feeling like, 'Okay, all these great companies come from Silicon Valley. Wouldn't it be cool to spend the summer out there and get that experience?'"[36]

Silicon Valley worked its magic, however. At the end of the summer and as successive new semesters approached, the team considered returning to Harvard and then thought: Why not stick it out a little longer? By December 2004, around the time to consider returning for spring semester, thefacebook had a million registered users. Also, the company had already lined up a $500,000 loan from Peter Thiel, after Thiel's friend Reid Hoffman passed on the opportunity of being the first outside investor because of his own social network LinkedIn. Thiel's loan would convert into a 10 percent share of the company assuming thefacebook had grown to 1.5 million users by the end of 2004. It didn't quite reach that goal, but Thiel still decided to convert his loan into an investment.[37] (Hoffman didn't entirely abstain, either. He invested $40,000 for a share of the company that today would be worth hundreds of millions of dollars.)

For someone of Zuckerberg's generation, Thiel was a much more attractive investor than a traditional VC. He had already run a successful company and was outspoken in his belief that a founder should be entrusted with guiding the company he created. Yet for all his faith in Zuckerberg's ability, Thiel also splashed some cold water. He wanted to shake Zuckerberg out of his lackadaisical approach toward running a business. A couple of times in his career as CEO, Zuckerberg would need to have market realities made clear to him. First up was Thiel, who immediately put the twenty-year-old Zuckerberg back on his heels by pointing out that he had mangled how shares were allocated to his partners. "I really knew so little at the time," Zuckerberg recalled. "I mean, when Peter Thiel came in to invest, one thing that he demanded was that all of the founders be on vesting schedules. And I didn't even know what a vesting schedule was. I'd never heard of that."[38] Thiel did leaven his criticisms with rewards, like his gift of an Infiniti FX35. The luxury car could be seen parked outside Zuckerberg's modest apartment, which had a living room with a mattress on the floor and a shower without a curtain.[39]

Facebook became the ideal candidate to test Thiel's theories about the network effect and monopoly power. Even in 2005, Zuckerberg imagined that he was creating a service that the public needed to access every day, unthinkingly, like water or electricity. "We're not trying to create something that people use for a specific purpose," Zuckerberg said at a talk at Stanford barely a year in. "This is a utility that people can use to just find relevant information socially to them."[40] In other words, a social good. Thiel saw a financial good, however, a potential monopoly that could sit above the hypercompetitive marketplace where no one makes any profit.

Thiel's persistent message to Zuckerberg was to grow and grow fast, the equivalent of a traditional utility rushing to lay pipe or cables in order to expand its customer base. "He was good at saying, 'Here's the one thing that matters,'" Zuckerberg recalled about Thiel, who remains on Facebook's board. And what was that one thing? "Connecting everyone as quickly as possible, because network effects were a massively important part of this."[41] During this growth spurt, however, Zuckerberg's project went from a self-supporting site to a project that required large outside investments, the first of which came from Accel Partners in April 2005—more than $12 million for a 15 percent stake, supplemented by $1 million from the partner at the firm, Jim Breyer.[42]

Facebook would need the money to add new programmers and equipment as it kept scaling. Zuckerberg explained his hiring practices at the time, which were exactly what you would expect from a young, privileged hacker and typical for Silicon Valley start-ups. The first quality he sought was "just raw intelligence," that elusive big brain who can build things. Youth, too. Young big brains. "You can hire someone who's a software engineer and has been doing it for 10 years, and if they're doing it for 10 years, then that's probably what they're doing for their life. And I mean, that's cool . . . but if you find someone whose raw intelligence exceeds theirs, but has 10 less years of experience, then they can probably adapt and learn way quickly and within a very short amount of time be able to do a lot of things that that person may never be able to do."[43] The second quality, he said, was devotion to the company's cause so that they will be willing to work really hard.

Here was the typical staffing method of a Silicon Valley start-up that cared not a whit for diversity, racial or gender, or an outside life, and wasn't afraid to tar someone as young as thirty-two as washed up. It's a sobering description of how to staff for a small company, focused on this prized if elusive quality "raw intelligence," which emerges from test scores or an intense interview. But that approach becomes downright scary when you consider that this company now has thousands of employees. There was an awkward scene, too, when a *Rolling Stone* reporter was visiting Facebook's headquarters early on and heard Dustin Moskovitz, Zuckerberg's roommate and cofounder of Facebook, joke about trying to use their Facebook powers to meet attractive women back at Harvard. "Dude, we just got out of a sexual harassment seminar," Zuckerberg snapped at him. These were kids who were still college age, grappling with adult responsibility. The disconcerting fact, however, was that the grownup in charge was Peter Thiel.[44]

Zuckerberg enthusiastically adopted Thiel's advice of pursuing runaway growth, which meant coming to terms with a profound shift in the purpose of his social network. Rather than running a service centered on a particular location, Facebook would increasingly be based on relationships, whether formed online or off. Back in 2005, he expressed his doubts about spreading thefacebook too far, too fast and made a case that a social network should focus intensely on a particular community. "There is a level of service that we can provide when we were just at Harvard that we can't provide for all of the colleges," he said, "and there is a level of services when we're a college network that we wouldn't be able to provide if we went to other types of things."[45]

Once Facebook made this shift from colleges to high schools to particular companies to the wider world, it sought ways to re-create the feelings of connection that came from living close by. The immense amounts of data Facebook collected provided some clues. There was the "ten friend rule," for example; it revealed itself as a pattern among new users as they explored the site, particularly the main newsfeed containing updates about Facebook friends' lives. "Once you had 10 friends," Zuckerberg observed, "you had enough content in your newsfeed that there would just be stuff on a good enough interval where it would be worth coming back to the site. . . . We re-engineered the whole flow of having someone sign up to get all this extraneous shit out of the way and just make it so that the only focus at the beginning is helping people find people to connect with. And we honed what the tools were to get them to do that."[46]

For a puzzle solver and amateur psychologist like Zuckerberg, the access to so much information about people was thrilling. The company put this data to other uses as well. Like PayPal under Max Levchin's guidance, Facebook designed algorithms to determine if a registered user was a real person or a bot accessing the site as part of some scam. "We actually compute how, like a percentage of realness that a person is, and if they fall below a threshold then they're gone," Zuckerberg said in 2005, describing how the algorithms treated humanness fluidly. "It's actually pretty funny. This is something that my friends and I like to do. We just go through and like see how real certain people are who we know are actually real people. We're like, you're only 75 percent real."[47] Another purpose for its algorithms was more akin to what Google does; that is, to help users sift through piles of information to get to what is most relevant. For example, Facebook's algorithms had to determine who among three hundred friends should have his photos shoot to the top of a newsfeed, and whose should largely be ignored.

This Google-like question—what are the most relevant photo results for a particular Facebook user?—points out the similarities between the missions of the two companies. Both are in the information-organizing business. The information that Google organizes is everything that appears on the Web, as well as the material on its own sites, while the information that Facebook organizes is whatever people are willing to share about themselves on its site. Google's initial hurdle was to locate, copy, and store immense amounts of data, using computers that "crawl" the Web; Facebook's hurdle is to persuade the public to be more forthcoming. "You can't just send a Web crawler around and learn what's going on with people," Zuckerberg said, "you have to build tools that give people the power to share that content themselves."[48]

In July 2006 Yahoo offered a cool billion for Facebook, which Thiel pushed Zuckerberg to at least consider. Marc Andreessen says he was a rare voice encouraging Zuckerberg to follow his instincts and keep trying to expand Facebook. "The psychological pressure they put on this 22-year-old was intense," said Andreessen. "Mark and I really bonded in that period, because I told him, 'Don't sell, don't sell, don't sell!'"[49] When Zuckerberg walked into the board meeting that considered the Yahoo offer, Thiel recalled, he said, "Okay, guys, this is just a formality, it shouldn't take more than 10 minutes. We're obviously not going to sell here."[50]

Looking back, Zuckerberg says he regrets that he even entertained the idea of selling. "I mean if you don't want to sell your company, don't get into a process where you're talking to people about selling your company," he said, laughing. But the entire experience, he says, gave him a way to assess the core values of his team, and then shed those who tipped their hand that they were motivated exclusively, or primarily, by getting a share of a billion-dollar fortune. "That's an awesome outcome, but that's not what I was in it for and I wanted people around me for whom that's what they were in it for was to build a company for the long term," he said.[51] Thiel wasn't tarred by his association with the Yahoo offer. He remains a key advisor to Zuckerberg, though Zuckerberg clearly enjoys needling him about what a mistake selling Facebook would have been, even worse than selling PayPal for $1.5 billion.[52] On the other hand, Andreessen was invited to join Thiel on the Facebook board two years later, in 2008.

The Yahoo offer was so scarring because it confirmed what Zuckerberg distrusts about the predominant view in Silicon Valley—so many there appear to be in it for the money! "If I were starting now, I just would have stayed in Boston I think," he told an interviewer in 2011, when he was still in his mid-twenties. Silicon Valley clearly had the experienced hands to help a nineteen-year-old scale his college project—the accountants, the lawyers, the data centers, the programmers, the steely minded VCs. But, he adds, "there's aspects of the culture out here where I think it still is a little bit short term focused in a way that bothers me. You know, whether it's like people who want to start companies . . . not knowing what they like, I don't know, to like flip it."[53] Zuckerberg is clearly conflicted by the idea of running a business. A year earlier, in 2010, he defended the role of the market in Facebook's growth, speaking in engineering terms. "Building a company," he said, "is one of the most efficient ways in the world that you can kind of align the incentives of a lot of smart people, towards making a change."[54]

In May 2012, these abstract considerations suddenly became real. Facebook stumbled through its IPO, and the scenario was similar to what Google's founders were put through when they acted as though they were running a computer lab rather than a business with investors who were only interested in profits. Their resistance to carrying advertising on their beloved search engine, or to accepting an outside CEO, melted away. Likewise, when Facebook was failing to deliver the expected level of profits after the stock offering, Zuckerberg was forced to adjust his attitude. He assigned a top engineer to the task of giving a boost to advertising, just as the Google guys had. "Wouldn't it be fun to build a billion-dollar business in six months?" Zuckerberg asked the engineer, Andrew Bosworth.

Like Brin and Page, Zuckerberg made a big concession on advertisements, reversing his view that they should not be permitted in the main newsfeed unless a friend had "liked" the product. The newsfeed had been sacrosanct—a process that had its own logic, flowing from the interests of your particular set of friends, independent of business considerations—much the way Brin and Page had treated search results. Interestingly, when Zuckerberg bent on this principle, he, like Brin and Page, later cited research showing that users were actually happier with the new ads.[55]

These detours into business calculations must have struck a blow to the egos of Know-It-Alls like Zuckerberg and Brin and Page. From the start, they have been the indispensable ones; they called all the shots. Yet when the market turned, a hard truth emerged: in fact, others were calling the shots. You could take the long view and see this as nothing more than the Tesla lesson, which taught that even the most free-thinking innovators had to spend some serious brainpower pleasing investors lest they lose the freedom to work on the really important questions. In Google's case, those questions involve applying artificial intelligence in ever more elaborate ways, which was what brought them to the Stanford computer science department in the first place.[56] Zuckerberg seems to have even more ambitious goals that he wants to be free to pursue: connecting the world "so you have access to every idea, person and opportunity."[57]

In the immediate years that followed, Zuckerberg returned to the goal of global connection and communication, something his company pursues through technical improvements, like the algorithms designed to entice users to share more data or the drones and satellites that provide rudimentary Internet access to remote areas so that new users can share personal information about themselves. At times, too, Facebook has relaxed the privacy settings for the information stored in its computers, confident that once more material is being shared, its users will be pleased and accept the new standards. Users have at times objected, however, and then Facebook apologizes and returns to some version of the old settings.[58] But it keeps trying, confident that, as the ten-friend rule suggests, once people experience the benefits of sharing information they will want to share more, too. In fact, Zuckerberg has observed that the amount of information being shared online has doubled every year—a discovery his friends have called Zuckerberg's law, in a tip of the hat to Moore's law, which predicted the steady increase in microchip processing speed.

This new law, Zuckerberg believes, has a disruptive potential similar to that of Moore's law. As we share more information via digital tools like Facebook, we as a species are enhancing our ability to connect and feel empathy for others. If a computer is about extending a person's ability to think—providing what Steve Jobs called "a bicycle for our minds"[59]—a social network "extends people's very real social capacity," Zuckerberg argues.[60] As evidence, he points to a change Facebook has detected in the so-called Dunbar number, which was originally proposed to suggest that there is a cap to the number of close friends a person can have at one time. Based on observations of other primates and correlating brain size to the number of members in a species' social group, the anthropologist Robin Dunbar argued that humans were capable of maintaining genuine, empathetic relationships with up to about 150 people.[61]

Facebook, Zuckerberg contends, has raised that number because of the ease and efficiency in making and keeping online friendships. "Naturally when people sign up the average amount of friends that they get is around 150," he said, "but then over time it can expand and you can keep in touch and stay in touch with many more people."[62] This is an oddly quantitative way of suggesting that there has been an "improvement" in the human ability to feel empathy. To start, this presumes that maintaining many good friendships is superior to nurturing just a few. But this bias shouldn't necessarily be surprising. Silicon Valley is a culture that evaluates intelligence with a number and business success with a number and attractiveness with a number. Why not sociability, even if it means draining friendship of all that is unquantifiable—the depths of shared history, a mysterious sympatico?

In a letter Zuckerberg and his wife wrote to their daughter, Max, they explain how expanded Internet access will help the public in so many ways, extending life spans, lifting hundreds of millions out of poverty, broadening educational opportunities. They are expressing a generous impulse, but it necessarily comes in a disturbing package: a world filled with isolated individuals—geographically and emotionally—who are expected to fend for themselves rather than look to the community for sustenance. In the Zuckerbergian vision, an Internet connection becomes a lifeline: "It provides education if you don't live near a good school. It provides health information on how to avoid diseases or raise healthy children if you don't live near a doctor. It provides financial services if you don't live near a bank. It provides access to jobs and opportunities if you don't live in a good economy. The Internet is so important that for every 10 people who gain Internet access, about one person is lifted out of poverty and about one new job is created."[63]

This seems a strange way to think of helping a person, as opposed to helping, say, a computer. For better health care, we must build clinics and hospitals and train doctors, as well as improve access to self-treatment via the Internet. For a better education, we must build schools and hire more teachers and train and compensate them better, as well as introduce self-teaching via the Internet. For a better work experience, one that ensures that workers are treated fairly and given responsibility as part of a motivated team, we must promote unions and mutual support in the workplace rather than encourage an individual to become a "start-up of you" forced to sell her services online at the whim of the market. Any path to health, education, and wealth must include neighbors, the people who are part of an actual community, not just a virtual one. Even the great Zuckerberg needed a personal tutor at first to learn how to program.

Education has been a particular focus of Zuckerberg's philanthropy, and he has brought his familiarly individualistic, mechanistic view of how people behave to both teachers and students. There was his well-publicized foray as a donor to the Newark, New Jersey, school system, when he tried to tie his $100 million gift to a series of policies toward teachers, like awarding bonuses of up to 50 percent of salary to teachers based on performance. An educational algorithm, if you will. He also proposed eliminating certain other policies—algorithms that he didn't like—like teacher seniority, which is an automated way of saying that age and experience should entitle you to advantages.

Zuckerberg's positive program of using bonuses to extract better performances from teachers, and encouraging more ambitious people to become teachers, faced a few problems and was never adopted by the school system. First, the district would be unable to sustain such a program once Zuckerberg's donation ran out—it was too expensive, when applied to a unionized school system. Furthermore, there was no precise way to measure the quality of a teacher; test results can be gamed and can reflect the preparation and home life of the students rather than the performance of the teacher. Finally, bonuses were not likely to be as effective as Zuckerberg imagined in motivating a group like teachers, as opposed to members of a Silicon Valley start-up. Teachers explained that the money wasn't such a direct influence—it wasn't that they didn't want or believe they deserved more pay, it was just that bonuses wouldn't lead to "better teaching" perforce, as Zuckerberg's view of human motivation would expect. Having a supportive principal was the greater motivation for a teacher to work hard than money.[64]

Zuckerberg viewed students, not only teachers, as individuals who approached education in isolation. "You'll have technology that understands how you learn best and where you need to focus," Zuckerberg and Chan write in their letter to their daughter about how education should improve. "You'll advance quickly in subjects that interest you most, and get as much help as you need in your most challenging areas. You'll explore topics that aren't even offered in schools today. Your teachers will also have better tools and data to help you achieve your goals." What Zuckerberg and Chan call personalized learning—guided by algorithms applied to a student's work—"can be one scalable way to give all children a better education and more equal opportunity."[65] When the term *scalable*, which defines something unbound by all-too-human frailties, is applied to a something as human as preparing a child for life, perhaps a warning flag should go up.

Interestingly, however, when Zuckerberg and Chan discuss a school they are planning in East Palo Alto, California, after the debacle in Newark, they include working with health centers, parent groups, and local governments to ensure that "all children are well fed and cared for starting young." In order to improve the quality of education, they write, "We must first build inclusive and healthy communities."[66] A sensible approach, no doubt, but also one that won't scale and is more traditional than disruptive. In fact, traditionally, we would expect this kind of work to be carried out by local, state, and federal governments rather than concerned billionaires dipping into their monopoly profits.

Assistance for the developing world from Zuckerberg is still stuck in the earlier, algorithmic, phase. For example, he expresses mathematical certainty in the benefits from Facebook's Free Basics, which offers a free, stripped-down version of the Internet, including Wikipedia and Facebook, to those who can't afford any access to the Internet. Zuckerberg again cited his one in ten formula for poverty reduction from Internet access: "There are more than 4 billion people who need to be connected and if we can connect them, then we'll raise hundreds of millions of people out of poverty," he said in defense of Free Basics.[67] The Indian government nonetheless rejected the idea, in part motivated by more than 750,000 emails complaining that the service would create a poor Internet for poor people.[68] Critics in India, like one group called Savetheinternet.in, saw a more nefarious purpose behind Facebook's offer, which it described as "Zuckerberg's ambitious project to confuse hundreds of millions of emerging market users into thinking that Facebook and the Internet are one and the same." All children, even poor children in India, the group wrote, "deserve the same experience and opportunities when it comes to an open and free Internet, as much as their urban or richer peers."[69]

Facebook board member Marc Andreessen was enraged and shared his feelings, via Twitter. The Indian government clearly didn't know what was best for its people. "Another in a long line of economically suicidal decisions made by the Indian government against its own citizens," read one Andreessen tweet. Another, which drew the most complaints, "Anti-colonialism has been economically catastrophic for the Indian people for decades. Why stop now?"[70] Like Thiel, another Facebook board member, was known to do, Andreessen was merely stating what everyone around him thought, though he later apologized to the nation of India and the Indian people. Because Andreessen's medium was Twitter, he couldn't say he was misquoted or misunderstood by an interviewer; rather he insisted that he was "100% opposed to colonialism, and 100% in favor of independence and freedom, in every country, including India."

Zuckerberg quickly condemned Andreessen's comments and stated his objection to the Indian government's decision on Free Basics with much more finesse. He wasn't criticizing the Indian people, but, on the contrary, was speaking up for those without the power to speak for themselves. "Remember," he said, "that the people this affects most, the four billion unconnected, have no voice on the Internet. They can't argue their side in the comments below or sign a petition for what they believe. So we decide our character in how we look out for them."[71] Zuckerberg, along with his wife, makes a similar pledge to his daughter: "We must engage directly with the people we serve. We can't empower people if we don't understand the needs and desires of their communities."[72]

Of course, another way to empower people is simply to give them power. Power to use or even misuse. But Zuckerberg wasn't speaking as a politician. Or even as an entrepreneur. His vision of an interconnected humanity, whose members share details of their lives within the Facebook platform, wasn't something that emerged organically from the people, or even with some gentle nudging from the people's representatives, the government. Zuckerberg was conceiving a new online civilization before our eyes and, if he succeeded, he would be responsible for something grander than Julius Caesar or even Bill Gates could ever have imagined.

THE FUTURE

"Local, small-scale, active"

In college, I used to marvel at American history books that explained panics like the Salem witch trials or religious revivals like the Second Great Awakening by pointing to social and economic shifts that were profound but largely undetected by the people living through them: new shipping routes linking up to the Caribbean, say, or the settlement of the West. What must it be like to be buffeted by such forces and be none the wiser? Poor fools. Yet the past twenty-five years of radical social, political, and economic change since Tim Berners-Lee introduced the Web have given me new sympathy for such pawns of fate. Our behavior has changed, too. Extremist mass movements and social panic are gathering strength. People are distrustful and angry, they feel isolated and vulnerable to exploitation. The Web itself has encouraged this troubling state of affairs, yet we rarely stop to question how and why the Web developed the way it has. If *The Know-It-Alls* can achieve one thing, it will be to demystify the origins of the harsh market-based values being pumped out by Silicon Valley, which can seem irresistible. They are not. At crucial moments, a relatively few well-positioned people made decisions to steer the Web in its current individualistic, centralized, commercialized direction, rejoicing at the profound disruptions this has produced along the way.

Berners-Lee intended the Web to be something like the opposite—decentralized, collaborative, and minimally commercial. He assumed a generosity of spirit that would drive people to work together to help their neighbors; in this way, the Web would add to the world's all-too-thin connective tissue. And he was not alone in those values. Google's founders, Sergey Brin and Larry Page, saw the Web as having the potential to revolutionize the world's access to knowledge and warned in biting language about the harm that would come from the commercialization of search engines. At the start, they viewed market-based competition as the enemy of their chosen task of organizing the world's information, not its friend. Likewise, Mark Zuckerberg originally saw Facebook as being most effective as a local tool that supplemented real-world relationships, the way it worked when it was still called thefacebook.com and only operated on university campuses.

The founders of Google and Facebook were seduced by the power and money offered by venture capitalists and agreed to reorient their socially minded designs to become profit generators. Turns out that idealistic projects from ambitious, talented young people can become quite lucrative after their leaders have ditched the idealism. The tracking of users' Web searches, which Google initially deployed in the name of "perfect" search results, became tools for placing the most effective advertising. Facebook's fascination with its users' interests and preferences, originally intended to forge friendships, also became grist for highly targeted advertising. Other, less-idealistic entrepreneurs, like Marc Andreessen, Peter Thiel, and Jeff Bezos, managed to inject just enough tech idealism into their profit-making schemes—about empowering consumers, for example—to create lucrative companies of their own. Together, these Know-It-Alls represent a sixty-year climbdown in the goals for computer science and artificial intelligence, from teaching machines to think like humans to teaching them how to help some humans make money by imitating how other humans think.

Thiel likes to describe those diminished ambitions in today's Silicon Valley by saying, "We wanted flying cars, instead we got 140 characters."[1] Well, Thiel may want flying cars, but computer pioneers like John McCarthy wanted something much more extravagant, a new form of intelligence that could make its way through the world. This was a goal worth pursuing not only because artificially intelligent machines would be so cool—more cool, even, than flying cars—but because they would be so profound. Just think of the things these thinking machines could think. But you can't. They've never been thought before. McCarthy and his peers weren't focusing on how to profit personally, but on how society would benefit from having a supreme intelligence to guide it.

In a lecture back in the 1960s, McCarthy made clear that he wasn't worried about a time when computers would be smarter than people, as many tech leaders are today. So what does he suggest we do during our first encounter with these superior machines? Well, obviously, we should ask the machine itself for advice: We created you, oh wise machine, now how should we get along? Armed with the answer, whatever it may be, "we could act accordingly and with greater intelligence than now."[2] In this ultimate sense, McCarthy and his idealistic hackers were laying the groundwork for intelligence to be the most important quality in a leader. He wasn't building an empathy machine that "felt" more intensely than humans. But McCarthy at least presumes a gentleness within these great new intelligences. Of course they will want to help us with our troubles.

By contrast, here is how Peter Thiel reacted to the prospect that genuine artificial intelligence would arrive one day. "The development of AI would be as momentous as the landing of extraterrestrials on this planet," Thiel told an audience on Reddit, shuddering at the thought. "If aliens landed, the first question would not be about the economy!" Presumably, the first question would be about our safety, as in, "Will AI be friendly?"[3] If you see great intelligence, at its heart, as about the power to control and dominate others, you understandably would tremble at encountering a bigger brain. Suddenly the tables would be turned. This reflects the Know-It-All playbook, which closely resembles the Donald Trump playbook, with its emphasis on domination and disruption and life as a competition. McCarthy and the early AI pioneers conceived of their research as part of a collective human quest—funded by the government, destined to help all of us. The current crop of tech leaders, however, see these civilization-altering quests as personal. Consider how the billionaires Elon Musk and Jeff Bezos are taking on the ultimate collective human quest, space exploration, through private companies, SpaceX and Blue Origin.

McCarthy isn't blameless, of course, when it comes to the online culture we all endure these days. Hiding behind their reverence for supposed "raw intelligence," he and his hacker acolytes created a computer lab ethos that was unwelcoming to people who were different, particularly women and minorities. As we've seen, hacker-led tech companies re-created those patterns. McCarthy and the hackers were fierce toward those who couldn't cut it, and today the Web is overrun with aggressive, nasty comments, which are tolerated by large companies like Twitter as being part of a robust debate. Furthermore, by challenging the very idea of authority, McCarthy and the hackers gave comfort to the most destructive impulses of start-up founders.

But the early hackers' indifference to wealth and personal power meant that the harm from these toxic ideas was largely contained within the walls of the computer lab. In the 1970s, McCarthy's artificial intelligence lab was five miles off campus, its members' heads even higher in the clouds. "In those old glory days at SAIL," wrote the cognitive scientist Douglas Hofstadter, "speculations about the undecidability of Fermat's Last Theorem mingled freely with pictures of Cantor sets, Cantor dusts, Sierpinski gaskets, snowflakes, flowsnakes, blinkers, traffic lights, gliders, and glider guns, while somewhere down the hall, Principia Mathematica, Gödelian incompleteness, the halting problem, and other Ouroborous-like diagonalizations nestled up to Stanislaw Lem's 'Cyberiad,' Newcomb's problem, teleportation fantasies, and free-will puzzles, and elsewhere, Necker Cubes, Soma cubes, Go boards, impossible objects."[4] McCarthy's lab knew its place—it was part of a system of open research conducted at university labs with the support of government grants. Even the great anti-censorship fight at Stanford championed by McCarthy was an attempt to protect the early Internet, which he considered home turf. McCarthy wanted the lab's ideas tested, challenged, and ultimately used to help the public; he didn't will his or someone else's ideas to run the world single-mindedly. And that, in short, is what changed.

Who would have thought to impose the values of the lab on the world, anyhow? That person was Frederick Terman, Stanford's ambitious provost who didn't understand why his university and its students and faculty shouldn't profit from their brilliant ideas. He promoted the idea that engineers should become rich and powerful, starting with two of his early students, William Hewlett and David Packard. Stanford benefited. Shareholders benefited. Society benefited. If engineers set the agenda for the country, and the world, then at last we would be certain that the brightest would be in charge, as his father, Lewis, the student of "gifted children," had dreamed. Ordinary folks wouldn't need to be weighed down by questions they couldn't understand, anyhow. On efficiency grounds, Terman's vision might make sense. On humanitarian grounds, less so. Do we really want engineers—and their hyperrational comrades—to determine how we live? Democracy, for all its faults, is the best way to ensure that the public is being served by its leaders. No one can look out for your interests as diligently as yourself and no engineer is so unemotional as to be acting purely rationally without bias or self-preservation.

And, let's face it, an un-self-aware engineer is really the best-case scenario. The people who populate *The Know-It-Alls* have dreams of world domination and seem especially poor candidates to set the priorities for society. Consider Peter Thiel, who was once asked if the super-rich were happier than the rest of us. He first answered by saying enormous wealth can cut both ways when it comes to happiness, and then added, "I've always questioned the premise of the question. I'm not sure whether subjective happiness should be the most important metric at which we evaluate things. There's many other metrics we can use." His personal crusade has been to harness science to forestall death. Life span is a favorite metric. Whether Thiel is happy or not with existence, he is certain that he wants more of it. "I actually think life is something that's worthwhile in and of itself," he told an interviewer. "Death is kind of a bad thing, in and of itself, so even if I was adrift and had no sense of what I was doing at all, I would still all else being equal, hopefully prefer to live a lot longer."[5] His vision of the future represents a slight improvement on Hobbes—nasty, brutish, and long.

Then there is Mark Zuckerberg, who in a letter written with his wife, Priscilla Chan, in 2015 to his newborn daughter, Max, laid out what he hoped for her future and our future. His aspirations were oddly quantitative. Max's birth was the occasion for Zuckerberg and Chan to announce that they were creating a private corporation, the Chan-Zuckerberg Initiative, to invest and donate the billions of dollars he had made from Facebook. The purpose of the initiative, they wrote in the letter to Max, was to advance human potential and promote human equality. And, in detailing the kind of work they would be supporting in those causes, Zuckerberg and Chan proposed "pushing the boundaries on how great a human life can be," including the goal of being able to "learn and experience 100 times more than we do today."[6]

What a beguiling notion! A hundred times more to experience and learn than is typical today—like suddenly living your life in high-def. Facebook is helping to bring about that future as best it can. Already, people have more close friends than once was thought possible, according to Zuckerberg, and those friends are sharing more about themselves, stories, photographs, new hobbies, new relationships. You do the math. Based on your access to Facebook, how many more experiences have you already experienced, how many more facts have you learned? With its investment in virtual-reality technology, Facebook is hoping to bring more of the world in front of our eyes and with life-like clarity.

This line of reasoning does inevitably raise a few questions, such as: Are experiences really so fungible? Is watching a hundred sunsets a day through a virtual-reality headset, for example, one hundred times the experience of lingering over the sun as it sets once and only once outside your window? On first blush, this quantitative approach to life is more peculiar than pernicious. Why exactly would someone want a life overstuffed with experience as Zuckerberg with his social networks and virtual-reality devices and Thiel with his life-extension research are promising? What is pernicious, however, is the incidental destruction, the collateral damage, as these leaders pursue their dreams by centralizing our relationships—personal, economic, political. Local stores, local newspapers, local unions, local political organizations are swept away as tech companies centralize profits.

We are lonely and crave connection. We are confused by life and crave meaning. We are anxious and crave the feeling of being cared for. We are angry and crave the ability to trust. Internet giants like Facebook are eager to step in. In a 2017 manifesto, Zuckerberg described the online communities facilitated by his social-networking platform as "a bright spot" in the darkening global landscape. Not only can Facebook "strengthen existing physical communities by helping people come together online as well as offline," he wrote, but "in the same way connecting with friends online strengthens real relationships, developing this infrastructure will strengthen these communities, as well as enable completely new ones to form." Facebook is nothing less than our salvation. Of course, the reason Zuckerberg was writing this particular statement to the world was the criticism of Facebook's role in encouraging extremist, hate-filled political movements during the 2016 presidential election and what he himself described as "surveys showing large percentages of our population lack a sense of hope for the future."[7]

The one connection that Zuckerberg wasn't prepared to make was between the growth of a centralized, commercialized Web and the lack of hope and sense of isolation he sees all around him. But that connection is what the preceding pages have been about. When you have been isolated and treated as a commodity by big companies, whether as a target of advertisers or as a potential "start-up of you"; when you lose the ability to protect your fellow citizens online and off because of the assault on business regulations and a social safety net; when you see obscene wealth delivered to the hands of a few; when hostility and incivility is the coin of the realm in online conversation; when racial, ethnic and gender inclusion are considered assaults on freedom. . . . Well, naturally, you lose hope and feel unprotected.

Where do we go from here? Looking to Facebook and the other tech giants for solutions would be madness. Europe provides a model, with its greater protections for individuals against tech companies' ability to exploit the information it collects. European governments have also tried to prevent Silicon Valley companies from holding monopoly power in the marketplace, in part to support their own start-ups. These are all steps in the right direction.

But rather than offer a set of policy proposals, I would repeat a prescription for a just society that begins with "a commitment to the local, the plural, the small scale and the active."[8] Those are the qualities the Web must have, even if it means cutting off the flow of revenues to giant companies like Google, Facebook, Amazon, and eBay. We can't tolerate an Internet, or a society, led by a few self-proclaimed geniuses claiming to serve mankind. The Internet can and must work for us, instead of the other way around, through a diversity of voices and platforms free to organize and collaborate on their own rather than through a few centralized services. This way the Internet can help build the social connective tissue we so desperately need, as Berners-Lee originally intended.

A NOTE TO THE READER

Careful readers will notice that in *The Know-It-Alls* I have tried hard not to use gender-neutral pronouns or mix up the "shes" and "hes" in some sort of equalized fashion. Certainly, such an effort would send a message of inclusion, and that is precisely why it would be so inappropriate for a book like this. The story of how Silicon Valley leaders came to their libertarian worldview is the story almost exclusively of men: the hackers who first mastered computers and promoted extreme individualism, as well as the venture capitalists and tech start-up leaders who brought those innovations to market. Fittingly, the political theory they promote is one that necessarily belittles the contribution of women as part of its fantasy of extreme individualism, in which adult men arrive in the world magically with no debt to anyone. We, author and reader alike, must not lose this thread of systematic exclusion even if it is intended to promote a fairer world going forward.

I am not the first to bring this argument to my writing about Silicon Valley. In her review of *The Hard Thing About Hard Things*, a business advice book written by Ben Horowitz, founding partner of the venture capital firm Andreessen Horowitz, Diane Brady took pains to praise Horowitz for his work in support of women's rights, but nonetheless expressed her bafflement at phrases like "tough times separate women from girls" and other conspicuous efforts by Horowitz to treat the sexes the same in his writing. "Horowitz's persistent use of 'she' comes off as social satire in a world with so few actual women," Brady writes in *Bloomberg Businessweek*, a world where "'her' is more likely to refer to your operating system than to your business partner."[1]

Not surprisingly, this call for self-reflection by the men who lead Silicon Valley was met with contempt, most notably by Marc Andreessen, Horowitz's business partner, who wrote with typical subtlety on Twitter: "Mind-bending review of known misogynist pig @bhorowitz's new book :-):"[2] Yet surely there can be a system inherently unfair to women without each of its leaders being "known misogynist pigs." Calling out superficial attempts at equality is a vital first step toward promoting real change in a field where there is so much self-satisfied resistance.

ACKNOWLEDGMENTS

This book grew out of my writing and editing at the *New York Times*, particularly the six years or so when I was responsible for the Link by Link column, which tracked the influences—amusing, wrenching, terrifying—of Internet culture. Bruce Headlam, the media editor at the time, saw that this column would suit my interests and shepherded me and my copy expertly. When I turned my focus to *The Know-It-Alls* I had a number of inspiring discussions: Lee Vinsel was generous with his time as he helped me understand how my book could fit into the larger critique of the cult of innovation; Paulina Borsook walked me through her experiences writing *Cyberselfish*, which was prescient in describing the deficiencies of a society led by Silicon Valley entrepreneurs; Sue Gardner gave me encouragement that I was on the right path based on her own time in the Bay Area; and my cousin Carl Shapiro, who died as I was writing the book, was my special guide through the history of computers and the Internet.

I had the benefit of old and new friends and family members who either read drafts or heard outlines and interrogated my premises: Robert Mackey, Todd Schiff, Martha Bridegam, David Malaxos, Alan Cohen, Lori Cohen, David Crossland, Kevin Kolben, Jenna Wortham, Liam Wyatt, Joseph Reagle, Sarah Szalavitz, Victoria Baranetsky. Jeff

Wise hashed through the ideas in this book week upon week. Eric Kaplan and Joseph Tedeschi were invaluable close readers of the entire manuscript, always encouraging, always questioning. My agent, Rafe Sagalyn, kept this neophyte on the right path.

My former *Times* colleague, John Markoff, kindly shared his recordings of his interview with John McCarthy. Thanks, too, to Michael Zimmer, whose Zuckerberg Files, hosted by the University of Wisconsin, Milwaukee, expertly tracks and transcribes the talks and interviews of Mark Zuckerberg. The *Stanford Daily* should be commended, too, for its excellent digital archive.

I relied on the reporting of many fine technology writers and historians to make my case about the Know-It-Alls, even if these reporters wouldn't necessarily agree with my conclusions. Steven Levy's pathbreaking work, *Hackers*, is the ur-text for understanding the young men who caught the computer programming bug and convinced themselves these machines could save the world. C. Stewart Gillmor's chronicle of Frederick Terman at Stanford manages to be a deeply reported history of a man and a university. In *Once You're Lucky, Twice You're Good*, Sara Lacy created an indelible portrait of the ferment of the so-called Web 2.0 years. George Packer is insightful in explaining how Peter Thiel belongs in the story of Silicon Valley values. My arguments were shaped by the detailed research of, among others, Rebecca Lowen and Paul Edwards, and, more overarchingly, by the intellectual history of Daniel T. Rodgers, whose *Age of Fracture* captures the hyperindividualism of America at the end of the twentieth century even if the words "Internet" and "Web" never appear. The humane values of Joseph Weizenbaum, the world-weary, lapsed artificial intelligence believer, were a touchstone.

At The New Press, my editor, Carl Bromley, was a steady hand and ready guide for me on this project, starting with the inspired title. His colleague, Jed Bickman, was an important early reader of my drafts. Diane Wachtell has long been a friend and advocate. Jessica Yu has been a model in getting the ideas in this book in front of the public, while Emily Albarillo has been a model in getting the words in this book in front of the public.

My father, Stuart Cohen, is my example of being open to what the world has to offer; for as long as I have known him, he unfailingly accentuates the positive. Harlan Cohen and Adam Cohen are both a spur and a safety net, as only older brothers can be. My wife, Aviva Michaelov, is a source of joy, pride, and profound friendship, the pillar in my life supporting so much more than the writing of a book, as all-encompassing as that task may have seemed at times.

During the writing of this book, I lost my mother, Beverly Sher Cohen. Her questioning spirit and joy in life and language surrounded me as I was writing, much the way I see her vividly in the smiles, giggles, and occasional words of reproach from her granddaughters, Kika and Nuli.

NOTES

INTRODUCTION

1. "To Serve Man," teleplay by Rod Serling, based on a short story by Damon Knight, *The Twilight Zone*, aired March 2, 1962.

2. "Minimum Viable Product," by John Altschuler, Dave Krinsky, and Mike Judge, *Silicon Valley*, season 1, episode 1, aired April 6, 2014.

3. "Proof of Concept," by Clay Tarver, *Silicon Valley*, season 1, episode 7, aired May 18, 2014.

4. Google Privacy and Terms, "Welcome to the Google Privacy Policy," last modified August 29, 2016: http://www.google.com/policies/privacy.

5. Originally called Internet.org, the project's home page is: https://info.internet.org/en/story/free-basics-from-internet-org.

6. Video, May 4, 2015, available at Mark Zuckerberg's Facebook page: https://vimeo.com/126762664.

7. Adi Narayan, "Andreessen Regrets India Tweets; Zuckerberg Laments Comments," Bloomberg.com, February 10, 2016.

8. Susan Moller Okin, *Justice, Gender and the Family*, New York: Basic Books, 1989, p. 75.

9. Reid Hoffman and Ben Casnocha, *The Start-up of You: Adapt to the Future, Invest in Yourself, and Transform Your Career*," New York: Crown Business, 2012, pp. 159–161.

10. Ibid., pp. 8–9.

11. Tim Berners-Lee with Mark Fischetti, *Weaving the Web: The Original Design and Ultimate Destiny of the World Wide Web*, New York: Harper, 2000.

12. David Streitfeld and Malia Wollan, "Tech Rides Are Focus of Hostility in Bay Area," *The New York Times*, February 1, 2014, p. B1.

13. "Inside the Extravagant Wedding of Sean Parker and Alexandra Lenas," *Vanity Fair*, August 1, 2013.

14. Peter Fimrite, "Vinod Khosla Wants $30 Million for Martins Beach Access," *The San Francisco Chronicle*, February 23, 2016.

15. Katherine Bindley, "David Sacks, Yammer CEO, Hosts Extravagant Birthday Party," *The Huffington Post*, June 19, 2012.

16. Steven Bertoni, "Instagram's Kevin Systrom: The Stanford Billionaire Machine Strikes Again," *Forbes*, August 20, 2012.

17. Rich McCormick, "Ghostbusters Star Leslie Jones Calls for Stronger Twitter Guidelines after Racist Abuse," *The Verge*, July 19, 2016.

18. Peter Thiel, "Address to Republican National Convention," Cleveland, OH, July 21, 2016, C-Span: https://www.c-span.org/video/?c4612796/peter-thiel-addresses-republican-national-convention-proud-gay.

19. David Streitfeld, "Peter Thiel to Donate $1.25 Million in Support of Donald Trump," *The New York Times*, October 15, 2016.

20. Elon Musk, post to Twitter, Jul 31, 2012, @elonmusk.

21. Erik Wemple, "Peter Thiel's Media Critique: Reporters Take Trump's Statements 'Literally' but Not 'Seriously,'" *The Washington Post*, October 31, 2016.

22. See Dylan Matthews, "Jeff Bezos Is Buying the Washington Post. Here's What You Need to Know About the Sale," Wonkblog, *The Washington Post*, August 6, 2013; David A. Graham, "The Politics of New Washington Post Owner Jeff Bezos," *The Atlantic*, August 5, 2013.

23. See Steven Levy, *Hackers: Heroes of the Computer Revolution*, Penguin Books, New York, 2001 (original 1984).

24. Richard W. Lyman, *Stanford in Turmoil: Campus Unrest, 1966–1972*, Stanford, CA.: Stanford University Press, 2009, p. 5.

25. Barbie Fields, "Frederick Terman—A Living Bay Area Legend," *The Stanford Daily*, October 7, 1977, p. 1.

26. Carolyn E. Tajnai, "From the Valley of Heart's Delight to the Silicon Valley: A Study of Stanford University's Role in the Transformation," Stanford University, Department of Computer Science, 1996: http://forum.stanford.edu/carolyn/valley_of_hearts.

27. See C. Stewart Gillmor, *Fred Terman at Stanford: Building a Discipline, a University and Silicon Valley*, Stanford, CA: Stanford University Press, 2004.

28. David Orenstein, "Computer Science@40: Faculty, Alumni Celebrate Life-Changing Advances," *Stanford News*, April 5, 2006.

29. Telephone interview with Richard Weyhrauch, May 23, 2016.

30. See Steven Levy, *In the Plex: How Google Thinks, Works, and Shapes Our Lives*, New York: Simon and Schuster, 2011.

31. Ken Auletta, "Get Rich U.," *The New Yorker*, April 30, 2012.

32. Tonya Garcia, "Amazon Will Account for More Than Half of 2015 E-Commerce Growth, Says Macquarie," *MarketWatch*, December 22, 2015.

33. Max Chafkin, "What Makes Uber Run," *Fast Company*, September, 8, 2015.

34. Ginia Bellafante, "Airbnb's Promise: Every Man and Woman a Hotelier," *The New York Times*, December 17, 2014.

35. Statistics from Facebook's Newsroom: http://newsroom.fb.com/company-info.

36. Stanford University, "James Breyer/Mark Zuckerberg Interview, Oct. 26, 2005, Stanford University" (2005), Zuckerberg Transcripts.

37. Computer History Museum, "The Facebook Effect (interview with Mark Zuckerberg and David Kirkpatrick)" (2010), Zuckerberg Transcripts.

38. Douglas Bowman, "Goodbye, Google," March 20, 2009, at Stopdesign: stopdesign.com/archive/2009/03/20/goodbye-google.html.

39. Alex Hern, "Why Google Has 200m Reasons to Put Engineers over Designers," *The Guardian*, February 5, 2014.

40. Marc Andreessen, Tweet, December 12, 2014 (since deleted). On September 24, 2016, Andreessen, whose handle on Twitter is @pmarca, announced that he was "taking a Twitter break!" and deleted more than 100,000 posts to Twitter, leaving that one tweet. The quotes from his Twitter account that appear here were copied by the author during research. Intriguingly, some 72,000 of his Tweets, starting in 2015, have been reposted by a Twitter account called "I retweet pmarca."

41. Sarah Lacy, *Once You're Lucky, Twice You're Good*, New York: Gotham Books, 2008, pp. 126–127.

42. Ben Horowitz, *The Hard Thing About Hard Things*, New York: Harper Collins, 2014.

43. Lessley Anderson, "Elon Musk: A Machine Tasked with Getting Rid of Spam Could End Humanity," *Vanity Fair*, October 8, 2014.

44. James Douglas, "Star Lords," *The Awl*, December 15, 2015.

45. To be precise, Google's tech workforce is 18 percent women and Facebook's is 17 percent women, while women hold 24 percent of Google's leadership positions and 27 percent of senior leadership positions at Facebook.

Amazon doesn't break down its tech workforce numbers, but the percentage of women in management positions was in the same area, 25 percent. The percentages of African Americans and Hispanics within Google's and Facebook's tech workforce were identical: 1 percent African American, 3 percent Hispanic. Uber recently released its first diversity numbers—tech workers were 15.4 percent women, 1 percent African American, and 2.1 percent Hispanic.

See Google Diversity Web site, accessed February 20, 2017: https://www.google.com/diversity/; Maxine Williams, "Facebook Diversity Update: Positive Hiring Trends Show Progress," July 14, 2016 Facebook Newsroom: https://newsroom.fb.com/news/2016/07/facebook-diversity-update-positive-hiring-trends-show-progress/; "Our Workforce Demographics," Diversity at Amazon, data as of July 2016: https://www.amazon.com/b?node=10080092011; Uber Diversity, data as of March 2017, https://www.uber.com/diversity/.

46. Robert Pogue Harrison, "The Children of Silicon Valley," *The New York Review of Books* blog, July 17, 2014.

47. Marc Andreessen, "Why Software Is Eating the World," *The Wall Street Journal*, August 20, 2011.

1. John McCarthy

1. Joseph Weizenbaum, *Computer Power and Human Reason: From Judgment to Calculation*, New York: W.H. Freeman and Company, 1976, pp. 226–227.

2. Weizenbaum, *Computer Power and Human Reason*, p. 227.

3. "Speaking Minds: Interviews with Twenty Eminent Cognitive Scientists," edited by Peter Baumgartner and Sabine Payr, Princeton, NJ: Princeton University Press, 1995, p. 253.

4. Ibid., p. 116.

5. John McCarthy, "An Unreasonable Book," appearing in Benjamin Kuipers, John McCarthy, and Joseph Weizenbaum, comments on *Computer Power and Human Reason*, in *ACM Sigart Newsletter* (Association for Computing Machinery, Special Interest Group on Artificial Intelligence) no. 58, June 1976, p. 8: http://www-formal.stanford.edu/jmc/reviews/weizenbaum.html.

6. Cheryl Zollars, "Scientists Discuss Role of Technology in Society," *The Stanford Daily*, May 19, 1978, p. 1.

7. John Markoff, interview with John McCarthy, July 19, 2002, personal copy.

8. There is no book-length biography of John McCarthy, and when asked later in life if he would write a memoir, he said he wouldn't because he was "not prepared to be honest" and address "what I could have accomplished if I

hadn't been lazy." However, he has given many retrospective interviews and written prolifically about his life. His extensive personal Web site, with links to papers, talks, essays, popular science articles, favorite sayings, and so on, is www-formal.stanford.edu/jmc/, with Stanford running its own site: http://jmc.stanford.edu/index.html.

A number of works describe McCarthy's life, including: Philip J. Hilts, *Scientific Temperaments: Three Lives in Contemporary* Science, New York: Simon and Schuster, 1982; John Markoff, *Machines of Loving Grace: The Quest for Common Ground Between Humans and Robots*, New York: HarperCollins, 2015, particularly chapter 4, "The Rise, Fall and Resurrection of A.I."; Nils J. Nilsson, *John McCarthy, 1927–2011: A Biographical Memoir*, Washington, D.C.: National Academy of Sciences, 2012, pp. 1–17; Patrick J. Hayes and Leora Morgenstern, "On John McCarthy's 80th Birthday, in Honor of His Contributions," *AI Magazine*, Winter 2007, pp. 93–102.

The oral histories are Nils Nilsson and John McCarthy, interview, September 12, 2007, Computer History Museum: http://www.computerhistory.org/collections/catalog/102658149; and William Aspray and John McCarthy, interview, March 2, 1989, Palo Alto, CA, Charles Babbage Institute, University of Minnesota, Minneapolis: purl.umn.edu/107476.

9. Markoff and McCarthy interview.

10. Kathryn Cullen-DuPont, *Encyclopedia of Women's History of America, Second Edition*, New York: Facts on File Inc., 2000, p. 184.

11. Susan McCarthy, "What Your Dentist Doesn't Want You to Know," part of Celebration of John McCarthy's Accomplishments, Stanford University, March 25, 2012: http://www.saildart.org/jmc2012.html.

12. M. Ilin, "100,000 Whys: A Trip Around the Room," translated by Beatrice Kinkead, Philadelphia: J.B. Lippincott Company, 1933, p. 9.

13. Markoff and McCarthy interview.

14. John McCarthy, "What Is Artificial Intelligence?," November 12, 2007, John McCarthy Web site: http://jmc.stanford.edu/artificial-intelligence/index.html.

15. Paul N. Edwards, *The Closed World: Computers and the Politics of Discourse in Cold War America* Cambridge, MA: MIT Press, 1996, p. 159.

16. "Hixon Symposium on Cerebral Mechanisms in Behavior," California Institute of Technology, Pacific State Hospital, Pomona, CA, September 20, 1948, accessed at Linus Pauling Day by Day Web Site, Oregon State University Libraries Special Collections: http://scarc.library.oregonstate.edu/coll/pauling/calendar/1948/09/20-xl.html.

17. Nilsson and McCarthy interview.

18. Markoff and McCarthy interview; Sylvia Nasar, *A Beautiful Mind: The Life of Mathematical Genius and Nobel Laureate John Nash*, New York: Simon and Schuster, 2001, p. 146.

19. Markoff and McCarthy interview.

20. See John McCarthy, "What Was Attractive About Marxism?," May 10, 2005: http://jmc.stanford.edu/commentary/progress/marxism2.html; and John McCarthy, "Marxism," August 27, 2008: http://jmc.stanford.edu/commentary/progress/marxism.html.

21. Nilsson, *John McCarthy*, p. 4.

22. Nilsson and McCarthy interview.

23. J. McCarthy, M. L. Minsky, N. Rochester, C. E. Shannon, "A Proposal for the Dartmouth Summer Research Project on Artificial Intelligence," August 31, 1955, reprinted in *AI Magazine*, vol. 27, no. 4 (2006), pp. 12–14.

24. Aspray and McCarthy interview.

25. Margaret Hamilton, interview with author, October 2, 2015.

26. John McCarthy, "The Well-Designed Child," 1996: http://jmc.stanford.edu/articles/child.html.

27. John McCarthy, "Information," *Scientific American*, September 1966, pp. 65–72.

28. John McCarthy, "The Little Thoughts of Thinking Machines," *Psychology Today*, December 1983, pp. 46–49.

29. John McCarthy, "Artificial Intelligence and Creativity," Century 21 lecture, January 30, 1968, audio file in KZSU Collection, Stanford Archive of Recorded Sound, Stanford University Libraries.

30. John McCarthy, "An Example for Natural Language Understanding and the AI Problems It Raises," 1976: http://jmc.stanford.edu/articles/mrhug.html.

31. Nilsson, *John McCarthy*, p. 11.

32. Steven Levy, *Hackers: Heroes of the Computer Revolution*, New York: Penguin Books, 2001 (original 1984), p. 24.

33. Louis Fein, oral history interview conducted by Pamela McCorduck, May 9, 1979, Charles Babbage Institute, retrieved from the University of Minnesota Digital Conservancy: http://hdl.handle.net/11299/107284.

34. This paper was later published in an academic journal: Louis Fein, "The Role of the University in Computers, Data Processing, and Related Fields," *Communications of the ACM*, vol. 2, no. 9, September 1959, pp. 7–14.

35. Ibid., p. 13.

36. Quora, "How did Mark Zuckerberg become a programming prodigy," https://www.quora.com/How-did-Mark-Zuckerberg-become-a-programming-prodigy?redirected_qid=2886003.

37. Paul Graham, "Some Heroes," April 2006: http://paulgraham.com/heroes.html.

38. Levy, *Hackers*, pp. 26–27.

39. Tung-Hui Hu, *A Prehistory of the Cloud*, Cambridge, MA: MIT Press, 2015, p. 46.

40. Edwards, *The Closed World*, pp. 257–258.

41. Ibid., pp. 55–56.

42. Ibid.; see chapter 2, "The Hacker Ethic," pp. 39–49; quote appears on p. 67.

43. Ibid., p. 83.

44. Hamilton, author interview.

45. Levy, *Hackers*, pp. 40–49.

46. George E. Forsythe, "What to Do till the Computer Scientist Comes," Technical Report No. CS 77, Computer Science Department, School of Humanities and Sciences, Stanford University, September 22, 1967, p. 4.

47. Ibid.

48. McCarthy and Markoff interview, 2002.

49. Ibid.

50. Steven G. Ungar, "AI Goal: A 'Thinking' Machine," *The Stanford Daily*, January 26, 1971, p. 1.

51. John Markoff, "Optimism as Artificial Intelligence Pioneers Reunite," *The New York Times*, December 8, 2009, p. D4.

52. Bard Darrach, "Meet Shaky, the First Electronic Person," *Life*, November 20, 1970, p. 64.

53. Ungar, "AI Goal."

54. Classified advertisement, *The Stanford Daily*, May 25, 1971, p. 4.

55. Bruce Guenther Baumgart, "Saildart Prolegomenon 2016": www.saildart.org/book/0.pdf.

56. Stewart Brand, "Spacewar: Fanatic Life and Symbolic Death Among the Computer Bums," *Rolling Stone*, December 7, 1972.

57. Ungar, "AI Goal," p. 1.

58. John McCarthy, "The Home Information Terminal," appearing in "Man and Computer," Proceedings of the International Conference, Bordeaux, 1970, pp. 48–57 (Karger, Basel 1972).

59. John McCarthy, "The Home Information Terminal—a 1970 View," June 1, 2000: http://www-formal.stanford.edu/jmc/hoter2.pdf.

60. McCarthy and Markoff interview.

61. McCarthy, "The Home Information Terminal," p. 7.

62. McCarthy and Markoff interview.

63. Jim Wascher, "SRM Protest: Council Meeting Halted," *The Stanford Daily*, April 3, 1972.

64. Cheryl Zollars, "Scientists Discuss Role of Technology in Society," *The Stanford Daily*, May 19, 1978, p. 1.

65. John McCarthy, "Prophets—Especially Prophets of Doom," October 17, 1995: http://www-formal.stanford.edu/jmc/progress/prophets.html.

66. Lee Dembart, "Experts Argue Whether Computers Could Reason, and if They Should," *The New York Times*, May 8, 1977, p. A1.

67. John Markoff, "Joseph Weizenbaum, Famed Programmer, Is Dead at 85," *The New York Times*, March 13, 2008, p. A22.

68. Diana ben-Aaron, "Weizenbaum Examines Computers and Society," *The Tech*, vol. 105, no. 16, April 9, 1985, p. 2: http://tech.mit.edu/V105/N16/weisen.16n.html; Howard Rheingold, *Tools for Thought: The History and Future of Mind-Expanding Technology,* Cambridge, MA: The MIT Press, 2000, pp. 163–164.

69. Ben-Aaron, "Weizenbaum Examines Computers and Society."

70. Weizenbaum, *Computer Power and Human Reason*, p. 115.

71. The identity of the "patient" in this conversation is hard to pin down. In his academic paper on Eliza, Weizenbaum describes the conversation as "typical." See Joseph Weizenbaum, "ELIZA—A Computer Program for the Study of Natural Language Communication Between Man and Machine," *Communications of the ACM*, vol. 9, no. 1 (January 1966): 36–35. In *Computer Power and Human Reason*, however, he describes the computer's interlocutor as a "young woman." (Based on the dialogue, that appears to be the "part" being played.) In a *New York Times* account, which includes the same sample conversation, Weizenbaum is identified as typing in the statements himself: "In one test of Eliza's instructions, the following typewritten conversation took place between Mr. Weizenbaum, the patient (P.) and an IBM 7094 computer (C.) in the role of the doctor, with the latter 'unaware' of what the specific questions would be." John Noble Wilford, "Computer Is Being Taught to Understand English," *The New York Times*, June 15, 1968, p. 58.

72. Wilford, "Computer Is Being Taught to Understand English."

73. Joseph Weizenbaum, comments on *Computer Power and Human Reason*, in ACM Sigart Newsletter, p. 13.

74. "Speaking Minds: Interviews with Twenty Eminent Cognitive Scientists," edited by Peter Baumgartner and Sabine Payr, Princeton, NJ: Princeton University Press, 1995, p. 260.

75. Ibid., pp. 257–258.

76. *Plug and Pray*, directed by Jens Schanze, Mascha Films, 2010.

77. Joseph Weizenbaum and Reid Hoffman, "Virtual Worlds—Fiction or Reality?" Davos Open Forum 2008, January 26, 2008: https://www.youtube.com/watch?v=E198IynGbg0.

78. Jason Bloomstein, "Racial Slurs Cause University to Shut down Bul-

letin Board," *The Stanford Daily*, January 30, 1989, p. 1. A summary of the controversy from McCarthy's perspective can be found on his Web site: "The Rec.Humor.Funny Censorship at Stanford University," May 12, 1996: http://jmc.stanford.edu/general/rhf.html. The digital archive at the Stanford Artificial Intelligence Lab preserved the emails within the Computer Science Department: http://www.saildart.org/FUNNY.89[BB,DOC].

79. See Daniel T. Rodgers, *The Age of Fracture*, Cambridge, MA: Harvard University Press, 2011, p. 210.

80. David Sacks and Peter Thiel, *The Diversity Myth: "Multiculturalism" and the Politics of Intolerance at Stanford*," Oakland, CA: The Independent Institute, 1995, p. xxi.

81. McCarthy, "The Rec.Humor.Funny Censorship at Stanford University."

82. John McCarthy email to su-etc@SAIL.Stanford.EDU and faculty@SCORE.Stanford.EDU, January 29, 1989.

83. John McCarthy <JMC@SAIL.Stanford.EDU>, email to su-etc@Sail.Stanford.edu, February 7, 1989: http://www.saildart.org/FUNNY.89[BB,DOC].

84. William Brown, Jr. <wab@sumex-aim.stanford.edu>, email to su-etc@sumex-aim.stanford.edu, February 14, 1989: http://www.saildart.org/FUNNY.89[BB,DOC].

85. Ibid.

86. Mark Crispin <mrc@sumex-aim.stanford.edu>, email to William Brown Jr, February 15, 1989: http://www.saildart.org/FUNNY.89[BB,DOC].

87. Andy Freeman <andy@gang-of-four.stanford.edu>, email to su-etc@score.stanford.edu, February 15, 1989.

88. William Brown, Jr. <wab@sumex-aim.stanford.edu>, email to Andy Freeman, February 15, 1989.

89. W. Augustus Brown Jr., telephone interview with author, February 13, 2017.

90. John McCarthy <JMC@SAIL.Stanford.EDU>, email to J.JBRENNER@MACBETH.STANFORD.EDU, February 8, 1989: http://www.saildart.org/FUNNY.89[BB,DOC].

91. Oren Patashnik <op@polya.stanford.edu> email to su-etc@SAIL.Stanford.EDU and faculty@SCORE.Stanford.EDU et al., March 1, 1989.

92. John McCarthy, "Computer Science 40th Anniversary: A Symposium & Celebration Arrillaga Alumni Center," March 21, 2006: https://itunes.apple.com/us/itunes-u/department-computer-science/id385659431?mt=10.

93. McCarthy, "Computer Science 40th Anniversary."

2. Frederick Terman

1. Frederick Terman, letter to Paul Davis, December 1943, in Stuart W. Leslie, *The Cold War and American Science: The Military-Industrial-Academic Complex at MIT and Stanford*, New York: Columbia University Press, 1993, p. 44.

2. Rebecca S. Lowen, *Creating the Cold War University: The Transformation of Stanford*, Berkeley: University of California Press, 1997, p. 15.

3. Ibid., p. 148.

4. C. Stewart Gillmor, *Fred Terman at Stanford: Building a Discipline, a University, and Silicon Valley*, Stanford, CA: Stanford University Press, 2004, p. 491.

5. Carolyn E. Tajnai, "From the Valley of Heart's Delight to the Silicon Valley: A Study of Stanford University's Role in the Transformation," Stanford University, Department of Computer Science, 1996: http://forum.stanford.edu/carolyn/valley_of_hearts.

6. Ibid, p. 8.

7. Lowen, *Creating the Cold War University*, p. 173.

8. Gillmor, *Fred Terman at Stanford*, p. 379.

9. Lowen, *Creating the Cold War University*, p. 159.

10. Gillmor, *Fred Terman at Stanford*, p. 419.

11. Richard W. Lyman, *Stanford in Turmoil: Campus Unrest, 1966–1972*, Stanford, CA: Stanford University Press, 2009, p. 6.

12. Orrin Leslie Elliott, *Stanford University: The First Twenty Five Years*, Stanford, CA: Stanford University Press, 1937, pp. 16–17: https://archive.org/details/stanfroduniversi009361mbp.

13. Ibid., p. 12.

14. Elliott, *Stanford University*, pp. 15–16.

15. Stanford Facts 2016, "The Campus Plan," http://facts.stanford.edu/about/lands.

16. Gillmor, *Fred Terman at Stanford*, p. 17.

17. Stanford University, "The Founding Grant with Amendments, Legislation, and Court Decrees," 1987, p. 24.

18. Elliott, *Stanford University*, p. 39.

19. Ibid., pp. 21–22.

20. Richard Hofstadter and Walter P. Metzger, *The Development of Academic Freedom in the United States*, New York: Columbia University Press, 1955, p. 413.

21. Ibid., p. 414.

22. Elliott, *Stanford University*, pp. 50–51.

23. Stanford University, "Birth of a University": https://www.stanford.edu/about/history/.

24. W. B. Carnochan, "The Case of Julius Goebel: Stanford, 1905," *The American Scholar*, vol. 72, no. 3 (Summer 2003): p. 95.

25. Margo Davis and Roxanne Nilan, *The Stanford Album: A Photographic History, 1885–1945*, Stanford, CA: Stanford University Press, 1989, p. 47.

26. Elliott, *Stanford University*, p. 270.

27. Ibid., p. 272.

28. Hofstadter and Metzger, *The Development of Academic Freedom in the United States*, p. 436.

29. Elliott, *Stanford University*, "The 500 Limit," pp. 132–136.

30. Stanford University, Founding Grant. The cap at five hundred women was first reached in 1903 and continued until 1933, when it was revised to a 40 percent quota, which reflected the ratio in 1899, when Mrs. Stanford made her change to the founding grant. In 1973, Stanford petitioned a court to have the grant amended to remove any limits on the number of women attending the university.

31. Elliott, *Stanford University*, p. 132.

32. Ibid., p. 135.

33. Elliott, *Stanford University*, p. 160.

34. Susan Wolfe, "Who Killed Jane Stanford?" *Stanford Alumni* magazine, September/October 2003: https://alumni.stanford.edu/get/page/magazine/article/?article_id=36459.

35. Carnochan, "The Case of Julius Goebel," p. 108.

36. Wolfe, "Who Killed Jane Stanford?"

37. Peter Hegarty, *Gentlemen's Disagreement: Alfred Kinsey, Lewis Terman, and the Sexual Politics of Smart Men*, Chicago: University of Chicago Press, 2013, p. 3.

38. See John D. Wasserman, "A History of Intelligence Assessment: The Unfinished Tapestry," in *Contemporary Intellectual Assessment, Third Edition*, edited by Dawn P. Flanagan and Patti L. Harrison, New York: The Guilford Press, 2012.

39. Ibid., "Lewis Terman: Trails to Psychology," pp. 297–331.

40. B. R. Hergenhahn and Tracy Henley, *An Introduction to the History of Psychology, Seventh Edition*, Belmont, CA: Cengage Learning, 2013, p. 304. The full title of Terman's dissertation: "Genius and Stupidity: A Study of the Intellectual Processes of Seven 'Bright' and Seven 'Stupid' Boys."

41. Wasserman, "A History of Intelligence Assessment," p. 17.

42. Henry L. Minton, *Lewis M. Terman: Pioneer in Psychological Testing*, New York: New York University Press, 1988.

43. Ibid., p. 20.

44. Alfred Binet and Théodore Simon, *The Development of Intelligence in Children*, Baltimore: Wilkins & Wilkins Company, 1916, pp. 42–43.

45. L. M. Terman, "Were We Born That Way?" *World's Work*, October 1922, vol. 44, no. 6, p. 659.

46. Edwin G. Boring, "Lewis Madison Terman (1877–1956)," Washington, D.C.: National Academy of Sciences, 1959, p. 429.

47. Daniel Goleman, "75 Years Later, Study Still Tracking Geniuses," *The New York Times*, March 7, 1995, p. C1.

48. Mitchell Leslie, "The Vexing Legacy of Lewis Terman," *Stanford Magazine*, July/August 2000: https://alumni.stanford.edu/get/page/magazine/article/?article_id=40678.

49. See Adam Cohen, *Imbeciles: The Supreme Court, American Eugenics, and the Sterilization of Carrie Buck*, New York: Penguin, 2016.

50. Walter Lippmann, "The Abuse of the Tests," *The New Republic*, November 15, 1922, p. 297.

51. Lewis M. Terman, "The Great Conspiracy, or the Impulse Imperious of Intelligence Testers, Psychoanalyzed and Exposed by Mr. Lippmann," *The New Republic*, December 27, 1922, p. 119.

52. Mitchell Leslie, "The Vexing Legacy of Lewis Terman."

53. Boring, "Lewis Madison Terman," p. 440.

54. See Gillmor, *Fred Terman at Stanford*, chapter 1, "California Boy," pp. 11–69.

55. Stuart W. Leslie, *The Cold War and American Science*, p. 49.

56. Gillmor, *Fred Terman at Stanford*, p. 90.

57. Stuart W. Leslie, *The Cold War and American Science*, p. 53

58. Gillmor, *Fred Terman at Stanford*, p. 251

59. Lowen, *Creating the Cold War University*, pp. 130–131.

60. Lyman, *Stanford in Turmoil*, p. 9.

61. Lowen, *Creating the Cold War University*, p. 135.

62. Quoted in Lowen, *Creating the Cold War University*, p. 137.

63. Gillmor, *Fred Terman at Stanford*, p. 341.

64. Gillmor, *Fred Terman at Stanford*, p. 333.

65. Lowen, *Creating the Cold War University*, pp. 14, 104.

66. Lyman, *Stanford in Turmoil*, p. 8.

67. Nils Nilsson and John McCarthy interview, September 12, 2007, Computer History Museum: http://www.computerhistory.org/collections/catalog/102658149.

68. Allison Tracy and Edward Albert Feigenbaum interview, Stanford Historical Society Oral History Program, 2012, p. 20.

69. Stanford News, "Neuroscience Pioneer Marc Tessier-Lavigne Named Stanford's Next President," February 4, 2016: http://news.stanford.edu/features/2016/president-named/.

70. Stanford University, "OTL and the Inventor: Roles in Technology Transfer," retrieved October 22, 2016: http://otl.stanford.edu/inventors/resources/inventors_otlandinvent.html.

71. Lisa M. Krieger, "Stanford Earns $336 Million off Google Stock," *The San Jose Mercury News*, December 1, 2005, p. A1.

72. Stanford News, "Jen-Hsun Huang Pledges $30 Million for Innovative Engineering Center at Stanford," September 10, 2008: http://news.stanford.edu/pr/2008/pr-building-092408.html.

73. See Stanford University, "Fact Sheet: Sustainable Demolition—Frederick E. Terman Engineering Center": http://sustainable.stanford.edu/sites/default/files/documents/FactSheet_SustainableDemolition.pdf.

74. Kathleen J. Sullivan, "Excavator Tears down Walls, Ceilings and Floors of Terman Engineering Center," Stanford News, October 18, 2011.

3. Bill Gates

1. David K. Allison, "Transcript of a Video History Interview with Mr. William 'Bill' Gates," National Museum of American History, Smithsonian Institution: http://americanhistory.si.edu/comphist/gates.htm. "A major milestone for us was when we were walking through Harvard Square, one time, and saw this *Popular Electronics* magazine. And it was kind of in a way, good news and bad news. Here was someone making a computer around this chip in exactly the way that Paul had talked to me, and we'd thought about what kind of software could be done for it, and it was happening without us."

2. Walter Isaacson, "Dawn of a Revolution," *The Harvard Gazette*, September 20, 2013.

3. Stephen Manes and Paul Andrews, *Gates: How Microsoft's Mogul Reinvented an Industry—and Made Himself the Richest Man in America*, New York: Touchstone, 1994.

4. James Wallace and Jim Erickson, *Hard Drive: Bill Gates and the Making of the Microsoft Empire*, New York: Harper Collins, 1993, pp. 46–47.

5. Allison and Gates interview.

6. Ibid.

7. Ibid., p. 33.

8. Isaacson, "Dawn of a Revolution."

9. See Steven Levy, *Hackers: Heroes of the Computer Revolution*, Penguin Books, New York, 2001 (original 1984), pp. 224–243.

10. Allison and Gates interview.

11. Manes and Andrews, *Gates*, p. 26.

12. Daniel Golden and John Yemma, "Harvard Amasses a Colossal Endowment," *The Boston Globe*, May 31, 1988, p. A1.

13. Allison and Gates interview.

14. Scott Malone, "Dropout Bill Gates Returns to Harvard for Degree," Reuters, June 7, 2007: http://www.reuters.com/article/us-microsoft-gates-idUSN0730259120070607.

15. William Henry Gates III, "An Open Letter to Hobbyists," Homebrew Computer Club Newsletter, vol. 2, no. 1, January 31, 1976, p. 2.

16. *Homebrew Computer Club Newsletter*, vol. 1, no. 1, March 15, 1975.

17. Y Combinator, "Mark Zuckerberg at Startup School 2013" (2013), Zuckerberg Transcripts, Paper 160: http://dc.uwm.edu/zuckerberg_files_transcripts/160.

18. Bill Gates, @billgates, Twitter, May 15, 2017.

4. Marc Andreessen

1. Computer science's roots in artificial intelligence were a persistent concern for IBM, according to John McCarthy. "IBM thought that artificial intelligence was bad for IBM's image—that machines that were as smart as people and so forth were bad for their image. This may have been associated with one of their other image slogans, which was 'data processing, not computing.' That is, they were trying to get computing into business, so they wanted it to look as familiar and unfrightening as possible." John McCarthy, oral history interview with William Aspray, 1989, Charles Babbage Institute.

2. See Matthew Lyon and Katie Hafner, *Where Wizards Stay up Late: The Origins of the Internet*, New York: Simon & Schuster, 1999.

3. Tim Berners-Lee with Mark Fischetti, *Weaving the Web: The Original Design and Ultimate Destiny of the World Wide Web*, New York: Harper, 2000, pp. 12–13.

4. Tim Berners-Lee, "Frequently Asked Questions," on personal home page hosted by the World Wide Web Consortium (W3C): https://www.w3.org/People/Berners-Lee/FAQ.html.

5. See Tad Friend, "Tomorrow's Advance Man," *The New Yorker*, May 18, 2015.

6. Ben Horowitz, annotations to Tad Friend, "Tomorrow's Advance Man," at Genius.com: http://genius.com/summary/www.newyorker.com%2Fmagazine%2F2015%2F05%2F18%2Ftomorrows-advance-man?unwrappable=1.

7. Joshua Quittner and Michelle Slatalla, *Speeding the Net: The Inside*

Story of Netscape and How It Changed Microsoft, New York: Atlantic Monthly Press, 1998, pp. 12–13.

8. Marc Andreessen, Tweet, May 10, 2015.

9. Quittner and Slatalla, *Speeding the Net*, p. 14.

10. James Romenesko, "Netscape's Wonder Boy Says of His Wisconsin Life: Oh, Yuck!" St. Paul Pioneer Press, June 1, 1998, p. 3E.

11. Matt Beer, "Net Scope," *The San Francisco Examiner*, May 23, 1999.

12. Friend, "Tomorrow's Advance Man."

13. Marc Andreessen, Tweet, September 4, 2015.

14. Quittner and Slatalla, *Speeding the Net*, p. 15.

15. Beer, "Net Scope."

16. Ibid.

17. The National Science Foundation, "Cyberinfrastructure: From Supercomputing to the TeraGrid": https://www.nsf.gov/news/special_reports/cyber/fromsctotg.jsp.

18. Quittner and Slatalla, *Speeding the Net*, pp. 9–15.

19. Julie Bort, "Marc Andreessen Gets All the Credit for Inventing the Browser but This Is the Guy Who Did 'All the Hard Programming,'" *Business Insider*, May 12, 2014.

20. David A. Kaplan, "Nothing but Net," *Newsweek*, December 25, 1995, p. 32.

21. Marc Andreessen, "New 'XMosaic' World-Wide Web Browser from NCSA," January 23, 1993, message forwarded by Tim Berners-Lee to newsgroups alt.hypertext and comp.infosystems: http://www.bio.net/bionet/mm/bio-soft/1993-February/003879.html.

22. David K. Allison, "Excerpts from an Oral History Interview with Marc Andreessen," Smithsonian Institution, June 1995: http://americanhistory.si.edu/comphist/ma1.html.

23. John Markoff, "A Free and Simple Computer Link," December 8, 1993, p. D1.

24. Berners-Lee, *Weaving the Web*, p. 68.

25. Scott Laningham, "DeveloperWorks Interviews: Tim Berners-Lee," IBM, August 22, 2006: http://www.ibm.com/developerworks/podcast/dwi/cm-int082206txt.html.

26. Walter Isaacson, *The Innovators: How a Group of Hackers, Geniuses, and Geeks Created the Digital Revolution*, New York: Simon and Schuster, 2014, p. 417.

27. Berners-Lee, *Weaving the Web*, pp. 70–71.

28. John C. Thomson Jr., "Privatization of the New Communication Channel: Computer Networks and the Internet," Web paper on Internet privatization, Fall 2000: http://johnthomson.org/j561/index.html.

29. Ibid.

30. See Paul Andrews, "Profit Without Honor," *The Seattle Times*, October 5, 1997.

31. Laningham, "DeveloperWorks Interviews: Tim Berners-Lee."

32. Berners-Lee, *Weaving the* Web, p. 57.

33. Isaacson, *The Innovators*, p. 417.

34. Ibid.

35. Brad Stone, *The Everything Store: Jeff Bezos and the Age of Amazon*, New York: Little, Brown, 2013, p. 25.

36. Quittner and Slatalla, *Speeding the Net*, p. 74.

37. Allison, "Oral History Interview with Marc Andreessen."

38. John Markoff, "A Free and Simple Computer Link," *The New York Times*, December 8, 1993, p. D1.

39. Michael Lewis, *The New New Thing: A Silicon Valley Story*, New York: W. W. Norton, 2000, p. 81.

40. Andrews, "Profit Without Honor."

41. Kaplan, "Nothing but Net."

42. Adam Lashinsky, "Remembering Netscape: The Birth of the Web," *Fortune*, July 25, 2005.

43. Lewis, *The New New Thing*, p. 40.

44. Andrews, "Profit Without Honor."

45. Lou Montulli, interviewed by Brian McCullough, Internet History Podcast, episode 5, March 6, 2014: http://www.internethistorypodcast.com/2014/03/chapter-1-supplemental-1-an-interview-with-lou-montulli/.

46. See Jamie Zawinski, "The Condensed and Expurgated History of the About:authors URL": https://www.jwz.org/doc/about-authors.html. An early feature of the Netscape browser was the address about:authors, which would take users to a page listing the programming team responsible for the browser. The passage continues, "Thus it amounts to the same thing whether one gets drunk alone or is a leader of nations. If one of these activities takes precedence over the other . . . it will be the quietism of the solitary drunkard which will take precedence over the vain agitation of the leader of nations." Jean-Paul Sartre, *Being and Nothingness*, translated by Hazel E. Barnes, New York: Washington Square Press, 1993, p. 797.

47. Matthew Gray, "Measuring the Growth of the Web: June 1993 to June 1995," 1995: http://www.mit.edu/people/mkgray/growth/.

48. W. Joseph Campbell, "The '90s Startup That Terrified Microsoft and

Got Americans to Go Online," *Wired*, January 27, 2015: https://www.wired.com/2015/01/90s-startup-terrified-microsoft-got-americans-go-online/.

49. Marc Andreessen, Internet Gazette Multimedia Conference, San Francisco, November 5, 1994.

50. Ibid.

51. Allison, "Oral History Interview with Marc Andreessen."

52. Andrews, "Profit Without Honor."

53. Marc Andreessen, Twitter, January 12, 2014.

54. Andrews, "Profit Without Honor."

55. Andreessen, Internet Gazette Multimedia Conference.

56. Berners-Lee, *Weaving the Web.*

57. Lou Montulli, "The Reasoning Behind Web Cookies," The Irregular Musings of Lou Montulli Blog, May 14, 2013: http://www.montulli-blog.com/2013/05/the-reasoning-behind-web-cookies.html.

58. See Rajiv C. Shah and Jay P. Kesan, "Recipes for Cookies: How Institutions Shape Communication Technologies" (July 15, 2004), *New Media & Society*, May 1, 2009, vol. 11, no. 3: 315–336.

59. Lou Montulli, interviewed by Brian McCullough.

60. See Shah and Kesan, "Recipes for Cookies."

61. See user profile of blue_beetle, aka Andrew Lewis, who has made T-shirts featuring the phrase: http://www.metafilter.com/user/15556.

62. Tim Jackson, "This Bug in Your PC Is a Smart Cookie," *Financial Times*, February 12, 1996, p. 15.

63. Lee Gomes, "Web 'Cookies' May Be Spying on You," *The San Jose Mercury News*, February 13, 1996.

64. Montulli, "The Reasoning Behind Web Cookies." See also Lou Montulli, "Why Blocking 3rd Party Cookies Could Be a Bad Thing," The Irregular Musings of Lou Montulli Blog, May 17, 2013: http://www.montulli-blog.com/2013/05/why-blocking-3rd-party-cookies-could-be.html.

65. Lashinsky, "Remembering Netscape."

66. Ibid.

67. Ted Greenwald, "How Jimmy Wales' Wikipedia Harnessed the Web as a Force for Good," *Wired*, March 19, 2013.

68. Lashinsky, "Remembering Netscape."

69. Estimates vary about market share, but one reliable tracker at the time based at the University of Illinois, Urbana-Champaign, came up with these figures. Accessed via the Wayback Machine, which takes snapshots of Web sites: https://web.archive.org/web/20010507150536, http://www.ews.uiuc.edu/bstats/months/9710-month.html.

70. Campbell, "The '90s Startup."

71. Quittner and Slatalla, *Speeding the Net*, pp. 76–77.

72. John Perry Barlow, "A Declaration of the Independence of Cyberspace," February 8, 1996: https://www.eff.org/cyberspace-independence.

73. Lashinsky, "Remembering Netscape."

74. Kaplan, "Nothing but Net," p. 32.

75. Marc Andreessen, "Why Software Is Eating the World," *The Wall Street Journal*, August 20, 2011.

76. Todd Rulon-Miller, who became Netscape's vice president of sales, described his interview with Andreessen, who was twenty-three at the time. "He was on a workstation staring intently into the screen. I don't think he looked at me. I sat in a chair next to him. He was playing Doom." In Lashinksy, "Remembering Netscape."

77. Friend, "Tomorrow's Advance Man."

78. Mary Anne Ostrom, "From Peak to Valley; Andreessen Offers Perspective on Good Times and Hard Times in Tech," *The San Jose Mercury News*, March 6, 2003, 1C.

79. Marc Andreessen, posts to Twitter, July 13, 2014.

80. Sam Biddle, "Deep Thoughts with Marc Andreessen: The Poor Have It Pretty Good!," *ValleyWag*, June 4, 2014.

81. Maya Kosoff, "Marc Andreessen Quit Twitter and Now He Feels 'Free as a Bird,'" VanityFair.com, September 30, 2016.

82. Berners-Lee, *Weaving the Web*, p. 2.

83. Ibid., pp. 107–108.

84. Ibid., pp. 30–31.

5. Jeff Bezos

1. Marc Andreessen, Internet Gazette Multimedia Conference, San Francisco, November 5, 1994.

2. Charles King, "1995: The Year the Internet Transformed Business," Pund-It blog, July 15, 2015: http://www.pund-it.com/blog/1995-the-year-the-internet-transformed-business/.

3. Jessica Livingston, *Founders at Work: Stories of Startups' Early Days*, Berkeley, CA: Apress, 2008, pp. 248–249.

4. Craigslist, "About: Expansion": https://www.craigslist.org/about/expansion.

5. Livingston, *Founders at Work,* p. 250.

6. Jessica Mintz, "Craigslist Chief Executive Tells Investment Community Users, not Money, Drives Business," Associated Press, December 7, 2006.

7. See Adam Cohen, *The Perfect Store: Inside eBay*, New York: Little, Brown, 2003.

8. Ibid., p. 25.

9. Ibid., p. 76.

10. Our History, eBay Web site: https://www.ebayinc.com/our-company/our-history/.

11. Cohen, *The Perfect Store*, p. 76.

12. Randall Stross, *eBoys: The First Inside Account of Venture Capitalists at Work*, New York: Crown Publishing Group, 2001, p. xv.

13. Peter de Jonge, "Riding the Wild, Perilous Waters of Amazon.com," *The New York Times Magazine*, March 14, 1999.

14. Les Earnest, "Automatic Investments," SAIL Sagas, December 13, 2009: https://web.stanford.edu/~learnest/spin/sagas.htm.

15. David Shaw, email re: 2009 SAIL Reunion, October 29, 2009, accessed via Regrets Web page: https://web.stanford.edu/~learnest/spin/regrets.htm.

16. "Biophysicist in Profile: David E. Shaw," Biophysical Society Newsletter, January 2016, pp. 2–3: https://biophysics.cld.bz/Biophysical-Society-Newsletter-January-2016/2#2/z.

17. James Aley, "Wall Street's King Quant David Shaw's Secret Formulas Pile up Money. Now He Wants a Piece of the Net," *Fortune*, February 5, 1996.

18. Michael Peltz, "The Power of Six," Institutional Investors' Alpha, March 2009.

19. Stone, *The Everything Store*, p. 27.

20. Aley, "Wall Street's King Quant."

21. Ibid.

22. Joel Shurkin, *Broken Genius: The Rise and Fall of William Shockley, Creator of the Electronic Age*, New York: Macmillan, 2006, p. 164.

23. C. Stewart Gillmor, *Fred Terman at Stanford: Building a Discipline, a University, and Silicon Valley*, Stanford, CA: Stanford University Press, 2004, p. 11.

24. See "The High Cost of Thinking the Unthinkable," in Shurkin, *Broken Genius*, pp. 241–256.

25. Stone, *The Everything Store*, p. 20.

26. Jeff Bezos, "We Are What We Choose," Baccalaureate Remarks at Princeton University, May 30, 2010: http://www.princeton.edu/main/news/archive/S27/52/51O99/index.xml.

27. De Jonge, "Riding the Wild, Perilous Waters of Amazon.com."

28. Department of Computer Science Alumni News, University of Illinois, Urbana-Champaign, Summer 2001, vol. 2, no. 6, p. 10: http://www.cs.uiuc.edu/sites/default/files/newsletters/summer01.pdf.

29. Craig Cannon, "Employee #1: Amazon," Y Combinator blog, September 6, 2016: http://blog.ycombinator.com/employee-1-amazon/.

30. Ibid.

31. John Cook, "Meet Amazon.com's First Employee: Shel Kaphan," *GeekWire*, June 14, 2011: http://www.geekwire.com/2011/meet-shel-kaphan-amazoncom-employee-1/.

32. Stone, *The Everything Store*, p. 40.

33. Stone, *The Everything Store*, p. 37.

34. Cook, "Meet Amazon.com's First Employee."

35. Cannon, "Employee #1."

36. De Jonge, "Riding the Wild, Perilous Waters of Amazon.com."

37. Tonya Garcia, "Amazon Will Account for More Than Half of 2015 E-commerce Growth, Says Macquarie," *MarketWatch*, December 22, 2015: http://www.marketwatch.com/story/amazon-will-account-for-more-than-half-of-2015-e-commerce-growth-says-macquarie-2015-12-22.

38. "Amazon.com Announces Fourth Quarter Sales up 22% to $35.7 Billion," *BusinessWire*, January 28, 2016: http://www.businesswire.com/news/home/20160128006357/en/Amazon.com-Announces-Fourth-Quarter-Sales-22-35.7.

39. Jodi Kantor and David Streitfeld, "Amazon's Bruising, Thrilling Workplace," *The New York Times*, August 16, 2015, p. A1.

40. See, e.g., Spencer Soper, "Inside Amazon's Warehouse," *The Morning Call* (Allentown, PA), September 18, 2011; Spencer Soper, "Amazon Workers Left out in the Cold," *The Morning Call* (Allentown, PA), November 6, 2011; Hamilton Nolan, "True Stories of Life as an Amazon Worker," *Gawker*, August 2, 2013: http://gawker.com/true-stories-of-life-as-an-amazon-worker-1002568208.

41. Jeff Bezos, "Amazon Chief's Message to Employees," *The New York Times*, August 18, 2015, p. B3.

6. Sergey Brin and Larry Page

1. Sergey Brin and Lawrence Page, "The Anatomy of a Large-Scale Hypertextual Web Search Engine," Seventh International World-Wide Web Conference (WWW 1998), April 14–18, 1998, Brisbane, Australia.

2. Marc Andreessen, Internet Gazette Multimedia Conference, San Francisco, November 5, 1994.

3. Ibid.

4. Katherine Losse, *The Boy Kings: A Journey into the Heart of the Social Network*, New York: Free Press, 2012, p. 6.

5. Steven Levy, *In the Plex: How Google Thinks, Works, and Shapes Our Lives*, New York: Simon and Schuster, 2011, pp. 19–20.

6. Brin and Page, "The Anatomy of a Large-Scale Hypertextual Web Search Engine."

7. Christopher Lyle and Ravi Sarin, "Googles of Dollars," *The Stanford Daily*, April 11, 2000, p. B1.

8. Levy, *In the Plex*, p. 21.

9. Brin and Page, "The Anatomy of a Large-Scale Hypertextual Web Search Engine."

10. Lawrence Page, Sergey Brin, Rajeev Motwani, and Terry Winograd, "The PageRank Citation Ranking: Bringing Order to the Web," Technical Report (1999), Stanford InfoLab, pp. 11–12: http://ilpubs.stanford.edu:8090/422/.

11. Levy, *In the Plex*, p. 35.

12. John Markoff, interview with John McCarthy, July 19, 2002, personal copy.

13. Brin and Page, "The Anatomy of a Large-Scale Hypertextual Web Search Engine," p. 3.

14. Ibid.

15. Ibid., p. 18.

16. Ibid., p. 19.

17. Google Inc. press release: "Google Receives $25 Million in Equity Funding: Sequoia Capital and Kleiner Perkins Lead Investment; General Partners Michael Moritz and John Doerr Join Board," June 7, 1999: http://googlepress.blogspot.com/1999/06/google-receives-25-million-in-equity.html.

18. Stanford School of Engineering Web site, "Gates Computer Science Building": https://www-cs.stanford.edu/about/gates-computer-science-building.

19. Levy, *In the Plex*, p. 23.

20. Eli Pariser, *The Filter Bubble: How the New Personalized Web Is Changing What We Read and How We Think*, New York: Penguin, 2011, p. 31.

21. Levy, *In the Plex*, p. 27.

22. Ibid., p. 13.

23. David K. Allison, "Excerpts from an Oral History Interview with Marc Andreessen," Smithsonian Institution, June 1995: http://americanhistory.si.edu/comphist/ma1.html.

24. John F. Ince, "The Lost Google Tapes: Conversations Tape-Recorded in the Early Years with Google's Founders Illuminate How Their Actions Forged the Growth of a Silicon Valley Giant," *The San Francisco Chronicle*, December 3, 2006.

25. Jessica Livingston, *Founders at Work: Stories of Startups' Early Days*, Berkeley, CA: Apress, 2008, p. 128.

26. Ibid., p. 134.

27. Ibid.

28. Peter Sinton, "Sequoia Grows Ventures," *The San Francisco Chronicle*, April 17, 1996, p. B1.

29. David F. Salisbury, "Yahoo! Founders Endow New Stanford Chair," Stanford News, February 12, 1997: http://news.stanford.edu/pr/97/970212 yahoo.html.

30. Mark Shwartz, "Alumni Couple Yang and Yamazaki Pledge $75 Million to the University," Stanford News, February 15, 2007: http://news .stanford.edu/news/2007/february21/donors-022107.html.

31. Ince, "The Lost Google Tapes."

32. Levy, *In the Plex*, p. 33.

33. Jacob Jolis, "Frugal After Google," *The Stanford Daily*, April 16, 2010, p. 3.

34. Levy, *In the Plex*, p. 34; and Jolis, "Frugal After Google."

35. Ince, "The Lost Google Tapes."

36. Ken Auletta, "Googled: The End of the World as We Know It," New York: Penguin Press, 2009, p. 44.

37. Levy, *In the Plex*, p. 74.

38. Ince, "The Lost Google Tapes."

39. See Levy, *In the Plex*, pp. 136–142.

40. Auletta, "Googled," p. 56.

41. Levy, *In the Plex*, p. 79.

42. Auletta, "Googled," pp. 66–68.

43. Levy, *In the Plex, Part Two: Googlenomics*, pp. 69–120.

44. Stefanie Olsen, "Google Files for Unusual $2.7 billion IPO," CNet, April 30, 2004.

45. Brin and Page, "The Anatomy of a Large-Scale Hypertextual Web Search Engine."

46. Harvard University, "CS50 Guest Lecture by Mark Zuckerberg" (2005), Zuckerberg Transcripts, Paper 141: http://dc.uwm.edu /zuckerberg_files_transcripts/141.

47. Lisa M. Krieger, "Stanford Earns $336 Million off Google Stock," *The San Jose Mercury News*, December 1, 2005, p. A1.

48. The Thiel Fellowship Web site home page: http://thielfellowship.org/.

7. PETER THIEL

1. For Thiel biography, see George Packer, *The Unwinding: An Inner History of the New America*, New York: Farrar, Straus and Giroux, 2013, pp. 120–136, 209–216, 381–397.

2. Stanford Technology Ventures Program, Thiel and Levchin, "Entrepreneurial Thought Leader Speaker Series," January 21, 2004.

3. Max Levchin and Peter Thiel, "PayPal Cofounders Met in Terman at a Seminar," Stanford eCorner, January 21, 2004: http://ecorner.stanford.edu/videos/1022/Paypal-Cofounders-Met-in-Terman-at-a-Seminar.

4. Eric M. Jackson, *The PayPal Wars: Battles with eBay, the Media, the Mafia, and the Rest of Planet Earth*, Washington, D.C.: WND Books, 2012, p. 5.

5. "A Conversation with Max Levchin," *The Charlie Rose Show*, August 1, 2013.

6. Jessica Livingston, *Founders at Work: Stories of Startups' Early Days*, New York: Apress, 2008, pp. 1–16.

7. Jackson, *The PayPal Wars*, p. 19.

8. Peter Thiel, "Address to Republican National Convention," Cleveland, OH, July 21, 2016, C-Span: https://www.c-span.org/video/?c4612796/peter-thiel-addresses-republican-national-convention-proud-gay.

9. Packer, *The Unwinding*, pp. 120–121

10. Peter Thiel with Blake Masters, *Zero to One: Notes on Startups, or How to Build the Future*, New York: Penguin Random House, 2014, p. 37.

11. Isaac Barchas, "The Voice of the Right," *The Stanford Daily*, February 23, 1989, p. 4.

12. David O. Sacks and Peter A. Thiel, *The Diversity Myth: "Multiculturalism" and the Politics of Intolerance at Stanford*, Oakland, CA: The Independent Institute, 1995, p. xxi.

13. Ibid., p. 152

14. Ibid., p. 140.

15. Ibid., p. 238.

16. Brad Hayward, "Report Explores Motives of Frosh," *The Stanford Daily*, January 18, 1989, p. 1.

17. Sacks and Thiel, *The Diversity Myth*, p. 41.

18. Ibid.

19. Brad Hayward, "Ujamaa Case Ends Without Charges," *The Stanford Daily*, February 10, 1989, p. 1.

20. See Sacks and Thiel, *The Diversity Myth*, pp. 169–174.

21. Keith Rabois, "Rabois: My Intention Was to Make a Provocative Statement," *The Stanford Daily*, February 7, 1992, p. 5.

22. Juthymas Harntha, "Two Students Can't Be Charged for Hurling Homophobic Slurs," *The Stanford Daily*, February 3, 1992, p. 1.

23. See Sacks and Thiel, *The Diversity Myth*, p. 174.

24. Jackson, *The PayPal Wars*, p. 204.

25. Sacks and Thiel, *The Diversity Myth*, p. 147.

26. Owen Thomas, "Peter Thiel Is Totally Gay, People," *Gawker*, December 19, 2007: http://gawker.com/335894/peter-thiel-is-totally-gay-people.

27. Connie Loizos, "Peter Thiel on Valleywag; It's the 'Silicon Valley Equivalent of Al Qaeda,'" *PE Hub*, May 18, 2009.

28. Jeffrey Toobin, "Gawker's Demise and the Trump-Era Threat to the First Amendment," *The New Yorker*, December 19–26, 2016.

29. Ibid. and Andrew Ross Sorkin, "Tech Billionaire in a Secret War with Gawker," *The New York Times*, p. A1, May 26, 2016.

30. Julia Carrie Wong, "Peter Thiel, Who Gave $1.25m to Trump, Has Called Date Rape 'Belated Regret,'" *The Guardian*, October 21, 2016.

31. Ryan Mac and Matt Drange, "Donald Trump Supporter Peter Thiel Apologizes for Past Book Comments on Rape," Forbes.com, October 25, 2016.

32. Sacks and Thiel, *The Diversity Myth*, p. 59.

33. Ibid., pp. 58–59.

34. "Undergraduate Senators," *The Stanford Daily*, April 9, 1987, p. 6.

35. Katie Mauro, "4 Groups Denied Spot on Fee-Request Ballot," *The Stanford Daily*, February 27, 1992, p. 1.

36. Elise Wolfgram, "Groups Cry Foul on Granting of Funds to Review," *The Stanford Daily*, May 29, 1992, p. 1.

37. Thiel, *Zero to One*, pp. 36–37.

38. Peter Thiel on the Future of Innovation with Tyler Cowen, "Conversations with Tyler," Mercatus Center, April 6, 2015: https://medium.com/conversations-with-tyler/peter-thiel-on-the-future-of-innovation-77628a43c0dd#.bav03wzih.

39. Kevin Wacknov, "Championship Stanford Chess Team Never Board," *The Stanford Daily*, December 2, 1986, p. 7.

40. Thiel, *Zero to One*, p. 141.

41. "A Conversation with Max Levchin," *The Charlie Rose Show*.

42. Peter Thiel, *Zero to One*, p. 173.

43. See PayPal slide show at Max Levchin Web site: July 1999 staff photo: http://levchin.com/paypal-slideshow/2.html.

44. Thiel, *Zero to One*, p. 122.

45. Jackson, *The PayPal Wars*, p. 19.

46. Ibid., p. 92.

47. Peter Thiel with Tyler Cowen, "Conversations With Tyler."

48. Levchin and Thiel, Stanford eCorner.

49. Jackson, *The PayPal Wars*, p. 33.

50. Ibid., pp. 44–46.

51. Levchin and Thiel, Stanford eCorner.

52. See Jackson, *The PayPal Wars*, passim 51–126.

53. Livingston, *Founders at Work*, p. 10.

54. Levchin and Thiel, Stanford eCorner.

55. Jackson, *The PayPal Wars*, p. 152.

56. Max Levchin, "Data and Risk," DLD13 Keynote, January 21, 2013.

57. Bloomberg News, "EBay Settles Suit by PayPal Customers," *The Los Angeles Times*, Junc 15, 2004, p. C5.

58. PayPal, S-1 Filing with the S.E.C., September 28, 2001: http://www.nasdaq.com/markets/ipos/filing.ashx?filingid=1557068.

59. Jackson, *The PayPal Wars*, p. 189.

60. Ibid., p. 212.

61. Margaret Kane, "EBay Picks up PayPal for $1.5 Billion," Cnet, August 18, 2002.

62. Jackson, *The PayPal Wars*, p. 228.

63. Brian Caulfield and Nicole Perlroth, "Life After Facebook," *Forbes*, January 26, 2011.

64. Andy Greenberg and Ryan Mac, "How a 'Deviant' Philosopher Built Palantir, a CIA-Funded Data-Mining Juggernaut," *Forbes*, August 14, 2013.

65. Peter Thiel, "Ask Me Anything," Reddit, September 11, 2014: https://www.reddit.com/r/IAmA/comments/2g4g95/peter_thiel_technology_entrepreneur_and_investor/.

66. See Timothy B. Lee, "Peter Thiel Thought About the Election like a Venture Capitalist," *Vox*, November 11, 2016.

67. Casey Newton, "Mark Zuckerberg Defends Peter Thiel's Trump Ties in Internal Memo," *The Verge*, October 19, 2016.

68. George Packer, "No Death, No Taxes," *The New Yorker*, November 28, 2011.

69. Peter Thiel with Tyler Cowen, "Conversations with Tyler."

70. Nathan Ingraham, "Larry Page Wants to 'Set Aside a Part of the World' for Unregulated Experimentation," *The Verge*, May 15, 2013.

71. Peter Thiel, "The Education of a Libertarian," *Cato Unbound* blog, April 13, 2009.

72. Thiel, *Zero to One*, p. 24.

73. Ibid., pp. 24–25.

74. Farhad Manjoo, "Why Facebook Keeps Beating Every Rival: It's the Network, of Course," *The New York Times*, April 19, 2017.

75. Thiel, *Zero to One*, p. 32.

76. Max Levchin, *The Charlie Rose Show.*

77. Thiel, *Zero to One*, p. 26.

78. *Time* magazine cover, February 19, 1996.

79. Jeffrey M. O'Brien, "The PayPal Mafia," *Fortune*, November 26, 2007.

8. Reid Hoffman et al.

1. Gary Rivlin, "If You Can Make It in Silicon Valley, You Can Make It . . . in Silicon Valley Again," *The New York Times Magazine*, June 5, 2005, p. 64.

2. Internet Live Stats, "United States Internet Users, 2000–2016": http://www.internetlivestats.com/internet-users/us/.

3. Internet Live Stats, "Internet Users," http://www.internetlivestats.com/internet-users/.

4. D. Steven White, "U.S. E-Commerce Growth: 2000–2009," August 20, 2010: http://dstevenwhite.com/2010/08/20/u-s-e-commerce-growth-2000-2009/.

5. Scott Laningham, "DeveloperWorks Interviews: Tim Berners-Lee," IBM, August 22, 2006: http://www.ibm.com/developerworks/podcast/dwi/cm-int082206txt.html.

6. John Cloud, "The YouTube Gurus," *Time*, December 25, 2006.

7. Matt Richter, "Napster Appeals an Order to Remain Closed Down," *The New York Times*, July 13, 2001, p. 4.

8. Katie Hafner, "We're Google. So Sue Us," *The New York Times*, October 23, 2006, p. C1.

9. Jeffrey Rosen, "Inconspicuous Consumption," *The New York Times Book Review*, November 27, 2011, p. 18.

10. Miguel Helft, "It Pays to Have Pals in Silicon Valley," *The New York Times*, October 17, 2006, p. C1.

11. Rivlin, "If You Can Make It in Silicon Valley."

12. Eric M. Jackson, *The PayPal Wars: Battles with eBay, the Media, the Mafia, and the Rest of Planet Earth*, Washington, D.C.: WND Books, 2012, p. 24.

13. Ibid.

14. Reid Hoffman and Ben Casnocha, *The Start-up of You: Adapt to the Future, Invest in Yourself, and Transform Your Career*, New York: Crown Business, 2012, pp. 159–161.

15. Thomas Friedman, "The World Is Flat: A Brief History of the 21st Century," New York: Farrar, Straus and Giroux, 2005, p. 75.

16. Hoffman and Casnocha, *The Start-up of You*, p. 15.

17. Ibid., p. 19.

18. Ibid., p. 36.

19. Ibid., p. 239 (footnote 4, chapter 1).

20. Packer, "No Death, No Taxes."

21. Ibid., p. 19.

9. Jimmy Wales

1. Ted Greenwald, "How Jimmy Wales' Wikipedia Harnessed the Web as a Force for Good," *Wired*, March 19, 2013.

2. Bomis Sign-Up Page, accessed through the Wayback Machine, May 8, 1999: http://web.archive.org/web/19990508174513/http://my.bomis.com/member/signup.

3. Stacy Schiff, "Know It All," *The New Yorker*, July 31, 2006; Katherine Mangu-Ward, "Wikipedia and Beyond," *Reason*, June 2007.

4. See Zach Schwartz, "An Interview with the Founder of Wikipedia," Zach Two Times Blog, November 19, 2015: http://zachtwotimes.blogspot.com/2015/11/an-interview-with-founder-of-wikipedia.html.

5. Larry Sanger, "The Early History of Nupedia and Wikipedia: A Memoir," *Slashdot*, April 18, 2005: https://features.slashdot.org/story/05/04/18/164213/the-early-history-of-nupedia-and-wikipedia-a-memoir.

6. Terry Foote, e-mail with author, July 19, 2016.

7. Schwartz, "An Interview with the Founder of Wikipedia."

8. Wikipedia: Multilingual ranking January 2002: https://en.wikipedia.org/wiki/Wikipedia:Multilingual_ranking_January_2002.

9. Larry Sanger, "What Wikipedia Is and Why It Matters," talk to Stanford University Computer Systems Laboratory EE380 Colloquium, January 16, 2002: https://meta.wikimedia.org/wiki/Wikipedia_and_why_it_matters.

10. Larry Sanger, "The Early History of Nupedia and Wikipedia, Part II," *Slashdot*, April 19, 2005: https://slashdot.org/story/05/04/19/1746205/the-early-history-of-nupedia-and-wikipedia-part-ii.

11. Terry Foote, e-mail with author, July 22, 2016.

12. Larry Sanger, "Announcement About My Involvement in Wikipedia and Nupedia," February 13, 2002: https://meta.wikimedia.org/w/index.php?title=Announcement_about_my_involvement_in_Wikipedia_and_Nupedia--Larry_Sanger&action=history.

13. Nathaniel Tkacz, "The Spanish Fork: Wikipedia's Ad-Fuelled Mutiny," *Wired UK*, January 20, 2011.

14. Terry Foote e-mail, July 22, 2016.

15. "Wikia Continues Global Expansion with $15 Million in D-Round Funding," *PR Newswire*, August 27, 2014: http://www.prnewswire.com/news-releases/wikia-continues-global-expansion-with-15-million-in-d-round-funding-272899031.html.

16. Wikimedia Foundation Inc., "Financial Statements," June 30, 2016 and 2015 (With Independent Auditors Report Thereon): https://upload.wikimedia.org/wikipedia/foundation/4/43/Wikimedia_Foundation_Audit_Report_-_FY15-16.pdf.

17. "Wikipedia Founder Jimmy Wales Responds," *Slashdot*, July 28, 2004: https://slashdot.org/story/04/07/28/1351230/wikipedia-founder-jimmy-wales-responds.

18. Jimmy Wales, "Keep Wikipedia Free": https://wikimediafoundation.org/wiki/Keep_Wikipedia_Free.

19. Sarah Mitroff, "Craig Newmark Sits at the Top and Bottom of Craigslist," *Wired*, July 16, 2012: https://www.wired.com/2012/07/craig-newmark/.

10. Mark Zuckerberg

1. Michael M. Grynbaum, "Mark E. Zuckerberg '06: The Whiz Behind Thefacebook.com," *The Harvard Crimson*, June 10, 2004.

2. Joseph Weizenbaum, "Computer Power and Human Reason: From Judgment to Calculation," New York: W.H. Freeman and Company, 1976, p. 115.

3. Jose Antonio Vargas, "The Face of Facebook," *The New Yorker*, September 20, 2010.

4. Designing Media, "Designing Media: Mark Zuckerberg Interview" (2010), Zuckerberg Transcripts, Paper 73: http://dc.uwm.edu/zuckerberg_files_transcripts/73.

5. Synapse promotional copy found on Myce.com, April 24, 2003: http://www.myce.com/news/Intelligent-MP3-player-plays-the-right-song-at-the-right-moment-5776/.

6. "Machine Learning and MP3s," *Slashdot*, April 21, 2003: https://news.slashdot.org/story/03/04/21/110236/machine-learning-and-mp3s.

7. S. F. Brickman, "Not-so-Artificial Intelligence," *The Harvard Crimson*, October 23, 2003.

8. Mark Zuckerberg interview, Y Combinator, Startup School 2013, October 25, Zuckerberg Transcripts, Paper 160: http://dc.uwm.edu/zuckerberg_files_transcripts/160.

9. Mark Zuckerberg interview, Idea to Product Latin America, October 13, 2009, Zuckerberg Transcripts, Paper 92: http://dc.uwm.edu/zuckerberg_files_transcripts/92.

10. Mark Zuckerberg interview, Y Combinator, Startup School 2012, October 20, Zuckerberg Transcripts, Paper 161: http://dc.uwm.edu/zuckerberg_files_transcripts/161.

11. Zuckerberg, Y Combinator (2013).

12. Bonnie Goldstein, "The Diaries of Facebook Founder," *Slate*, November 30, 2007.

13. Bari M. Schwartz, "Hot or Not? Website Briefly Judges Looks," *The Harvard Crimson* November 4, 2003.

14. Luke O'Brien, "Poking Facebook," *02138*, November/December 2007, accessed via Wayback Machine: https://web.archive.org/web/20080514021019/http://www.02138mag.com/magazine/issue/58.html.

15. Zuckerberg, Y Combinator (2013).

16. The Harvard Crimson Staff, "M*A*S*H," *The Harvard Crimson*, November 6, 2003.

17. Matthew Shaer, "The Zuckerbergs of Dobbs Ferry, New York," *New York Magazine*, May 6, 2012.

18. Mark Zuckerberg, interview for Justin.tv's Startup School 2010, October 19, Zuckerberg Transcripts, Paper 35: http://dc.uwm.edu/zuckerberg_files_transcripts/35

19. See Richard Pérez-Peña, "To Young Minds of Today, Harvard Is the Stanford of the East," *The New York Times*, May 30, 2014, p. A1.

20. Ibid.

21. See O'Brien, "Poking Facebook," for the history of the development of Harvard Connection and thefacebook.com.

22. Grynbaum, "Mark E. Zuckerberg '06."

23. Alan J. Tabak, "Hundreds Register for New Facebook Website," *The Harvard Crimson*, February 9, 2004.

24. O'Brien, "Poking Facebook."

25. Brad Stone, "ConnectU's 'Secret' $65 Million Settlement with Facebook," *The New York Times*, Bits blog, February 10, 2009.

26. Matt Welsh, "In Defense of Mark Zuckerberg," Volatile and Decentralized blog, October 10, 2010: http://matt-welsh.blogspot.com/2010/10/in-defense-of-mark-zuckerberg.html.

27. John Cassidy, "Me Media," *The New Yorker*, May 15, 2006.

28. Tabak, "Hundreds Register for New Facebook Website."

29. Bianca Bosker, "Facebook's Mark Zuckerberg, Barefoot with Beer: 2005 Interview Reveals CEO's Doubts (VIDEO)," *The Huffington Post*, August 11, 2011, http://www.huffingtonpost.com/2011/08/11/facebook-mark-zuckerberg-2005-interview_n_924628.html; Transcript via Zuckerberg Transcripts, Paper 56: http://dc.uwm.edu/zuckerberg_files_transcripts/35.

30. Henry Blodget, "Mark Zuckerberg on How Facebook Became a Business" (2010), Zuckerberg Transcripts, Paper 8: http://dc.uwm.edu/zuckerberg_files_transcripts/8.

31. Welsh, "In Defense of Mark Zuckerberg."

32. Grynbaum, "Mark E. Zuckerberg '06."

33. Cassidy, "Me Media."

34. Zuckerberg, Y Combinator (2012): "Q. Why did you choose ones that had school specific social network?

Mark Zuckerberg: Because I wanted to—

Q: Because they could become competitors?

Mark Zuckerberg: Well I wanted to go to the schools that I thought would be the hardest for us to succeed at."

35. Zuckerberg, Y Combinator (2013).

36. Blodget, "Mark Zuckerberg on How Facebook Became a Business."

37. Brian Caulfield and Nicole Perlroth, "Life After Facebook," *Forbes*, January 26, 2011.

38. Zuckerberg, Y Combinator (2013).

39. David Kushner, "The Baby Billionaires of Silicon Valley," *Rolling Stone*, November 16, 2006.

40. Stanford University, "James Breyer/Mark Zuckerberg Interview, October 26, 2005, Stanford University" (2005), Zuckerberg Transcripts, Paper 116: http://dc.uwm.edu/zuckerberg_files_transcripts/116.

41. Zuckerberg, Y Combinator (2013).

42. Dealbook, "Tracking Facebook's Valuation," *The New York Times*, February 1, 2012.

43. Stanford University, "James Breyer/Mark Zuckerberg Interview."

44. David Kushner, "Being Mark Zuckerberg," IEE E Spectrum blog, September 16, 2010, http://spectrum.ieee.org/tech-talk/geek-life/profiles/being-mark-zuckerberg.

45. Biana Bosker, "Facebook's Mark Zuckerberg, Barefoot With Beer: 2005 Interview Reveals CEO's Doubts (VIDEO)."

46. Mark Zuckerberg interview, Y Combinator, Startup School 2011, October 30. Zuckerberg Transcripts, Paper 76: http://dc.uwm.edu/zuckerberg_files_transcripts/76.

47. Stanford University, "James Breyer / Mark Zuckerberg Interview."

48. Zuckerberg, Y Combinator (2013).

49. Tad Friend, "Tomorrow's Advance Man," *The New Yorker*, May 18, 2015.

50. Peter Thiel with Blake Masters, *Zero to One: Notes on Startups, or How to Build the Future*, New York: Penguin Random House, 2014, p. 80.

51. Zuckerberg, Y Combinator (2011).

52. Sarah Lacy, *Once You're Lucky, Twice You're Good*, New York: Gotham Books, 2008, p. 182.

53. Zuckerberg, Y Combinator (2011).

54. Mark Zuckerberg, interview for Justin.tv's Startup School 2010.

55. Evelyn M. Rusli, "Profitable Learning Curve for Facebook CEO Mark Zuckerberg," *The Wall Street Journal*, January 5, 2014.

56. Gideon Lewis-Kraus, "The Great AI Awakening," *The New York Times Magazine*, December 14, 2016.

57. Mark Zuckerberg and Priscilla Chan, "A Letter to Our Daughter," December 1, 2015: https://www.facebook.com/notes/mark-zuckerberg/a-letter-to-our-daughter/10153375081581634/.

58. Mark Zuckerberg, "Our Commitment to the Facebook Community," note to Facebook's Facebook page, November 29, 2011: https://www.facebook.com/notes/facebook/our-commitment-to-the-facebook-community/10150378701937131/.

59. Video interview with Steve Jobs, "Memory and Imagination: New Pathways to the Library of Congress," directed by Julian Krainin and Michael R. Lawrence: https://www.youtube.com/watch?v=ob_GX50Za6c.

60. Zuckerberg, Y Combinator (2012).

61. Robin Dunbar, "You've Got to Have (150) Friends," *The New York Times*, December 25, 2010, p. WK15.

62. Ibid.

63. Ibid.

64. See Dale Russakoff, *The Prize: Who's in Charge of America's Schools?*, New York: Houghton Mifflin Harcourt, 2015.

65. Zuckerberg and Chan, "A Letter to Our Daughter."

66. Ibid.

67. Mark Zuckerberg, video, May 4, 2015, available at Mark Zuckerberg's Facebook page.

68. See Mahesh Murthy, "Internet.org Is Just a Facebook Proxy Targeting India's Poor," *Firstpost.com*, April 17, 2015.

69. Savetheinternet.in Coalition, "Dear Mark Zuckerberg, Facebook Is Not, and Should Not Be the Internet," *Hindustan Times*, April 17, 2015.

70. Adi Narayan, "Andreessen Regrets India Tweets; Zuckerberg Laments Comments," Bloomberg.com, February 10, 2016.

71. Mark Zuckerberg, video, May 4, 2015, available at Mark Zuckerberg's Facebook page.

72. Zuckerberg and Chan, "A Letter to Our Daughter."

THE FUTURE

1. George Packer, "No Death, No Taxes," *The New Yorker*, November 28, 2011.

2. John McCarthy, "Artificial Intelligence and Creativity," Century 21 lecture, January 30, 1968, audio file in KZSU Collection, Stanford Archive of Recorded Sound, Stanford University Libraries.

3. Peter Thiel, "Ask Me Anything," Reddit, September 11, 2014: https://www.reddit.com/r/IAmA/comments/2g4g95/peter_thiel_technology_entrepreneur_and_investor/.

4. Douglas Hofstadter, email re: 2009 SAIL Reunion, October 29, 2009, accessed via Regrets Web page: https://web.stanford.edu/~learnest/spin/regrets.htm.

5. Peter Thiel on the Future of Innovation with Tyler Cowen, "Conversations with Tyler," Mercatus Center, April 6, 2015: https://medium.com/conversations-with-tyler/peter-thiel-on-the-future-of-innovation-77628a43c0dd#.bav03wzih.

6. Mark Zuckerberg and Priscilla Chan, "A Letter to Our Daughter," December 1, 2015: https://www.facebook.com/notes/mark-zuckerberg/a-letter-to-our-daughter/10153375081581634/.

7. Mark Zuckerberg, "Building Global Community," Facebook, February 16, 2017, https://www.facebook.com/notes/mark-zuckerberg/building-global-community/10103508221158471/?pnref=story.

8. Daniel T. Rodgers, *The Age of Fracture*, Cambridge, MA: Harvard University Press, 2011, p. 194, discussing Michael Walzer, *Spheres of Justice: A Defense of Pluralism and Equality*, New York: Basic Books, 1983.

A NOTE TO THE READER

1. Diane Brady, "In Ben Horowitz's New Book, Women Are Markedly Absent," *Bloomberg Businessweek*, March 12, 2014.

2. Marc Andreessen, post to Twitter, March 12, 2014.

INDEX

ABOUT THE AUTHOR

Noam Cohen covered the influence of the Internet on the larger culture for the *New York Times*, where he wrote the Link by Link column, beginning in 2007. He lives in Brooklyn with his family. This is his first book.

CELEBRATING 25 YEARS OF INDEPENDENT PUBLISHING

Thank you for reading this book published by The New Press. The New Press is a nonprofit, public interest publisher celebrating its twenty-fifth anniversary in 2017. New Press books and authors play a crucial role in sparking conversations about the key political and social issues of our day.

We hope you enjoyed this book and that you will stay in touch with The New Press. Here are a few ways to stay up to date with our books, events, and the issues we cover:

- Sign up at www.thenewpress.com/subscribe to receive updates on New Press authors and issues and to be notified about local events
- Like us on Facebook: www.facebook.com/newpressbooks
- Follow us on Twitter: www.twitter.com/thenewpress

Please consider buying New Press books for yourself; for friends and family; or to donate to schools, libraries, community centers, prison libraries, and other organizations involved with the issues our authors write about.

The New Press is a 501(c)(3) nonprofit organization. You can also support our work with a tax-deductible gift by visiting www.thenewpress.com/donate.

BROTHER TERMITE

BROTHER TERMITE

PATRICIA ANTHONY

HARCOURT BRACE & COMPANY
NEW YORK SAN DIEGO LONDON

ISBN 0-15-114422-2

Designed by Lori J. McThomas
Printed in the United States of America

For Pat LoBrutto.
He always believed.

1

THE BULLETPROOF GLASS IN THE Oval Office windows cast a gloom over the day, the sort of greenish pall associated with bad storms. Appropriate clouds rose from the Ellipse, pluming easterly in the late autumn breeze. On E Street a string-straight line of troops prepared to advance. The White House chief of staff knew that had the French doors been open he would be hearing the chuck-chuck of the tear-gas guns, the rattle of the Uzis' rubber bullets, and the screams.

Eisenhower had warned him this would happen.

Doggedly he swiveled away from the riot, his leather chair squeaking, to face the mantelpiece and the portrait of Millard Fillmore that hung above it.

The door behind him opened with a click. His secretary announced, "Sir. The NSC's finally arrived through the Treasury Building tunnel. They're waiting for you."

Wearily he rested his chin on his hand. The President, in one of his frequent tutorials on politics, had assured his chief of staff that governments existed only by the apathy of the governed. The people outside, with their placards and Molotov cocktails, seemed troublesomely unapathetic.

With a surge of will he pictured himself as a pool. The riot and

the oil painting of Millard Fillmore were pebbles tossed into water. The ripples they made widened until the warm waves of their company gently rocked him.

The roundness of stones in the bottom of a stream; the circular pattern of fishes' scales. He sat in the silence of the huge office but pictured the triangular thrust of the Rockies with their beards of conical firs, shapes within shapes within shapes. Perhaps soon he would take a needed Colorado vacation. Perhaps one day he would do the unthinkable and retire.

"Sir? You hear me?"

"Yes." He refused to turn around.

Muffled footsteps on the thick wool carpet. Natalie came into view behind his left shoulder, just inside the range of his peripheral vision. Her blouse, sewn from a material of disorderly, multicolored shapes, sent chills of disquiet down his neck. To avoid the sight of that blouse, he moved his gaze toward the window and the riot again.

"Who are the demonstrators?" he asked.

"Germans, French, some Scandinavians," she replied, seating herself in the Louis XV chair next to his desk.

"What are they protesting?"

"The tariff bill. They think the Chinese and Koreans are about to undermine their economic freedom."

There was a new box of pencils on his desk. He picked up the container and slid off the top. Inside, pencil ends nested like flat, hexagonal atoms. He drank in the scent of wood and graphite, running his finger down the first queue. "This," he said fondly, "is freedom."

Holding the corner pencil down, he upended the box, letting the others spill onto the desk. Then he righted the case and lifted his opposable claw from the single survivor. The pencil toppled from its pleasant upright alignment and fell against the side of its container. "That is freedom to you," he said.

Natalie pondered the box, then picked up a pencil from the heap and dropped it, with a dull tap, in with the other. "It looked lonely," she explained.

In the box the two pencils lay at an antagonistic angle. Yes, he had missed the point. Two crossed pencils were more symbolic of what humans judged to be freedom.

"There are plots to kill me," he told her.

"I know."

"Who could be behind it?"

"Anyone," she said with a shrug. "Everyone."

He peered down the long velveteen spread of the south lawn to the single army tank at the barricade and the advancing troops behind it. The helmets of the UN peacekeeping forces were an inappropriately cheerful sky blue. "They expect me to do something, but I don't understand tariffs. And why should economics be so important?"

"Pocketbook issues always get people into a sweat."

The White House chief, like all Cousins, was used to concrete answers. Good data, he felt, should line up in neat rows like pencils in a new box. "What specific pocketbook issues?" he asked, hoping she would come to the point.

"Oh, cheaper cars."

In the window his own image was superimposed on the riot, as though he had given it a seal of approval. His eyes were huge onyx almonds on a pale hot-air balloon of a head that seemed tethered above his black uniform. On his shoulder his insignia and nameplate gleamed.

"Cheap cars are unimportant," he told her, "when compared to the peace of Communal thought."

Light as a leaf drifting onto the surface of a pond, his attention settled on her. The colors of her blouse were hectic blues and reds and greens, the shapes ill-formed triangles that pointed, higgledy-piggledy, in all directions. "This blouse," he said.

She touched her collar in evident surprise. "New. You like it?"

"Don't wear it again. Muted colors, as I told you. Grays and blacks and navies."

"Gray makes me look ten years older," she argued. "And I spent good money on this blouse. You know, I could make a lot more in

the private sector. I have great front-office appearance. Not, of course, that *you* would ever notice, but the senators do. You don't pay me enough—"

He stood and lifted his hand as a signal that she had won the fight. Natalie, at five feet one-half inch tall, had been one of the few applicants his size. "Use the White House credit card to buy yourself another."

"And a new pair of shoes."

He cocked his head to the right in query.

"I bought shoes to match this blouse. So you owe me."

"All right."

"And a purse." Natalie's mouth was in a tight line. It was a dangerous expression, he knew. A sign of anger. Perhaps the blouse was a pocketbook issue.

"Buy whatever you like," he said. She bared her teeth in a smile, and he began to wonder if he was being overly generous.

"Sir? Better get down to the basement."

As he turned to go, the room assaulted him with its disorganized design, one that had no relationship at all to nature. Humans had a primitive idea of harmony. Only once had he seen the order of fractals in a piece of human art: a Renaissance oil that showed the subject standing next to a painting of the same subject and the same painting, copies of the large painting growing smaller and smaller until the final one was done in a suggestion of tiny brushstrokes.

Chaos, he thought as he strode across the presidential seal woven into the dark blue carpet. Chaos was going to kill him.

2

A brooding William Hopkins and a nervous Speaker of the House were lurking at the West Wing stairs. Dropcloths were spread nearby, and Secret Servicemen were gathered in a somber knot watching a pair of painters apply eggshell latex over three lines of graffiti on the wall. The red paint was stubbornly bleeding through the beige.

The sharp, aggressive strokes of the letters were plain enough, but the White House chief found the message bewildering:

BLACK UNIFORMS,

LIGHTNING BOLT INSIGNIA.

REMIND YOU OF ANYTHING?

Reen idly fingered the outline of the white lightning bolt on his chest.

"Reen," Hopkins called. The FBI director was smiling as he walked across the carpet. It looked as though his hand was fighting an urge to pop out of his pocket and grasp Reen's own, but Hopkins had worked with the Cousins long enough to have learned reticence.

"Director." The chief of staff nodded. Then his gaze fell on the man behind Hopkins's broad back. Of late the two habitually traveled together, the huge Bureau director and the diminutive congressman, as though the latter were a dog on his leash.

Reen searched his mind for the congressman's name and then remembered the word association Marian had taught him: What was the sound a Chihuahua would make, dropped from a twelve-story window?

Oh, of course. "Speaker Platt," Reen said before the FBI director's form eclipsed that of the other man.

Hopkins's sloping shoulders ballooned out into a puffy midsection, and his feet seemed too small to balance his bulk. As the man leaned over, Reen had the unsettling notion that he was about to be engulfed by a sofa.

Hopkins breathed whiskey-and-mint-scented breath into what he incorrectly imagined to be Reen's ear. "Wanted to talk with you for a minute before we had to go down to the meeting."

"Yes?"

"You know, I appreciate how you've adapted to us, but there's some stuff that, talking man-to-man so to speak, you're doing all wrong."

Reen glanced around Hopkins's looming bulk to the graffiti on the wall. The spiked letters, like slashes in the plaster from which blood oozed, bothered him more than the oblique message. There was implied violence in that calligraphy.

"Not your fault, of course. But I feel when you have things mixed up, it's my job to set you straight. For example, it's a well-known fact that if you give a woman any power at all, she'll either cave in at the first sign of trouble or else turn into a ball-breaking bitch. Bless 'em, they just can't help it. You understand 'ball-breaking'?" the director asked helpfully.

"Yes," he replied. Hopkins's references to body parts never ceased to fascinate Reen.

"The CIA," Hopkins said. "You have to do something about the CIA. Cole's on the rag, the vindictive bitch. Or maybe she's menopausal or something. You have to back me, Reen-ja. She's ripped the *cojones* right off some of my best agents. Probably made a victory necklace out of them."

Hopkins was so tall that Reen was eye-level with the man's tie. It was a nice tie, done in dark blue with small pink seashells lined up in neat rows across it. The only thing about the tie Reen found bothersome was that the lines were angled rather than horizontal or vertical. Why, he wondered, would the designer want to tip the pattern that way?

"Someday you're going to look up," Hopkins said, "and see she has a pair of gray *cojones* on that necklace, figuratively speaking. You understand the word *cojones*?"

Reen wondered how much the FBI knew about himself and Marian Cole. Skirting Hopkins, he quickly descended the stairs.

The FBI director hesitated a moment before following, Speaker Platt at his heels.

"Cole's got something on you, doesn't she, Reen-ja?" Hopkins asked when he caught up. "You can tell me what it is. Maybe I can persuade the Bureau to help."

Hurriedly, Reen changed the subject. "Why haven't we been able to find out who is painting the graffiti on the walls?" Not much that was human frightened Reen; but the graffiti had him worried. It meant that someone close to him, someone in the White House itself, hated him enough to be a dangerous foe.

"Secret Service have their heads up their collective butts," he said, deftly combining two body parts into a single image. "You know, one time when the downstairs was open, a tourist wandered in on Kennedy when he was having breakfast. Can you imagine?"

"I don't wish to discuss Kennedy," Reen said sharply. He wondered if Hopkins carried a pocket of hero worship in the multizippered, confusing organ that was his human heart. If Hopkins loved the memory of Kennedy, he could be the author of the graffiti. Reen glanced at the director's manicured hands but could see no evidence of paint.

When they reached the bottom step, Hopkins gave a quick, abashed grimace. He was huffing from the unaccustomed exercise, and his jowled face was an alarming shade of red. "Sorry.

Nothing personal. So are we going to get together on this CIA thing?"

Without answering, Reen hurried to the cavernous situation room. The National Security Council had had time to become bored. Vilishnikov, head of the Joint Chiefs, was brushing dandruff from his red epaulets. Hans Krupner, the education advisor, was making an origami giraffe from a paper napkin. Krupner, it appeared, had gotten closest to the riots. His hands were still atremble, disturbing his efforts at folding. There was a bruise on his forehead.

At a corner of the U-shaped table, Marian Cole was carrying on a listless conversation with DiSecco of Finance. When she caught sight of Hopkins and Reen together, she shot the White House chief a suspicious look.

Marian was dressed in brilliant crimson, a color chosen to annoy him. And she was spotlighted by one of the ceiling's recessed bulbs. The light, Reen noticed, was kind. The translucent skin of her cheek glowed pink, like the tender hue of the seashells on Hopkins's tie.

Faced by her silent accusation, Reen hesitated. An instant later her blue eyes darted away, releasing him from the pain of her scrutiny.

Reen took his usual seat at one prong of the U to avoid being bracketed by the taller humans. Platt was standing indecisively, considering the only empty seat: the President's. Finally the Speaker grabbed a folding chair from the wall and, with murmurs of apology, squeezed between Hopkins and an environmental consultant from MIT.

Vilishnikov began pulling papers from his briefcase and setting them on the table. "I have here a copy of the Tariff Regulation Bill. I thought we might go over it point by point. The President has five days left in which to sign. Five short days. Then it becomes a pocket veto, and I assure you, when that happens, Europe intends war."

No one on the east side of the U was aware that the door was swinging open behind Vilishnikov. The west side instantly froze. DiSecco slid lower in his chair, as though preparing to duck under the table.

A marine sergeant in full-dress uniform stepped into the room. "Ladies and gentlemen," he announced, "the President of the United States."

In a show of conformity, the humans all stood, DiSecco having to pull himself up from his crouch. A Secret Serviceman was at the doddering President's elbow. Age and the crush of responsibility had bowed Womack's once ramrod-straight back. The face had withered to a deceptively sweet-expressioned skull. For a moment the Secret Serviceman and the President fought a small war over which way Womack was to turn. At last, gentle but persistent, the agent won; he led Womack to his seat at the head of the table, and the rest of the National Security Council took their chairs.

Reen stared down the table at the only other human he loved. Womack was drooling.

"War in Europe," Vilishnikov continued.

Womack snored once, loudly. Everyone turned to the President. Womack's eyes were closed; his mouth hung open; his head bobbled precariously. Quickly the Secret Serviceman eased him into a position where the presidential face would not drop to the National Security Council table.

"So. War in Europe," Vilishnikov began once more, clearing his throat. "As a precautionary measure I have ordered our troops in this hemisphere to full alert—"

"Why?" Hopkins interrupted. "If the Europeans move, they'll move east. To China. To Japan. To Korea. Who cares? What's important are the disappearances. This month five of Reen's people have turned up missing. That makes twelve so far this year."

Marian Cole put down her coffee cup and smiled at the frustrated head of the Joint Chiefs. Her swept-back blond hair seemed to be rebelling against that morning's hairspray. A lock of it hung above her right eye. "Don't you worry, Arkady, honey. Billy takes over meetings the way a hog takes over an acorn patch. We'll talk about your war if you want to."

Hopkins's small eyes narrowed further, to be nearly buried in

frowning flesh. “Maybe Director Cole doesn’t want to talk about the disappearances because the CIA’s behind it. I suggest we start investigating over at Langley.”

“Try it. You talk a good game, Billy, but you’re proud-gelded.” Marian Cole coolly regarded the ceiling. “The will’s there, but the bang’s a dud.”

Hopkins smacked the table with his open palm. All the members of the NSC but Marian Cole, Reen, and the snoring President jumped in place.

“Two Cousins,” said the White House chief.

Hopkins turned to Reen, his jowls shivering, his expression that of utter disbelief.

“Ten Loving Helpers have gone missing this year, but only two Cousins.”

“Shit!” Hopkins shouted. “They’re still your people, aren’t they?”

Reen could not fathom why Hopkins was so enraged. “Yes, but—”

“Billy,” Marian said in an indulgent voice, “why don’t you just let me handle this? The CIA was taking care of all the alien business before. We have kind of a historical caveat.”

“Listen, Reen-ja.” Hopkins rose from his chair like a mountain thrust upward by plate tectonics. “The CIA has been working on ways to get rid of your people ever since the Truman administration. You know that. And they would have kept on if the budget had been funded.”

Reen took in the appalled faces around the table. Marian Cole was the only one who seemed calm. The lock of hair had fallen another quarter of an inch. There was a smile on her red lips.

“Oh, sit down, Billy,” she said with a wave of her hand. “The thing we should be talking about here is what the Cousins intend to do if Europe declares war and if the domestic terrorism isn’t stopped. What about it, Reen?” Her denim blue eyes twinkled. “You have the obvious weapons superiority. We’re a bunch of wing-clipped ducks in a lake. Why don’t you finish us off?”

Around the table a breathless, terrified silence. Krupner spasmed, accidentally decapitating his origami giraffe. He looked down at his guilty hands and the torn paper in dumbfounded woe.

"Jesus Christ," Hopkins whispered to Cole. "Will you shut up."

"Somebody's got to have the balls to say it. What about it, Reen?" Marian asked.

Reen stiffened, feeling the tug of her nearness as a star feels the thieving pull of a black hole. Each time they were together, she stole more and more of him. He was a small creature growing even smaller, a being on the very edge of disappearance.

He fought to keep his treacherous mouth shut. Had they been alone, he would have told her. He would have answered any question, no matter how ugly the truth.

"Come on," she said. "What are you guys waiting for?"

Hans Krupner burst into tears. "We have always the same meetings. Threats. Shouting. Everyone at one another's throats. So this is the peace the Cousins promised us? I tell you, I cannot stand such peace anymore."

At that moment the President rose. The NSC looked expectantly, encouragingly to Womack. Vilishnikov stared at the President with the wonder of a blind man catching his first glimpse of the sun.

Womack fumbled with his fly, took out his penis, and, before the Secret Serviceman could stop him, voided his bladder on the tariff bill. Urine splattered. Krupner forgot his tears and inched away from the spreading wet.

"Meeting adjourned," Reen said, rising and heading quickly to the door. There he stopped and looked back. The members of the NSC were standing, gazing down at the urine-splattered papers. The humans were differing shapes, differing colors. Even in physical appearance they were chaotic. He felt he could read idiosyncratic fears and individual ambitions behind their tiny eyes.

"Does that count?" DiSecco asked. "Listen. Could we somehow construe that as a signature?"

Reen called, "Director Cole."

Marian lifted her head.

She was angry with him, he knew; and that was to his great regret. On the other hand, she didn't have the courage to refuse his direct order.

"I will see you now in my office."

3

Reen waited in the Oval Office fifteen minutes before opening the door to the huge reception area to find Marian Cole talking to Natalie as though they were old friends. The two women, one tall and blond, the other short and blond, turned. Natalie, he noticed, had exchanged her irritating blouse for a cream-colored sweater.

"I told you I wanted to see you," Reen said to Marian.

Natalie spoke up: "But you said first thing this morning to hold all calls."

"You might have announced Director Cole was here."

"That would have been a call. You tell me 'Hold all calls' when you don't want to talk to anyone; and then you're supposed to say, 'Hey, I asked so-and-so to come over, so forget the holding-the-calls thing.' That's how you're supposed to talk to a secretary." She rolled her eyes.

"Hold all calls while the director and I are speaking," Reen told her.

Natalie went back to her typing. "Okay."

When he reentered his office, Marian followed. He closed the heavy oaken adjoining door, his claw clicking on the brass knob.

"So. What's Billy Hopkins been saying about me?" she asked.

Reen walked to the windows and peered out. The riots were over, and a sanitation department truck was washing the blood from the streets. "I don't talk about him to you or you to him. That would be disloyal."

"Disloyal?" she asked in amusement. "I thought maybe Billy was babbling again."

He was glad that she was standing directly at his back, right in the sixty-degree dead spot of his three-hundred-degree vision field. He didn't want to see her face. "Angela asks about you."

Behind him there was silence. Reen, who ached no less for Marian's approval than four-year-old Angela did, longed to turn to see if she was smiling or frowning. "It's been nearly a month. I thought we would go see her."

"I'm tired of this, Reen." Marian's voice was so weary that it frightened him. Humans aged in too short a season, like the fleeting Appalachian fall. From the past year to this it seemed that her moistness and energy had gone. There were new lines on Marian's face, more silver in her hair. She was slipping from him too quickly.

Marian moved slightly to the right and entered his peripheral vision. She stood as she stood when they had first met: hands clasped, chin lifted. The other children, stolen in their sleep and awakened to alien surroundings, had screamed. But not five-year-old Marian.

That one, he told the doctors. *I hope it will be that one.*

"Don't fight me, Marian," he told her.

She gave Millard Fillmore an appraising look. "How can I? You always get your way."

He knew he should apologize but didn't. Too many years, too many chances for apologies had passed. He opened the French doors for her, and together they walked to the south lawn.

In the Rose Garden the crisp air held the tangs of autumn and cordite. Down the spread of grass, on the other side of the fence, stood two knots of humans encumbered by still cameras and minicams. Reen would have found it difficult to distinguish reporter from tourist

but for the frenzied shouting from the media and the CNN truck parked nearby.

His eye lit on a solitary figure between the throngs: a young man with a purple Vespa and a backpack. For two days now, each time Reen had ventured onto the south lawn, he had seen the boy. And even from that distance Reen could feel the disquieting intensity of his stare.

What could be so important to demand such a single-purposed vigil? The boy's pose was taut, his expression that of barely contained fervor. Reen pictured the boy reaching in the backpack, bringing out a gun, a bomb. Head down, Reen hurried his stride.

Past a knee-high barrier of ornamental shrubbery the ovoid commuter waited as it always did. And there waited Thural, a head taller than the three Loving Helpers at his side. His black eyes were pools of calm. The Loving Helpers' eyes were dark, abandoned wells.

"Cousin Reen-ja," Thural said, speaking quietly in Cousin language. "Jonis went with two Loving Helpers to observe the riot and has not yet returned."

Reen entered the shelter of the ship's doorway, just out of the backpacked boy's possible line of fire. "But the riot has been over for some time."

"Yes, Reen-ja. It causes me to wonder."

"Inform the Community, then," Reen said. "Maybe they can find him. In the meantime we will be taken to West Virginia." He motioned to Marian, who was standing on the lawn, well out of the shadow of the ship's overhang. Well out of the Loving Helpers' reach.

"Keep those things away from me," she said.

After a self-conscious glance at Marian Cole, Thural told the Loving Helpers, "Go." In unison the three about-faced and marched toward the command room, Thural at their heels.

When they left, Marian entered. Reen led her down the right-hand corridor.

"I hate them," she said. "I can't stand the way they move, like

little robots. I hate the blank way they look at me. Ninety-three percent of your people. Doesn't that scare you?"

Reen stopped in the middle of the hall and looked back, searching her expression for pity. Her face was hard. "We live with it."

"No, you don't."

Embarrassed, he continued down the hall to the lounge. Marian gave the monochromatic, minimalist room a sweeping glance and then tried to make herself comfortable on a chair that was too short for her legs. Reen perched on a sofa opposite her and contemplated the wall. There was a falling sensation as the ship's gravity changed.

When Reen glanced at Marian, he found himself staring into the side of her cheek.

"I want you to be happy," he told her.

"That's great, Reen. You rape me, then insist I enjoy it."

Humans always muddied the clear water of emotion; and in that murk the handsome, darting shapes of love swam with ugly creatures of lust.

Once she had loved him as a playmate. Then he took the place of her absent father. *I'm going to marry you,* Marian, at six years old, had told him. And the psychologists, accustomed to the caprices of human children, had laughed.

But neither Reen nor the psychologists had been prepared for her determination. It was Marian, not Reen, who always got her way.

Remembering that touch was important to humans, he leaned forward to grasp her beautifully wrought hand. The Cousins, in their twelve hundred centuries of civilization, could have created splendor with hands like those. With their three stubby fingers and claw they had managed only to produce utility.

He noticed the aging lizard texture of her skin and tried, with helpless dismay, to smooth it. His claw gently traced the raised white scars at her wrist, the evidence of her earlier disappointment with her husband. Once, he reminded himself, she had loved Howard, too.

"It's my fault you're so bitter. If I had known that remembering would . . ."

She slipped her hand from his. "You never come by anymore. But you got what you were after."

"Angela." He rolled the name in his mouth like candy. "Wasn't Angela worth it?"

Her eyes narrowed, her lips twisted. The savagery in her face unnerved him. "Women are made to be brood mares, is that what you're saying?"

"No," he replied, wondering what he could do to make things right. He suddenly realized how deluded he had been. And how tragically his experiment was turning out.

Thural poked his head into the lounge to say they had landed. Marian got to her feet.

"You will hug her," Reen blurted.

She looked at him blankly.

"I don't care how you feel about me. And it doesn't matter whether you wanted Angela or not. She is here, and you are her mother. Angela is a mammal. She needs to be hugged. I'm not practiced at touching. And I suspect I'm no good at it."

But Marian knew that, didn't she? Their own shy, awkward embraces had led to—what? he wondered. A sterile thing that surely hadn't been enough for her and had been nearly too much for him. No, theirs had been a laboratory mating, not warm limbs wrapping warm limbs but a petri-dish entwining of DNA.

As he followed her off the ship, he wondered dismally if she needed more and if that was the reason for her anger.

It had snowed in the West Virginia mountains. The sun was struggling to peek out from behind a layer of cirrus clouds. Reen slogged through the drifts on the walkway and kicked his boots clean on the mat before he entered the house.

A knot of gray, large-headed, and huge-eyed children were playing ball on the living room floor. As soon as Marian entered, one popped up from the group and darted her way, as dramatically and hopelessly drawn to Marian as an iron filing to a magnet.

Love, Reen thought. One day his daughter would choose another

of the recombinants to mate with, and when they mated, they would do so with love. Perhaps they would talk after the act was over, the way humans so often did. Angela's children would grow up under the sunny indulgence of both mother and father, and her life would be sweeter than Reen's had been.

As Angela hugged Marian's legs, Marian stood immobile, gazing into the distance, seemingly unaware or perhaps embarrassed by the show of adoration. After a heartrending wait, Marian bent, pried the child's grasping hands from her thighs, and picked her up.

Reen relaxed and studied the perfect five-fingered gray hand now clasped in Marian's pink one. Angela's nose was tiny and well formed, her mouth a small bow. On the top of her head was a dusting of hair as pale as the snow on the hills outside. Despite her color, despite her huge eyes, she was mostly Marian's child.

"Reen," Angela said and blinked.

The ice of Reen's earlier annoyance thawed. He put out his hand to his daughter, and she grabbed his claw.

Sandra Gonzales, the caregiver, and Quen, the Cousin overseer, ambled up.

"Such a good child," Mrs. Gonzales was saying. The caregiver had the plump roundness of bread dough. Gray children trailed in her wake like eager gulls behind a tugboat. "Angela's such a kind, sweet little thing, Ms. Cole. She plays with the other children so well."

Marian had not ceased her vague contemplation of the room. Although she held Angela in her arms, she had not once looked at her child. "You should have some colors in the house. Children like bright colors."

"Distracting," Quen said. "They must learn to focus. They are human, but they are Cousin as well."

Marian put the little girl down. "I want to take her outside. Does she have a coat or something?"

Mrs. Gonzales fluttered her hands. "Yes, yes. A coat." She bustled out of the room, the children following.

The two Cousins and Marian Cole stood in uneasy silence until

Mrs. Gonzales came back and began to bundle Angela into a zippered windbreaker. "Your mother wants to take you outside. Won't that be fun? And then you can tell all the other children about it."

"What will she tell them about?" Marian asked sharply. "About having a mother that she knows or about playing in the snow?"

The smile slid like melted frosting from Mrs. Gonzales's sweet roll of a face.

"The other children have no idea who their parents are," Marian said.

"Not important," Quen told her.

Mrs. Gonzales was studying the zipper intently, much more intently than the job deserved.

"Then why is it so damned important that Angela know who I am?" Marian asked Quen with such ferocity that the Cousin blundered backward.

"Why is it so important?" Marian demanded.

No one answered her. Quen stood where his backward flight had taken him, his gaze averted. Mrs. Gonzales, lips puckered, was still fiddling with the coat zipper.

"They're killing us off," Marian told Mrs. Gonzales. "All very quietly. We're being sterilized, lady. Did you know that? Look at the statistics. The birthrate is down eighteen percent, and no one realizes what's happening."

"Not in front of the children," Reen said.

She gave him a brief glance and turned to Mrs. Gonzales. "Can't you see? In a hundred years or so, there won't be any humans left. These children will take over the world."

Quen stiffened. "These children," he said with pride, "will inherit the universe."

Giving the seam of the zipper a last tug, Mrs. Gonzales said in firm, quiet benediction, "There now," as though she were an elderly marzipan queen sending her champion into battle.

The tension in the room evaporated; an inevitable sadness took its place. Marian took her daughter's hand and led her to the door.

"Reen," Angela called, flapping her fingers at him. "Reen."

He followed a discreet step or so behind. Outside, in the wind, a blush rose on Angela's cheeks, pink human color, from either the cold or her excitement.

Reen remained on the porch while Marian walked the child to the edge of the forest. Picking up a handful of snow, Marian packed it into a ball. Her voice drifted across the frozen yard. "Like this, kid. Here."

Quen stood at Reen's side. "Do you not want to be with her, too, Reen-ja?"

"Later." After three unsuccessful tries, Reen finally managed to grasp his own meager clump of snow.

By the evergreens, Marian was bending down to Angela's height. The wind carried Marian's faint voice to him. "Come on. Every kid should know this. Body heat. That's what makes the snow pack down." Whirling, Marian threw the snowball. It sailed across the glade and, before Reen could duck, slammed into his chest, shattering into a thousand glittering pieces.

He staggered back. Quen asked anxiously, "Are you all right?"

"It didn't hurt." Reen brushed the snow from his uniform with his free hand. The snowball hadn't been meant to injure. What hurt were Marian's icy glances, her hard-packed words.

She was laughing. Reen knew enough about human children to realize that, had Angela's mind been as human as her looks, she would have been laughing, too. Instead his serious little girl bent and, dogged as any Cousin, packed her own snowball.

"That's a good girl," came the shadow of Marian's voice. "Now throw it at your daddy. Throw it hard."

Reen stood, an easy target. He would not have moved even if his daughter had been holding a gun. Angela threw overhand as her mother had done. The snowball rolled off her fingers and dropped to the ground a couple of feet in front of her shoes.

"That's okay, kid," Marian was saying. "We'll make another one. You can always make another snowball."

Reen looked at the snow he held. When he relaxed his grip, it slipped through his fingers like sand.

"She knows a great deal about us," Quen said.

Reen nodded.

"Will she talk?"

"No."

In her red dress Marian was a cardinal in the trees, a holly berry among the green of the pines.

"But what if she is not so much under your control as you believe?" Quen asked, skirting the edge of indelicacy.

Reen dusted his hands. "She has revealed nothing important. The programming is working."

But was it? Perhaps her new coldness toward him was the first symptom of rebellion. It had been years since Marian was under the power of the Loving Helpers, and time had a way of blunting things. Probably he should put her under Communal control again, to make certain, but he hadn't the heart. No. He would stand, vulnerable and still, and accept the snowballs of her rage.

Marian, all warmth and brightness, was bending down to Angela, his gray, quiet child. She was speaking too low now for him to hear what she was saying, but Angela was staring into her mother's face as though all the wisdom of the prophets was hidden there.

"But what if that is not enough?" Quen asked. "What if she is capable of breaking the programming?"

Reen's heart, too, had its secret compartments. In the largest compartment lay the Community. In the next, Angela. Marian and Jeff Womack resided in their own places. But Reen knew what should be important and what should not.

"Then she will have to be killed," he said.

4

AFTER LANDING AT THE WHITE House, Reen followed Marian down the ship's ramp to the south lawn. The shouts from the reporters at the fence were a wordless cacophony, distant as Marian's laughter across the Appalachian snow, muted as the cries of the gulls swooping in from the Potomac.

Reen noticed with relief that the boy with the Vespa and backpack had disappeared. And he saw that, near a boxwood hedge, Tali was waiting.

Reen lifted a hand in greeting. "Cousin Brother."

Tali didn't reply. There was something important to be discussed, Reen realized, and Tali wouldn't talk until Marian left.

Reen took a hasty and somewhat ungracious leave of Marian. Pensively, he watched her stride across the grass to her limo parked in the circular drive.

"Cousin Brother Firstborn," Tali said without preamble as soon as she was out of earshot, "Jonis is missing. The Loving Helpers who were with him have been found dead."

Reen regarded his Second Brother, by birthright the guardian of his conscience. "Where were the Loving Helpers found?"

"They were put into trash bags and placed by a newspaper stand on Constitution Avenue."

"Such a thing has never happened before."

"As soon as one human pattern establishes itself, another pattern supersedes it. Therefore we should not trust patterns."

It was Tali's right to give advice to his First Brother, but Reen also had a right to ignore it. "How were the Loving Helpers killed?"

"I thought it tasteless to ask, Reen-ja. Hopkins seemed very distressed at having to tell me, and I myself was uncomfortable hearing the news."

Reen lifted his face to the clouds scudding across the pallid December sky. "Why should that make you uncomfortable? By now the others have all died in captivity anyway."

"But no one is aware of our weakness, Cousin Brother."

"The kidnappers know. Does Director Hopkins have any idea why this crime was different?"

"Hopkins believes something went wrong and the kidnappers were afraid of being seen. That is why they took Jonis and murdered the Loving Helpers. But then he understands these things better than I," Tali said with unconvincing humility. Humility was something Reen's Second Brother had never been very good at.

"Does he have suspects?"

Tali watched Marian's limo nose its way through the iron gates and the barricade. "He says the CIA."

Reen gazed after the limo as it rolled out into the E Street traffic. "Hopkins accuses the CIA of everything, Cousin Brother."

Tali suddenly faced Reen. "You tell her too much."

A fractious breeze shadowboxed with a bed of chrysanthemums nearby, making the heavy-headed flowers duck and weave. Only Tali, Cousin Brother Conscience, had the right to address Reen so sharply, and he exercised that right too often for Reen's taste. "She has been implanted, Tali. She's been under my control since she was a child."

"Control or not, what she knows will make her hate us. Why do you insist on telling her?"

It would have been foolhardy to explain. The fact was that Reen couldn't help himself. Time had knit them. Unravel the thread of Marian, and the weave of Reen's life would fall apart.

"Remember, duty is to the Community, Reen-ja," Tali said.

Reen dipped his head in acceptance of the criticism. "And I realize it is your duty to remind me." Reen made his way to the West Wing, leaving his conscience standing in the watery sunlight by the boxwood hedge, staring after him.

The Rose Garden was littered with wet brown leaves. As he picked his way through the rosebushes, which had been cut back and bagged like corpses for the winter, Reen noticed Hopkins watching from a window. By the time he opened the French doors and entered the Oval Office, Hopkins caught up with him.

"You talk to Cole?" the director asked.

Reen took a deep breath. The Oval Office was redolent with the smells of lemon oil, peach potpourri, and old smoke from the fireplace. "Of course I have talked to Cole. You must have seen us come off the ship together."

Reen felt crowded by everything: Marian, the threat of war, the dark undercurrents in the Congress. And he was terrified above all else of being stalked. His fear made him feel so lonely, he nearly confessed it to Hopkins.

"It'll be all over the six-thirty news," Hopkins complained. "Marian gets all the media attention. How do you think that makes me look? Where do you two go, anyway?"

Reen curtly changed the subject. "Tell me about Jonis."

"Jonis? Oh, the last kidnap victim. Listen, Tali tells me Jonis was in charge of your defense. What if he talks?"

Reen thought of Marian and the flat indicting look in his Cousin Brother's eyes. "He won't talk."

"If the CIA's behind it, Jonis is going to spill his guts."

"He won't talk." Reen pointedly looked away from Hopkins and at an enameled table, a state gift from India.

"You want to give me permission to search Langley?"

"No." Reen strode out of the office, through the reception area, and to the colonnade.

"Well, okay. So don't worry. If he doesn't talk, we're home free. I've got the thing under control."

"If things are under control, where is Jonis?"

"He has to be with the rest of them, right? We're trying to get them back, but solving a kidnapping is slow."

"If solving a crime goes slowly, things are not under control." They entered the main building at nearly a trot. Reen passed the White House pantry where a dark-suited member of the kitchen staff looked at him curiously.

"We're talking to witnesses. That's all we can do for the moment."

In the elevator vestibule Reen paused.

"Where are you going?" Hopkins asked.

The nice thing about the FBI director was that he wore pleasingly dark suits and somber ties. But there were times Reen wished he could replace him. The White House chief tired of the man's inane questions. "Upstairs."

"To see Womack?"

"Is there anyone else upstairs I might want to see?"

"No."

"Then it is obvious I plan to visit the President." The elevator arrived. As Reen stepped into the car, Hopkins put his hand to the door.

"He's losing it bad. He's hired another medium. Did you know that? And his whipping it out in front of the whole NSC . . ."

Reen moved to the back of the small paneled elevator. "The President acts senile, but I know better. Get your hand off the door."

The director shook his head. "Our collective butts are in a sling, and he's not doing a damned thing about it. If Womack had any sense left, he would have signed that tariff bill this morning instead of pissing on it."

"Did you ever stop to think at what point the President upset

the meeting? He planned the interruption. Get your hand off the door."

Hopkins pulled his hand away. "He *planned* that? What are you talking about?"

Reen hit the button. "He tells me he's on strike."

5

JEFF WOMACK HAD MADE THE OVAL room on the second floor his study, and through his terms in office he had succeeded in changing its decor to one designed to make Reen's visits torturous and brief.

In the crowded, eclectic room, fleur-de-lis wallpaper did battle with Early American and Santa Fe; and Womack sat in a maple rocking chair, an afghan tucked around his sweat-suited legs. At a heavy table in front of him was a Domino's box containing the messy, aromatic remains of a pizza. Womack's long, lushly wrinkled face was lowered, his chin tucked to his chest. Pink scalp shone through his thinning white hair. He was regarding the floor with dull interest.

"Jeff?" Reen said.

The head snapped up. The brown eyes narrowed slyly. "Hi there, termite. Grab yourself some pizza."

Reen glanced into the box. The pizza was a thick-crusted combination: sausage, green pepper, and black olives scattered at random over the cheese. Reen preferred the dishes that the White House kitchen prepared: asparagus in rows with a neat stripe of hollandaise; circles of scalloped potatoes, all the same size. "No, thank you."

"So how'd I do this morning?"

Reen walked to the President's side. "You annoyed me."

Womack's smile brightened. "Which bothered you more? The pissing or the drooling? I've been practicing, see?" He opened his mouth. A glistening thread of moisture dropped from his lips.

"May I ask you a question?"

"Ask away." Womack wiped the spittle with his sleeve.

Reen took a deep breath. "Does menopause affect women's ability to deal with logic?"

Womack gave him a sharp look. "Knotty problem."

Reen steeled himself for the answer. All morning he had been haunted by Marian's puzzling anger. He had always believed she was intelligent, but females, after all, were females. Perhaps her intelligence was as much of a house of cards as his own.

"Where'd you pick up that idea?"

"Bill Hopkins."

"Hah!" The President lifted a forefinger. "I guessed as much."

Whipping off the afghan, Womack stood, then shuffled quickly to the bar. The President was a tall, frail gnome of a man who, when the mood hit him, could move with alarming speed. He took a cigarette from a crushed pack on the fireplace mantel and lit it, leaning gracefully against the wall.

"I wish you wouldn't smoke."

"Why? You can grow me another set of lungs like you usually do." Womack opened a cabinet, took out a fifth of Wild Turkey, and poured himself a drink. "Grow me another heart," he said grumpily into the glass, "so I can outlive another vice president."

Shifting uncomfortably on his feet, Reen asked, "And as to my question?"

"Hopkins is after Marian Cole again, right? He's jealous. Good. Keep 'em guessing. Just be careful not to show too much favoritism to Marian. If Hopkins discovers you're in love with her, he'll use that as ammunition."

"Thank you. I'll be more careful," Reen said, queasily contemplating the chaos inside the pizza box. "Should I also be careful not to show my love for you?"

Womack scowled. "Do me a favor. You *like* me, okay? You're *fond* of me. You'd like to go *bowling* with me. But let's not have a kid together like you and Marian."

As though Womack had taken a swing at his face, Reen flinched. "You know?"

Womack tapped a finger against the side of his patrician nose. "I make it my business to know things. My old political enemies used to call me a snake. But snakes, you know, they see all the dirt. Don't pay attention to what Hopkins says about Marian. Hopkins is jerking your chain."

Reen wondered how Womack had learned about Angela. A too-talkative Cousin? Or was he simply guessing? The President was superb at speculation.

"Listen, I'm still on strike, mind you," Womack said, "but about that meeting—I thought a little free advice might be in order." He studied the level in the glass before he lifted it to his mouth.

"Yes?"

"Get rid of Krupner. He's going to fold under pressure. Anyone who cries in the middle of an NSC meeting . . . give me a break."

Reen moved to the windows and looked past the Truman balcony's folding chairs to the Jefferson Memorial, a white marble pimple on the chin of the Ellipse. "The Germans want him."

"The Germans want a German. Tell them the problem. They'll replace him. If you want my advice, take it. If you don't, fuck you. By the way, I'm low on booze."

A spot of color near the White House fence drew Reen's attention. That color. That jolly grape–Kool-Aid dot of color. The purple Vespa was back.

"Termite? You listening? My world's crumbling, don't you hear? My liquor's almost gone, and all you can do is stare out the window."

Reen tore his gaze from the scooter and the watchful, motionless figure beside it. "All right. I'll send Thural up. You can tell him what you need."

"Yeah, Thural or Jonis. I like old Jonis. Thural, he just gets one of the Secret Service guys to do it. Jonis is *creative*. There's this bum—I guess the hell *that's* insensitive—okay, a street person. Okay? A homeless son of a bitch. Old Jonis meets him at the fence, hands him enough money to get me and the bum a bottle. Scratches both itches at the same time, Jonis says." Womack lifted his glass. "Great guy, Jonis."

"Jonis has been kidnapped."

The glass paused at Womack's lips.

"Who is the homeless person?" Reen asked.

"Never saw him. Don't know his name." Womack stared bleakly into the fireplace, then threw the remains of his cigarette onto the burning logs. "Poor Jonis. Think you'll get him back alive?"

"If he is not back within three days, we may consider him dead."

The President's intent eyes flicked to Reen. "Why three days especially?"

Reen dodged the questioning look. "Did Jonis have other connections we were not aware of?"

"Oo!" The President clapped a hand to his head. "Oo! I wanted to show you something!" Womack rummaged around in the bar's cabinet. "Shit. Where'd I put it?" Turning away from the bar, he scanned the room.

"What?"

"Something I found in the West Wing." In four rapid, arthritic strides he was at his knotty pine desk. Sliding open the top drawer, he brought out a folded piece of paper.

With one arm Womack swept the Domino's box from the Santa Fe table and onto the floor, sending the remains of the pizza tumbling facedown onto the carpet. He opened the paper carefully. On the white page rested a yellowish translucent cone.

Reen cringed.

"Know what it is?" Womack asked.

"Of course I know what it is."

"Is it yours?"

Reen stiffened. "No! When I shed a claw sheath, I shed it in private. Then I dispose of it, just as any Cousin should."

"Pick it up. Take a real good look at it."

"No. And stop playing with it. You don't know where that's been." But he had already caught sight of what Womack wanted him to see. A raised line ran down the cone's center: the adolescent ridge. There were no more young Cousins, and only one thing left had a claw like that.

"You see?" Womack asked. "How'd *that* get into the White House?"

"It dropped off. The Taskmaster didn't notice—"

"Don't be a dunce! I found it while I was crawling around under the furniture in the West Wing, like I told you. And no one brings Loving Helpers into the building."

"Yes, yes. This is all very interesting—"

"It's a *mystery*," Womack said, a gleam in his eye.

Reen lowered his gaze. "Congress is insisting that you choose a vice president." When he glanced up, he was astonished to see dread shadow Womack's gaunt face.

"There is only so much that regeneration can do. One day you *will* die, Jeff, and we will be unable to stop it." They had been friends for Womack's entire term, fifty-one long years. Never would Reen know another human so well. Despite his special relationship with Marian Cole, never would he love a human so perfectly.

"You said Congress wanted me to. How do *you* feel about it?"

Reen fought the upwelling of resentment in his chest, hoping that Womack, who sensed things so well, would not suspect that he chafed under the congressional pressure. "Something could happen to you."

Again those brown eyes picked him apart. "Could it?"

"I hear you have hired another medium."

"Marian tell you? Or Hopkins?"

Reen raised his head.

"Ah," Womack said with the heartfelt satisfaction of a glutton sitting down before a seven-course meal. "So it was Hopkins. It

doesn't matter much, though, termite. As many mediums as I hire, as much as they tell me about the other side, the thought of dying still scares me." He laughed. "It scares me to death."

With his claw and forefinger Reen plucked the sleeve of Womack's velour sweat suit. "The mediums are frauds. No one can call up spirits that way. Besides, the Appropriations Committee threatens to make your expenditures public."

"What? Ted Long behind this? That bastard doesn't scare me. The press is saying I'm senile. The gossip inside the Beltway is I'm dead. So what? I haven't stepped outside this room in three months, and my approval rating's eighty-seven percent. Now *that's* what I call presidential. Let Ted Long shove *that* Harris poll up his ass."

"Jeff, please. What if war breaks out? Can't you just sign the bill and have it over with? Must I bring Loving Helpers here to force you?"

Womack yanked his sleeve from Reen's grasp. His jaws were clenched, his words strangled, his gaze terrified. "Let go of me, you little gray shit!" He lumbered to the rocking chair and sat. "Christ, what a mess. What a bunch of goddamned bad karma. I'm the guy who handed the Earth to you fuckers. Then you stab me in the back."

A chill fury seized Reen by the nape of the neck. "You've never forgiven me for pressuring you to appoint Hopkins. Well, my Brother wanted Hopkins, and it has always been easier for me not to displease Tali. I give you back your own advice: Grow up, Jeff. This is politics."

For a breathless moment the two glared at each other. Reen was aware of the sickly, jailhouse pallor of the President's face, the distinctive garlic and tomato odor of the pizza. Then Womack's expression softened. "Hey. Consider this a learning experience. If you get in over your head . . . well, I have plans. I have agendas. You'll see."

"I hate your agendas." Reen's shoulders slumped as if the weight of the planet had descended on him.

From the rocking chair a contemplative, wry silence. "Don't trust me, do you?"

"You taught me every lie, every trick. How can I help but not

trust you?" Reen's voice trembled with the conflict of emotions he felt for the man. Womack had been one of Reen's longest-running trials—the cost, Reen had always figured, of victory. And yet, for all their arguments, he loved him, loved him with the same despairing love he felt for Marian Cole.

"You know, when push comes to shove, termite, you won't have the heart to get rid of me. But your Brother will."

Reen walked hastily out of the room. In the vestibule of the elevator he punched the button hard with his claw. He wanted to get away from Womack, but he wasn't sure what drove him: anger at Womack or fear of the truth.

"Hey, termite," Womack called.

Reen peeked around the corner. The President was framed in the doorway of his study, the pizza at his feet, a monarch amid the ruins of his kingdom. "Okay, so you don't believe in mediums. But you believe in spirits, right? I mean, we picked this spiritualism up from you guys. You're not just jerking me around?"

The elevator opened with a rumble and shush. "Of course there are spirits." Reen stepped into the car and let it take him down to safety, away from the torment in Jeff Womack's eyes.

6

Back in his office Reen sat at his terminal while the shadows of the trees outside lengthened and the day faded to night.

At six-thirty Natalie came in, her coat on her arm. "I'm going."

"Yes." He nodded, barely looking up from his work.

She hesitated at the door. "I mean, I have to go home now, you know? Sam'll want dinner."

He stopped scrolling the report, the cursor blinking on an item concerning unrest in Italy. "I understand," he said, although he didn't so much understand as accept. After years of frustration at his secretaries' holidays and vacations, he'd stopped trying to change them. He'd discarded the idea that humans were lazy. He'd even once, not long ago, taken a sort of vacation himself.

He expected her to leave, but she didn't. She stood with one hand on the jamb. "You want me to turn on the light?"

"No." He went back to his work but then looked up again. Natalie hadn't moved. "Is anything wrong?"

She took a breath to speak, then let out the air and the thought in a barren sigh. "Well. Don't work too late."

"I always work late."

"It makes me feel guilty. Thural's usually with you. I don't feel so bad when he's here."

"Thural is seeing about Jonis." Reen lifted his hands from the computer and set them primly in his lap. The room slowly darkened. The spill of light behind Natalie tossed a rectangle of gold across the carpet like an abandoned evening wrap. "You've worked for me now, what?" he asked. "Two months? When you work here long enough, you'll get used to my hours and the fact that I often work alone."

She scratched idly at the doorjamb with one long fingernail.

With a kind smile he said, "What would I do when I go home other than sleep?"

"You could watch TV. Sometimes they have great stuff on TV. Sitcoms. True-life murder stories. Ought to try it. I'll tell you when something good is coming on, and maybe you can bring in the portable."

"That would be nice," he said vaguely, thinking how distasteful it would be to watch a program on crime. Human life was short enough without other humans bringing it to a premature close. He'd known twelve presidents, had loved three of them, and now had outlived all but one.

"Sam," he said finally, because apparently she was not leaving. "Is that your husband?"

Natalie walked forward. Reached into her purse.

Startled by the unexpected gesture, Reen shrank back against his chair. He thought of the graffiti, of the boy with the backpack, and expected to see a gun in Natalie's hand. Instead she took out her wallet.

"My kid." She flipped open her wallet and held it toward him.

Reen took the wallet and switched on his green-shaded desk lamp. In the photo it was high summer. A blond boy with a smile and a baseball cap stood in the batter's box, bat in hand.

Sam had the doomed, sad beauty of his dying breed. The pool of light under the lamp washed the freckled face with brass. His hands

held the bat with nonchalant grace. There was arrogance in the set of his shoulders, a fearlessness in his eyes.

"He's a good kid."

Reen handed back the photo. "Such photos are to be valued." He knew Natalie could not understand what he meant and that she would never be allowed to. One day his own daughter would look at such pictures to remind herself of the debt she owed the past. When the Cousins died out, as they one day surely would, and when Reen, for her sake, made humans extinct, he wanted Angela to remember.

Natalie tucked the wallet back into her purse. "His dad, the son of a bitch, never sends us any money. That's why I got a little upset with you today about the blouse."

Reen folded his hands. "You must have a raise. Thural will see to it."

Her mouth fell open. Even in the dim light of the reading lamp, he could see her cheeks blanch. "I didn't mean—"

"I know. Go home to Sam. Don't worry about me. Mothers and fathers should concern themselves with their children."

"Okay. But stress can get to you. All work and no play . . ." Her voice wavered in indecision or perhaps in futility. Without finishing the thought she turned and made her way from the room. Reen watched her go, thinking of the photo of the boy, of the baseball game.

All work and no play.

He didn't understand the concept of baseball; he didn't understand games. *Take the snow and pack it,* Marian had said. His daughter, so instructed, had thrown the snowball with somber dedication and only because her mother had told her to. Angela had the wide shoulders of a brachiator, the generous musculature of her mother. But Reen knew she would never stand in a batter's box, her face agleam with joy.

All work.

He lifted his hands diligently to the keyboard. After a few moments of reading, his mind immersed itself in the Italian crisis, and

Natalie and her son were forgotten. At eight o'clock a maid wordlessly brought his dinner. By eleven he was so tired, the letters on the screen began to blur. He checked to see that the French doors were locked, flicked off the terminal and the reading lamp, and left his office.

The Secret Serviceman on duty in the colonnade gave him a brief glance. Other than that quick, furtive movement, nothing stirred.

Reen paused at the open doorway of the pool that Roosevelt had constructed, Nixon had made a press room, and reporter-weary Womack had reconverted. The White House was otherwise quiet, but something by the pool was making a sound. He entered. The lights in the pool were on, reflecting blue ripples across the ceiling. The filtration system gurgled. Water lapped the tiles.

On a lounge chair lay a bundle of old clothes, and from it came a noise like a buzz saw. And an arm. The hand, clutching an empty bottle of Mogen David, rested knuckles-down on the concrete.

Reen tiptoed to the guard. "There is a man sleeping by the pool."

"Yes, sir. The President's new medium."

"Why is he sleeping here?"

"Passed out, sir."

The guard looked away. An oppressive silence fell. Reen waded through it to the exit. Outside, the night air was cool, and sparse traffic growled down Pennsylvania Avenue.

Reen walked across the grass, nervously searching for the boy with the backpack. The fence was empty. Beside the West Wing the commuter ship gleamed dully in the full moonlight, Thural a ghost beside it. Reen trudged up the ramp. At the door he paused.

"Jonis bought liquor from a homeless man. Were you aware of this, Cousin?"

Did Thural's gaze shift in alarm? The movement was so quick that Reen couldn't be sure. "Yes, Reen-ja. Although I never personally—"

"Keep this information from the FBI but order the Guardians of the Community to find the man and bring him to me."

"I will give the Guardians his name and description—"

"Good." Reen turned his back on Thural and marched into the ship.

The lounge seemed perversely vacant without Marian there to vex it with her colors. He sat. A few minutes later Thural came to him.

"Reen-ja? We have landed at Andrews, and I have alerted the Guardians about Jonis's human friend."

Reen stared at his feet. Stress will get you, Natalie had said.

All work.

Every part of Angela functioned. Her hands were marvels, her brain clear. But had he made some terrible mistake? Quiet, shy Angela had the strength of a human in her body and the stamina of a Cousin in her mind. How would she handle the stress that was bound to follow her as an unkempt dog its master? As countless parents had before him, Reen wondered whether she would be happy. And if she could not find peace, he wondered, would she ever forgive him?

"Reen-ja?"

Without meeting his aide's gaze, Reen stood and followed Thural down the ramp.

7

When Reen walked into the Cousin Place, the first thing he noticed was the peppery acid smell of sleep. The second thing stopped him, brought him up short with a jolt of pleasure: the blandness of the gray monolithic room. The room was empty but for one Cousin. The Sleep Master sat quietly, his dark eyes full of slumber.

Reen, Thural at his heels, turned to enter the right-hand room.

"Wait."

The raspy voice came from behind. Hand to the soft wall, Reen turned. The Sleep Master's gaze was focused on him.

"You may not go forward."

Reen stood back to let Thural pass. He cast one look of longing into the chamber, at the Cousins packed quietly into their niches, before he made his way across the floor to sit at the Sleep Master's feet.

A light airy silence settled around them like mist.

"I am very tired," Reen said pointedly.

"I know. But you bring humanity with you when you come. Wash yourself of the humans, and I can allow you in with the others."

Reen fixed his eyes on the curve between wall and floor, willing his mind blank; but his brain fussed against rest like a recalcitrant

child at bedtime. Gradually he became aware he was thinking again, picking at the problem of Marian, sorting through his worries about Womack and Jonis.

"Even in here, Reen-ja, you disturb the sleepers. I feel them stir."

"Should I leave?" he asked dully, hoping the Sleep Master wouldn't take him up on the offer. His tiredness was ponderous and inescapable, like a weight about his neck. More than anything he wanted to crawl into a niche, feel the stiff embrace of the close walls, and relinquish, for a few hours, the strain of individuality.

"No. Talk to me. If you talk to me, perhaps your mind will not shout."

Reen looked into the Sleep Master's pocked gray face. "What do you wish to discuss?" he asked, wondering if this would lead to another lecture.

"I have found that if you talk about your day, you steal the power from it."

Reen dropped his weary eyes to the old Cousin's black boot. "Jonis has been kidnapped, Europe threatens war with China, and President Womack is still on strike."

"Yes?"

The room was cloying with the spice of sleep, and Reen found himself nearly dozing where he sat. *And I love my daughter and her mother to my own detriment.* "That is all."

"Those are small things to disturb the sleepers so."

"Complications are made of small things."

"Better that you put these small things away to come here."

As though I could put my troubles in a pocket. But the Sleep Master, insulated from human minutiae, could not understand. Reen tried to relax again, his mind peeling away the day in tiny patches, as though it were the clinging skin of an orange. Suddenly his consciousness lay stripped in his palm, tender and naked to the veins.

"Go, Reen-ja. Go before you fall asleep on the floor."

Reen staggered as he stood. He shuffled his way through the chamber door and into the blue-lit niches beyond. Finding a vacant hole,

he clambered in and lay down, unblinking eyes to the ceiling, arms rigid at his sides, as comfortable as a larva in its egg.

Angela slept like a human. Standing over her bed, Reen would often marvel at the way her lids shuttered her eyes. Her arms would curl to her side, her legs bend. She would press her head into the pillow and give herself to the dark.

The idea of darkness terrified Reen. It was darkness that bred human dreams. The closest Reen came to dreaming was when he felt the ghosts of long-dead consorts near him and heard their whispery voices.

Reen, the Old Ones said, and he knew he was sleeping.

Reen, you disappoint us.

They didn't speak with the anger he had been expecting but with a serene sort of dismay. Within arm's length of his niche stood three gigantic shadows.

The people are dying, Reen. Who will guard the eggs? Who will guard the sleepers?

Go away. Reen wished that he could sleep as Angela did. He would close his eyes on the ghosts. *We are all dying, and the egg cases are barren.*

The shadows at his shoulder began to dissipate into the gloom. *You are a father. You should understand,* the Old Ones hissed.

"Reen-ja?"

The Old Ones were back again for more of their fruitless lectures, only this time the ghosts were small.

"Reen-ja?"

A curt sound. A *ssst.* "Quiet, Thural," Tali said. "You will wake everyone."

Putting his hand to the close roof, Reen slid himself out of his niche. Thural and Tali were standing in the hazy blue aisle, the Sleep Master behind them, wringing his hands.

"Yes?" Reen whispered, wondering what time it was and whether their interruption of his sleep meant that Jonis and the rest of the kidnapped Cousins had been found.

"The police have discovered a body, Reen-ja," Thural said, keeping his voice down.

"The body of Bernard Martinez," Tali added importantly.

Around the three talkers, Cousins began to wake.

"The homeless man that Jonis often spoke with," Thural said. "He has been found strangled. I think it best you get up."

8

Outside the Cousin Place a rain fine as an aerosol was falling. Lights glistened on the tarmac. To the east a lethargic dawn was bleaching the sky. Tali, Reen, and Thural walked past a mothballed B-1 bomber to a four-seater Cousin craft. As they climbed into the ship, his Brother resumed what must have been an earlier lecture.

"It was embarrassing to the Keepers," Tali grumbled, appropriating the front passenger seat.

Thural plunked himself down gloomily at the controls, leaving Reen the back.

"Involving the police. Looking for a man only to find him recently dead," Tali went on.

The ship, not sensing other passengers, closed its transparent canopy. Thural grasped the control ball and pulled, drawing the craft upward a few feet, where it paused, wobbling.

"I had no way of knowing he had been murdered. And if the Keepers were more skilled at hiding the truth, the police would have never found out we were looking for him." With unCousinly petulance, Thural slammed the control ball right. The craft skipped northwestward like a flat stone across water.

Past the white egg shapes of the Anacostia Cousin Center the

Capitol dome rose through a thorny crown of trees. Beyond that, the Washington Monument stood gravestone sentinel over the Mall.

Tali swiveled toward Thural. "I think you know more than you are telling. That this man was found strangled means the President is involved in a conspiracy against us."

Alarmed by the direction of the conversation, Reen leaned forward, inserting his body between the two Cousins. "You jump to conclusions, Brother Conscience. That there is a conspiracy is obvious, but perhaps the President, not the Cousins, is the target."

"Gullible Reen." Tali's vitriol stung. "You trusted Eisenhower. You signed his silly Vandenberg treaty. And you see how he lied to us."

Reen sat back, perplexed. "Lied to us? Eisenhower might have delayed our landing, but even as he signed the treaty he vowed his people would never accept our leadership. And so it is. It was we with our arrogance who misjudged the situation. The humans are thrown into chaos, Brother, even fifty years after contact."

Tali sniffed. "It is not chaos. It is anger you see. The humans rage as Eisenhower did the first time he saw our ships. The man smiled and smiled, but still he raged."

Reen recalled Eisenhower's fixed, tense grin; how the President's hands, held stiffly at his sides, had clenched with impotent, white-knuckled fury.

The ship banked over the drab Potomac. Ahead of them, a Delta airliner, landing lights blazing, descended from the low clouds toward National.

"But we were the ones who broke the Vandenberg treaty," Thural said. "We allowed the humans to think we could wage war against them."

"It is not our fault they jumped to conclusions. And who broke the treaty first, Cousin, when Kennedy plotted to have Reen killed? In the skill of lying the humans will always have the edge." Tali's gaze fell on his Brother with the finality of a guillotine. "Find us a

good man to take over the presidency, Reen-ja. Someone like J. Edgar Hoover. Someone we can trust."

Reen tried to avoid Tali's eyes but was only partially successful. The way the seating was arranged in the ship, it was impossible to turn his back.

"Where are we going?" Reen asked Thural.

"M Street," Thural muttered.

Reen glanced down. The quaint roads of Georgetown were constipated with rush-hour traffic. Ahead, where Wisconsin Avenue crossed M Street, strobes from a group of squad cars washed the morning sidewalk with festive red and blue. Thural inched the ship over the gold dome of the Riggs Bank and to an empty space near the curb.

"Both of you forget Communal Duty," Tali said as the ship settled at a slight angle.

The canopy peeled back. Reen lifted his face to the mist. His Brother's reedy whine and insolent clicks were beginning to tire him, and he was looking forward to the relative peace of talking with the policemen.

As soon as the door spread open, Thural hopped out, Reen at his heels. A frigid breeze from the nearby C&O Canal pressed the fungal scent of river water into Reen's face. Traffic was backing up behind the parked ship, and frustrated commuters were leaning on their horns. A gathering of people at a bus stop turned to eye the three Cousins darkly.

A human with skin the fine texture and rich brown of glove leather approached with circumspection.

"Morning." He scanned their chests. When his eyes fell on Reen's nametag, they widened. "White House Chief Reen. I didn't expect to see you here, sir."

Rain was condensing like liquid diamonds in the man's black curls. He flashed his badge. "Detective Rushing, D.C. police. Hear your people are interested in the victim." Rushing let the sentence dangle, as though hoping Reen might pick up the thread and weave something useful out of it.

An army of policemen were gathered around the door of the old Vigilant Firehouse.

"You've called out many policemen for the murder of an inconsequential homeless man," Reen remarked.

A few yards away a squad car's radio spat static as monotonously as a teakettle on the boil. The huge detective laughed. "Homeless man? Bernard Martinez wasn't a homeless man, sir. Or at least he was homeless by religious conviction. Karma seller. That's what Martinez was." Rushing took a plastic bag from his pocket; a roll of blue tickets was coiled at the bottom like a snake.

Reen took the bag.

"Five-and-dime-store tickets, like the kind you'd buy for a church carnival," the detective explained. "I recognized the victim, but the tickets were the clincher. We've picked up Martinez eight times for airport solicitation."

Rushing plucked the bag from Reen's hand.

Reen walked to the body, which lay under the plaque dedicated to the dead firehouse dog. The wet pulp of a *Wall Street Journal* was pulled down from Martinez's face. The eyes bulged like eggs. Stars of blood marred the whites. The cheeks were chicken-pocked with burst capillaries. The garrote was still embedded in the neck like a vindictive necklace.

"Saint Bernard," Rushing said.

Reen turned inquiringly.

"That's what they called the victim. Saint Bernard. Seems he had quite a reputation among the karma sellers." Rushing's lips stretched into a semblance of a smile; his eyes were quietly observant. "If I might ask the reason you were looking for him, sir?"

On M Street the volume of honking intensified. The detective raised his head and called, "Thomas!"

A uniformed policeman shouted back, "Lieutenant?"

"Get over there and direct traffic."

"Alien ship's in the way, sir. Maybe—"

"Just get the traffic moving! So—" Rushing dropped his voice

and looked skeptically down at Reen—"we got a helluva mystery here, sir. A religious corpse with all the marks of a professional hit. You'd be doing us a favor if you could—" The detective glanced over Reen's shoulder.

Reen turned. A green Plymouth compact sedan was making its way slowly down the sidewalk, herding the sullen people at the bus stop to the edge of the curb. The car halted, and four men in dark suits climbed out.

"Shit." Rushing ran a hand through his cap of black hair. "I goddamn don't *believe*—"

"Kapavik, FBI," one of the approaching quartet said, flipping open his ID. "We'll take over the investigation from here, officer." He whirled to a shorter man behind him. "Call the lab to pick up the body."

A metallic crash.

The driver of a cherry red Jaguar, patience lost, had rammed the Cousin ship with his car. As Reen watched, the Jag backed into a Seville behind, then roared forward. Headlights broke with a wind-chime tinkle. The Cousin ship scraped a few feet along the sidewalk.

"Thomas!" Rushing shouted. "Handcuff that man!" Bending to Reen, the lieutenant said, "Maybe you should move your ship, sir."

"They can't hurt it."

A grimace passed over Rushing's face, as though from a twinge of indigestion. Quickly he turned to Kapavik, who was observing with professional interest how the driver was being dragged from his Jaguar.

"The Bureau doesn't have jurisdiction, Kapavik."

The FBI man's eyes were a pale wintry blue. "I believe we do."

Tali caught Reen's sleeve with a claw and pulled him away from the humans. "A karma seller, Reen-ja," he said with breathless alarm. "I begin to suspect terrible things. Was Jonis not aware karma selling is illegal? What could Jonis have been thinking, Cousin Brother? And what other illegalities could he have been involved in?"

More officers had run to Thomas's aid. The owner of the Jaguar

was struggling; it was taking three men to subdue him. Reen's eyes met Thural's, and he saw remorse there. "Did you know this?"

Thural wrung his hands. "Cousin Reen-ja, I would never—"

"Did you *know*!"

Faced with the First Brother's wrath, Thural groaned. "Yes. Forgive me, but President Womack is anguished. Jonis felt pity for him and bought him things: karma and liquor and pizza. He arranged meetings with mediums. Cousin Reen-ja, believe me. Jonis was foolish but kindhearted. It was an innocent—"

A glint of grape purple at the edge of Reen's vision. The Vespa was speeding down the sidewalk. Reen sucked in a startled breath and took a quick step backward, stumbling over the bare concrete, over his own mortality.

He tried to shout for help. Only a croak emerged. So stupid. Why hadn't he mentioned the boy to Hopkins? To Marian? They could have stopped it. They could have . . .

At the corner of his vision Reen could see Rushing and the FBI men. They were too far away to stop what had become inevitable, too absorbed in their argument to notice what was happening.

The boy parked and hurried to the trio of Cousins, his stride purposeful, his gaze intent. He was reading nametags.

Less than ten feet away now—point-blank range. The boy took the backpack from his shoulder, unzipped it, shoved his hand inside. Across the black plastic, cheerful yellow letters: GEORGE WASHINGTON UNIVERSITY LAW SCHOOL. Reen's world compressed until the boy filled it, horizon to horizon. The youthful pink-cheeked innocence, the rain-soaked hair, the brown eyes swollen from lack of sleep.

Closer. Close enough so that a weary and unsteady hand wouldn't miss the shot. Close enough to shove the muzzle against Reen's chest as he pulled the trigger. This near doom, a human would have fled. Reen froze. His pulse slowed. His vision blurred.

Through the hum in his ears, a voice, softer and more musical than fate's voice had a right to be: "White House Chief Reen? This is from the Senate Appropriations Committee."

The Senate. Had Reen been wiser, had Womack taught him better, he might have sensed the direction from which danger would come.

"Sir?" The boy again. "Sir? You're required to take this. With all due respect, sir, it's not within your right to ignore a subpoena."

Reen's vision slowly cleared. The boy's hand was outstretched toward his chest. There was a piece of paper in it.

With trembling fingers Reen took the subpoena and stuffed it into his pocket. The boy nodded and trudged to his scooter. Numb, Reen watched him drive off into the rain.

"A subpoena?" Tali's voice dripped contempt. "First Jonis embarrasses the Community, and now you, First Brother. Do you see what your laxity has done? It is your function to lead, and lead with morality. Not—"

Rushing's voice rose in a shout. He was livid. "You are obstructing a homicide investigation."

Kapavik shook his head. "This isn't one of your holdups or drug shootings. This homicide is directly related to a kidnapping, and that makes it a federal matter."

Reen's attention wandered, his disoriented mind still trying to grasp that he was alive.

Then he saw the mob.

They had emerged from their cars to gather on the slick cobblestones. Some were holding folded umbrellas like clubs.

Temper lost, Rushing drove a forefinger into Kapavik's chest. "It doesn't matter if twenty aliens were kidnapped, the stiff is mine."

The crowd was ominously silent. Their eyes were on the three Cousins. The policemen, sensing the crowd's mood, left the irate motorist lying against his Jag's hood and retreated west, toward Potomac Street.

Reen thought it prudent to point out the glowering mob to Rushing. He was opening his mouth to speak when Kapavik snapped, "How the hell did you hear the kidnap victim was an alien?"

A man in the crowd cocked his arm and let fly with a coffee mug, his pitching style even more beautiful and fluid than Marian Cole's.

The mug whizzed through the air, a blur of white. It sped past Reen and, with a meaty thud, knocked Tali off his feet.

"Tali!" Reen cried. He dropped to his knees beside him. "Brother!"

Tali's cheek lay against the sidewalk, his eyes dull and sightless. Reen put his hand to his Brother's back, then jerked away as he touched sticky blood and the ravenous suck of Communal Mind.

Rushing inserted his bulk between the trio of Cousins and the mob.

"Alien down!" Kapavik screamed to his men. "There's an alien down!"

Somewhere from the circle of FBI and police a gun boomed.

"Cousin Reen-ja!" Thural cried in a piping, hysterical voice. "Is he dead?"

"No. Not yet." Frantically Reen tried to drag his Brother toward the ship with his claw. Tali's head lolled; his flaccid arms hung; the body rolled out of Reen's grasp and tumbled heavily to the pavement.

Over the screams of the crowd and the shouts of the policemen, Reen heard the stuttering rattle of a machine gun. One of the FBI agents was firing warning shots with his Uzi. Poofs of dust ran along the wall of the Riggs Bank.

"Help me, Thural! Please! Won't you help me carry him?" Hooking his claw under the seam at Tali's upper arm, Reen jerked the body to its knees. Thural mastered his stunned confusion enough to grab the Cousin Conscience by the belt. Staggering under the dead weight, they dragged him to the ship.

The door parted as they approached. Thural let go of Tali and threw himself into the pilot's seat. Reen eased Tali's slumped form into his lap.

It was as though he were falling into a pillowy well. Reen dimly felt the ship jerk sideways, heard a metallic clunk as it slammed the red Jaguar into the grille of the Cadillac behind. He struggled to think. If he didn't fight the Communal Mind, he would end up as useless as a Loving Helper. "Up! Go *up!*"

Thural pulled on the ball. The ship wrenched itself into the air.

And silently, helplessly, Reen dropped. He fell toward a colorless place where nothing was important: the Vespa, the riot, the coming war. Then Reen's weakening grip loosened even the cherished: Womack, Marian, Angela.

With a moan Reen sat up. The ship was hovering above the Victorian mass of Georgetown Park, quivering as much as Thural himself. "The Potomac," Reen said.

Thural slewed the craft over the elevated Whitehurst Freeway until it was seesawing above the river.

Again Reen tumbled down, down, this time into a darkness where Tali's secret thoughts lurked, an unexpected and unexplored den of monsters. Startled, he pushed away his Brother's frightening thoughts. "Andrews. Get us to Andrews," he mumbled.

"Yes, Cousin." Thural lifted the craft high enough to miss the bumper-to-bumper traffic on Theodore Roosevelt Bridge.

Tali's hand twitched. Thural glanced over in surprised relief. "I think he is coming out of it, Reen-ja."

Tali heaved himself upright in Reen's lap, drunkenly fumbling at the wound on his shoulder. Caught in the undertow of oblivion, Reen held his Brother tight so the childhood comfort of Cousin flesh against flesh would call him back.

"Cousin Conscience," Thural said. "Tali. Listen to me. You must stir yourself. The little death nibbles at you."

A few nonsense syllables dropped from Tali's mouth. Then he said in a muddy voice, "They hurt me."

"Yes. Do you remember now?"

Tali's eyes were suddenly clear, the gaze piercing. He twisted out of Reen's grip and the bonds of Communal Mind dropped away so suddenly that the onrush of freedom made Reen gasp.

"I remember. Get your hands off me, Cousin Brother. We are not children anymore."

He shoved past Reen with such force that he bumped Thural, sending the ship into a brief, alarming dive toward the Capitol. Tali

did not notice. Breathing hard, he dropped into the rear seat. "They hurt me."

Reen remembered when they were children—when thoughts were innocent and life was less constrained. Centuries before, he and Tali had touched. Then, when they were grown, touching became taboo. As much as the Communal Mind repulsed Reen, he'd once mourned its loss, and Tali had mourned with him.

Now his Brother sat, arms rigidly at his sides, disgust in his face.

"Are you all right, Cousin?" Thural asked solicitously.

Tali curled his claw underneath the bar of his nameplate and savagely tore it off. The bit of plastic flew past Thural's head and pinged off the canopy. "They do not bother to learn our names."

Reen stared at the rectangle of black plastic lying on the control panel. The hook of the nameplate was bent at a furious angle.

Thural told him, "They don't see as we see, Cousin. We all look alike to them."

The ship swept over the congestion on Suitland Parkway.

"I will never wear the nameplate again. Not ever."

Reen turned to study his Brother. Tali was glaring down at the traffic below as though he wished he were an alien from an old science fiction movie and the scene they were playing with the humans was from "War of the Worlds." He stared down at the pedestrians and the cars like Godzilla, wanting to crush them all.

Reen's heart skipped a beat. "As you wish, Cousin Brother."

9

When they arrived at Andrews, Tali, still wobbly from his brush with the little death, climbed down from the ship. On the tarmac he pulled his sleeve free from Thural's steadying claw and marched into the Cousin Place, leaving Thural and Reen standing alone.

Thural said, "It must be a small wound. Tali will be all right, Cousin First Brother."

But would he? Remembering the ugliness he had sensed in his Brother's mind, Reen wondered if the wound was deeper than Thural knew. "Yes, I am sure he will," he told him. "I would like you to take me to the White House now."

As they lifted off again, Reen noticed that some of Tali's blood had splattered on his tunic. He brushed at the stiffening stain, knocking off a few brown flakes.

In a low, diffident voice Thural said, "Cousin Tali is too full of anger, Reen-ja."

"It is wrong to criticize the Conscience," Reen said curtly, hoping Thural would change the subject.

"Yes. Still, the humans have done nothing to us, and Tali has too much anger."

They banked over the Tidal Basin and passed the Washington

Monument. Reen took his Brother's broken nameplate from the control panel and closed his fist over it.

Troops had been called out to the White House. The men by the tanks looked up as the craft passed over their heads. On landing, Reen jumped from the ship without exchanging another word with Thural. As he walked to the West Wing, he slipped Tali's broken nameplate into his pocket.

Hopkins was waiting for him in the colonnade. "Reen? That you?" The man bent over to read the tag on Reen's chest.

"It's me."

The director's beefy face sagged in relief. "Thank God. My guys phoned me to say an alien was down, but they weren't sure which of you it was."

"Tali." Reen strode past the director and down the hall toward the main building.

"Tali? Oh, Jesus Christ. Not Tali. Hey, where are you going?"

"To see the President."

"Oh, that won't do you any good." Hopkins panted as he kept up with Reen's quick pace. "I went up a minute ago to talk to him, and the man was *drooling*. He was drooling all down his shirt. Must be a bad day or something. Say, I'm sorry about Tali. My guys did all they could, considering that—"

"Tali is recovering."

Hopkins put one hand to his chest. "God. The stress, you wouldn't believe. I thought I had my right nut in the wringer."

Near the kitchen was new graffiti.

AT GROVER'S MILL.

BRING CHICKEN POX.

"*War of the Worlds,*" Reen whispered.

"Huh?"

"I'm not fond of fiction, but I felt I should study all fictionalized aliens. Whoever wrote the graffiti has heard about the radio play *War of the Worlds*. That should give you a clue about who is doing this."

"Oh." Hopkins squinted at the message. "Grover's Mill. Now I

get it. But everyone and his dog's heard about that. Won't do us much good."

From the other end of the carpeted hall Marian Cole called Reen's name.

"Bitch," Hopkins muttered.

She approached at a saunter. "And good afternoon to you, too, Billy. Reen, I know you're going up to visit the President, but I need to talk to you now."

Out of the corner of his mouth Hopkins told Reen, "Watch yourself with her. I don't know what she's got on you, but—"

"Now, please," Marian said, and led Reen down the wide red-carpeted hall to the Map Room. A fire had been banked in the hearth, and a plate of food had been set out.

"Go ahead," Marian told him. "I know you're hungry. If no one bothers to remind you, you forget to eat."

Touched, he sat down. She took a chair opposite and rested her chin in her hand. "Detective Rushing is one of ours. I want you to make sure he gets a good look at the body before the FBI takes over."

Reen cut into a stuffed tomato. "So that's how he knew a Cousin had been kidnapped. Certainly he may have the body, if you like."

"I like. How's Tali?"

He was moved, too, that she asked about his Brother, and pleased that Rushing had been perceptive enough to notice which Cousin had fallen. "Better, thank you."

"Shit," she said with guttural anger. "Rushing told me he was down. I hoped he was dead."

He lowered a forkful of chicken salad. The heavy silverware chimed against the porcelain. Reen looked into her eyes and was cast adrift in the turbulent ocean of their blue. "I have never wished harm on any human, as you have just wished on my Brother."

She took a breath. "Vilishnikov has taken the precaution of calling out the army. You probably saw the troops in front of the White House. We've picked up new satellite data. German tanks are massing on Russia's border with China."

He wanted to touch her. Was afraid to. "Sometimes I wish I had treated you like the others. You could have been any one of hundreds of women, never knowing, never remembering . . ."

"Reen!" Her cheeks were flushed; her tone sharp. "Germany is heading up a European invasion of China. What do you plan to do when the missiles start flying?"

With his claw Reen pushed a potato chip to the side of his plate. "I don't know. I don't know anything. Is it Howard? Is that what the problem is?"

Her laugh was short and ironic. "Howard?"

"Something has happened between us. Are you still in love with Howard?"

"Oh, Reen. Love dies. It's no big deal," she said softly. "It happens every day: People fall in love, they fall out of love. Relationships end."

He clutched her hand. It was warm, warm as the glow from the fire. He squeezed her so tightly, he could feel her pulse. "I don't understand endings."

The room was hushed, the air heavy with the scent of lemon oil and furniture polish. She fought to pull free of his grip. After a moment he opened his fingers and let her go.

"I used to hold your hand and you clung to me. Do you remember?" he asked. "During the experiments, we shared things, as Brother bonds to Brother. Cousins live centuries, Marian. And love is the only neverending thing we have."

He had searched for that Brother union in Marian. Too late, he understood the consequences of what he had done. He made Marian remember the pain so that she would grow to need the comfort of his touch.

"It was a long time ago." She sat back. "What's in your pocket?"

He had forgotten the subpoena. Now he took it out and handed it to her. She read it, chuckled, and gave it back. "Get a good lawyer."

"I've never been before a Senate subcommittee. What will they do?"

Suddenly her smile failed. He stiffened in alarm.

"Reen, you're in danger. So's the President. And Tali's behind it."

Reen made an irritated click-click with his tongue. "Only humans are so fickle."

"Tali's involved. And Jonis has to be found."

She must have noticed him flinch because she asked, "What's the story with Jonis?"

He picked at the gold rim of the plate with his claw. "I was afraid I would find the kidnapper was you."

Love, Reen thought. It was the only neverending thing he had. It didn't matter that Tali gave Reen his disapproval. He also gave him love. As Brothers that was something neither Reen nor Tali could help.

"I didn't take Jonis," she said. "But your Brother knows who did."

He got up quickly and walked to the door, stuffing the subpoena in his pocket.

"Reen? Your Brother knows who did."

As he left, his hand touched the edge of his Brother's nametag, and he fingered it thoughtfully.

10

BEFORE GOING TO SEE THE PRESIDENT, Reen went to the West Wing to order the FBI to hand over Martinez's body. On his way out, the House majority whip waylaid him.

"Do you realize how hard it was to get that bill passed?" Barbara Yates was not much taller than Reen. Eye level. Her anger was visceral and barbaric.

"The Eastern bloc outnumbers us two to one. The Chinese delegation is so big, most of them have to vote electronically. Do you realize how many arms I had to twist? We're in a recession. This bill could get the economy moving. When does the President plan to sign?"

"I'm sorry." He was sorry about Marian's bitterness, about the impending war. He was sorry for it all.

"I hear you were served the subpoena. Six days from now the hearing will be broadcast live on C-Span. It'll be picked up on the networks. Womack's too popular to target, but *you* . . . You're dead meat. That black budget of Womack's—you know how much he spent this year? Two million! What in hell is he doing that costs two million dollars? And what's important enough about his veto to make our boys go to war?"

"I don't know. I don't—"

"Well, you'd better just find out, hadn't you. And you'd better be ready to answer, or you'll be found in contempt of Congress. And tell Womack to stuff his executive branch power play up—"

Reen fled. Barbara Yates's shouts followed him out the door.

Hopkins had either given up waiting for Reen or had decided, uncharacteristically, to go back to work. Reen passed a Secret Service agent standing at wordless attention in the cross hall and took the elevator to the second floor.

In the presidential study a fire was lit against the chill of the misty day. Womack and a weak-chinned, bespectacled man in a T-shirt were seated at the Santa Fe table having coffee.

"Hi, Termite," Womack said. "Meet Lizard."

The man lifted an emaciated arm in greeting. Lizard had horn-rimmed glasses and the sort of skin that looks as though it can be used for polishing silver.

"Can we talk in private?" Two million dollars for mediums. The sum sounded exorbitant.

"You can talk in front of Lizard," Womack said.

Reen shook his head. "I would rather not."

Lizard tucked his thumbs into his belt and slumped with insolent indifference.

"What'd you want to talk about?" Womack asked. "Go ahead. Don't mind Lizard. He's dead."

Lizard nodded sagely, his glasses glinting in the light. "Laid my hog down in 1972 doing eighty-five on Highway 20. So I don't have no stake in no live people shit."

Confused, Reen took a seat close to Womack. "Bernard Martinez was found strangled."

"Oh, bummer," Lizard groaned. "Me and Bernie were tight." He shoved an entwined fore- and middle finger into Reen's face. "Like fucking brothers. I mean, even though Bernard was shitting corporeal and all."

"Why don't you call Bernard and see who killed him?" Womack suggested.

Lizard's eyes rolled back into his head. Reen sat selfconsciously, watching the bloodshot whites. Finally the medium's irises returned to their normal position and he gave Reen a lupine smile. "Bernie ain't talking, man. He's ascended, you know. An important fucker in the spirit world."

Reen glanced down at Lizard's torn jeans. Little of the two million, apparently, had been spent on clothes. A tab of blue protruded from a begrimed pocket. Lizard must have bought his karma tickets the same place Bernard had.

"How well did you know Jonis?" Reen asked the medium.

Lizard darted a glance at him, then looked away. "Man, *everybody* knew Jonis. Jonis got around." After a pause he said softly, "Some shit happening in the basement of the West Wing. Heavy shit. While Jeremy was sleeping it off by the pool, he heard something."

"Who's Jeremy?" Reen asked.

With a wave of a gnarled hand Womack motioned him silent. "Jeremy's the medium. Lizard's the spirit guide. Let him talk. Go on, Lizard."

Lizard's eyes were the still, muddy color of algae in a shallow pond. "He heard something he wished he hadn't, man. And then he drank and hoped he'd forget it. Hoped God would forgive him for getting shit-faced, and prayed nobody'd seen him there."

"What'd he overhear?" Womack asked.

"Heavy, heavy shit."

Weary of this, Reen turned to Womack. "Thural tells me Jonis arranged to buy karma for you, Jeff. Who else was he involved with other than the karma sellers?"

Instead of Womack, Lizard answered. "Wasn't no karma sellers who offed Jonis. And they didn't mean to ice him."

"Why do you think Jonis is dead?"

Lizard turned those hazel eyes on Reen. The pools were muddier and deeper than he at first imagined. If he fell into Lizard's eyes, those dank waters would close over him. "His ghost comes to me, man.

That's how I know. He says they was real surprised how easy you guys die."

A thrill of fear ran down Reen's back like a rivulet of rain.

"You want to talk to him?"

"No," Reen said sharply.

"Funny. Jonis wants to talk to you," Lizard said. "He keeps trying to get your attention. Wants to apologize, he says. Wants to warn you. But he says you only listen to those old farts. The big shadows."

Startled, Reen blundered up from his chair. He was sure he had never described the Old Ones to Womack.

Womack caught Reen's wrist. "Remember what I found in the West Wing, termite? The thing that had no business being there?"

Reen pulled out of Womack's grip.

Lizard said, "They killed Bernie but not before he found out what they was doing. And they kidnapped Jonis because Jonis knew it all."

Womack leaned over the table. "It's coming to a head. I can feel it. Teddy Roosevelt tells me so. Cut your losses, termite. Get people close to you that you can trust. Fire Cole and Hopkins before it's too late."

Reen jumped to his feet and ran for the elevator, Womack following in his fast old-man shamble. "Reen! Reen!"

Reen plunged into the safety of the car, but before the door could close, Womack slapped a hand on the jamb. "Get rid of them, termite."

Reen pounded the row of buttons frantically, by accident setting off the alarm. Womack stepped into the elevator, and the car started its descent. "You'll have the Secret Service crawling all over us."

Reen turned his back.

"I know you don't want to hear it," Womack said.

Reen concentrated on the whirls of the wood paneling, how they nested into one another, shape into shape, like waves seen from a height. He lost himself briefly in the comfort of its pattern.

The elevator stopped. The doors rumbled open. A worried voice: "Sir? Is everything all right?"

"Elevator goes up," Womack chirped in his official-idiot voice. "Elevator goes down."

"Yes, Mr. President."

The doors rumbled closed. The car lifted.

"Are you still talking to me?" Womack asked.

"No."

"You trust people too much, termite."

"You and my Brother should get together, since you both enjoy lecturing me."

The door opened. Reen walked out of the vestibule and headed to the stairs.

"Your Brother's in the middle of it," Womack said, grabbing his arm.

In the study Lizard was sitting calmly in his chair, drinking his coffee. Their gazes met. Lizard's eyes had the tranquil self-assuredness of a man twice his size.

The President marched Reen back to the elevator, pulled a key from his pocket, inserted it into a brass plate, and turned. The car stayed put; the doors stayed shut.

"Did you hear me?" Womack asked.

"Yes. But I don't believe you."

The President leaned back against the wall, crossing his arms. "I'm scared to death, termite."

Reen was frightened, too. Frightened by the voices the medium had heard in the night; by Womack's lunacy.

"Get rid of Cole and Hopkins. They're spiders. You can't walk around Washington without getting a faceful of web."

"But only you can fire them."

"Forge my signature like you usually do."

"If you're so worried about them, why don't you abandon your strike and fire them yourself?"

"You took my office."

"I will give it back."

"No thanks."

Ordinarily Reen liked tight places, but the small elevator car was beginning to suffocate him. Womack was close enough for Reen to feel the heat of his body.

"You fire Krupner yet?" the President asked.

"Do you think he's in on it, too?"

"Not Krupner. But you'd better fire him all the same. It'll give you some practice. Never fired anyone before, right? Okay. First, you go in and sit on his desk. He sits in his chair. That gives you the advantage of height. Then you say something like, 'You know we're all fond of you, Hans.' That way he won't be able to bitch about it being personal. You tell him, 'But lately you haven't been pulling your own weight.' You with me so far?"

"You haven't been pulling your own weight," Reen repeated dubiously.

"That's the way. Then you say, 'We need a good halfback, someone who can carry the ball. You just haven't been advancing the offense upfield.' Understand?"

"No."

"Doesn't matter. You tell him. He'll get the idea. Then you call the Germans and tell them you fired Krupner. Don't tell them before. Work from a position of strength, otherwise the bastards will think they can yank your dick every time you turn around."

"Are you sure it's wise to make the Germans angry right now? An army is mobilizing on the border of China, and the CIA says the Germans are behind it."

Womack clapped his palms together with glee. "That's perfect! If the Germans are planning to invade China, they won't dare give you any grief over Krupner." The President took the key from its plate and pocketed it. Before he left, he leaned toward Reen, his eyes abnormally wide, mouth pursed, forefinger to his lips. "Shhh. Don't tell anyone what we talked about. It's dangerous."

Reen wondered which was more dangerous, Womack's paranoia or discussing Womack's paranoia with a third party.

In the hall he paused, undecided. In the fifty years since the

landing, Jeff Womack's guidance had been invaluable, consistently astute. But Reen was beginning to see it was now necessary to separate the President's kernels of reason from their demented chaff. Firing Krupner seemed logical when Womack had first suggested it. Now Reen wasn't so sure.

"May I help you, sir?" the man on duty asked.

Reen ignored him and walked to the West Wing.

Once in the first level of the basement, Reen looked for Krupner's office and found the nameplate, HANS KRUPNER, EDUCATION COUNSEL, at the end of a dark corridor next to the bathrooms. He opened the door. Krupner's tiny office was a riotous origami zoo.

"Dr. Krupner?" Reen called.

Past a barrier of varied animals on the desk, a voice answered: "Yes?"

As Reen approached, Krupner's balding pate came into view, followed by his round, questioning brown eyes. Reen searched for a place on the desk to sit, failed, and at last took a seat on a steel folding chair.

"Hans," he began, peering over a spread-winged eagle. "We're all very fond of you."

Brows rose over Krupner's bonbon eyes. "Yes?"

Reen, leaning forward to bring more of Krupner's face into view, nearly crushed a paper horse. "But I've noticed lately that you're not pulling weight."

Krupner's face became very still.

Reen blundered on. "We need a good half to carry a ball. You don't advance the field."

Blood had drained from Krupner's cheeks, leaving them the color of paper, as if the man had become an origami self-portrait. A line of perspiration salted his upper lip.

Reen wanted more than anything to flee from the tiny office and Krupner's agonizing stare. It hadn't been his intention to hurt the man's feelings. He had expected that Krupner would protest the firing, would perhaps indignantly resign. Instead the silence in the room

was a soft but inescapable pressure, like a pillow forced against the face.

The corners of Krupner's mouth trembled. He was bent forward, straining; but Reen couldn't tell what exactly he was straining for. Could the man be in pain? Could he be—God forbid—voiding his bowels in the chair? Then the answer hit Reen. What he was seeing was intense confusion. "*Bitte?*" Krupner asked uncertainly. "I'm sorry. I don't—"

"You're fired."

Tears sprang to Krupner's eyes. His head dropped into the cage of his hands. "*Gott in Himmel. Gott sei dank,*" he said. "I'd thought—"

Reen backed quickly to the door. "Have your resignation on my desk in an hour."

Up and down went Krupner's head. Up and down. He stared around the room, as though already planning how to pack his animals.

"I'll call Germany for you."

"*Ja, ja,*" Krupner agreed in a lackluster voice.

Reen hurried upstairs to the Oval Office. The House majority whip, he noticed with relief, was gone. "Call Germany," he ordered as he passed the reception area where Natalie sat reading a novel.

Still clutching her book, finger marking the page, she stood and followed him. "Do you realize what time it is there?"

"Call the governor—what's his name?—at home."

"All right," she replied doubtfully. "Werner Hassenbein."

"What?"

"The governor's name is Werner Hassenbein. You should at least know his name if you're going to get him out of bed. You know, it'd be better if this could wait until morning. The Germans have been real agreeable. No sense pissing them—"

"Just place the call." Reen sat behind the uncluttered rosewood expanse of his own desk.

"Videophone hookup?"

"Yes, yes." He waved her out.

As she stalked from the room, he heard her mutter, "Your

funeral," and he wondered what she meant by that and if he should be afraid of her, too.

A few minutes later Natalie's voice came over the intercom: "Hassenbein's on hold."

Reen swung around to his credenza and tapped a command on the AT&T unit. REFUSED VIDEO SEND flashed across the screen.

"Governor Hassenbein?" Reen asked.

A mumble came over the receiver. "Yes?"

"I have just fired Hans Krupner."

"What?" The governor was awake now.

"I must ask you to arrange a replacement for him immediately."

"Oh." There was a long pause. "All right. Nothing scandalous, I hope."

Reen thought hard, wondering what the Germans would consider scandalous. Invading China? "He just wasn't . . . pulling his weight."

"*Ja, ja.* All right. Yes. These things happen."

The intercom buzzed. Natalie said, "Call on line two."

Reen ignored her. "When can you send a replacement?"

"Well . . ." Hassenbein said judiciously, as though he were counting the days on his fingers.

Natalie: "Emergency call, sir."

The governor said smugly, "We have, you know, a pool of good applicants to choose from."

"Yes, I'm sure. Let's set up a time. I can send one of my ships to get you. There is a great deal I wish to talk to you about. The tanks you have sent to Russia, for example—"

"What?" Hassenbein blurted. "What tanks?"

A burst of static from the intercom. "Quen on line two, sir. He says there's a medical emergency in West Virginia, and you're to pick up the line immediately."

"What ta—"

Reen punched the red square at the edge of his phone, neatly clipping the end of Hassenbein's question. Hand shaking, he pushed the pulsing light on two. "Quen?"

The Cousin Caretaker's voice was frantic. "Angela is sick, Reenja. Very sick. You must come to West Virginia at once."

"She—"

"*Now,* Reen!" Even over the phone lines, Reen could hear the hysteria in his Cousin's voice. "Come quickly."

Reen was out the door and halfway across the anteroom when Natalie called, "Governor Hassenbein's still on hold. What should I tell him?"

Cold terror rose in Reen's chest like water from a broken pipe. Distantly he wondered if the little death was coming for him as it had come for Tali.

"Sir?"

He turned blindly to Natalie, for a moment wondering where he was and what he had been about to do.

"Sir?" she asked in a hushed voice.

He remembered. Angela. Angela needed him. "Tell him anything," Reen gasped as he ran to the ship.

11

QUEN MET HIM AT THE DOOR TO THE children's house. "Oh, Reen-ja," he said, wringing his hands. "She is very sick."

Reen brushed him aside, ran past a clump of wide-eyed children entranced by a puppet show, and burst through the doorway to the female dormitory. Angela's bed was empty.

Some part of him had always known it would happen. The combination wouldn't work; the mixture of genes would be unstable. A few years of life, and some unseen mistake, some fatal error in planning, would kill her.

"Reen-ja," Quen said, his voice thick with pity.

Shut up! Reen's mind screamed. If Quen didn't speak, Angela would still be there. She would come running to him the way she always did. Reen stood frozen, one hand on the door, his disbelieving eyes on the barren bed, the vacant pillow, the way the late afternoon sun cast a river of brass across the empty floor.

Quen touched Reen's sleeve with a claw. "Reen-ja," he whispered sadly. "She . . ."

Reen's mouth widened until he felt it had opened a tunnel through his chest. He should have known never to fall in love with anything so fragile. "Shut up!"

In the living room the high silly voice of the puppet hushed. The children, startled by the shout, began to cry.

Warm human fingers grasped his shoulders. "Sir," Mrs. Gonzales said quietly. "She's in a room by herself. We're keeping her away from the other children."

Reen found himself being pulled around. He tripped over his numb feet. Behind Mrs. Gonzales's doughy bulk stood an assembly of curious, large-headed children and Quen, his black eyes wide.

"Are you all right?" Mrs. Gonzales asked, steadying Reen with a strong hand, a hand made for cooking gingerbread and wiping children's greedy faces.

Reen didn't have the strength to answer.

"It's just the flu, sir," she told him in her soothing voice. "Here. Let me take you to her. She's been asking for you."

Reen let her lead him down the hall and through a door. On a twin bed Angela lay inert and unmoving, her huge eyes closed.

"Her fever spiked," Mrs. Gonzales was saying. "We had a little convulsion and it alarmed Quen, but she's all right now. We gave her an alcohol rub, and her temperature's down."

Reen walked through the fog of Mrs. Gonzales's voice and looked down at his daughter. Her face was pinched. There was a hectic flush high on her cheeks: twin spots of clown color. Her mouth was open, her breathing labored.

"Seizures happen to small children with high fevers sometimes." Mrs. Gonzales's calm voice brushed at Reen's sticky anxiety. "It's frightening to watch, but nothing to get alarmed about."

Tentatively, Reen touched his daughter's arm. The skin was hot and dry, as though banked coals were baking her from the inside out. Quen was right: His daughter was very sick, and Mrs. Gonzales, as all humans eventually did, was lying to him.

Angela's eyes opened a slit.

"Your daddy's here, Angela," Mrs. Gonzales said. "See? Your daddy came to see you."

"Daddy." Angela grabbed Reen's hand. He lightly squeezed back,

fearful of injuring her. Suddenly her face drew up into a mask of misery, and she was crying. "Hurts. It hurts, Daddy."

Reen whirled to Mrs. Gonzales. The caregiver was smiling and checking her watch. "She seems to do well on Tylenol. Let's give her another child's dose and some orange juice. Her throat's been bothering her." Mrs. Gonzales made her way from the room, shooing away the inevitable crowd of children.

Quen walked in. "She believes it is a minor human disease, Reen-ja, but I am not so certain."

Reen turned his back on Quen. If Mrs. Gonzales said it was a minor disease, that was the explanation Reen chose. He would hold that explanation and wring sugared comfort from it.

But Quen was a Cousin, and Cousins weren't given to lying. And he was a scientist; he should know. As Reen gazed at his daughter, sour anxiety came oozing back.

"Hurts," Angela said in a demanding pipe, as though she expected her father to send the pain away as easily as he might order a junior senator to leave the room.

"Mrs. Gonzales has gone to get you Tylenol," he told her helplessly.

Mrs. Gonzales came in with the Tylenol bottle and a glass of orange juice. "Here, sweetie." She put two tiny pink pills on Angela's tongue. "Raise her head," she told Reen.

Putting a hand behind the child, Reen gently lifted. Mrs. Gonzales slipped the end of a straw into the child's mouth. Angela took a sip but then wrenched her head away. Orange juice dribbled onto her pajamas. "Hurts."

"Children always get a little cross when they're sick," Mrs. Gonzales said with a forbearing smile. "Come on, sweetie. Just a little more."

"If it hurts her . . ." Reen said, unsure. Angela pressed her face protectively into his arm.

Mrs. Gonzales ignored him. "If you drink your orange juice, honey, you can have some ice cream."

Pouting, Angela turned to Mrs. Gonzales. When the caregiver put the straw back into her mouth, Angela drank almost half.

"Good girl. Quen? Why don't you go get Angela a scoop of ice cream. Chocolate. She likes chocolate."

With a glare, Quen left.

Mrs. Gonzales pulled Reen aside. "Quen may be the geneticist," she said firmly, "but I'm a pediatric RN. I know children. Angela's going to be just fine."

Reen wanted to believe her. But when Quen brought the ice cream, Reen noticed that Angela ate only a few spoonfuls before becoming weepy and demanding again. Mrs. Gonzales put a palm to the child's brow. Then she took Reen to a rocking chair in front of the window and set the blanket-wrapped Angela on his lap.

"Hold her," she said.

Reen cautiously slipped his arm under his daughter's head. Unlike Tali, nothing moved in Angela's mind, neither dark, hateful creatures nor ghosts of the Community.

"If her fever climbs," she said, "call me."

Angela filled Reen's arms with warmth. Outside, a gunmetal sky was sifting a fine snow that obscured the gray winter hills. "Snow," Angela whispered before lolling her head against her father's shoulder and drifting into an uneasy sleep.

Awkwardly, wishing he were more practiced at embraces, Reen rocked his daughter as the day blurred into night. On his lap Angela twisted and whimpered. In the main part of the house Reen could hear the sporadic laughter of children, could smell dinner on the stove.

It was dark when Quen made his way quietly into the room. "Reen-ja?" he whispered. "Will you be staying the night?"

Reen shifted his weight to ease a cramp in his leg. Angela stirred restlessly. "Yes."

Kneeling at Reen's side, Quen studied the little girl. "It is interesting that she called you Daddy when she hadn't before."

"Yes," Reen said faintly. "Interesting." He'd never demanded that

she love him, never encouraged her to call him anything other than his name, but the fact that in her misery she had acknowledged him as her father brought a raw ache to his throat.

"There are niches," Quen went on. "Not so many Cousins as in Washington, but enough to sleep well."

A cold draft from around the windowpane caressed Reen's arms and face. "I will stay here in her room." He gently wiped the glaze of perspiration from his daughter's forehead. Her skin was like and yet so unlike his own: gray, but supple and moist as a human's. Her curled hand was a marvel of engineering. Miraculous, dusky eyelashes shadowed her cheeks.

"But Reen-ja . . ."

"One night won't hurt me."

In the darkening bedroom there was a quiet sound, the sound of Quen's sigh. "Should I stay with you?"

From his tone Reen could tell that Quen hoped his offer would be refused. "Go sleep."

"If you tire, Cousin . . ."

"I know," Reen said curtly.

After a moment Quen rose and padded away, leaving Reen holding his daughter. In the glow of the outside lights the snow drifted, settling on the gentle curve of the ship, on the branches of the trees. Several times Reen felt himself dropping off to sleep, but then some unexpected movement of the snow or of the wind-nudged trees would wake him.

Around midnight a cramp seized his right arm, and he carefully moved Angela's head to his left shoulder. At three in the morning, by the luminous numbers of the digital clock on the bedstand, the snow stopped. In the hush a raccoon, foraging for an early morning meal, trundled through the pool of light between the house and the ship, the wind ruffling its thick fur. Pausing just at the edge of the light, the raccoon turned its bandit eyes toward the window where Reen sat in silent vigil over his daughter.

Reen dozed and was roused by the low, mournful hoot of an owl.

As dawn broke vague and blue, he stretched his shoulders to ease the ache in his back.

At six-thirty Mrs. Gonzales came in the room and stood in the pink sunrise from the window, looking down at Reen and his child. Angela's smooth face was still. Reen couldn't remember when the feverish twitching of her body had ceased.

"Her fever's broken," Mrs. Gonzales whispered. "She's fine now." Reaching down, she lifted Angela from Reen's arms. The child muttered in her sleep.

"We'll put her in her own bed. Are you all right?"

"Yes," he said, but when he stood up, he nearly fell. He was weak. There was a hot ache from his neck to the middle of his back. His left leg was numb. Holding on to the wall for balance, he limped out to the common room where Quen and Thural were waiting.

"Reen-ja," Thural said anxiously. "You didn't come to the niches."

"I know." Reen tried to bring his Cousin's face into focus.

"Will you sleep now, Reen-ja? A few of us will go back with you to make a Community."

Reen lifted his hand in negation, then let it drop as he forgot what the gesture had been for.

"Reen-ja. You will become ill yourself," Quen said sharply.

Thural said, "He becomes stubborn, and there is no way to deal with him. Let me take him to the Cousin Place at Andrews. Once he smells sleep he will go into a niche soon enough."

Reen knew he should be irked by what was said, but the moment the words were uttered, he tried and failed to grasp them. They drifted from his clutch like leaves in a stream.

"Come, Reen-ja." Thural grabbed Reen's sleeve with his claw. Obligingly, like a large, dimwitted dog, Reen let himself be led out of the children's house to the ship.

12

As Reen walked into the Cousin Place, the odor of sleep hit him, and he started to sag. Thural grabbed his tunic and tried his best to hold him upright without coming in contact with his body.

"Reen," the Sleep Master said.

Bleary-eyed, Reen turned the old Cousin's way, wondering what was wrong.

"Repeat the first covenant."

Thural nudged Reen against the wall with his boot and hooked a claw in his sleeve to prevent him from sliding to the floor.

For convention's sake Reen kept the irritation out of his voice, but it annoyed him that the Sleep Master would choose such a time to review catechism. "Work," he replied.

"And work's brother is?"

"Sleep," Reen said dully.

"Humans often ignore both, Reen-ja. Cousins cannot afford to. There is too little time left us for work, and too great a price to pay for forgoing sleep. See that you remember that."

When the Sleep Master turned again to gaze at the wall, point apparently made, Thural guided Reen into the chamber.

Reen straightened his body against the hard confines of a vacant

niche. The interlocking plates in his back relaxed. Now that it was permitted, he pulled the edge of the Communal Mind up to his neck like a secure blanket, and in a few moments he was asleep.

Thural woke him. "Reen-ja?"

Reen inched himself onto his side and saw his aide, a specter in the hazy blue of the aisle.

"Have you rested enough, Cousin?"

Reen wasn't sure. No time had seemed to pass from the instant he had lain down to the instant he had awakened. "What is it?"

"Hans Krupner is missing."

Reen was fully awake now. He slid out of the niche and was suddenly aware that Thural wasn't alone. Tali was standing by the door. "Kidnapped also? When?"

"I think not kidnapped. But I should tell you all of it, Cousin," Thural said. "While you were asleep the Germans called. I was training Sidam to replace Jonis as your second aide, so I took the call and spoke to Werner Hassenbein. He says they received a fax from Hans Krupner, a fax of an interoffice departmental study of baby food production at Gerber. He asked me where all the strained peas are disappearing," Thural said, twisting his upper body miserably, "and I did not know how to answer."

Reen looked at Tali, but his Cousin Brother was giving no hints. "Strained peas?"

"Missing food, Cousin, between the raw ingredients bought and what appears on the shelves. I told the Germans to delay their flight, but they are on the Lufthansa supersonic to Washington. Hassenbein says he will call you over the Atlantic. I fear they may have caught on at last, and I believe Hans Krupner may be hiding from us."

"Call Michigan and tell—"

"Yes, Cousin," Thural said breathlessly. "Already done. He is on his way."

Grumbling, Reen padded through the doorway of the baths to wash the gummy residue of sleep from his skin. While he was changing, the Sleep Master came in.

"Your mind becomes glass while you sleep, Reen-ja," the Sleep Master said. "I look through the glass and see the torment there. So do the other Cousins, and it robs them of their rest."

Reen lifted his arms into the sleeves of his uniform and caught a whiff of the tannic acid the bathwater had left on his body. "What should I do, then, Cousin, when work is the first covenant and torment is part of my job?"

"It is not work that causes your torment, Reen," the old Cousin told him, "but the love you feel for strangers."

"Humans," Reen corrected him. "We can't call them strangers anymore."

"They do not share the Mind when they sleep, Reen. Therefore they will forever be strangers."

It was quiet in the baths except for the splash some awakening Cousin made in the pools beyond the doorway. Reen dropped his dirty uniform near the bench for the Loving Helpers to pick up. As it hit the floor, something rustled. The subpoena. He bent, grabbed the paper, and shoved it into his pocket. Then he sat on a bench and pulled on his boots, hoping the Sleep Master would go away.

"I have spoken with Tali of the matter," the Cousin said.

Reen muttered, "As though he would understand love," and jerked his right boot on angrily.

The Sleep Master apparently decided to ignore Reen's rudeness. In a tolerant voice he said, "The sleep grows weak, Cousin First Brother. The female should be bred. Eggs would soothe her and help the Community sleep better. Tali agrees."

Reen stood and stomped his left foot into his boot. "There are too few of us left, Cousin. I will not choose one to die simply because the female should be happy."

"Tali suspects the breakdown in DNA can be reversed and that we should try breeding again."

The smell of tannic acid and moisture lay heavy in the room. Reen turned his back on the old Cousin and rummaged around in his locker until he found an extra nametag. "The DNA inviability cannot be

reversed. If it could be, the humans might then undo what we have done. We use the breakdown as a weapon, Cousin, and both we and the humans now die of the same malady. No race has lived as long as we. All species run to extinction. That we have run more slowly is a lucky thing that should be celebrated and not mourned."

"You give all our worlds and goods to these mongrel children, Reen-ja."

Angry now, Reen snapped his head around. "They are our children! The only children we will ever have."

"They are not Cousins. We should try breeding again."

Reen made a derisive click-click with his tongue. "The geneticists all agree that if we breed now, we will only breed more Loving Helpers. We might find ourselves in the unenviable position of having to destroy the larvae."

Behind Reen came a sharp gasp. When he turned, the disgust in the old Cousin's eyes hit him like a blow.

"Tali is right. You *are* a monster."

"I am a monster for loving; and Tali is not a monster for his hatred. Perhaps you could explain the ethics of that." Hands shaking, Reen fumbled at the nametag, pricking himself with the pin. In frustration he threw the tag to the floor. "Tell me. When Tali comes to the Community, do you see the ugliness behind his glass mind, Cousin Master of Sleep? Because Tali carries much ugliness in him."

The Sleep Master stared back impassively. Controlling himself, Reen knelt and picked up the nametag.

"Tali puts his untoward thoughts away for the night, as a good Cousin should," the Sleep Master said. "You might learn that from him. But perhaps you are too mired in strangers' lives to learn anything."

Reen rose to his feet, studying his finger. A bead of dark brown blood welled from the wound. "If you are displeased with me, take your displeasure to the Community."

"I have."

For a moment Reen fought to breathe.

"The Community is tearing itself apart very quietly, Reen-ja. I will not permit it. Perhaps one day you will wish to enter the chambers, and I will turn you away—you and Thural and the others who care too much for strangers. Then you can make your own Community where you can sleep and share non-Cousin things."

Who had the Sleep Master spoken with? Reen wondered as he pinned the nametag unsteadily to his chest. And who had agreed with him? "Tell me if you decide this," he said with careful, artificial calm. "But let me know ahead of time so arrangements can be made."

He dared not look at the Sleep Master as he hurried from the room. Instead he looked at his own chest. His nametag was crooked.

13

WHAT HE HAD LEARNED IN THE BATHS so disturbed Reen that he hoped his Brother wouldn't accompany him to the White House; but accompany him Tali did. He sat with Reen in the lounge. Instead of preaching more Communal law, he kept silent; and Reen was too angry to ask him what he had told the Sleep Master. Normally silence between Cousins was comfortable. This was torment.

When they sailed over the tanks gathered at the fence and landed at the side of the West Wing, the trio of Cousins followed Reen to the Oval Office. As soon as they entered, Natalie started reading nametags. "Oh. The whole group, huh? Hi, Thural. Welcome back, Sidam. The job training couldn't scare you off yesterday? Listen, Reen. Governor Hassenbein's been calling every five minutes. What's going on?"

Reen opened his mouth to answer, but Tali snapped, "Go back to your work immediately. There is nothing here you need to concern yourself with."

Natalie's face shut down. Her eyes scanned Tali's nameless chest as though wondering who he was and if he had the power to address her so curtly.

"It's about the firing yesterday," Reen said, hoping to defuse a showdown.

Luckily the buzz of the phone drew her attention. "Chief of staff's office," she said, picking up the receiver. There was a pause. "Just a minute, Governor. I'll check." With one red fingernail she hit the HOLD button. "It's Hassenbein. You in?" she asked Reen.

Tali, who had not yet learned the wisdom of silence, said nastily, "Of course he is in. Are you blind or merely stupid? Do you not see him standing in front of you?"

Thural and Sidam exchanged winces.

"Look, mister whatever the hell your name is," she told Tali, tapping a fingertip against the desk for emphasis. "Unless you sign my paychecks—"

"Thank you, Natalie. Tell him I'm here," Reen said hurriedly. "I'll take it inside."

At his desk Reen engaged his speakerphone. Natalie put the call through. He could hear the rumble and whine of the supersonic's engines. "Governor?"

Hassenbein shouted over the plane's noise: "Reen? I received a most interesting fax last night."

"Ye—"

"And it causes me to wonder, *ja?* So many tons of peas to Gerber Foods in Michigan, so few bottles of strained peas on the shelves. Production of bottled peas, of *bottled* peas, you understand, has dropped from one and a half million per day to merely seven hundred thousand over the last three fiscal years, yet the production of product, that is to say, the strained peas themselves, has remained the same. I was hoping you could clear up this discrepancy."

Reen waited a long time to answer. As he waited he cast a worried glance at his Brother who, head cocked, was listening intently to the conversation.

"What do you suppose this means?" Reen finally asked.

At the other end he could hear chimes and a garbled announcement from the plane's loudspeakers. The Lufthansa flight was de-

scending, and the passengers were being called to their seats. "It must mean something, yes? For Dr. Krupner to fax me the information."

"We were having a few problems with Krupner. Emotional problems."

"Ah, of course. But still it is an interesting development. Where do these strained peas go? We land in an hour. Perhaps you can find out by the time you pick me up at the airport. I would prefer to be picked up in the White House Mercedes. Your ships sometimes cause me to be . . . indisposed."

Reen looked at Tali. His Cousin Brother was standing rigidly, as Cousin custom dictated, his expression carefully blank. "This Gerber question, Governor Hassenbein. Are you using it to lure my attention away from your plans to invade China?"

A cough. "As much as the deregulation has hurt our manufacturing base, we have no plans to invade China."

"But—"

"Who told you that? The CIA? I have it on good report that your CIA cannot be trusted. And after this Gerber development, I must now be suspicious of you as well."

"I don't understand why developments at Gerber would trouble anyone but an employee of Gerber. Do you see it otherwise?"

He said, "I think maybe I do."

With a click the line went dead. Reen leaned back in his chair and sighed.

"You see what I am talking about, Cousin Reen-ja?" Thural said. "They apparently have discovered something. I fear they have found the component, and if so—"

Reen's intercom beeped. "The CEO of Gerber Foods is here, sir," Natalie said with a huff. "I tried to explain to him that without an appointment—"

"Send him in."

Before Reen could reach the door, Oomal was already entering, one hand burdened by an attaché case, the other outstretched in welcome.

Instantly Reen recoiled. "Oops," Oomal murmured and slipped the offending hand behind his back. "Good to see you, First Brother."

Reen shut the door. "I think the Germans have caught on to what is happening," he said, not bothering to keep accusation from his voice. "They talk about discrepancies with production, but—"

"Oh, that. *That's* no surprise. It's like trying to hide an elephant in the middle of a party, you know? The humans were bound to catch on sooner or later."

At this bombshell the other Cousins froze.

Oomal looked around the room. "Why don't we all sit down? I've been running around the home factory all morning."

Tali turned to the two aides. "You will not be needed in this discussion, so it is best that you go to the ship."

Thural was astonished. Sidam, though, simply turned and left the room. After a hesitation Thural followed him.

"So, Brother," Oomal said to Tali when the two aides had left. "How are you doing? And where's your nametag?"

"You wished to sit," Tali said. "So we will sit."

"Fine with me." Oomal threw a questioning glance at Reen.

Reen sat down in his swivel chair; Oomal slumped into the Louis XV antique and regarded the standing Tali.

"You know, if you hate keeping up with that nametag, Tali, you ought to have this done." Oomal ran a finger lovingly across the gold-embroidered *Oomal* above his left chest. "A little place up in Chicago sews these for me. Here." He pulled a wallet out of his pocket. Under a corporate Visa Oomal found what he was looking for: a blue-embossed card. "They ship UPS."

Tali reluctantly took the card and scowled at Oomal's diamond pinkie ring. "Reen-ja is right to accuse you, Third Brother." He took a chair a few feet to Reen's left and regarded both Brothers with poorly concealed contempt. "He believes you have been left too long to your own devices and that you have failed our trust. He is sure this has put the entire Community in danger."

Reen winced. He hadn't meant to accuse Oomal at all. Polite

inquiry would have been enough. But the Brother Conscience was giving him no way out. Tali wanted to see Oomal's blood on the floor, and he expected Reen to inflict the wound. Reen linked his hands and sat back, trying to decide what to do.

Oomal tapped his claw against the chair's cherrywood frame. Tick-tick went the claw. Tick-tick. "Failed? What makes you think that?"

Oomal was sprawled, legs apart. Tali's back was straight, several inches away from the human comfort of the cushion. Reen studied their different postures for a moment, until he became aware of his own. He was leaning back in his leather chair, rocking slightly. He stopped rocking and sat up.

"We now have a ninety-eight and a half percent birthless rate among women under the age of twenty-four," Oomal went on. "And human science and technology are pretty much at a standstill. You must have seen the reports."

"The Firstborn agrees with me on all Community matters, and he wishes me to warn you: This new generation of humans may be incapable of reproduction and may be partly under our control, but they understand what is happening to them," Tali said. "That is the danger."

A tense silence was broken only by the tick-tick of Oomal's claw. Reen studied the body language, the tiny annoyed gestures, the candid disdain on Oomal's face. Confronted by the censure of both First and Second, a Third Brother should have been humbled. Oomal wasn't. Reen was surprised how human Oomal had become during his years in Michigan. And confused to find that he admired him for it.

Tick-tick. "They don't understand, Brother Conscience. They don't understand anything. They see their engineering is fifty years stale, and they see the drop in the birthrate, sure. Only we make certain they can't think about it very long. We stopped the statisticians' reports at an eighteen percent decline. As far as any humans know, that's bottom line, okay? Listen. Humans under the age of twenty-four used to breed like rabbits, so I have to juggle catastrophic

drop-offs in the use of hospital maternity wards and soothe pediatricians and ob-gyn people. It's hard. And nobody's screamed yet. So, Cousin Brother, don't give me this 'they understand' crap. The truth is, you can only hide an elephant so long at a party. You can see that, can't you, Reen-ja?" Oomal turned to his First Brother for help.

"What was Hans Krupner doing at Gerber?" Reen asked mildly.

"A report on preschool nutrition. He came up to Michigan and went over our home office facilities for about a month."

"And you let him?" Tali asked.

"Why not? We're proud of our quality control. Besides, it's not as if we have problems at Gerber with corporate espionage. It would have looked suspicious if we refused."

Reen asked, "What is all this talk about the strained peas?"

"We buy more raw material than we need, and the excess production is sent via orbital mass driver into the sun. At Gerber," Oomal said solemnly, "we're environmentally correct."

Oomal, noticing Tali's disapproval, went on: "Look. You have to see the big picture." He leaned back and described an arc in the air with his hands, as though painting a rainbow. The diamond on his finger flashed. "We have a responsibility to the consumer, and we have to be careful the ingredient won't show up in FDA tests. Compassion Comes First, remember? Remember that ad campaign?—Those warm, fuzzy commercials showing us donating product because Cousins hated to see little babies starve? God! Was that high concept or what?" Oomal saw Reen cringe, and his delight floundered into embarrassment. "Well. So. We're not completely insensitive. The birthrate might have plummeted, but the infant mortality rate did, too."

"About the peas," Reen prompted.

"I'm getting to that, First Brother." Oomal set what looked like an attaché case on the desk and popped the snaps. It was not a briefcase, Reen saw, but a laptop computer.

Oomal was pleased by Reen's interest. "Nice, isn't it? My employees gave it to me for Christmas last year, along with a Roach Motel

as a gag gift. They're a lot of fun, my employees." The Toshiba laptop beeped as it automatically booted its program.

"I fail to see the humor in a Roach Motel," Tali said.

Oomal gave him a long, steady look. "Well, Cousin Brother Conscience, I guess you would." Hitting a key, he brought up a bar graph. Reen's interest wandered to Oomal's Piaget: the soothing pattern of diamonds around the bezel, the distressing clutter of the nugget band.

"Production," Oomal said, turning the screen so Reen could see it and pointing to the tallest bar. "Profits." He pointed to the smallest. "We're going to need more price supports, Reen-ja."

"You should simply close the factory," Tali said.

"What?" Oomal turned to Reen in horror. "Reen-ja! You're not thinking of closing Gerber!"

Tali said, "The Brother Firstborn sees the problem as clearly as I do. It is illogical to continue throwing money into a dying company."

Oomal made an exasperated hand motion. "Look. Neither of you knows anything about economics, but let me see if I can put it in terms you can understand. First of all, Gerber's not a dying company. In the third quarter of the fiscal year, when the bottom literally dropped out of baby foods, we diversified into frozen tartlets aimed at the adult consumer. The peach and apple were hits, although I'll admit the strained pea frozen tartlets and the strained carrot surprise didn't move well. But we're doing a brisk business with our strained veal and chicken pâté, which comes prepackaged with a cracker assortment."

Reen saw, next to Oomal's keyboard and *Forbes* magazine, a half-finished Snickers bar. The tough cartilage that served the Cousins for teeth was adequate to chew most foods, but Reen found himself wondering what Oomal did with the peanuts.

"Second, Cousin Brother Reen," Oomal said, "Gerber has a Japanese-style management. The employees think of the company as their home. We do not, as a corporate rule, lay off. I have a hundred thousand employees, sixty-eight plants. If I close them, I put family farmers

all over the world out of business." He pulled his wallet out again and shoved pictures across the desk: Oomal in a hard hat smiling amid grinning humans with hard hats; Oomal shaking hands with a pudgy, balding man. "That's Harry Bell, salesman of the year. Harry's a great guy, a real company man. Old Harry could sell diets in a famine. He has three kids and a mortgage. Look at that face, just look at it. How could you put that man out of a job?"

Reen studied the photo: the human hand grasping Oomal's own; the broad grins on both faces. His Third Brother seemed to have overcome the Cousin aversion to touching. Handing the picture back, he asked, "But what can be done?"

"It's simple, Cousin First Brother. We all know the free market economy will eventually go belly-up, and I've done a feasibility study in which I outline the problem we'll have when the zero birthrate hits home. I believe I've found the answer." Oomal gave Reen an unCousinly smirk.

Reen leaned his elbows on his desk. "And what is that, Brother Economist?"

"Bring back communism," Oomal said. "The object of capitalism is to capture market share, anyway. The Cousins will simply become the ultimate multinational corporation."

"And the goods?"

Oomal shrugged. He returned his wallet to his pocket. "We sell what we can and discard the rest. The worst part of the waste will peak inside another fifty years. At that point we can retire the few workers left, give them lake cabins and motorboats, and allow them to enjoy the remainder of their lives."

"Yes. That sounds perfect." Reen had always pictured himself as the benevolent caretaker of the last of humanity.

"I see no point in wasting resources," Tali said. "I suggest we begin the process of euthanasia."

Oomal clapped his palm to his brow. "God, Tali! How can you say that?"

"Before we landed, the First Brother gave us a promise—did you

not, Reen-ja?—that if the situation began to get out of hand, the viruses would be used. The situation is now deteriorating."

"Oh, come on," Oomal said. "Reen was pandering to our xenophobia. Those viruses were never intended—"

Tali leaped to his feet. "Do not listen to him, Firstborn! See how he has become human himself! And this has gone too far! Your first responsibility is to the Community, Reen-ja. Must I remind you of that?"

Reen was startled by his Second Brother's vehemence. Oomal simply groaned, "Tali, Tali. Haven't you seen enough murder?"

Tali was apoplectic. "Murder! Third Brother, how do you accuse me of murder?"

"Our ancestors," Oomal said, "wiped every sentient race but the humans off the face of the galaxy."

Tali said heatedly, "The Community expanded, yes. It is in the nature of the Community to expand. Do you have a problem with that, Cousin Brother Economist?"

Reen studied his hands, imagining blood on them. He, like Oomal, had always disliked Cousin history. Reen's people were cowards, but in the depths of their fear cowards could be deadlier than heroes.

"Of course I do. Don't you?" In a quieter, more reproachful voice Oomal asked Reen, "Cousin Brother Firstborn, don't you?"

Reen had no answer. Perhaps his ancestors had been right. Contact was a perilous thing—Reen had never before realized how perilous. Other cultures were so alluring. Tali's humanity was more subtle than Oomal's, but it was there nonetheless. At M Street, Reen had felt a very human darkness in Tali's touch. He could now sense hidden agendas in his demands.

Had he made a mistake by landing? Reen was young when he first met Eisenhower, barely out of the Communal attraction of adolescence, that time when he and Tali and Oomal and the rest of his Brothers slept side by side, locked in shared thought. When he was a child, Reen had only to lift his hand for the others to lift theirs, too.

That was when the fraternal bond had been made. Now Third Brother argued with Conscience. Conscience forced decisions on First.

Oomal said, "Our ancestors murdered without cause. Those other species didn't even get a chance to protest. Bang, and they were gone. Just like that." He snapped his forefinger and claw together. Reen knew Oomal had practiced diligently to get that gesture right. "What our ancestors chose to do is done, but we have a chance to make amends. We'll eradicate the humans, fine. Since they're a warlike species, I can see the reasoning in that. But if we want to have our children's respect when we die, let's please get it right this time. Because our children are half human," he said quietly, "and they will judge us."

Slowly, reluctantly, Tali took his seat. Into the abrupt and unsettling quiet Reen wondered aloud, "In the meantime what do I tell the Germans?"

Oomal snapped his eelskin case closed. "Put something else on the plate." He noticed Reen's confusion and explained: "Find something else to talk about. Accuse them of something. When in doubt, attack."

Reen nodded slowly. "They *are* planning to invade China."

"That's wonderful! Hit them with the invasion of China! And if the production discrepancy comes up, blame it on me. Tell them you have a Cousin up there running Gerber who doesn't know his ass from straight up. Tell them Cousins aren't used to money. Tell them you think Gerber will be run into the ground inside of three years and that corporate raiders are circling over the bones. Next week sometime I'll get the governor into one of our ships and explain to him just how uninteresting strained peas really are."

Oomal started for the door but paused in the center of the presidential seal to give Reen an encouraging look. "Don't worry. I'll take care of everything, Cousin Brother Firstborn. Hassenbein will forget about the strained peas."

Then with a wry smile and a shake of his head he told Tali, "And, hey. Call the toll-free number on that card, Second Brother. Tell them I sent you. And lighten up, okay?"

14

When Oomal left, Tali turned to Reen. "Behold the danger of consorting too much with humans, Reen-ja. You see how the Cousin Brother Economist has given in to slothful habits of speech and thought. He has copied the body language to make the humans accept him more easily. They probably trust him, yes, but only because they no longer see him as Cousin."

Reen ignored him.

"It will ruin our race," Tali said with a Cousinly gesture of his hand which, after Oomal's expansiveness, seemed awkward and self-conscious.

Reen said firmly, "What is there left to ruin, Cousin Brother? Aren't we the last of our kind? It seems to me that Oomal finds enjoyment in acting human, and I for one am glad for him. We must all find our solace where we may." He hit the intercom button. "Natalie. Have the Mercedes brought around. I'll be going to Dulles to pick up the Germans." Then he asked Tali, "Will you come with me, Brother Conscience?"

Tali's curt, negative reply was the best news Reen had had all day. "No. Thural will take me to Anacostia in a few minutes, Reen-ja. Go ahead."

But there was something in the way Tali lowered his eyes that

caused Reen to wish he could stay and see what business Tali had at the White House while he was gone. "I will walk you to the ship," Reen offered.

"Oh, I am in no hurry, First Brother," Tali said in a pitiful attempt to sound casual. "Do not fret about me."

"As you wish." With a final backward look, Reen proceeded to the anteroom where Natalie was standing, a mink-collared pink coat over her shoulders.

"Let's go, sir. The Mercedes is in the driveway."

Had she actually said, "Let's go?" Reen looked at the briefcase in her hand. It was a tattered brown thing, an old government issue that even the seal of the President of the United States couldn't make respectable.

"*You* can't go!" Then he softened his tone. "Hassenbein and I are going to be speaking about sensitive issues."

"I'm not letting you out of my sight. You have a whole stack of documents to review and sign, and you were gone all morning. If you insist, I'll take a taxi back from Dulles after you pick up the Germans."

"All right."

Natalie prattled all the way down the hall and through the exit. "I mean, it'd be an inconvenience to get a taxi, but if that's what you want. . . . Don't forget, though, I have the highest security clearance. Probably higher than the governor himself. Who types your memos, anyway?"

The limo was poised like a slick black cat in the afternoon light. Reen walked past the juniper border and climbed in without answering. When Natalie was seated, too, the chauffeur shut the door, sealing them into a leather-scented silence.

As the limo purred around the circle and down the drive, Reen looked out the window at the lawn made an eerie chartreuse by the bulletproof glass. Beyond the army troops at the gate the limo picked up its police escort.

The speaker at Reen's shoulder gave a spit of static. "The sirens bother you, sir?" the chauffeur asked. "You want the radio on?"

"No, thank you."

The click of the snaps on Natalie's briefcase brought his head around. "Here," she said, putting a two-inch stack of papers in his lap.

He switched on the reading lamp and began at the top of the first page.

Pursuant to the agreement made April fifth was as far as he got before the rushing of the scene outside and the slower movement of his eye over the page began to make his stomach churn. He returned the page to the stack and pulled down the blind at his window.

Natalie reached over him and raised the blind. "I'm claustrophobic."

"Oh." After an uneasy glance at some gawking tourists near the ramp at the Roosevelt Bridge, Reen wondered what time it was and checked his watch. He always wore the Rolex that Oomal had given him, but he wore it more for memory than as a timepiece. It wasn't a digital, so he had difficulty deciding whether the little hand was closer to the two or the three. The three. Three forty-five.

On Route 66 the limo speeded up. Reen slumped back into the leather seat and thought about his visit to Michigan, how the few Cousins there had fit into the company party Oomal threw like round pegs nestled happily in square holes.

It had been a nice party, Reen remembered, much more festive than what he was accustomed to in Washington. The humans wore blue jeans and, after a great deal of beer and barbecue, laughed very loud. And when Oomal handed Reen the pretty package and explained to the humans in such a simple way that Reen was his big Brother whom he loved very much, one of the women cried. "That's so sweet," she said. "Isn't that sweet?"

Sweet, he thought, staring at the Rolex and wishing he had made a note of the time Hassenbein had called.

As the limo leaned into a long right turn, Reen saw that they were exiting onto the Dulles Access Road. He would probably be early.

Natalie asked, "You going to sign those or what?"

"I can't read them in the car."

She snatched the top inch of papers. "Pursuant to the agreement of April fifth," she began.

With a stomach-lurching jolt the limo braked and veered. Reen heard the crunch of gravel as it slowed to a stop.

Natalie punched the speaker button. "What's going on?"

With a hum the tinted glass between driver and passenger compartments began to lower. Reen saw the usual sparse traffic on the Dulles Access whipping by and noticed that the motorcycle escort had parked their bikes on the shoulder.

The policemen were walking toward the car, their guns drawn.

The chauffeur was facing Reen, his elbows planted on top of the opposite seat. "Get down on the floor," he said.

Reen's attention snagged on the chauffeur and the silver revolver in his hand. He couldn't believe it. The man was pointing a gun at him.

"You, too," the chauffeur said, waving the black well of the barrel in Natalie's face.

Reen decided it would be wise to comply with the chauffeur's wishes. The man's expression was inflexible. But Reen couldn't get his body moving. The policemen were very close now, and they looked remarkably like real policemen.

"Get *down*!" the chauffeur bellowed. Reen jumped.

Something shoved Reen in the back and toppled him to the carpet. "The man said down, sir," Natalie said sharply. "Didn't you hear him?" To the chauffeur she said, "Listen. You're kidnapping us, okay? But I'm dying for a cigarette. You got a light?"

Reen was on the floorboard where Natalie had pushed him, and her shoes were in his face. New shoes, he thought stupidly, wondering if she had bought them with the White House credit card. They were navy high heels with small gold bows. Natalie was rummaging in her purse. It was a big beige purse and it didn't match the shoes. That wasn't at all like Natalie.

"On the *floor*!" the chauffeur shouted.

Three popping sounds, one right after the other. Natalie bounded to the opposite seat and wriggled through the partition. The limo jerked forward, the sudden acceleration pushing Reen's shoulder into the upholstery behind.

Clunk, clunk, clunk went the limo as it slammed into metal. The motorcycles, probably, judging from the way the big car bounced.

He heard a hum and sat up. The partition's opaque glass had been raised. The Mercedes was rushing up the Dulles Access, weaving in and out of traffic.

"Natalie!" Reen cried, punching the intercom button.

No one replied. He hit the lever to lower the partition's glass. Nothing happened.

Reen lay down on the floorboard again. The Mercedes was so heavy that, without looking at the gray screen of winter trees rushing by the window, he might have thought they were gliding along at a sedate twenty.

The car slewed. Brakes screamed. Reen was flung toward the door. There were four jarring bumps as the big car mounted the curb, and four more as it dropped to street level again.

Reen sat up and saw they were headed in the opposite direction from the airport. The Mercedes skidded across three lanes, cutting off a green pickup. Ahead was the red-striped toll barrier and a small gesticulating figure in a booth. With a muted bang and a shudder, the Mercedes plowed through the barrier, knocking it several feet into the air and over the car. Reen looked out the rear window and saw it lazily falling, a candy cane from heaven, before a thicket of leafless hickories hid it from view.

They whipped through a residential section of Tyson's Corner and took Chain Bridge Road toward Wolf Trap, weaving in and out of traffic, running red lights. Somewhere near Vienna they turned west onto a winding lane with woods on one side and pastures on the other. Then they were deep in Virginia horse country.

Reen punched the intercom button. "Natalie?"

The limo was flying down the secondary road, going much

too fast for him to jump to safety, even had his paralyzing fright allowed.

"Natalie? Are you there? Please. Are we going back to the White House now?"

The ammoniac smell of urine and the copper-penny smell of human blood spread through the heating ducts like a contagion.

"Natalie?"

Reen sat back, linked his hands in his lap, and, to keep the little death from taking him, began frantically thinking of pleasant things: Oomal and the party. Oomal handing him the present. Reen not knowing quite what to do with it because no Cousin had ever given him a gift. He remembered his Brother saying gently, "Open it, Reen-ja." How thc humans and Cousins had gathered around, the woman crying, "How sweet." And Oomal, because he could not embrace him, had hooked his claw into Reen's sleeve and asked, "Do you like it?"

Reen looked long and hard at the Rolex. *My big brother whom I love.*

The Mercedes squealed to a halt. The door opened. A man in a white hard hat reached in and grabbed Reen's arm. The workman was huge, his hands enormous. Reen found himself being dragged from the Mercedes, and he hit his side painfully on the green phone receiver the man wore at his belt. The workman slammed the Mercedes door and gave the side a sharp slap.

The limo sped away. In horror, Reen watched it disappear around the next curve.

Feeling the man's grip momentarily relax, Reen tore himself free and ran across the road toward the woods. He was thigh-deep into a patch of thorny blackberry bushes when the man flailed in after and grabbed him again. Reen struggled. The man fought to hold on. The subpoena dropped from his pocket.

"Come on, sir," the man said as he grasped Reen about the waist and pulled him to a white and green Chesapeake Bell panel truck.

The man threw Reen facedown onto the truck's carpet. The rear

doors banged shut, and a moment later they were speeding down the road, the opposite way the limo had gone.

Huge hands grabbed Reen and pulled him up onto a cushion. "How many fingers?" the phone company man asked, holding three stiff fingers before Reen's face.

Reen looked away. If he had to die like Jonis and the rest, then he would do the best his small courage allowed and at least keep silent.

The man sat back, sighed, and unfastened a walkie-talkie from his belt. "Domino's delivers," he said into it. Then he crawled away and sat with two other phone company men who were checking their Uzis.

Yes, Reen decided, the best thing to do now, the easiest thing, was die quickly before they caused him pain.

The three linemen were too alike to tell apart, all broad-shouldered with slim waists. Their hard hats hid their hair. One of them crawled forward and held four fingers up to Reen.

"How many fingers, sir?"

Reen turned his head away. Right now they were elementary questions; later the questions would get more difficult. *Why are you here? What are your plans for us?* And then would come the agony. To protect the humans, Reen had hidden his suspicions from the Community. In fact, his suspicions were so terrible, he himself had dismissed them. The kidnapped Cousins had not died gently in those three allotted days. Reen knew they had died tortured.

"You hear me," the man said. "I know you can hear me." The man went back to the others. "I think he's okay."

No, Reen thought, seeing his death as clearly and as close as the carpeted wall before him. *I am not okay.* When they had held him long enough, they would see his life seep from him, and they would wonder. With perverse satisfaction he wished he could see the astonishment on their faces.

The truck braked. Reen heard the slam of the driver's door. He glanced warily at the three men in the back, but they were intent on

their guns. The door slammed again. The vehicle inched forward and stopped.

Reen's heart faltered. If only he had been able to overcome his own squeamishness and bring some Loving Helpers along. The Helpers, condemned to a life sentence in Communal Mind, were an uncomfortable reminder of the ancient Cousin past, the declining Cousin future; but a touch from them could send human consciousness to a place where free will did not exist. Reen loathed the panic he had seen on human faces when they found themselves sinking into that dark well of compliance. At this moment, however, he would have given anything to see his kidnappers wearing that same powerless look.

Someone flung open the rear doors. They were in a barn. Late afternoon sunlight streamed through weathered slats. Reen took a breath and smelled the dry, prickly scent of hay, the earthy aroma of long-vanished horses.

A man dragged Reen out and unceremoniously dumped him on a pile of straw.

Reen sat quietly, watching the bars of sun slant through the gaps in the wood. He listened to the ticking sounds of the van's engine, the quiet murmur of the kidnappers' voices. Then a man threw a blanket over Reen's legs and set a chilled can of Coca-Cola beside him.

After a brief hesitation Reen picked up the can and popped the top.

"Don't give him that," another man said, knocking the can out of Reen's hands, spilling cold, sticky Coke over the front of his uniform. "I thought I told you not to bring any carbonated drinks."

So they knew something about Cousins, Reen thought in disappointment as he watched the remainder of the Coca-Cola Classic being taken out of his reach.

The man came back with a bottle of orange juice, which Reen ignored.

"He wanted the Coke," the first man said.

Reen watched as the second man poured the contents of the can

into the hay. "Carbonation kills them. He was trying to commit suicide. If you have any more carbonated drinks, get rid of them now." Then he called over his shoulder, "A helluva painful way to go, sir."

Oh, but nothing was painful to a Cousin for very long. In that, Reen had the advantage over a human. He had seen humans die.

He looked at the kidnappers, wondering if they would end up screaming in hospital beds or bubbling their lives away in car crashes. Better to be a Cousin, he thought, and die without much pain. Better to be fragile and long-lived. The Sleep Master was a four-century Cousin; Reen himself had seen two centuries pass.

When Reen died, the Earth Community would never be the same. The Cousins were scattered in sparse knots across the galaxy, with not enough firstborns to send, as Reen himself was sent when Thural's First Brother had died. No, the Community on Earth would not recover from the shock, and secondborn Tali would hold a precarious and uneasy dominion.

He waited for the men to begin the torture, but instead they sat down, took fried chicken from a cooler, and started to eat.

"You hungry, sir?" one of them called.

Reen turned his head away to stare at the back of the old barn and the shafts of dying sunlight. It was the last he would see of Earth, he figured, and the sight was a good one—not as good as the Rockies would have been, or Angela's face, but under the circumstances the dust motes dancing like gold flakes in the sun were enough.

There were things left undone. For one, he wished he could keep Tali from Community rule. But the humans and Cousins would have to fend for themselves now. Reen had lived long enough to see his child born, ensuring some sort of continuation of his species. There was no sense at this late date in accepting any more pain than he had to; no point in struggling, as a human would, to persevere. After all the intrigue at the White House, his life had suddenly become very simple. Sighing, almost content, he sat back against the straw and watched the evening taper into night.

15

OUTSIDE THE BARN, THE SUN SET IN shades of pink and violet. The dust motes gave one last glimmer before they turned to ash. The kidnappers lit a Coleman lantern, and by its acidic glow three played a card game while the fourth sat watch over Reen. At either six forty-five or seven forty-five by Oomal's Rolex, Reen heard the sound of a car. Blinding white light blared through the boards at the front of the barn like the loud opening chord of a symphony.

One of the men threw the barn door open, and a BMW drove inside. Reen sat straighter.

The interrogator had arrived.

Shielding his eyes from the headlights, Reen watched as the car door opened and a figure emerged. Self-assured footsteps swished on the straw as they approached; the weighty sway of a full-length mink coat; the smooth curve of legs in nylon hose.

"Hi, Reen," Marian Cole said.

Heartbroken, he turned away, putting her in that blank spot in his vision, the place where he wished he could now send her forever.

The straw rustled as she sat. "Not going to talk to me?"

He would have talked to her without this, and she knew it. But perhaps she wanted the witnesses Reen had never allowed her to have.

There would be no torture, Reen realized with a sinking sick sensation. Marian wouldn't need it. She would simply ask him the questions over and over until love pried his lips ajar and he began to speak.

"Well, at least look at me, okay? It's hard talking to your back."

He couldn't.

"Please," she said softly.

Without wanting to, he whirled. "Why did you do this to me, Marian?"

The men by the Coleman lantern had turned to stare.

"Shhh, shhh." Marian trailed cool fingertips across his mouth. "Don't."

With a furious jerk Reen turned his back on her again. "Is this what you meant by endings?"

She fumbled for his hand. He tried to snatch it away, but she held him tight. "Shhh. Don't be afraid. Isn't that what you used to say to me when I was the one who was helpless? God, Reen. Do I have to be a Cousin before you can trust me? Natalie was one of ours. Since I've been director, all your secretaries have been agents. And their only job is protection. I knew your Brother and Hopkins were going to make their move, and once Jonis was kidnapped, I knew they'd do it soon." She tugged at his hand. "Come on. I want to talk to you in private."

She pulled him, his reluctant feet stumbling, toward her car. Once in the backseat, she closed the door, fumbled in her purse, and took out a pack of cigarettes.

"I gave these up three years ago; did you know that?" She fished a Carlton out of its box with her fingernails and lit it. The warm glow from the lighter washed her face free of the small wrinkles around her eyes, making her seem, for an instant, magically young. Flicking the lighter closed, she took a drag. The enchantment ended. Age and worry claimed her face again.

"Natalie called just after she handed you off. That was the last we heard from her before she headed to the safe house. They must

have gotten to her a little after that. We found the Mercedes. There was blood on the front seat. We don't know yet if all of it came from the chauffeur."

Chagrined, Reen mumbled, "I'm sorry about not trusting you. And no, you don't have to be a Cousin for that. I trusted you before, but lately . . ."

"Just listen." She tapped the cigarette against the ashtray, dislodging a small column of ash. "Two hours ago a bomb exploded at Gate Six at Dulles. The Germans were killed instantly. Whoever arranged that meeting set you and Hassenbein up for murder."

"Krupner told them," Reen said. "He sent a fax—"

"Forget Krupner," she said with such confidence that it gave Reen pause. "He works for the Germans. We've known that for a long time. Poor Hans wasn't much of a spy. No, this was bigger than Krupner. The usual White House chauffeur was called by someone posing as the head of the serving staff and told not to come in today. Right now we're looking for the police escort, but the cops who were assigned to you have vanished." She took a deep breath. "There's something else I need to tell you."

There were two deep furrows on either side of her mouth. Her lowered eyes were lusterless. Was it about Angela? His heart skipped a beat. No, that was impossible. None of the West Virginia Cousins would have told her anything about Angela. "What?"

She took another drag before replying. "This afternoon, just about the time the bomb went off at Dulles, the White House commuter fell into the Watergate Complex and exploded." Leaning forward, she tapped the ash into the ashtray. "Nobody on the ship survived." After a pause she asked, "Who was on board?"

"Thural," he whispered. Cousin Thural, almost close enough to be Brother.

"I'm sorry."

"And Tali," he remembered. Odd how he had thought of the Cousin first and the Brother after.

"I ordered this made for you. Here."

She pressed a hard rectangular piece of plastic into his hand. A nametag. He opened his fist and read the letters: TALI.

"No one knows who was on the ship so we're going to a party. In separate cars, of course. I'm leaving in a few minutes to pick up Howard. Tali wasn't invited, but if he shows up, the hostess won't make a fuss. It's very *in* to have a Cousin as a guest."

His Cousin Brother was dead, and Reen was being asked to impersonate him. He wasn't sure he could.

Marian reached over and unpinned his nametag. "Keep your ears open for anything anyone tells you. Act like Tali if you can. Pretend you have a rod up your ass. Don't talk much, and when you do, don't, for God's sake, be your usual charming self."

Taking Tali's nametag from his open palm, she replaced his with his dead Brother's.

He looked up at her. She was staring at him strangely, as though trying to memorize his face, as though picking out the tiny differences between his features and the cookie-cutter features of the others.

Warm human hands on his neck pulled him close. A kiss on his cheek.

"I got lipstick on you. Here." She scrubbed her thumb over the spot her lips had touched.

Stunned, he lifted his hand to his face.

Her laugh was smooth cream with a bite of lemon sorrow in it. "Just like a kid, you know that? Sometimes you're just like a little kid."

Grabbing his hand, she took an unsteady breath, then reached across him and opened the door. He would have fallen out if she hadn't still had hold of him. "A car's here for you, and a chauffeur. Don't speak to me at the party. Tali and I hated each other."

He stumbled away, and she slammed the door. Her chauffeur jumped up, got behind the wheel, and backed the BMW out of the garage.

Reen watched the car pull onto the farm-to-market road. He stood there long after she was gone.

16

THE PARTY WAS HELD IN ONE OF THE larger houses on Georgetown's Q Street. When Reen rang the bell, a butler answered and was obviously nonplussed to see a Cousin standing on the stoop.

His eyebrows rose. "Whom may I announce?"

"Tali," Reen replied, feeling a pinprick of guilt for having momentarily snatched his Brother from an untidy grave.

The eyebrows rose another, seemingly impossible notch.

"Tali, sir? And will that be all?" he asked with the air of a man accustomed to royalty.

"Second Brother and Conscience to White House Chief of Staff Reen."

The brows lowered. "Very good, sir. Please come this way." With a bow he ushered Reen into the marble foyer. There was another hesitation as the butler scrutinized Reen's small body to see if he was hiding a coat.

From a wide, arched doorway to the right came the sounds of a Brahms sonata nearly drowned out by the strained gaiety of party conversation. Disconcerted by Reen's lack of an evening wrap, the butler paused at the entrance, Reen just to his back.

"Tali," the man announced. "Second Brother and . . ." He cleared

his throat and continued gamely, but as though suspecting he had it wrong, "Conscience to White House Chief of Staff Reen."

The babble stopped. The pianist missed the next bar of music. In the back of the huge room, his bulk competing with the Steinway grand beside him, William Hopkins stood with Speaker Platt. The FBI director's mouth was agape; a canapé was crushed in his startled fingers.

Reen trudged down the steps, wading into the pool of stunned guests.

"How nice to see you," a woman corseted in a beaded dress exclaimed as she unfroze from her confusion and sailed across the carpet to greet him.

The hostess, Reen assumed, wishing Marian had thought to give him her name.

"And what a *surprise!*"

Had Reen been there as himself, he would have inquired whether the surprise was pleasant or unpleasant, and had he any suspicion of the latter, he would have stayed only long enough to make his exit less obvious as an escape. But he was Tali now, and Tali never used social graces when rudeness would do just as well.

The woman approaching was tall and broad. Reen received a too-complete view of her décolletage.

"Yes," he said sharply and swiveled away.

And found himself eye-to-eye with Hopkins, who had circled from the piano to make a flank attack. The usual smile was absent from the FBI director's face. He was staring fixedly at the nametag on Reen's chest.

"Mr. Hopkins," Reen said. "Is there something you want?"

Hopkins gave him a flat smile. "No. Nothing," he replied before gravitating back to the small Speaker of the House.

Reen stared hard at the director's broad shoulders, his mind turning that smile over and over, as his hands might have toyed with an interesting objet d'art. Cousin ships had too many fail-safes for the crash of the commuter to be an accident. Sabotage, then. And if

Hopkins had been behind it, he would know the Cousin at the party wasn't Tali.

A passing waiter pushed an ornate silver platter into Reen's face. Reen admired the orderly rows of canapés for a moment, then selected a shrimp on toast, the only food he recognized.

"What about that Gerber?" a voice asked from behind Reen.

Reen nearly dropped the shrimp. The questioner was a pudgy man, his black formal dinner jacket spread wide to either side of his ample belly, as though he were offering his gut up for sacrifice.

"Who are you?" Reen asked.

"Ralph Bitterman, CEO of Heinz," the fat man said. "I remember when you guys undercut us and Beechnut out of the baby food business."

"And?"

"Running it into the ground, I hear." The man, Reen saw with dismay, was quite drunk. Bitterman pulled a stray guest into the conversation. "Say," he said, gloating into the captured woman's face, "did you hear Gerber's going broke? The White House is supposed to hold a news conference about it tomorrow."

A waiter lowered a tray of drinks into Reen's view. Without thinking, Reen took one.

"Now why do you suppose the only baby food manufacturer still in existence is going broke?" the fat man from Heinz asked the woman.

Reen glanced at the stemmed glass and noticed it held champagne. He toyed with the idea of drinking it down and ending all his troubles quickly. No one had told him about a press conference.

"What about it, uh . . ." Bitterman leaned over drunkenly to read the nametag. "Tali? Eighteen percent decline in the birthrate. Cousins buying up and ruining baby food manufacturers. Hey. There has to be a story there somewhere."

Reen remembered Oomal's metaphor about the elephant at the party. He looked numbly around the room to see if there was anyplace to hide.

"You going to answer me, or what?" Bitterman asked, switching from boisterous to pugnacious without any transition. He reached out and grabbed the front of Reen's uniform. "Are you going to answer me?"

At the head of the stairs the butler cleared his throat. "Marian Cole-Franklin, director of the CIA," he announced, "and husband, Dr. Howard Franklin, professor of biology, Georgetown University."

As the hostess moved across the carpet to greet her new guests, she slid between Bitterman and Reen, adroitly plucking the CEO's fist from Reen's uniform. "How *nice,* Marian! And don't you look *lovely!*"

Foiled, Bitterman slunk away and was soon engulfed by the party. Marian stood with her husband at the top of the stairs. Howard's handsome face was slack, his nervous laugh too shrill, his eyes glazed. He had been drinking again.

And Marian. Marian. The butler had taken her mink. Her dress was a filmy white thing that reminded Reen of lilies. The color in her cheeks was high, her mouth curled in welcome. She kissed the hostess's cheek with vacuous duty as her gaze swept the crowd, resting on Reen for a moment in pique before it moved on.

Then Marian's blue eyes widened on something pleasant a few yards to the right of Reen. Her arm rose in greeting. A bright smile spread her lips. "Director Billy. Get me a drink, will you?"

Reen watched her leave her husband and stride across to the fireplace, to the now-solitary Hopkins, who was either playing a part like Reen or was genuinely delighted to see her.

"Bourbon straight up?" he heard Hopkins murmur intimately as he ran a possessive hand down her bare back.

Resentfully Reen watched them disappear into the adjoining room. Vilishnikov appeared from the same open doorway, clutching a mixed drink with a cherry in it. Reen, relieved to catch sight of someone he knew, almost waved but stopped himself in time.

Vilishnikov set out toward him anyway. A few feet away he halted in surprise. "Oh, Tali," he said. "I am thinking you were your

Brother." The head of the Joint Chiefs was wearing his dress uniform, and the weight of his medals seemed to make him list to one side.

"I was wishing to speak to Reen about Krupner."

Reen was so startled that he almost took a sip of his champagne. When the drink waiter passed, he rid himself of the glass and picked up a tomato juice with a celery stick buried in its heart. "What about Krupner?"

"I am not, as you may be aware, happy at the Pentagon," Vilishnikov said. "Such a bad commute. Perhaps now that he has disappeared, I may have his office?"

"Ask Reen."

Vilishnikov, rebuffed by the sharp answer, lifted his chin and began searching the room for possible deliverance. Apparently he saw someone familiar because his smile widened. Intent as a heat-seeking missile, he made for the French doors.

At the Steinway the pianist thundered into a loud piece which Reen, whose musical knowledge began with Bach and ended with Beethoven, didn't recognize. He admired the skill of the pianist, however, and there was something disturbingly familiar about the man's face.

Reen caught a snippet of conversation next to him. "So nice to hear a composer play his own work," a woman in pink said, touching the hostess's arm.

"Yes," the hostess murmured. "Rachmaninoff has always been one of my favorites. He does Pavarotti with lesser success, you know. Something about the vocalization."

They wandered away toward the room with the bar.

Glancing around, Reen saw that Marian was back with her elegant gray-haired husband. The lids over his large brown eyes were at half-staff. ". . . that lard-assed Hopkins's hands on you," he growled. Suddenly he reached out to grab Marian's arm. She pulled away, hissing something Reen couldn't hear. She had a fixed half-smile on her face and her blue eyes were hot with embarrassment.

Howard's voice, thick with self-deprecation, rose over the crowd:

"No, I don't think I've had enough. I never get enough. Poor Howard doesn't get anything anymore." He turned to a man beside him and brayed a laugh that turned heads. "She's in love with a dickless gray alien."

People froze. Marian's tense smile disappeared, and for a moment she stood as Reen himself stood, alone and defenseless in the turmoil of the party.

Abruptly the embarrassed gathering shifted. One man in the crowd turned to another. "So," he said, "what's new over at Justice?"

Reen ducked and weaved his way through to the open bar. As he passed the piano, the pianist finished the piece, stood, and shot his sleeves. Their eyes met.

"Hi." Rachmaninoff suddenly wasn't as self-assured. The man seemed to have shrunk inside his formal attire. "I'm Jeremy Holt." He offered his hand.

Reen regarded the hand dubiously. "Holt? I thought you were Russian."

The refused hand jerked back to the safety of the suit and dallied around a pocket for a moment before deciding on a few simple twitches at the man's side. "Oh, no," the pianist said with an edgy squeak of a laugh. "I'm the President's new medium."

Reen took a step back to study the horn-rimmed glasses, the chamois-soft skin.

"I sleep in the Lincoln bedroom. He drops in on me every once in a while to see how I'm doing."

"President Womack?" Reen asked.

"President Lincoln. I sort of met your Brother, but I was someone else at the time. I wanted to tell him that I'm available for funerals and weddings and bar mitzvahs."

Reen looked at the business card Holt thrust into his hand and wondered how he could steer the conversation to the karma sellers without making the man suspicious.

Holt laughed again, his chortle going over the heads of the guests like a wayward fly ball. "You want a composer? A rock star? A dead

president? I can be anybody you want. It's because I have a go-between like Lizard. Lizard's great. When he asks spirits to come through, they don't refuse."

"The karma sellers . . ." Reen began.

But abruptly the hostess was there, taking Holt's arm and propelling him away. Her voice trailed behind her like strong flowery perfume. "Marvelous, darling. For the rest of the evening, how about Van Cliburn?"

Abandoned, Reen meandered past the open bar and found a door that led into the refreshing chill of the backyard. Following a curved path through ornamental shrubbery, he came to a gazebo. There he sat and nursed his tomato juice. Earth's moon, pale and wan, topped the roofs of the nearby houses.

So far the party had been useless, except for Hopkins's odd smile and the news of the press conference. That information, Reen thought glumly, might have waited until the morning. A few hours from now he would have to return to the Cousin Place, and the Sleep Master was sure to sense the anxiety in him.

"Tali," a voice whispered from the bushes.

Reen stood and looked around but saw nothing.

"Listen and don't talk," the voice said.

The bushes stirred in the night wind. The noise from the party was as faint as memory. Dead moonlight iced the flagstones, frosted the redwood railing and the evergreens.

The whisper was cold. "We fucked up getting your Brother today, but we'll try again."

There was a rustle of branches. A shadow separated itself from a tree trunk and, hidden by the night, left the garden.

The voice wasn't Marian's or Bill Hopkins's. It didn't belong to anyone Reen knew. He longed to run after the speaker, to ask how Tali could have betrayed him. He didn't dare. Not now. Not when everything, in its own way, had been settled.

From the house came the bell-like tones of a Beethoven sonata. A broken fragment of cloud scurried over the moon. Reen put his

hand over the nameplate and felt the sharp edges of the letters. Tali. Dead Cousin Brother. Tali, who had wanted Community rule so badly, he had been willing to do the human thing and kill to get it.

Reen sat down, upsetting his drink. Tomato juice spread like thick human blood over the gazebo's planked floor. He would leave the party now and go to the Cousin Place where Thural and Tali were not and never would be again.

He rose unsteadily. As he exited the gazebo, he heard a man weeping. The sounds were labored, as though the man were trying to bring to the surface a grief that had long ago congealed.

A dark form sat on a bench, its face in its hands. Reen passed without being seen. The man on the bench was Howard.

17

THE CHAUFFEUR DROVE REEN NORTH, away from the White House, taking winding residential streets to Rock Creek Park. Back and forth they threaded past thickets of trees and bicycle trails until Reen thought to check his watch, saw it was nearly midnight, and began to wonder whether he was being kidnapped again.

Fifteen minutes later the chauffeur pulled the Buick over to a wooded copse and stopped by a parked BMW. Marian, a phantom in the moonlight, got out of her car and climbed into the backseat with Reen. Wordlessly the chauffeur left the car and stood by the fender.

Marian's dress made a slithering sound against the leather seat as she moved toward him. She smelled of perfume and cigarette smoke. "Have fun at the party?" she asked.

"No. And you?"

"It was all right."

Reen gazed out the window into the moon-dappled shadows under the trees. Far across the park, streetlights gleamed in shades of topaz and aquamarine. "You were talking to William Hopkins, I noticed, and you seemed friendly."

"Jealous?"

Marian was a pale blur next to him: the glimmer of her dress, the glint of her blond hair. Was she smiling? "No. But it causes me to wonder."

"Billy and I keep friendly pretenses up. It's expected at parties."

Friendly pretenses. Was it only that? Reen asked himself again if it was sex she wanted. For him, Marian's company was enough. Still, the idea of her and Hopkins together was painful in an apprehensive way, like the beginnings of an inflammation beneath the skin.

"Did you find out anything?" she asked.

Reen was looking at the trees again. Under the streetlight a few stubborn leaves gleamed on dead branches like silver coins. "No."

He had learned nothing that would help Marian. His Conscience, the betrayer, was dead. During the drive through the park Reen had made peace with his Brother. Tali had plotted against Reen not for power but for sad, misguided duty to the Community. Reen could forgive him that.

"Too bad." Leaning over she unpinned Tali's nameplate from his chest and replaced it with his own. She was a warm shape in the dark, as nebulous and emotionally charged a presence as the Old Ones.

"I love you," he said.

Her form wavered. "What brought that on?"

Howard's words, he realized. The idea of sharing Marian with Hopkins.

"If you want someone else," he said, "I'll accept that. After all, I didn't stand in your way when you decided to marry. What I cannot understand is why you stay with Howard after the way he . . ." Reen stopped himself.

A suck of indrawn breath. "I don't want anyone else."

So Hopkins wasn't the usurper. Her tyrant was Howard. After all these years, still Howard.

"Why bring Howard into this?" she asked, suddenly irate. "Haven't you done enough?"

So what she felt for Howard was guilt, not love. Reen wondered which emotion was the stronger and which one she would heed.

"Oh, shit." She swiped at her eyes. "Poor, dumb Howard."

"What do you want of me, Marian?"

"Let's buy a house in the country, all right?" She laughed. "Maybe some horses and some dogs. Let's retire there. At night you can tie fishing lures. I can knit. At eleven o'clock we'll climb into bed and watch the news on TV. Forty-seven years, Reen. Don't you think you owe me that?"

He squeezed her hand. "I'm sorry."

"I know." She pulled away, opened the car door, and was gone.

"I'll take you back to the White House now, sir," the chauffeur said, getting into the front seat.

Reen didn't answer. He watched Marian's BMW disappear around a curve.

The Buick executed a three-point turn and headed south, taking Reen around the darkened zoo and down a nearly deserted Connecticut Avenue toward the White House.

They were stopped at the gate , and an army officer leaned into the car. "Yes, sir? Who shall I— White House Chief Reen! Sir!" he said in surprise, seeing Reen's nametag. "Everybody's been worried about you. Go ahead." He gestured to the marine guard in the gatehouse. With a buzz the gates slid back, and the Buick purred around the drive to the West Wing.

A commuter ship was parked at the side of the building, Reen noticed as he stepped from the car. Head down, he walked toward the Cousin who was standing at the door. The Cousin unexpectedly trotted down the lawn to meet him.

"Reen-ja!"

Reen's steps faltered. It was Thural standing there, elation in his ebony eyes.

Reen's throat spasmed. No words emerged. He walked to Thural's side and snagged a claw in his sleeve, pulling him as close as Communal law allowed. "Cousin."

Thural hooked the side of Reen's uniform, and Reen could feel the cold, welcome press of his claw. For a moment the two simply

stood, holding on to each other as the early morning traffic rumbled down Pennsylvania Avenue and the moon set behind the buildings.

To Thural's back another Cousin emerged from the ship. Stunned, Reen watched his Brother Conscience approach.

"Reen-ja," Thural said. "The commuter ship crashed with Sidam in it. It might have been Tali and me, but at the last minute Tali had business and sent the ship on."

What sort of business was that? Reen wondered as he watched his Brother stride across the lawn to them. *Was it accidental business or planned business that saved him?*

"Where were you?" Thural went on. "We were so worried when the bomb went off at Dulles and you did not return."

Ah, but was everyone worried? Reen felt the pull of his Cousin's claw as Thural gently prodded for an answer; but Reen only had eyes for his Brother.

When Tali stopped on the grass beside them, Reen's sharp gaze never left his Brother's face.

"Someone tried to kill me," he said.

18

For the ride to the Cousin Place, Tali chose to sit with Thural instead of with Reen. Reen lingered a while in the ship's lounge, then wandered to the circular hall and peered out the windows as the craft rose from the lawn. When they had gained some height, Foggy Bottom and the Potomac came into view. The searing halogen floodlamps that had been set up for rescue work were so bright that even at that distance they made Reen wince.

There was not much to rescue. One entire side of the Watergate was rubble, and what was left looked like a ruin awaiting demolition.

As the ship sailed east, the lights of the rescuers grew smaller and smaller until Reen couldn't pick them out from the blazing clutter near the river. He looked down at the Capitol, an illuminated pastry set on the dark starry tablecloth of the Washington streets. Over Maryland, the lights were sparser, with busy little angular embroideries at Woods Corner and Camp Springs.

When they landed, Tali hurried off the ship as though fleeing his Brother, fleeing the truth. Reen pursued him. By the time they reached the Communal chamber, the Brother Conscience was already heading for the niches.

Reen halted in the center of the room, glaring at Tali's retreating back.

The Sleep Master rose from his bench. "*Out!* Get out of here immediately!"

Tali paused at the door and turned—the Brother who plotted treachery with humans but chose to be, among them, the Cousin without a name.

Without a name. Reen suddenly understood the smile he had seen on Hopkins's lips.

"When I left for Dulles, you remained behind to talk with Hopkins, didn't you, Tali? You plotted with the FBI to murder me."

With a gasp Thural reached out and hooked Reen's sleeve. Reen flung his arm up, away from his Cousin's restraining claw.

The Sleep Master roared: "Get *out!*"

Reen faced the old Cousin. "Sidam died today! A Cousin is gone! Won't you feel that vacant place among the niches? Let us speak the truth, then, in the sleep place where the law forbids lies to hide. That ship was sabotaged." He could see fear in Tali's black eyes. "Why did you put a bomb on that ship, Cousin Brother?"

Something knocked Reen off his feet. He looked up from the floor of the chamber. The Sleep Master had butted him with his claws.

No Cousin strikes another, Reen thought. *But, then, no Cousin murders another, either.*

The Sleep Master leaned over him, claws held as though he wished to hit Reen again. "Leave! You walk through filth and then track it into the chamber!"

Thural interposed himself between them. "Reen-ja is tired, Cousin Master of Sleep. I will take him outside for a bit." And without waiting for the Sleep Master's reply, he pulled Reen up and marched him to the door.

Outside the Cousin Place, the damp air haloed the lights, and the breeze smelled of snow. Thural eased Reen onto the steps and sat beside him. Reen pulled his legs up and rested his arms on his knees. He stared at the tarmac, his rage gradually subsiding.

After a while Thural said quietly, "Tali is sometimes difficult to

deal with, but he is still Brother. You do not really believe your Brother plotted to kill you, Cousin Firstborn."

"I refused to believe it before, but I have reason to believe it now."

Resting his back against the smooth wall of the building, Thural contemplated the line of scrapped American warplanes. "Tali did talk to Hopkins. How did you know that, Reen-ja?"

Reen gave Thural a human shrug since no Cousin gesture seemed appropriate.

"I sometimes wonder about Jonis, First Cousin." There was a pensive, contrite look on Thural's face. "There was a time before he was kidnapped that Jonis no longer spoke to me, and we were Brothers, as you know. Why should a Brother stop speaking to a Brother?"

A pale blur of movement beyond the row of planes. A quartet of guardian Loving Helpers was making rounds about the perimeter, a Cousin Taskmaster at their heels.

And Reen thought of Tali. "Because of shame."

As though he had called him forth, the door spread open and Tali walked into the damp wind. Across the tarmac the first flakes of snow began to fall.

In his black uniform Tali was merely a floating head and bobbing hands. "I could not sleep," he said, "without making my peace with you."

"Sit, then," Thural offered when Reen refused to speak.

With a sigh not much louder than the falling snow, Tali sat on the stairs. "It *was* Hopkins I visited, Cousin Brother." The landing-strip lights were reflected in his huge eyes. "But we spoke only of his worry that Marian Cole steals too much of your confidence. This is all we spoke of, nothing more."

"Is it your right," Reen asked, "to judge my actions in the presence of humans?"

"It is my right to judge you at all times," Tali retorted, sounding more like himself. He shifted his body on the steps. "I come to make my peace with you before sleep, Brother, not to be told my duty."

"Let us have peace, then," Thural said, holding a hand toward

each of them as though he feared they might begin tussling on the ground like humans.

Reen looked away. Snow was falling faster now, and the wind drove the flakes around the lights like a horde of moths.

"Hopkins is a good man," Tali went on, "but a man of many words when just a few would do. The hour became late, and Sidam was tired, yet Hopkins talked. I sent Sidam on and kept Thural, who did not then need sleep, with me."

"You did not want to tell me you were meeting with Hopkins. You were ashamed to admit it." Cousins weren't bothered, as humans were, by small changes in temperature. But Reen felt cold. He hunched his shoulders and pressed his hands together in his lap to protect them from the wind.

"Yes, Cousin Brother Firstborn." Tali's voice was subdued, earnest, and uncharacteristically contrite. "I was ashamed."

Of course Hopkins had known the Cousin at the party was an impostor. By that time he knew Tali no longer wore a nametag. And he knew that the Cousin who had died was Sidam. But, then, who had whispered to Reen from the bushes? Perhaps someone sent by Hopkins to make Reen distrust his Brother.

"I forgive you," Reen said shortly.

"Then we will go inside, yes, Reen-ja? Yes, Cousin Conscience?" Thural asked. "It is getting late."

The three rose and walked into the warm, spice-scented chamber together, making their way to the niches. The Sleep Master glared at Reen but didn't stop him.

19

THE NEXT MORNING REEN SAT WITH Thural on the flight to the White House. A gray sky, soft as a goosedown comforter, was spread over the city, and from it a few flakes of snow still fell. It was the kind of day Reen liked, one in which sharp edges were softened, harsh colors subdued.

"You should not press Tali so, Cousin Firstborn," Thural said as they passed over the Tidal Basin.

Reen gave Thural a quick, searching look, but his aide was intent on the instruments. "Did you hear the conversation between my Brother and Hopkins?"

The Washington Monument loomed out of the mist. Below stretched the fog-swaddled lights on Constitution Avenue.

"No, Cousin. But I know they talked. I saw Mr. Hopkins and Tali go into a room together. They were there a long time. And it is true that when Tali came out, he looked at Sidam and me, saw that Sidam was tired, and told him he could go home."

They swept over the tanks, the south lawn, and Thural lowered the ship to its pad.

"He thinks your leadership is unsuitable, Reen-ja," Thural said before they disembarked. "And if he can, he will banish you from the Cousin Place. Do what you must, but guard your temper. If

you do not guard it well, others may turn from you as the Sleep Master has."

Reen nodded. The door spread apart, and the pair wordlessly trudged through the snow-dusted grass to the building.

When Reen entered the reception area that led to the Oval Office, Thural at his heels, a black man stood up behind Natalie's desk. He was clasping a steno book to his chest. "Good morning, sir. I'm Bobby Pearson, your *temp*-orary. I just can't tell you how delighted I am to be working in the White House."

Reen paused before the painted oak doors and gave the slender Pearson a once-over look. "CIA, I suppose."

Pearson waggled a brown finger in front of Reen's nose, and his pursed mouth delivered a string of tsks. "Now, now. That's supposed to be a secret. But since you guessed!—Well, not only am I proficient in Word Perfect and take dictation like a dream, but I also have a black belt in kar-*at*-e. And with a nine-millimeter automatic I can snuff out a candle at thirty yards. So"—he flipped open his steno pad—"I suppose we should get down to business. You have a news conference scheduled in an hour."

Reen's shoulders slumped. He had forgotten the strained-pea crisis. "Where is what's-his-name, the press secretary?"

A frown drew down the edges of Pearson's mouth. "What's-his-name, the press secretary, quit."

"Well, call my Brother Oomal in Michigan. Tell him to get down here right away. I have enough to worry about, and I refuse to face this press conference by myself."

Pearson lifted a finger to his lips. "Oomal in Michigan. Yes, I do believe I have that number." He was still flipping through the Rolodex when Reen went into his office and slammed the door.

"Do not fret, Cousin," Thural said in a soothing tone. "Oomal will know what to do."

"He'd better. If the humans learn the truth, there is no telling what will happen."

Pearson stuck his head through the right-hand doorway. Reen

stepped back guiltily from Thural. "Your Brother's on his way, sir. Says he'll be here in less than thirty minutes."

"Mr. Pearson," Reen said, recovering himself. "Don't ever barge into my office again. Use the intercom."

As quickly as he had materialized, Pearson vanished.

Thural shook his head and sat down on one of the two loveseats by the fireplace. "If the humans discover the truth, Reen-ja, there will be riots that will make the riots we have now seem small. And the Community will insist on euthanasia."

"It will be a great massacre, Cousin, one way or another." Gloomily Reen sat at his desk and booted his computer. But his anxiety made the words on the screen blur. After a few minutes of pointless scrolling, he turned off the IBM and sat on the loveseat opposite Thural. Hands in his lap, he listened to the pop and sizzle of the fire.

Secrets. The Cousins had so many of them. The secret of how vulnerable they were; the secret of past genocides. Cousins were made up of secrets. And the biggest secret of all was that they were taking humanity with them in their fall into oblivion, a little company for the end.

Pearson, ignoring Reen's previous order, bustled into the room unannounced, a tray of coffee and croissants in his hands. "Marian insisted I feed you. She says you always forget to eat."

Reen watched as Pearson buttered a croissant and handed the plate to him.

"Eat up," the man chirped.

Reen sat, limp pastry in hand, until the secretary left the room again. "I fear for us, Thural," he said, putting the croissant down.

"I fear for us, too," Thural said glumly, pouring himself a cup of coffee, which he then ignored.

Outside the French doors, snow gathered in the Rose Garden, drifted on the walk. Thural's nervous fingers tore a croissant into greasy golden crumbs. Reen checked his watch, then checked it again.

Twenty minutes later the intercom buzzed. In his eternally cheerful voice, Pearson announced, "Mr. Reen? Your Brother's here, sir."

Oomal burst through the door, a gray Mighty Mouse with an attaché case in his hand. "Press conference? Let me handle the whole thing. I can do a press conference, Cousin Brother."

He took a seat next to Reen. "I've been giving this some thought during the trip back to Washington, Brother Firstborn," he said, grabbing Reen's forgotten croissant from the plate. "And I think I've come up with an angle."

The fire snapped. A spark sailed like a meteor toward the blackened bricks.

"Trouble is, we have to come off that eighteen percent decline to make it work." Oomal spoke through a mouthful of pastry. "Here's the deal. The eighteen percent was a noncrisis figure. It's zero-worry level in human terms." He gestured with the croissant. "Twenty percent, that's the discomfort zone, because to a human twenty percent is close to twenty-five percent, and that means an entire quarter drop-off. We've done research."

Reen watched his Brother stuff the rest of the croissant into his mouth and wash it down with Thural's coffee. "Cold," Oomal said with a shudder, giving Thural an accusatory glance. "Okay. So here's the angle." He wiped his hands on the linen napkin that had been placed beside a crystal rose vase. Then, thoughtlessly, he tossed the napkin down, destroying the harmony of the tray. "We come off the eighteen percent and bring it up to twenty-seven percent. Get some anxiety going. There's no way to hide it, Cousin Brother. The shit's going to hit the fan. The thing to do is micromanage, micromanage, micromanage."

Reen stared bleakly at the crumpled napkin, wondering how far the situation would deteriorate and how close lay the brink of no return. The huge room was silent as Oomal poured himself more coffee.

From the intercom a shrill "Five minutes, sir."

Oomal stood up, adjusted his tunic. "I look okay, Cousin Brother?"

Wearily Reen stood up with him. "Can you handle it?" he asked, studying his Brother's face.

"If I can handle stockholders, Cousin Brother, I can handle reporters."

Leaving Thural behind, Reen and Oomal hurried from the West Wing and through the colonnade. At the main building Reen considered taking the elevator, decided against it, and walked to the stairs.

On the steps Oomal fell behind. He was clutching the ornate brass railing and wheezing a little. Reen looked back in alarm.

"You're walking too fast, Cousin Brother," Oomal said wanly. "If I'm going to field questions, at least let me catch my breath."

"What's the matter with you?"

Head down, Oomal told him, "Just a little stage fright, Reen-ja. Not to worry. I always get it, and then I'm always fine."

How could his Brother handle reporters if he was stricken by stage fright? To escape the oncoming disaster, Reen bolted down the steps. Oomal snagged him with a claw.

"Get back up there, Reen-ja, and introduce me. I'm fine. I'm just fine."

Reen hesitated. Oomal looked deathly ill, but he whispered, "It's not as easy as I make out, dealing with what I have to do, Cousin Brother. But my shame is no concern of yours. Go introduce me."

Reen, before any second thoughts could stop him, strode quickly around the door and into the blinding glare of television lights. He groped his way to the lectern, hearing the crowd noise subside into a low expectant grumble.

When his eyes adjusted, he saw that the reporters had dressed themselves, for Cousin notice, in shades of brown and gray. Looking past the television cameras to the anemic light that seeped through the tall windows, he cleared his throat. "I know you are here today about the situation at Gerber—"

A shout from the crowd: "Sir! Sir!"

Shielding his eyes with one hand, Reen peered out into the seated throng and saw a woman on her feet. He glanced nervously behind him and saw Oomal, his expression still numb and heartsick, waiting on the red carpet just past the door.

"Sir!" the woman called.

"Yes?" Reen would have to answer the strained-pea question himself or call the stricken Oomal from the wings.

"Bambi Feinstein, *Havana Libre*. I have a question and a follow-up, sir. Why did the commuter ship crash yesterday?"

Reen stared helplessly at the woman. What should he tell her but the truth? The crash was obvious sabotage. Every Cousin knew that. Yet if he admitted it was sabotage, who should he say was responsible?

The FBI? Because Hopkins had known enough to keep Tali from boarding. His Cousin Brother? Because even though Tali had denied having anything to do with it and even though Brother had a difficult time lying to Brother, Reen still distrusted him.

A murmur spread through the crowd. They were waiting for an answer. But, then, so was Reen.

"We're looking into it," came a whisper to his back.

On the other side of the doorway Oomal was motioning to him. "We're looking into it," he repeated.

Reen lowered his mouth to the microphones. "We're looking into it."

"Second part of my question, if you don't mind, sir," the woman from *Havana Libre* went on, leaving Reen stunned by her acceptance of his nonanswer. "The Watergate is of immense historical value. Are you planning to commit funds for rebuilding?"

"Yes," Oomal hissed.

"Yes," Reen said, glancing at Oomal, who seemed to have recovered and was anxious to get to the microphone. Ignoring the raised hands, Reen blurted, "The CEO of Gerber Foods is here and will answer your questions."

He stepped off the wooden box that had been positioned at the lectern for Cousin convenience and took his first deep breath since

facing the television lights. Oomal bounded to the vacated box and gave the press as wide a smile as a Cousin could manage.

"Good morning. I have bad news and some not-so-bad news."

Chuckles splattered around the crowd like sporadic rifle fire.

"Okay, the bad news," Oomal went on. "According to our studies at Gerber, human births are down a full twenty-seven percent."

Hands shot up. Oomal disregarded them. "The decline is highest in developed countries. At Gerber we believe there are two reasons for this. Number one, a decline in native births seems to follow a first contact. Why, we don't know. It may have something to do with stress in the native population. Second. Second," he said more loudly over the clamor, "we believe that Earth may have reached its optimum population level. Now, species don't simply get to that level and stop, you see." He marked an arbitrary boundary with his hand. "They surpass it"—his hand went up a notch—"and then experience a sharp decline in births." The hand lowered two notches. "A nonsapient population is naturally culled by lack of available food, but sapient species seem to work on a deep psychological level, a level we don't completely understand. After some study we have come to believe that Earth may be slightly overpopulated at the moment, and a decline in births is simply your way of dealing with it. Now I'll answer questions."

Reen stared up at Oomal, suddenly realizing how brave his Brother was and how schizophrenic the job he managed. It was clear now why the little death had brushed Oomal the moment before he took the podium.

"David Ching, CBS News," a tall Asian said, standing. "When you first took over Gerber fifty years ago, were you aware that such a drop might occur?"

"The possible drop in births was of some consideration in the buy-out, and it has given us the chance to monitor it closely."

"Do you have any plans to correct it?" Ching asked quickly, before any of the other reporters could break in.

"Correct it?" Oomal cocked his head. "You know, only mistakes

need correcting, David. This may be a natural process. We'll continue to monitor the situation, however, and if it appears that humanity is reaching the danger level, we will certainly do all we can to promote fertility. Yes?" he asked, pointing.

A familiar woman jumped up from her chair. "Harriet Standifer, *Washington*—" The *Post* reporter's question died in her throat. She was staring wide-eyed at a spot behind Oomal, as though God and a retinue of His archangels had materialized there.

Wheeling, Reen came face-to-face with Jeff Womack. The President winked at his chief of staff and tucked his tie into the jacket of his pin-striped suit. "Excuse me." Womack nudged Oomal from the stand.

"No, no, Jeff," Reen whispered, waving his hands.

But Womack kicked the box away and leaned down into the microphones. "Good morning, ladies and gentlemen."

The crowd came out of its trance with a thunderstorm of applause. Womack beamed into the cameras. Hands were shooting up all over the East Room.

Womack bent forward, and the audience went breathless with quiet. "I am pleased to announce that, at seven-thirty this morning, Eastern Standard Time, I signed the Tariff Deregulation Bill into law."

"What is this?" Oomal hissed, turning to Reen. "What's he doing?"

Reen was too stunned, too terrified to answer. The President was a loose cannon, and the Cousins were trapped with it on a small boat. One roll the wrong way, and they would be crushed.

Womack waited for the excited whispers to die down. "And I have another announcement, one of great historical importance."

Reen wondered frantically how he could remove Womack from the lectern. Did the President know about the sterilization plan? And if so, had he picked this moment to tell Cousin secrets? Reen and Oomal would be murdered where they stood. Not even the Secret Service would intervene to save them.

"I've served without a vice president for two years, and the time

has come to correct that. Right now," Womack went on, checking his watch, "the Senate is voting to approve my choice for a new vice president, and I would like to take this opportunity to introduce him."

Reen gasped. Someone was standing in the shadow beyond the door.

"He is a man with a great deal of political experience," Womack continued, "and someone I'm sure you will all recognize." He swept his arm to the side. "The spirit of John Fitzgerald Kennedy."

Bursting into the East Room, Jeremy Holt, the medium, held his hand high in greeting. Womack patted him on the back. The medium, needing no encouragement, bellied up to the microphones.

With a boyish, disarming smile Holt said, "Ah, thank you," even though no applause, not even a murmur, had been offered. "It's nice to be back."

Reen took in the broad Bostonian accent and the twinkle in the eyes, and even though it lay a century away, Camelot came rushing back. Of all the presidents he had known, he hated Kennedy the most. Dangerous Kennedy with his smiling eyes.

Those mannerisms: the tip of the head, the casual grace that only long-standing wealth could buy. Kennedy stood in Jeremy Holt's body. Kennedy, the once and future king.

"I've, ah, been privy to some interesting information on the other side."

Dizzily Reen felt Oomal grab his sleeve. There was a humming in his ears, a prickly dryness in his throat. He felt his mouth open and wondered if he was about to say something or simply scream.

"Ah, first of all, there *was* a gunman on the grassy knoll," Kennedy said with a pleasant smile. "The FBI marksman beyond the fence was put there by J. Edgar Hoover, while Lee Harvey Oswald, like Sirhan Sirhan later, was under total alien control. My brother's death was a payoff, ah, to the FBI for helping the aliens get rid of me. Now, I thank President Womack for his appointment, and I promise to bring

myself up to date on some of the history I've missed. I'm sure you, ah, have a great many questions, so I will take them now."

Except for an annoying buzz from one of the kliegs, the East Room was silent.

In the back of the room a hesitant hand rose.

"Yes?"

The reporter stood. The crowd craned their necks. "Uh, Gordon Appleton, *London Times.*"

"Yes?"

Appleton took a deep breath and brought his question out in a stammer: "S-sir? Is it true about you and M-Marilyn Monroe?"

20

As Kennedy answered questions, Womack turned and quickly left the East Room, Reen at his heels.

"How could you do this to me?" Reen cried.

On the steps Womack paused, his hand on the banister. "Everything's coming to a head, termite. There's blood on the floor in the basement. Watch your back."

Womack continued his climb. Reen followed. "You tell me to watch my back and then you nominate Kennedy as your vice president? You know when he was president I had him killed. How could you do this?"

"No time, termite. No time." Womack topped the stairs and scurried for his suite.

Pewter light from the high windows flooded the huge room. On the desk a McDonald's Happy Meal sat half eaten.

"You know I'm in danger," Reen protested as he watched Womack rummage through the dry bar's cabinet. "I was kidnapped yesterday. Don't you even care? A bomb went off at Dulles right where I was supposed to be. The commuter ship was sabotaged. You were the one who told me to fire Krupner. I cannot help but wonder what the Germans would have told me had they lived. I have been called to appear before a Senate subcommittee. The subpoena is

lying in a blackberry bush somewhere in Virginia, and you appoint *Kennedy*!"

Womack turned, a pistol in his hand. Reen staggered backward. His hip collided with the open door.

Womack's preoccupied eyes swept past him as though Reen were too insignificant to register. Turning to the mantel, he set the pistol on it. "Forget about the subpoena. I signed the tariff bill. They're not after you now. Besides, the Senate's not the problem. Something big is going on. I always tried to do the right thing. Well . . . nearly always. Do you think history will realize that?"

Although the President seemed to have forgotten about its existence, Reen stared at the pistol. "What are you doing with a gun?"

"Oh, God! I know too much, Termite!" Womack cried. His skin was taut over the bones of his cheeks. His eyes were so wide, Reen could see the halo of white around the irises. "All I wanted was gossip. You know how I love gossip. Now they're all after me. They know I have proof. So I had to choose a vice president, you see? There's danger ahead: bogs and quicksand and knee-deep shit. I mean, there comes a time when you have to put politics away and think about duty and morality and all that crap, you know? Jesus. I took an oath, didn't I? Nobody has the political skills to take my place but Kennedy." He cocked his head and said wistfully, "I always pictured myself as being a little like Kennedy, you know."

Reen approached Womack, holding wary hands up. "Sit down, Jeff. Let me call a doctor. Getting upset this way . . ."

Head still cocked, Womack asked, "Tell me, termite. All in all, don't you think I was a little like Kennedy?"

"I hated Kennedy," Reen moaned. "You know that. I can't believe you'd betray me like this." Tali. Womack. The Sleep Master. Everyone was turning on him.

Womack looked around the room.

"What are you looking for?"

"I forget," Womack said vaguely, patting his pockets. "I lose things. My ballpoint pens. My mind. My soul." He chuckled. "They'll

never find it. They don't know where to look. But they know I have evidence. Records. Pictures. I've got it all. So I have to keep the gun handy, termite. Maybe I'll kill a few of them first. Tell me, do you think life's worth living anyway? Listen." He bent down and whispered into Reen's ear. "The Secret Service can't be trusted."

Reen stiffened in alarm. "Do you think that is how the graffiti got on the walls? The Secret Service? Of course, you must be right. How else could someone have written that without being seen?"

Clapping his hands to his cheeks, Womack gave Reen a long-suffering sigh. "I mean they've gotten to the Secret Service. That's what I mean! I tried to tell you! I tried!"

"You tried to tell me what?"

"Shhh!" He put a finger to his mouth for emphasis. "There's bugs in the walls. Bugs in the walls. And they're listening through the window. They have stuff that can do that, you know."

"But who wrote the graffiti?"

"Jeee-sus! Important things are going on. Will you forget about the graffiti? I was the one who wrote the damned graffiti."

"You?" Reen asked dumbly. "You did it?"

"Get with the program, termite! Start thinking bad guys, okay? Start thinking assassinations."

Reen's indignation gathered. He could feel its chill weight at his neck. He backed away from Womack. "You no longer exist," he hissed, giving the President a level, malicious gaze. "You are in that place where the eye does not see."

Womack looked startled, but there was no way for him to fully understand what this meant. Only Marian could know. Marian, who understood endings.

"Come on. Don't be a jerk," Womack told him. "The graffiti—the Secret Service knew all about it. And we had a good laugh. I was messing with you, okay? I was getting under your skin a little, that's all. It's fun to get you rattled."

Reen would never forgive the President's treachery, just as he would never forgive his Brother's; but it would have taken a Commu-

nity decision to do with Tali what Reen was doing now with Womack. "I cannot identify your face. I do not recognize your voice." Reen turned and stalked from the room.

Womack's apology trailed after him down the hall. "I said I was sorry. You wishing I was dead or something? Come on, Termite. You sound like a three-year-old."

It would not be as if Womack was dead but as if he had never been. Even as Reen shoved that love away, he could feel it tugging at his sleeve, demanding attention.

"Reen!" Womack called.

Head high, back rigid, Reen walked to the stairs.

Womack hobbled after, threw himself in front of Reen. "I'm sorry, okay? I've got my sad face on, see?"

Reen stepped around him.

"Termite?" Womack's voice was thick with hurt.

Reen turned the corner and started down the stairs. His knees gave out, and he huddled there, mourning his loss.

Below, the press conference was breaking up. Jeremy Holt, Kennedy still occupying his body, swept down the hall at Reen's feet, a broad white grin on his lips. The rectangle of light on the carpet blinked out as a cameraman in the East Room extinguished the kliegs.

A moment later Oomal emerged, paused in the corridor, and looked up the steps. "Reen? Are you all right, Cousin Brother?"

"No," Reen replied. "Thural warned me of my temper, and he was right. My anger has caused me to do something stupid."

Oomal came and sat down beside him. "Tell me."

With a catch in his voice Reen said, "I threw Jeff Womack away, Brother, and I don't know how I will be able to bear it. From now on he will talk to me, and I can no longer hear. From now on I will look at him and no longer see. Our friendship is over." Reen peered through the brass banister rails to the floor below, imprisoned by his own decision.

"It'll get better as time goes on," Oomal said softly. "You'll get used to it. Can I do anything?"

"Leave me alone," Reen whispered.

Oomal hesitated, then got to his feet and padded quietly down the carpeted steps.

Love dies, Marian had told him. She was wrong. Love never died. Only relationships. And they left love festering behind.

He could hear the chairs in the East Room being folded for storage, the podium being put away. Soon the room would be cleared. Sitting, staring between the bars, Reen carefully folded and put away one by one the memories of Womack.

Jeff, a young President just two months in office, standing in the hot, whipping wind of the Vandenberg base, the aftershock of having learned of aliens and secret treaties still trembling in his face. His hand coming forward, a whispered word from an advisor, and the hand jerking back nervously to his side. Reen looking up at this new President and wondering how they would get along.

Fists pounding the table eight months later, Jeff's red-faced shouts of "No! No! You don't have the right!" and Reen telling him mildly that treaties were worthless and their landing inevitable. How much younger they had both been: Reen, unused to humans, pushing too hard; Jeff, unused to Reen, glaring at him as though he were a monster.

Less than a month later both of them facing each other across the oval doughnut of the UN's National Security Council table. The banks of cameras, the hush, the other members fearful and silent in their knowledge that the Cousin ships could outfly a plane and send conflicting messages into the brain of a missile. Reen, Loving Helpers around him like a living wall, because if a gun was fired, they would die for him—ten, twenty, a hundred, a thousand of them, if need be. Reen watching Jeff calmly as the new President shouted, "Why should these nations give up their sovereignty? It isn't in the interests of the united states that they become colonies." And Reen, who had learned to see behind human words into that dim region of what was left unsaid, recognizing the President's dark mirth.

A little show for the cameras. Jeff had taught him that. "Wave at the cameras," he said a year later as they stood on the White House

portico. And in the Green Room, before the fireplace, the crumbs of their finger sandwiches dusting their empty plates, the remains of brown coffee ringing the bottom of their cups, Jeff pointing to Reen's chair and telling him about all the heads of state who had once sat there.

Jeff was a student of history, a pupil of human nature, a scholar of vice. Jeff had taught Reen well.

Thinking back, Reen couldn't remember when partnership became love. Affection entered as stealthily as a cat into a strange room, until without warning there it was in Reen's lap, purring and warm.

Now he stood and brushed at his legs, as if shooing it away. Below him, the East Room was silent. A maid, dustcloth in hand, passed across the hall on her way to the pantry.

Jeff, slapping Reen lightly on the arm and laughing at something he said that he hadn't meant to be funny. Jeff, poking him lightly, playfully in the side with his finger and for the first time calling him termite.

When had that been? Reen wondered. The years flowed into each other like rain into a calm sea.

Upstairs, a clap—loud and sharp. Reen lifted his head curiously and heard swift footsteps from the elevator. Another clap, different from the first. The slam of a door. A slight clank as the elevator descended.

Somewhere in the quiet building a maid was running a vacuum cleaner. The smell of frying green peppers drifted up from the kitchen.

The elevator clanked again, once, as it ascended. More footsteps, slower now, but determined. A door above opened with a squeal of hinges.

Whispers, murmurs, a choked "Goddamn."

A thunder of steps, and a Secret Serviceman rounded the top of the stairs at a dead run. He nearly fell over Reen. His face was pale. His forehead and upper lip glistened with sweat.

"Go to the West Wing desk immediately, sir!" The man took Reen's arm forcefully, nearly pulling him off his feet. "Find Miller. Can you remember that? Agent Miller. Stay with him until we have the situation under control."

"What is it?"

"The President's been shot." Suddenly the man was gone.

Reen stumbled up the stairs.

In the study two men stood staring down at Jeff Womack. Jeff lay in that place where the eye did not see and yet, in the light from the windows that was the color of old silver, Reen saw everything clearly.

Jeff was sitting in the rocking chair, his neck crimped back hard against the rest. The McDonald's Happy Meal scented the room with onions; Jeff scented it with blood. His eyes were open, and he was regarding the ceiling with surprise. Behind him on the cheerful yellow carpet was a feathery spray of brains.

"Have somebody call the Senate and see if they've confirmed," one of the men said, glancing at his watch.

The other man hurried away. A doctor and a nurse ran in.

"Let's get him on the floor," the doctor said sharply, grabbing the President by the front of his jacket and pulling him out of the chair.

Jeff punching Reen in the side and calling him, for the first time, termite. Jeff tumbling bonelessly, heavily to the carpet, the back of his skull staining the yellow red. Jeff with the doctor tearing his shirt open, buttons flying, one button bouncing like popcorn off the gun that lay a few feet away.

"Get me an airway."

Brown eyes as wide and unblinking as a Cousin's. Hands curled, the palms perfect and pink as shells. The long, groaning, hopeless sigh from the dead chest as the heels of the doctor's rhythmic hands compressed the lungs.

"What time do you call it, Doctor?" the man in the suit asking.

The doctor snapping back, "I haven't called it yet."

"His goddamned brains are all over the floor."

The doctor, kneeling, pushed at Jeff's chest. But couldn't he tell that that wasn't what needed attention? Jeff's pink brain was pushing through his white hair as though some deformed creature were squirming its way to birth.

Put it back in, Reen thought. *Please put it back in.* They should, all of them, find the pieces scattered on the rug and put them back inside the splintered bone where they belong.

More footsteps pounding. A breathless voice. "Confirmed fifteen minutes ago."

"Shit." The man turning, fists raised impotently.

Reen could not see; but he did. He saw Jeff's blood on the floor. He could not hear; but he heard Jeff laughing in the Green Room, talking about history.

Suddenly Oomal and Thural were at either side of Reen, claws digging into his sleeves so hastily that they left stinging scratches. "Come away, Reen-ja," Thural said, tugging.

Reen felt his feet trip over each other, felt himself falling. Thural sucked in a breath as they collided, and for an instant both touched the oblivion of Communal Mind.

Thural struggled to get away, but Reen seized him around the waist, tumbling him to the floor where dim light and purposeful dark waited, where the young were in their nests and Brothers crawled unthinking through the smooth, cool tunnels of childhood.

"Reen!" Oomal was dragging him back. Thural was scrabbling across the carpet to escape Reen's grasping hands. The humans were staring.

Jeff was staring, his sightless eyes still fixed on the ceiling as his cunning, wry mind leaked across the floor.

Reen lay on the carpet, Thural crouched before him, the gaping hole of the pistol's muzzle a few feet away. One of Jeff's buttons lay near Reen's outstretched fingers.

He pushed himself unsteadily to his feet, and Oomal stepped back.

Quieter footsteps this time, hesitant footsteps. Men entered the room with a stretcher and a long green plastic bag. They looked curiously at the Cousins and somberly at the dead President.

The doctor, still kneeling, looked up at the men with the stretcher. "A suicide," he said.

21

Reen went down to the ground floor and sat in the Vermeil Room, his Cousin and Brother sitting silently by him but not too close lest he touch them again.

The ambulance left, lights winking, siren off. Thural walked to the kitchen and brought back a late lunch.

"You may return to Michigan if you wish, Brother," Reen offered finally, looking at his untouched food.

Oomal pushed his empty plate away. "I'll stay awhile, Reen-ja."

When dusk was settling across the lawn, Reen, without a word to the other two Cousins, left and made his way up the two flights of stairs.

Jeff's office was a yellow hearth of light kindled against the icy evening. A wall-to-wall strip of carpet had been pulled up, exposing the dun pad underneath. In the fireplace was a humped grave of smoldering ash. Jeff's rocking chair was gone.

Reen walked to the bar and stared at the half-bottle of Wild Turkey lying on the counter, the used glass beside it.

Jeff, eyes twinkling over the rim, telling him of Harding's mistress; of Brezhnev's scantily clad masseuse; of broken treaties and purposeless wars.

Jeff, too, had become part of history.

Among the row of books on the shelves above the dry bar, Sandburg's *Lincoln* and Kennedy's *Profiles in Courage* were upside down.

Someone had been searching the room.

Behind Reen came the sound of a drawer slamming shut. He pivoted. The door to Jeff's bedroom was slightly open. Quietly he went to the crack and heard the sound of shoes on carpet.

"I still can't believe the Senate confirmed him," a voice said.

There was a click, like a small box closing. A feminine sigh and a familiar voice, "Last night Womack telephoned all one hundred senators. He traded the signing of the tariff bill, and the vote passed by acclamation. You always underestimated him. I didn't. Womack was a devious son of a bitch."

The quick triple-pump of Reen's heart was so forceful, so loud, that he was certain the people on the other side of the door could hear it. He crept backward, bumping into a small table and catching a vase before it could fall.

Marian Cole was searching for Jeff Womack's evidence.

Reen tiptoed down the hall, down the stairs. He had known Jeff better than anyone, and he knew that if Jeff wanted to hide something, he would have been cleverer than to hide it upstairs.

He would have hidden it where he thought no one would look.

Reen passed the pantry and the Secret Service room at the end of the corridor. The colonnade was silent except for the gurgle and lap of the pool. Reen stole into the West Wing like a small gray wraith and turned left to the Oval Office.

The reception desk was vacant, with a single lamp left burning. The door of the dark office gaped like a mouth. Reen walked in, flicked on a light, and began his search.

It was behind the portrait of Millard Fillmore that he found it, taped to the canvas with black electrician's tape: a fat manila envelope. He tore it from its hiding place and spilled its contents on the desk.

Enough photos to fill an album. Neatly typed memoranda. Notes crumpled by nervous, sweaty hands. And a folded slip of paper with

a blue karma ticket stapled to the top. Reen picked that up and opened it. The paper was dry and old, and made a sound like dead leaves when he pulled the edges apart.

Under the blue ticket was the Xeroxed typewritten suggestion: WRITE YOUR SIN BELOW.

Under that was a Cousin's scrawled and difficult handwriting:

May God forgive us
for Killing you—
Jonis

Reen's fingers began to tremble. Paperclipped to the karma ticket was a typed note:

Jonis now an asset. —Bernie

Poor, deluded Jonis, whom guilt could not release. Reen traced his Cousin's painful scribbles with a numb finger. No wonder Jonis had avoided Thural. It was so hard for a Brother to hide truth from a Brother. And treason was so alien a concept that not even Thural would have understood.

Reen's eye lit on a slender manila folder marked TERMINATION PLAN. Inside, just under the heading CARBONATED DRINK, was a large cheerful yellow Post-it Note:

Eliminating Reen too precipitous. And too much bad karma involved. Advise first step putting Gerber out of business. See historical references re Tylenol Scare. —J.W.

J.W. Jeff Womack. So the President had known all along what the Cousin plans were, knew that Reen had deceived him. And he evidently was aware of the doomsday virus.

Setting the folder down, Reen forced himself to sort though more evidence. A photo this time. A happy group of scruffy people around a barbecue pit. The karma sellers at a picnic. Bernard Martinez smiled into the camera. His arm was around a huge man with a beard, knit cap, and smooth brown skin. To the photo was paperclipped a note:

> To J.W. Bernard M. frightened. Claims mole in organization. No proof this is true. Essential Martinez not flee from D.C. Advise funnel more money through Jonis to keep karma sellers fat and happy.
>
> —Agent Miller

Bernard Martinez, a grin on his face, terror in his eyes, his arm around the disguised Lieutenant Rushing. Reen let his breath out in a long sigh.

Quickly he leafed through the rest of the papers. An autopsy report and three postmortem pictures, photos so ghastly that Reen nearly flung them away. Then, above the bloodied, shattered jaw Reen recognized the corpse's eyes. Le Doux. Gentle, quick-witted Le Doux, easy to laugh, eager to please. A month earlier the Secret Service agent abruptly left White House security. Reassigned, Reen had been told when he asked about his absence.

The soles of Le Doux's feet were burned black. Welts lay in a houndstooth pattern across his legs, his chest. On the autopsy report the grim notation:

> Burns caused by application of electrical current. Cause of death: gunshot wound. Bullet entered medulla and exited center of mandible.

The letters blurred, an order from Reen's mind not to read further. An autonomic demand of blind love.

With the autopsy report was a Post-it Note:

Landis compromised. Fingered Le Doux. If they shot Le Doux, he talked.

Reen laid the autopsy report down and waited until his vision cleared. Humans were a mix of cold murder and warm laughter. Cousins walked a tepid middle path. It was Reen's own fault that he had underestimated them. Human violence had always seemed newspaper-story distant, television-drama unreal. Now he knew how sheltered the walls of the White House had been and how brittle and breakable they could become.

He forced himself back into the search. More photos. Grainy black-and-white photos taken by security cameras. Photos of Hopkins and Tali. Tali and Loving Helpers entering the Secret Service office at the end of the White House's cross hall.

The pictures halted Reen, his mind balking before the insurmountable barrier of Tali's own treason. Then he was searching hurriedly again, picking up memos, discarding them, their messages barely registering.

Joint Chiefs at Langley 1/17, 1/19, 1/28, 1/30. Miller

Jonis scared to death. Afraid Tali has caught on. Bernie

Don't you people understand? Look what you let happen to Jonis. Someone's following me. The last time I slept was in the Greyhound bus station three nights ago. I have to get out of town NOW. Get me some money or I'll go to Hopkins. I'll tell him everything. I'm not kidding. —Bernie

On the third page lay a wrinkled, unattached piece of paper. Reen opened it carefully. It was even more fragile and brittle than Jonis's petition had been. In Jeff Womack's slanted handwriting, a cryptic series of numbers: 7039713991.

Folding the page carefully, Reen gazed around the oval room. The logs had burned themselves out, and the fireplace seemed to be sucking warmth from the air.

He put the papers back into their envelope, hopped up on a chair, and taped the envelope again to the back of the portrait. Then he walked down the hushed corridor and the quiet stairs to the office of White House security.

He twisted the knob and pushed. The hinges creaked. The room, which should have been manned, was dark. Patting the wall to his right, he found the light switch and flicked it on.

On the worn carpet by the file cabinet Reen found three dime-sized drops of dried blood and four bloody parallel grooves in the beige paint—grooves that human fingernails must have scratched. *Landis compromised. Fingered Le Doux.* But before he gave in to the Loving Helpers, Security Chief Landis had fought.

"You found it, didn't you?" a voice said.

Reen turned and saw Pearson. Pearson who knew karate, who with a nine millimeter could put out a candle at thirty yards.

"The documentation, I mean." Pearson's dark eyes were somber, his voice shorn of its cheerful lilt. "Where is it?" Pearson oozed around the door and shut it behind him.

Reen stepped back.

Pearson's eyes tracked him. "What did you find out?"

Reen forced his dry lips apart. "Are you going to kill me?"

As though surprised, Pearson lifted his eyebrows. He seemed to be gauging how much force he would need to wrest the truth from Reen. How much torture it would take.

Reen said, "Do something, Mr. Pearson. Either kill me or let me go."

The dark eyes shifted in indecision. Then the agent stood away from the exit. Reen rushed past him and out the door, up the stairs, and into the dark, haunted colonnade, where the tingling smell of chlorine seeped from the open doorway of the pool.

In the Vermeil Room, Oomal and Thural still waited, talking in low tones. When Reen entered, they stood.

"What is it, Cousin Brother?" Oomal asked, seeing the look in Reen's eyes.

"Get a Taskmaster and three Loving Helpers," Reen told them. "Bring them here now."

22

When Reen pushed Jeff's bedroom door open, the light from the study revealed the figure of Marian Cole and the large hulking form of Lieutenant Rushing. The pair froze.

"Reen," Marian said, pressing a hand to her neck. "You scared me."

The half-light was kind to her face. She didn't look much older than she did at the time of her first rebellion, when she had run away to marry.

"Bring them," Reen said. Behind him was the patter of the Loving Helpers' soft boots, the heavier tread of the Taskmaster. When Marian saw the Helpers, she shrank back against a dresser, hitting her shoulder with a bruising thud.

"Don't, Reen. Just listen for a minute. Jeff was murdered." She eyed the Helpers who had drifted like ghosts into the room. "That was no suicide. The nitrate test on his hand came up negative. The autopsy showed two bruises on his jaw where someone held his head, and two chipped teeth where the gun was shoved in his mouth."

Jeff, his laughter ringing out from the Green Room, a sound as unforgettable as the clap of his death.

"I found Jeff's evidence, Marian," Reen said. "And I read it."

Her face, burdened by the weight of the inescapable, sagged. "What did it say?"

"That Detective Rushing murdered Bernard Martinez. That you knew all the time that Jeff was using the Secret Service and the karma sellers to spy on you and the FBI. Is that why you killed him?"

Rushing edged toward a window. "We didn't kill Womack. Hopkins did. Hopkins was behind it all: Jonis, the attempt on your life, all of it."

In a lockstep that was very much like the lockstep of their minds, the Helpers walked toward Marian.

She held her hands palms out, as though she might find the strength to push them away. "Reen! Please! Hopkins made plans with Tali. He traded your murder for the assassination of Womack. Hopkins figured once Womack was out of the way, Speaker Platt would become president. He squeezed Platt with one hand, Tali with the other."

The Loving Helpers stepped forward. Marian slid to the floor, hysteria constricting her throat. Her cry was that of a naughty little girl who has caught a glimpse of her father's punishing belt. "No! Listen! Hopkins snatched Jonis, and he wanted to take Bernard Martinez, too. Jonis wouldn't have talked, but he worshiped Martinez. He would have told Hopkins everything to save Bernie. I had to order Martinez killed before he gave himself up to the FBI. I *had* to."

"Don't let those things touch her," Rushing said. "Jesus Christ! Can't you see how scared she is? Can't you see that?"

The Helpers stepped forward again.

Rushing reached under his jacket. He drew his gun and pointed it at Reen's chest. His hands shook. "Order them back!"

Reen's heart galloped for an instant before going numb and still.

"No!" Marian rose to her feet with a scream. "No, Kyle! Don't shoot him!"

The gun barrel wavered. "How can you let him do this to you, Marian? You know how he hurt you. How he—"

"Goddamn it!" Her face was tight with anger. She was breathing

hard. "What happened between the two of us is none of your business. Put the gun away *now*!"

With a brusque gesture Reen ordered the Taskmaster and his trio of Helpers back.

Rushing slowly holstered his pistol. His voice was a low growl. "She could have had you killed a hundred times, but she didn't. Tali and even the Secret Service wanted to get rid of you. She stopped them. Didn't you know that? Don't you know how she feels about you? Goddamn. And haven't you hurt her enough?"

Marian slumped to a sitting position on the floor. Reen knelt beside her, so close that he could feel the heat from her body. "Do you know where Jonis is?" he asked.

Her knees were drawn to her chest, her skirt a waterfall around her legs. "Buried at Camp David."

Reen reeled back.

"I didn't do it. It wasn't me." Her words stumbled over each other. "I told you: Billy did it. We found out where they took the body. I got to one of his agents."

Her eyes met his. He wondered how he had ever thought they had depth. The irises were as blank as blue paper cutouts.

"Oh, God, Reen," she moaned. "Didn't I tell you that your Brother knew? Didn't I tell you we had to find Jonis?"

"Did they torture him?"

Her breath was moist and close against his skin, like an exhalation from a greenhouse. "Hopkins couldn't get Jonis to talk. He was getting sick, and Hopkins got so scared that he made a move to snatch Martinez. That's why Rushing had to terminate Martinez. Hopkins didn't understand Cousins. When Martinez was killed, he thought torture was his last chance. It confused Hopkins when Jonis died."

Reen stood. "We will get his body."

At his feet, Marian looked up. "My people are already there. We were going to find him and hide him again, hide him better. I was afraid the other Cousins would find out. Hopkins is stupid," she said bitterly. "He thought Tali had told him everything. He didn't know

about the doomsday virus. Poor Martinez. He was harmless, really. I didn't want him killed. But he should never have converted Jonis; and the President shouldn't have tried to play detective. Womack was getting too close to the truth."

"And Tali?" Reen asked, gazing down at the top of Marian's blond, disheveled head.

"Your Brother knows about Jonis," Rushing answered. "Hopkins told him. Tali might have gone to the other Cousins for help, but he found out the FBI could prove that the Loving Helpers had subverted the Secret Service and that Tali helped plot your murder. Tali didn't dare turn the Loving Helpers against Hopkins. Too many in the FBI knew. Still, Hopkins was scared shitless when Jonis died. He went to Tali and confessed. Your Brother promised he'd protect him. See? He knew who got to Jonis and why, and he just didn't care. To Tali, man, once Jonis had converted, he was just another human. And your Brother, he doesn't like humans worth crap."

Reen straightened, gazed at the misty cobalt square of window to Rushing's right. "Let's go to Camp David," he said.

Rushing nodded. "We'll drive you."

"You drive," Reen told him with a heartsick sigh. "We'll go in the ship." He looked down at the crouched and terrified Marian. "And we'll take the Loving Helpers with us."

23

"I HAVE LOST THE ONLY TWO HUMANS I ever loved," Reen told Oomal as he watched Marian's car roll through the barricades, past the waiting tanks, and out into the dark rush-hour street.

Oomal gave him a sidelong glance.

"So now there is no reason I cannot out-Cousin Tali," Reen said.

"If that's your goal, you'd best forget it." Oomal seemed amused. "Nobody can out-Cousin Tali." The BMW disappeared down Pennsylvania Avenue, into the river of red taillights. "Let the Helpers take over her mind, Brother. Let me ask her some questions. There are things she's lying about."

"I can't, Oomal." Reen spread his hands and looked at them: the chubby fingers, the stubby claw. No wonder guilt-ridden Jonis hadn't been able to manage a better penned note of apology. "I've begged her to let me prolong her life the way I did Jeff Womack's, but she says she would rather die than have the Helpers touch her. I can't put her under control again."

"I'm gentle with them, Cousin Brother," Oomal replied. "You know I'm gentle."

Reen nodded. Oomal was the gentlest of Brothers, making the descent into Communal Mind a cushioned fall. Yet during that fall,

even with Reen holding her hand, Marian had wept. Communal Mind was deep, much deeper than the shallow graves of Marian's eyes—its depths without light, its sides without handholds.

"So a karma seller converted Jonis? No shit," Oomal said in wonder as they started for the ship. "Poor Jonis. There *is* something seductive about the humans, you know. Give us a couple more generations with them, if we had them to give, and Cousins would start wearing three-piece suits and driving Volvos. Maybe Tali knows that. Maybe that's why he's playing Super Cousin. And," Oomal said, giving Reen a knowing glance, "maybe that's why he thinks you're dangerous."

"If he did not think like a human himself," Reen grumbled, "he wouldn't have plotted to kill me."

"Just my point." His Brother paused at the lighted ramp. "Another generation. That's all it would take. Two cultures don't merge without one coming out the winner. Some of us would be driving Volvos, all right, and some would be driving Chevy pickups with guns under the seat. Now I see why our ancestors acquired the bad habit of genocide."

Oomal tapped the shocked Reen playfully on the arm.

"Remember when we first landed and it looked as though things were going to go the other way? Remember you were on the *Today Show,* and you said the Old Ones spoke to you? Overnight it seemed as if every human became a damned spiritualist. That's where this karma seller stuff all came from, you know—that *Today Show* interview fifty years ago. I'll bet you anything that Womack was trying to call up the Old Ones and turn them against us."

Reen looked at his Brother with such shock that Oomal laughed.

"Trying to hook up an AT&T long-distance link with the Old Ones. Come on," he said, snagging his Brother's sleeve, "what do you expect? We took all Womack's power away. But screwing around with cardboard ghosts isn't important. What bothers me is what Marian said about Tali. And how Tali's been acting lately. As if he has a bug up his ass. It's only a matter of time before the Community

finds out what Second Brother was up to. And if Tali's panicking, Reen, we have a problem."

Thural came out and stood in the lighted rectangle of the ship's doorway. Reen trudged to him, and the three walked to the navigation room.

"How many humans do you figure know about the sterilizations?" Oomal sat down and hooked an arm over the back of his chair.

Reen fell heavily into his seat. Marian. The Secret Service. Certainly Bernard Martinez had known, and anyone else Jonis had confessed to. There could be hundreds.

"And when do you suppose the balloon's going to go up?" Oomal asked.

Reen looked worriedly toward the tanks surrounding the White House. He didn't reply.

"Maybe we ought to start making contingency plans, Reen-ja," Oomal said.

"Why hasn't someone leaked it already?" Reen wondered aloud. "Why aren't we seeing stories on the news?"

"They're too afraid of that doomsday virus. And so am I," Oomal muttered. "Come on. Let's get out of here. I want to follow that car and make sure they don't duck out on us."

Obligingly Thural took the ship up. Extinguishing the outside illumination so they would not be seen, they located Marian's BMW by its hidden beacon and tagged after the twin cherries of its taillights.

Cottage-cheese clouds sailed across the moon. The road below was a necklace of tarnished silver that some careless hand had tossed on the black, rumpled bedspread of the Maryland hills. Intent on his flying, Thural hunched over the controls. In a gesture copied from the human pantomime book, Oomal pretended to straighten a crease in his skin-tight pants and then crossed his legs.

Humanity was so seductive.

Reen looked down at the faint red dot-dot-dot tracer of the car's

lights as it shot past the trees. Marian had deceived him with her strength, her warmth. But Reen had deceived her first.

Come along, the Cousins had told her when the Helpers took her hand and dragged her to the ship.

We won't hurt you.

The murmured assurances of a nurse with a needle to a frightened five-year-old.

Just a little sting, and it will all be over.

Marian, naked on the table, the robot arm digging into her flesh as tears leaked from her eyes. The genetic combination had been so hard to get right. Ten, twenty, thirty years. And each year the same empty promise.

Rape. Yes, it had been something like that.

How fortunate, the Sleep Master's First Brother had written nearly three hundred years before, *to have found a species our ancestors ignored. With the decline in our own population, it may be that we can lift genetic material from them to strengthen our race.*

But Reen had taken that dream a step further than the Sleep Master's First Brother ever intended. Reen had created not stronger Cousins but Cousinly humans. Humans who would live four hundred years and breed like animals for the sheer exhilarating pleasure of it. Angela would probably live long enough to see her progeny cover the galaxy like a blanket.

By then, surely, the new species would find some way to defeat distance, and it would spread to the Magellanic Clouds, Andromeda.

Yes. If the purpose of his rape was Angela, Reen would choose Marian's suffering again even though he knew she still needed pills to sleep.

By the time she reached fifteen, he understood why she kept the lamp burning at her bedside, why she was afraid to be alone. And yet he went on capturing her, a fox mouthing a speechless, terrified rabbit.

He couldn't help himself. From the moment he first saw her he knew that he wanted his child to have her courage. And once he had

lost his heart, once the decision had been made, he kept to it through Marian's tears, through her pleas, through her bad marriage and attempted suicide.

There was no good reason why Marian should ever trust him, Reen thought as the ship now passed over the high fence of Camp David and flew over a group of humans gathered under a sparse forest of floodlights. Absolutely no reason.

Thural landed in a darkened, deserted part of the complex.

"You really want to do this?" Oomal asked, leaning over and laying a claw on Reen's arm.

Reen nodded.

"You sure? It's one thing seeing what humans did to Womack, Brother. It will be another to see what human has done to Cousin. As long as I've lived among them, as much as I like them, there are still some things about humans that I—"

Angrily shrugging off Oomal's claw, Reen stood and walked out of the ship. The air was calm, prickly with frost and the smell of pine. Above his head, clouds made a banded halo around the moon.

The Taskmaster herded the trio of Helpers out of the lounge and down the ramp. Oomal glanced around as though counting heads. "Okay. Let's go," he said quietly.

They made their way through the trees.

In the glare of the halogens Marian and Rushing were watching a pair of workmen dig a rectangular hole. At Rushing's feet a naked man lay, his right arm twisted under his body, one cheek pressed into the dirt. As Reen approached, he noticed the houndstooth pattern of burn marks, the ruined feet. And he recognized the bleached blue of the slain man's dumbfounded eyes.

Kapavik.

Rushing saw the Cousins. He tapped Marian's arm and nodded toward them.

Marian, seeing the direction of Reen's gaze, said, "We had to do it this way. There wasn't time for anything else."

So Marian had ordered the tortures. Did Le Doux and Kapavik scream? Did they beg for mercy? Marian always got what she wanted.

Reen peered into the open grave at his feet and saw what he first took to be the glint of dark water. *Only water,* he thought in relief. *Nothing to be afraid of. And in a minute all of this will be over.*

The workmen bent to lift the water, which turned out to be black plastic sheeting.

"Not yours," Marian told him, reading Reen's expression. "Ours. We're taking her home."

Rushing knelt and flipped back the plastic. Dirt tumbled down the gleaming sides. A gaseous stench escaped, spoiling the night air.

Natalie lay curled in her comfortless shroud, legs slightly bent, hands at her chest. The fingers were broken and bent backward. There were needle marks along her arms, some torn and jagged. The bullet that killed her had entered the back of her cranium and, leaving, took her forehead with it.

Reen looked down at Natalie's body, at which both worms and humans had plucked. Natalie of the bright clothes, all her color gone to a dull blue-gray. His throat closed. His voice emerged in a rasp. "Why?"

"Natalie died protecting you, Reen," Marian said. "Everything I've done was meant to protect you."

When he glanced up, she was giving him a speculative look.

"Jonis is over here, Reen," Marian said.

Jonis was wrapped in a soiled white sheet, and he lay, a cocoon without prospects, on the brown winter grass.

"I don't know if you should look," Rushing said gently.

Reen kept his eyes lowered until the sheet was peeled from the body.

Ants had visited Jonis. Disagreeable houseguests, they were crawling in and out of his punctured, wrinkled eyes.

"Where are his fingers?" Reen asked, his voice nearly failing him. "Where are his feet?"

Rushing went to the ambulance and returned with a small box.

A clumsy Pandora, he unfastened it, and from the opening came a thick puff of corruption.

"They buried the feet and fingers separately," Rushing said, closing the box. "Kapavik said they were planning to dismember the rest of him, to conceal what they had done. Jonis died before they pulled the third finger out of its socket."

Reen turned to Marian. "Where were you going to bury Jonis?"

"At the Virginia farm."

"Take him there. Take him there and bury him again."

Marian seemed surprised. "You don't want—"

"Take him!" Reen shouted. "Bury him, damn you! Don't you understand that the Community can't comprehend torture? That they believe the Cousins who were kidnapped died in peace, without a human raising a hand against them?"

She blanched. "We didn't have a thing to do with Jonis. We don't kill Cousins, Reen. That's not what we're after."

"You murdered Sidam, didn't you? You planted the bomb on the commuter ship. Tali was talking with Hopkins. Despite all we have learned from you, no Cousin could have murdered as coldly as that. And no other human could have got that close."

She drew back, as if fearing Reen would strike her. "I knew Tali and Hopkins were planning your kidnapping. I thought I could stop it."

He looked across the lawn to the two rectangular holes. The opening into Communal Mind was softer, its depths free from importunate insects and decay. "How did you get the explosives on board?" he asked. "Tell me on your own or I will bring the Helpers over and you won't have any choice but to tell me."

"I caught Sidam by the ship," Marian said, "and gave him a teddy bear for Angela. I told him you'd be going to West Virginia the next morning and that you'd give it to her then. There was an altitude-triggering device inside it. I never thought I'd kill Sidam, Reen. When Natalie called, I left for Langley. I thought it was Tali who died."

In a day and a night, Reen's entire life had soured. Marian turning

against him. Jeff's laughter gushing onto a yellow carpet. Hopkins and Tali conferring in the basement of the White House, planning Reen's destruction. And at his feet the shell of Jonis in its filthy shroud.

Abruptly Reen turned and walked away.

"Reen," Marian called. "Where are you going? What are you going to do?"

Reen didn't answer. Hopkins was the problem. Hopkins, who had ripped out Jonis's fingers by the roots to learn Cousin secrets; Hopkins, who had murdered Jeff and had led Tali down the twisted path of treason. As Reen stalked past the other Cousins and the three Loving Helpers, they swiveled and followed him to the ship.

Oh, yes. Reen was going to see Hopkins.

24

LIKE COUSINS, HUMANS SENT OUT SIGnals when they slept, signals so resonant that if a Cousin listened carefully, he could hear the mutters of their slumber.

Below the darkened ship Reen could hear that murmuring. He felt a woman in a neighboring house toss in a restless dream; sensed beneath him Hopkins's mind drifting like a boat across a dark sea.

When they landed and walked to the door, Oomal slid an opener into the key slot. Reen could hear its metal fingers probing the lock's tumblers. Beside him, the Taskmaster was fumbling a trace into an outside plug where it would send a command through the network of electrical nerves in the house telling the security system to slumber, too.

There was a soft click. Oomal turned the knob and opened the door to black, warm silence.

The floor was marble, and the hall smelled not of death but of peach potpourri. In the living room to the right, the glow from the VCR's clock cast an eerie deep-ocean green on the carpet.

Reen turned left and found the stairs that led to where Hopkins was riding the slow breakers of his slumber. Behind him, quiet as thieves, soft as cats, the Loving Helpers followed.

Five rooms, all open, the cobalt of night gathered in the door-

ways. Downstairs the furnace came on with a low rumble and an exhalation of heated air. Somewhere in the darkness a mechanical clock ticked. Reen chose the second of the right-hand doors, the one from which Hopkins's sleep licked at the edges of his mind.

Hopkins lay, a graveyard hump, under moonlit covers. Reen, whose ancestors had crawled in twilight tunnels and had eyes that pierced all shadows, saw Hopkins's hand curled innocently under his jaw.

Two bruises on the jaw, Marian had told him, where strong unexpected fingers had clutched Jeff's face. Reen could almost hear the sudden, frightened squeak of the rocking chair, the clink of teeth against metal, the felling explosion.

The Loving Helpers, dainty and elfin, were drawn by body warmth, by curiosity, to Hopkins. One grasped the man's hand. In a milky spill of moonlight from the blinds Reen saw Hopkins's eyes fly open.

"Who am I?" Reen asked, stepping to the bed.

"Reen," Hopkins whispered, not needing to read the nameplate, for now Hopkins could see as a Cousin saw. He could look past the unremarkable face straight into Reen where the soul itself murmured identity.

"Get up," Reen said.

With a thin moan Hopkins sat up in bed, the Helpers clustered around, touching him like street children in some strange Third World country.

"You murdered Jeff," Reen told him. "You murdered Jonis."

Humans responded in different ways to a Helper's touch. Marian quietly, steadily wept. Hopkins was the speechless type, his terror so profound that it couldn't be given tongue. He shuddered. His face poured sweat. His eyes were tender, moist, globular, like peeled plums.

"Tell me," Reen said.

"Yes."

"Do you have a gun in the house?"

Hopkins's reply came in a reedy squeal, the sound of a saxophonist hitting a bad note. "Yes."

"Get it."

The man's mind fought to escape; his body ignored it. When his feet hit the floor, he looked down at them in surprise.

"Get it now," Reen told him.

With trembling hands Hopkins slid open the nightstand drawer. In it lay a nickel-plated pistol.

Hopkins looked up at Reen in mute, apprehensive hope, as though praying the exercise was over.

"Pick it up."

When the hand obeyed, Hopkins's jaw dropped in slapstick surprise.

Against a wall of the darkened room sat a rolltop desk. Reen walked over and pulled out the chair. "Sit here," he said. "Bring the gun."

Hopkins's mind was obviously screaming for him to stop. He walked stiff-legged. The Helpers led him to the chair, and Hopkins collapsed into it.

"Put the muzzle in your mouth," Reen said.

A twitch ran through the muscles in Hopkins's cheeks. His breathing was shallow and rapid. Reen heard a drip-drip on the carpet. The man was urinating. His maroon pajamas were soaked.

Hopkins's face twisted grotesquely. His jaw worked. He was struggling to talk. "Tali. Tali."

"I know all about Tali. Put the muzzle in your mouth."

"The others . . . not me. Marian Cole. Yes. Yes. Jonis. But didn't mean—"

"Do what I said."

Hopkins's mouth twitched closed. His eyes bulged as he watched his hand turn on the pivot of its wrist. His lips parted in a rictus of a smile. His teeth stayed clenched, the only mutiny he could muster.

"Pull the trigger," Reen said.

Hopkins moaned. On his teeth the muzzle was playing frantic castanets.

The Taskmaster leaped forward. "No!"

Reen looked into the white-rimmed blank pennies that were Hopkins's eyes.

"Pull the—"

An explosion. The head snapped backward. The back of it blossomed open like an autumn-blown rose, strewing red petals of skull to the floor.

Hopkins's right foot kicked the desk once, hard. His arm jerked out away from him, flinging the pistol in an arc to smash the dressing-table mirror. His body heaved, then flopped wearily back into the chair.

After the boom of the gun, the silence of the room was so complete that it seemed to Reen he had been struck deaf. A sliver of mirror fell from the frame and tinkled on the dresser.

A Loving Helper shrieked, rubbing its hands as though Hopkins's death had left gummy acid on its palms.

"How could you do this?" the Taskmaster cried. "How dare you do this thing?"

The Helpers were screaming, screaming until the house echoed with their high-pitched cries.

In the Green Room, Reen knew, Jeff was laughing again, laughing to beat the band.

"Get them under control, damn it," Oomal said.

The Taskmaster glared. "I can't. They absorbed the death agony. No one can control them now."

Thural retreated. Oomal did, too. The noise the Helpers were making was the noise of forged steel as it bends.

"Someone will hear," Oomal said, glancing nervously out a window.

"They'll make every Helper we have go mad." The Taskmaster slipped a rod from his belt and touched one and then another of them. The small Helpers crumpled to the ground soundlessly, like crusts of

charcoal that, unnoticed, had burned to ash. Somewhere in the darkness of the house a clock chimed the hour.

"You killed them," the Taskmaster said as he contemplated the outcome of his sad, final chore.

At their feet the three Loving Helpers lay in a tumble, the obsessive light of Communal Mind extinguished in their eyes, their gray skin dim as smoke.

The furnace clicked off. The clock gave one last peal and then fell silent.

Reen thought he heard Hopkins's never-voiced pleas echo from room to empty room. And somewhere in the silent house he thought he heard a Helper scream, its cry like tearing metal.

25

REEN PICKED UP ONE OF THE CHILD-sized Loving Helpers and made his way down the steps, cradling his burden as snugly as he might have held Angela. Behind him he could hear Oomal, Thural, and the Taskmaster following, none of them speaking.

There was nothing to say. Reen walked across William Hopkins's dead lawn, the small head of the Helper nestled lifelessly against his shoulder.

They're not as intelligent as dogs, he had once admitted to Marian. But, oh, how much more loyal was this flesh of his flesh, Reen's skewed mirror. He pressed his cheek against the smooth cool cranium of the Helper, the bulbous case where no thought but duty had ever sparked.

Reen had never touched one, and now he marveled at the feel of that thick skin which was a copy of his own; he wondered at the solidity of its body and the twig-fragility of its limbs.

Halfway across the grass he stopped. Thural tried to take the body from him, but Reen pulled away. The others were now waiting with their own limp burdens at the ship's door.

"Come, Reen-ja. Come," Thural urged softly.

Reen twisted away. "No."

Reen wanted to weep for the Helper but couldn't. Cousins were made from emotionless clay. Only when they reached sapience did they discover there were things to weep for, but by then it was too late. They hadn't the genetic tools for mourning.

He heard Oomal's gentle voice, Brother to Brother. "Let me have the Helper, Reen-ja. It's time to go."

After a hesitation Reen put the corpse into his Brother's arms. The Helper's head lolled back, sharp chin pointed to the sky, eyes huge, opaque, and sightless. As Oomal turned, the Helper's arm swung like a heavy rope.

In the ship the others went to the lounge, but Reen sat alone in a small blue meditation room near the door. He fingered the lightning bolt at his chest, the symbol of his intelligence: a brilliant spark from earth to sky.

Fully ninety-three percent of his Brothers had been culled from the nest, raised separately from those who would have individual temperaments and individual names. Reen didn't know what his Helper Brothers looked like. He doubted he could pick them out from the others. Loving Helpers were interchangeable. They were the faceless night that surrounded the lightning.

Reen sat until Oomal came to tell him the ship had landed.

"Reen-ja, you're in no shape to go into the Cousin Place," he said after the door had closed behind him. "So let's talk for a minute. I have something I need to tell you."

Oomal sat beside his Brother, not slouching in the chair, as was his new style, but ramrod straight, his old.

"You're the First and I'm no Cousin Conscience, but I have to tell you that you fucked up."

Reen didn't bother to nod.

"Tali's going to crucify you with this. For a while tonight you had the upper hand. I mean, here Tali knows about Jonis, lies to the Community, and you kill your only goddamned witness."

"I have proof!" Reen said heatedly. "I have pictures: Tali bringing

Loving Helpers into the West Wing. I have names and dates. Everything, Oomal! Jeff had everything!"

"So you have pictures. So you have documentation. Photos don't tell the whole story. And the Community thinks all humans lie. We had to have Hopkins, Cousin Brother. They'd believe what Hopkins said if he was in the hands of the Loving Helpers. I thought you were just going to put a little scare into the man. Drag him back with us to the Cousin place, make him spill his guts. God, Reen, what a mistake."

"Do I disgust you?" Reen whispered.

Oomal stared at the wall. "You offend the hell out of me, First Brother. You and I and maybe Thural—we don't see the humans as strangers anymore. Christ. However much Hopkins conspired against you, how could you do it? How could you stand there and tell him to pull that trigger? Wasn't seeing Womack's body enough, and Kapavik's, and Jonis's? And you made me stand there and watch. It's something I'll never be able to forget. I don't know if I can forgive you for that."

"I'm sorry."

"Sorry doesn't cut it, First Brother. Nothing can make up for what you've done to me. And to yourself. Tali's been using Hopkins against you, and he probably thinks you've been using Marian Cole against him, like one of those old Third World wars by proxy the United States and the Soviet Union used to have. Now you murdered Hopkins. You upped the ante. Tali's not going to let you get away with it. So what did they do during the Cold War to keep it from heating up? They negotiated. You're going to have to negotiate with Tali, First Brother. As much as you hate it, you'll have to."

"Tali tried to kill me," Reen said.

"No, Reen. Tali didn't try to kill you. Cousins don't kill Cousins. He hired a human instead. Tali knows more about Communal law than you ever will. That's his job, and he's damned good at it. He knows that Cousins never dirty their hands, and they don't use Loving Helpers as weapons."

Reen looked away.

"Listen to me, Firstborn. Thural won't talk, but you can bet that the Taskmaster will. As far as he's concerned, you're *Tulmade*, you're egg-eater. He thinks you're crazy. That's all he talked about on the flight home. Now you're going to have to walk in there and give Tali something to make him happy. What does he want?"

"To breed the female."

Oomal was quiet. The lighting in the room was cool, blue, and lulling: nest color. Reen wanted to put his head down and go to sleep.

"That's stupid," Oomal said after a while. "You sure?"

"He can't accept what is happening to us."

"Yeah, well, Tali will quiet down once the first eggs are hatched and he has another thousand or so Loving Helpers to feed and house."

Reen turned to his Brother. "I can't allow the breeding of the female. Who would I choose? You? Thural? Any of the others? And as First, I would have to stand witness. I couldn't, Oomal. I couldn't watch that. I won't order a Cousin to die simply because our Brother can't accept reality."

Oomal spread his hands in defeat. "So what do you plan to do?"

"I will go in there," Reen said firmly, "and apologize for my actions."

"Oh, *that* should work. *That* should make everything all right."

"I'm not finished! Then I will tell the Community that Tali knew about Jonis. That he tried to have me murdered. I will ask Tali to step down as Conscience and put another in his place. You, perhaps, since you seem to like the job."

Oomal ignored the barb. "You're skirting the edge of disaster, Reen-ja. Brother bonding goes only so far. Tali may have your chains around him, but he chafes under their weight. If you don't play it very, very cautiously, you'll end up in rebuke, and Tali will be designated to make all your decisions for you."

Reen got to his feet. "The Community won't do that. At least not after a hearing. And I have you and Thural as witnesses to Hopkins's confession."

"Reen-ja, sit down. You can't—"

"Are you coming with me, Third Brother? Or are you afraid of Tali, too? When I call on you to speak up for me, will you lie?"

Oomal jumped to his feet, and Reen found himself slammed against the wall. He nearly fell. Oomal jerked him upright. "Listen, Cousin First Brother," he said in a low, deadly tone. "Get hold of yourself. You always had a bad temper, even when we were children, and time hasn't taught you shit. I'd jump off a cliff if you told me to, if you had a good reason, so don't take your rage at Tali out on me."

Reen felt as though he were under rebuke already, that every shred of authority had been taken from him. He was suddenly afraid of Oomal, afraid that his Brother would strike him as the Sleep Master had.

But Oomal let him go and stood back. Reen slid to the floor.

"Are you all right?" Oomal asked.

"No, I'm not. I'm sorry for everything. For trusting Marian Cole, for not suspecting Hopkins. I'm sorry for Jonis, for the Loving Helpers, for my anger."

"Quit saying you're sorry."

Reen looked up at his Brother. "What else can I do, Oomal?"

"Breed the female. Close your eyes and point. Choose somebody. Please point away from me."

Reen looked at the lozenges of blue light set along the tops of the walls. "Then I will have murdered five times tonight: Hopkins, the Helpers, and my own blood."

"Too bad that by law you can't choose Tali," Oomal mused. "That would be a sound executive decision. Come on. We'd better get inside and get it over with." He bent and helped his Brother to his feet.

It was late. The moon had set, leaving the sky adorned with a meager sprinkling of city stars. Oomal at his side, Reen walked into the chamber, stopping dead when he saw that a crowd of Cousins had gathered there.

Reen's arrival was met with silence. The Sleep Master, his face

grim, was standing next to the Taskmaster. Thural was frozen, one hand still out to Tali in entreaty.

The Taskmaster broke the spell. "Egg-eater," he spat.

Reen searched the crowd, found nothing but hatred or caution. Prudently Oomal stepped away from Reen's side.

"I . . ." Reen began.

The Sleep Master brought him up short. "We cannot identify your voice. We do not recognize your face."

Reen saw Thural's hand fall uselessly, wearily, to his side, all appeals abandoned.

"You are in that place where the eye does not see."

26

Reen staggered from the Cousin Place, looked around a moment, realized there was nowhere to go, and, dazed, sat on the steps.

A death sentence. The Community had given him a death sentence.

Along the dark horizon, the lights of Washington, D.C., painted a glowing dome on the bottom of the night. The air was brittle with frost. The moon, high and silent, was a lamp in the hands of Orion. Reen looked up, searching for home; but the star was too far and too faint to be seen.

Reen had misjudged how far and how fast Tali would go. *Now what?* he asked himself. There was no use going back inside and pleading. No one would listen.

Behind him, a quiet pop. The door opened, spilling light down the stairs. "Reen?" a low voice called.

Oomal. Oomal had called his name. Reen got to his feet. His Brother was looking at him, looking into his face as if nothing had happened.

Reen wasn't sure about the etiquette involved, if he should respond to his Brother's call.

Like a luminous eye closing, the door pressed shut. "You okay?" Oomal asked.

"Should we be talking?" Reen whispered. "If they hear us talking . . ."

"Tali already tried to rebuke me because I said he was the egg-eater and not you. He's in there shouting orders, and about half the Community is acting as if he were the one thrown away. It's a mess, Reen."

With a moist, kissing sound, the door parted again. Thural stumbled out. His dark gaze slipped past Reen and fixed on Oomal. "Tali cannot lead and be Conscience as well," he said. "Oomal, you must be Conscience. Go back in there and tell him."

Oomal shrugged. "I am already Conscience, Cousin Thural. Tali has nothing to do with the destiny of birth order. He'll understand that when he gets over his snit."

"But you are under rebuke, Cousin. How can Tali put his Conscience under rebuke?"

"He can't. Tali knows Communal law. He's bluffing. Go on back, Thural, before Tali tries to put you under rebuke, too. I'll let him cool off and then remind him how the Community works."

"He cannot be the First!" Thural shouted. "He cannot simply throw away his Brother and then take over his place! This has never been done! Another First should rule."

"We don't have another First," Oomal reminded him gently.

Thural's cry shattered the night as Hopkins's gun had shattered the mirror. "What he does is human, Cousin Conscience! This is a human thing Tali does, to murder a Brother in order to rule!"

"Yes," Oomal said with a malicious chuckle. "I agree. Very human. You might go back in and point that out to the Community, too."

Reen thought for sure that Thural, so full of indignation, would turn on his heel and march back to confront Tali. Instead his Cousin looked out at the dark landing strip and was silent for a long breathless moment. "What the Nameless did was evil, Cousin Conscience,"

he finally said, "but not evil enough for this. If the Cousin Who Has No Voice should ask for help, I might hear his request and sleep at his side."

Reen clapped his hand to his own cowardly mouth to keep from uttering an appeal. Enough murder had been done that night. A pair of Cousins didn't make a Community. If he accepted Thural's offer, they would spend the next three days in a sleepless wait for death.

"Never mind," Oomal told him. "The Nameless will be taken care of. I have some Gerber execs who like the Nameless a lot more than they like Tali. If he wants to come to Michigan, he has a sleeping place. Now go back in there before Tali starts plotting against you."

Reluctantly Thural went to the door and let it swallow him.

"I meant what I said." Oomal turned to Reen. "You come on up to Michigan. Tali can't do anything to me or my employees. Don't worry about us. We won't get thrown away just for hanging around with a Nameless Cousin."

A Nameless Cousin.

Reen took in a ragged breath that tasted of ice. There were difficult things he would have to remember: that he would never again be able to give an order; that he would make no more decisions other than his own.

Commuter ships and the smaller runners squatted on the tarmac like a gathering of toadstools. Soon he would leave in one and never be able to return.

There had been a time when the Cousins' obedience to him had been instinctive; when his Brothers, all but one, had loved him.

"I can't go just yet," Reen said.

"Don't be a jerk, Reen."

"If Tali does not have a consensus, he won't dare go against the humans. But he will go after Marian Cole. I must warn her," Reen said.

"Let her go. She hates us. Don't you see that yet? Someday, Reen, she's going to drink you dry."

As a child, when Reen had first felt the sightless nuzzle of his Brothers exploring him for allegiance, love had poured from him like milk. It wasn't just Marian who would drink him dry, it was the Community, it was the humans, it was Angela.

"I know," he said.

27

He had always come to her like a thief, sneaking into her house, rummaging through the closets of her mind. Down the hall, Howard wrestled with his nightmares, but Reen stood in the doorway watching Marian.

Her eyes opened. When she raised her head to look at him, he turned and went down the stairs to the kitchen. At his back a breathy whisper: "Reen?" He could hear her groping her drowsy way from the bottom of the steps to the hall.

"Here," he replied, pulling out a chair and seating himself in the breakfast nook.

She shuffled into the dark kitchen and fumbled for the light switch. The fluorescents came on with a chill dazzle, igniting color in the room: the turquoise countertops, the terra-cotta-tiled floor.

Marian had hastily tied a pink terry-cloth robe over her nightgown, and she was squinting in the glare. "You always come to me like a dream," she told him, rubbing her eyes with the tips of her fingers.

He sat, his hands linked on the tabletop. It was late, and the hours sagged around his shoulders. The colors in the room were painfully iridescent. Surreal.

"You want some coffee?"

Without waiting for an answer she went to the cabinets and pulled out an acid-green can of Folger's. A hiss of water from the tap. The clunk as the glass carafe was set on the Mr. Coffee hotplate.

"I murdered William Hopkins tonight," Reen said.

A crash. He turned and saw Marian staring down at a broken cup.

He reached for her, but she was too far away. In some ways she had always been. "There's no reason to be afraid."

"No, of course not." With a fussy gesture she pushed her hair back from her face. "How silly," she said, bending to pick up the pieces of shattered cup. "How clumsy."

On the counter the coffee maker spat. The aggressive scent of coffee pushed through the heavy air in the kitchen.

"Come here," he said. "Please."

She placed the shards of porcelain on the drainboard, then walked over, tucked her robe about her knees, and sat. "You look tired," she said.

She was the one who looked tired. Without makeup, her eyes seemed smaller, a more watery blue. Her cheeks were a wan, weary color. Tiny lines checkmarked the skin around her lips.

"Sit with me awhile," he said, his voice trembling a little. "I want to apologize."

She looked down at his hands and stroked the smooth gray surface of his fingers. "Don't feel guilty about Hopkins. He deserved it. The man was a shit."

"I know," he said softly. "I want to apologize for what I've done to you."

Her fingers halted in mid-caress. Her touch was warm but light as feathers.

"I've thought about what you told me, Marian. I've tried to understand what I did. I think that sometimes we fall in love with our opposites. Then we try to erase the differences. That's what I did to you."

"It was over a long time ago, Reen. It doesn't matter."

"Of course it matters," he snapped.

They looked at each other, and he saw that, despite everything, they were the same irascible Reen and the same vexing Marian that had existed from the beginning of the genetic experiments.

"When you married Howard, I should have left you alone, or at least not allowed you to remember. You and Howard could have bought that country house you always wanted. You could have had your dogs. Your horses. I kept you from that."

"Howard?" She was surprised. "You think I wanted Howard? You never told me I was putting on weight. You never noticed I was growing old. You never criticized the way I dressed or laughed at my opinions."

"There are things I am unable . . ."

"Don't!" she said sharply. "For God's sake, don't blame yourself. How do you think that makes me feel? I wanted things from you that I knew you couldn't give. You love as if everybody were important. As if everybody were the same. You know? Once I even slit my wrists so you would love me best."

He drew his hand away in shock. He always thought she slashed her wrists for Howard.

"If you didn't love Howard, you should have left him. You might have met someone else, someone who understood you . . ."

Her sour laugh stopped him.

"A *man* who understands me? Shit. Little boys grow up in some damned club called No Girls Allowed. And by the time they get to adolescence and start thinking about girls, they only want to know how to get into our pants. Later, when they're grown, they start trying to understand us, but by then it's too late."

Blinking hard, she said, "Women spend their whole lives wondering what we did wrong. Wondering why the ultimate insult for one eight-year-old boy to another is to call him a girl. Don't you dare apologize to me, Reen. You're no good at it. I've been apologizing my whole fucking life."

Bracing her hands on the table, Marian pushed herself to her feet. "Let's have some coffee."

Then she walked away. Reen heard the clinking sound of glass against china, the gurgle of coffee pouring. A moment later she was back, pushing a cup and saucer across the butcher-block table toward him.

He stared into the liquid, dark and brown as blood. "Oomal wanted to use Loving Helpers to find out why you were lying to me. I didn't let him."

There was a long silence. When he glanced up, he saw that she was watching him over the rim of her cup.

"I want to trust you," he said.

She put the cup down, turned it this way and that on the table, as if trying to find some perfect but elusive alignment.

"In a few days, I will die."

Her eyes rose.

"Tali is now First. Oomal is now Conscience. Oomal is strong enough to keep Tali from using the virus, or at least he will be if I stay away. But he either can't or won't stop Tali from coming after you. I want you to leave tonight. Pack a few things. Drive to some safe place. Surely you have one."

She gave a flat laugh. "Stop joking."

"I will die, Marian. There is no way to prevent it. The Sleep Master and Tali have ordered me from the Community because of what I did to Hopkins."

She grabbed at his arm, nearly spilling his coffee. "Don't leave me, damn it!"

Reen put his head in his hands. Lack of sleep was already getting to him. His arms shook; his head felt heavy.

Suddenly she was kneeling on the tiles, pushing herself into him, arms around his waist, head to his chest. He sat back in confused and awkward alarm.

Marian was so good at embraces. In all those years he had never really learned to hold her. He lowered his arms to her back.

Pressing his face into her hair, he smelled the apple scent of her shampoo.

When he lifted his head, he saw Howard standing in the shadowed doorway watching, just watching. Reen wondered how long the man had stood there and how much he had heard. For a moment they looked at each other, then Reen turned away and put his head again on Marian's silken, fragrant hair.

"We'll go away together," she said, "just the two of us. Let Oomal handle everything. I know how tired you've been lately, how the stress has gotten to you. Just walk away from it, can't you? Can't you do that for me?"

Reen looked up, but Howard was gone.

"I have to leave," he said.

She clung to him. Now it seemed that her hot, hungry arms were eating at him; that if he sat any longer, he would be consumed.

He shoved free. Her hands fell away. She sat back on her heels, her eyes shuttered with hurt. "I was never enough for you, was I?"

"Cousin is tied to Cousin, Marian. I can't help that."

"Since I was five years old you've been my whole goddamned world. You . . ."

He stood.

She stood, too. Her face was so twisted with anger that he thought she would strike him. "They always meant more to you than I did. Sometimes I hate you for that. Tali tells you to die, and you crawl off somewhere and stop living. Reen, you can learn to do without the other Cousins. I know you can."

"We are hive creatures, Marian!" he shouted in exasperation. "I have to have other Cousins around me to sleep! Listen to me. I want to know that you're safe. Pack some things. Leave the house."

She paled. "Wait. Stay here. Stay right here, just for a minute. I have something." She rushed into the next room.

Through the dark doorway, the slam of a drawer. A muttered "What are you doing up?"

"You're leaving, aren't you?" It was Howard in the shadows, his tone thick with hurt.

Marian's fierce whisper: "Where did you put it?"

"Just . . . don't do this. I know I can make things right. Just stay with me. Talk to me. Tell me what to do."

The bang of a cabinet. "Goddamn you. Where is it?"

A pause. A hollow reply. "In the blue vase."

Riffling sounds like paper. The clink of a diamond ring against porcelain. "Go to bed, Howard."

"Please. You—you'll be up in a few minutes, won't you? We'll talk. We'll—"

A hoarse "Go to bed."

A hesitation. Then Reen heard a heavy tread on the stairs. The squeak of a floorboard.

Marian rushed into the kitchen, her eyes wide. "Here! Take it! I killed for this!"

She shoved a cassette tape at him. He took it.

"You said you killed Hopkins, and it looks as if you didn't get anything out of it. If you're going to kill, Reen, at least do it right. This tape proves what Tali was up to. It proves everything." Her voice caught. "This will save you, won't it? They'll forgive you now, won't they?"

He turned and walked from the kitchen. Marian called his name. He closed the door on her voice, snapping it like a thread.

28

It was near dawn when Reen arrived at the White House. Alone, he parked his small ship at the edge of the landing pad and trudged past the darkened colonnade to the stairs.

He was the only thing moving in the halls. A four-in-the-morning hush had fallen over the White House, time holding its breath for the sun.

When he got to the second-floor study, he noticed the light was still on. He lifted a heavy hand to switch it off. Shuffling into Womack's adjoining room, he arranged himself on the bed. The mattress was so soft and so open that he couldn't decide whether he was in danger of being swallowed or of falling. After a few minutes of tossing he got on the floor and positioned his body between the safety of the bed on one side and the rigid frame of the dresser on the other.

There was no way he could sleep. The corners of the room were too sharp and hard, its Georgian design too fussy. Predawn light, the wrong shade of blue, seeped around the heavy curtains. The room smelled not of peppery rest but of potpourri.

With a little moan, Reen pressed his head closer to the dresser, gathering what comfort he could from the hard surface.

The first day would be the worst. The first day his struggle to

sleep would be frantic. After twenty hours or so, when his weary mind gave up the fight, the going would be easier. He would lie in dazed insanity until his heart gave out. Reen had never seen a Cousin die from *mitalet,* but he'd been warned enough by his elders.

Intelligence was too heavy a burden to carry alone.

Reen fought to drive out thought, but like a boorish dinner guest it refused to go. Lying there, he remembered the smooth tunnels of childhood. He pictured his Second Brother: the resolute victory in a face turned to cruel stone.

Memories assailed him. He pulled the pillow over his eyes, as though the press of the satin might keep out the visions.

But they paraded: Angela and Marian in the snow; Oomal, pity and revulsion in his gaze; Jeff Womack's head leaking pinkish gray brain; the fear in Hopkins's face.

Without the tether of the Community, his walleyed imagination bolted. Tali would find Marian and kill her. The Community would unleash the virus on the humans if the humans didn't revolt and kill the Cousins first. Thural, for his sympathy with Reen, would be chosen to die as consort.

Thural. Reen wished now that he had accepted his Cousin's offer. Two weren't enough to make a nest, but some of the edge might be blunted.

Thural. Reen tried to get up to go find him, but his body refused to move. Instead of rising, he flipped over on his side, his neck at an uncomfortable angle.

Reen heard a Cousin whimpering, then realized he was alone in the room and the whimpering came from him. Two more days.

The door hinges squeaked.

Reen lay in a tiny defenseless ball near the bed. Another squeak. Footsteps whispered across carpet.

"Reen?" Oomal called.

Reen rolled over. Oomal was standing at the corner of the bed, looking down.

Oomal should never have come. Reen's defenses were down,

and like Marian he would envelop the nearest victim in his own selfish need. He wanted to tell Oomal to run for his life, but he couldn't.

"I took a little nap when I got back to Michigan," Oomal said. "Then Sakan woke me up to say you hadn't arrived. I figured you'd do something stupid."

Another Cousin stepped around the side of the bed. "Hi, Reen," Sakan said. "You look like shit."

The two bent, grabbed Reen by his sleeve, and pulled him to his feet. Blearily he saw that four other Cousins were standing by the door, Louis Vuitton suitcases in hand.

"Oomal says we're camping out," Sakan said. "Like the time we went on the fishing trip."

Oomal made quick introductions. "You know Sakan. He's our director of marketing, the one who came up with the strained pea tartlets, remember?"

Sakan muttered, "Right. Bring that up again."

"Radalt," Oomal went on. "He's our controller. Kresom, vice president in charge of personnel. Zoor—the humans call him Zoomer—vice president of sales. And Wesut, production manager."

The Cousins gave Reen little waves of acknowledgment as they threw their suitcases on the bed.

"Zoomer," Oomal said. "Go find us some sheets."

Zoor nodded. "Where's the linen closet?"

Reen pointed to the hall, and Zoor left.

Oomal said, "Follow the logic, Reen. We evolved from tunneling creatures." He held up his opposable claws. "So we like semidarkness and confined spaces. Sleep's our way of getting back to the larval stage."

Radalt opened his suitcase and took out a blue light bulb.

"Communal Mind is part of it, but the ambiance has to be right, too," Oomal said.

Zoor came back in, holding up a sheet patterned with red and blue cartoon dinosaurs. "Hey, guys. Get a load of this."

Radalt stopped what he was doing. At the window, Kresom turned.

Looking down at the sheet, Zoor asked, "Our extinction or theirs?" Then he left on his quest again.

When the chuckles subsided, Oomal went on, "Anyway. The camping trip."

"Zoor kept asking why they didn't just cut out the middleman and eat the worms, remember?" Wesut said. "He popped a worm into his mouth, and Harvey Cohen from accounting fell over the side laughing and nearly drowned before we could get him back in the boat? Remember that? And then—"

"The humans kept telling us how much fun camping would be," Oomal said. "So, what the hell, we decided to try it. That night we pitched a tent and slept just fine."

Radalt switched on the lamp, flooding the room with blue. Kresom closed the heavy velvet draperies on the gray morning. Zoor came back with a sheet and tossed it to Sakan. "Colored sheets, but that's all I could find."

"If we wrap ourselves up tightly enough, we feel we're in the security of the nest," Oomal lectured as Sakan flapped out his sheet and rolled himself up in the material. His gyrations fetched him up against a nightstand with a thud.

"Comfortable, Sakan?" Radalt asked the pink cocoon.

A shiver went through Reen. He was looking at Sakan, he knew, but thought of Jonis, Jonis in his shroud.

Sakan's reply was muffled. "Just fine."

Zoor passed out sheets to the rest of them. Oomal helped Reen into his, showing him how to hold his arm down, demonstrating how to flip the end over his head.

"Sleep, Reen," Oomal said gently when his Brother was a tight cocoon in the corner.

Reen's sheet was a pale yellow, and once he was rolled up in it, the blue tinged the color light green. Arms pinioned at his sides, he caught the first whiff of spice. One of the Cousins had quietly and

without the least difficulty fallen asleep. A moment later the room was heavy with the dumb inescapable weight of Communal Mind. Reen fretted for a moment against the confines of his shroud before he, too, dropped into the dim, thoughtless regions of slumber.

Reen, the Old Ones called.

Reen couldn't see them, but he could hear them. His mind was falling, falling.

Reen, they said, but he was plummeting too fast to answer, his guilt wrapping him as tightly as the sheet.

He couldn't reply. He shouldn't. All ties with the Community were gone except for Oomal's unbreachable pity.

Aerodynamics, Reen thought giddily. The word dropped from his mind and fell with him, a small, round, heavy thing. Down and down and down. He imagined he could feel the edges of the sheet flutter.

Reen. The voices of the Old Ones echoed like thunder from the mouth of a well. And Reen knew they couldn't understand why he refused to answer.

29

Reen was yanked out of his doze by the clamor of angry voices. He was awake but couldn't move. He couldn't see. He tussled frantically until he remembered that he was wrapped in Jeff Womack's sheet.

"—back to Michigan!" Tali was shouting.

Oomal's reply was calm, but Reen could hear the anger in his voice like the throbbing bass note in a musical chord. "Order the other Cousins if you can, Tali. By law I don't have to listen to your shit."

Reen flipped the sheet from his head and wriggled his way out of the tangle. Tali and Oomal were standing in the doorway, the other Gerber executives watching, their empty, makeshift cocoons littering the floor.

Radalt smiled down at Reen. "Oh, hi. You awake? Want a bath?" he asked pleasantly. "We filled the tub with tannic water and set a fresh uniform out for you."

Tali's fury shifted from Oomal to Radalt. "You speak to the air! There is no one there! No one!"

It looked as though Radalt was longing to make some snappy rejoinder but couldn't quite work up the courage. Zoor bent and started picking up sheets.

"This is the law," Tali said, speaking into the averted faces of the Michigan Cousins, who seemed to be engaged in trying to pretend that Tali was invisible instead of Reen. "It is cleanliness to throw the dead from the Community because if the dead stay, they breed disease. And this Nameless Cousin, like a dead thing, will breed a terrible illness, a sickness of the soul."

Burdened with his pile of sheets, Zoor made his hesitant way past Tali and out into the hall, searching, Reen supposed, for a maid, for deliverance, or at least for a washer and dryer.

"Go back to work, Cousin Brother," Oomal said, snagging Tali's sleeve. "There's nothing to interest you here."

Tali jerked away. "You speak to me of *work*?" he shrieked. "You who bring your workers here with nothing for them to do? Where are we without purpose, Brother? Illness and insanity are the fruits of idleness."

"You know, Tali," Oomal said with amused irony, "you're just like a damned elderly Cousin looking for spots of fungus in his claw and telling scary stories to the young. But I'm grown now, and those Communal myths don't frighten me anymore." Turning, he motioned the other Michigan Cousins out of the room. "Go on down to the office we set up in the East Wing, guys. It's okay. Let my Brother and me scream at each other in private."

When the Gerber execs had all filed out, with backward looks of concern, Tali muttered, "Envy-eyed liar. Spiteful stomach for eggs. You want my place. It eats at you that I am First now and you are Second. Do not think I am blind to this."

"Paranoia is a human malady, Cousin Brother," Oomal said gravely. "You should add it to your list of diseases. As Conscience I thought you might need to hear that."

Tali pivoted on his heel and marched out of the room.

When he had left, Oomal said irritably, "Get up, Reen. Get off the floor, damn it! Take a bath. I have work to do." Then he slammed out the door.

In the bathroom Reen stripped off his uniform and lowered

himself into the water. There he sat, heartsick, knowing that Oomal still loved him but would never forgive him.

When he had sloughed off the coating of sleep, he dressed in a fresh uniform, and after a moment's thought pinned his nametag to his tunic. Then he walked into the study, the one room in the White House where Jeff Womack had always said he felt comfortable.

Reen didn't feel comfortable there. He went past the strip of bare carpet padding and out into the cold wind on the Truman balcony. An itchy sort of need crawled his spine. If sleep was drink to Cousins, work was food. Reen was hungry for something to do. He walked back through the warmth of the oval study and down the grand staircase to the colonnade.

It was as though an invasion had begun in the executive offices. Cousins were everywhere, striding purposefully down the halls, stacks of paper in their hands. They passed Reen without a glance. An unfamiliar Cousin was perched behind Natalie's desk. And in the Oval Office, Reen saw with bitter shock, Tali stood conversing with the Sleep Master and Thural.

For a heartbeat the conversation paused. Of the three, only Thural's gaze flickered as Reen entered and sat on one of the loveseats.

"We will bring the law to bear on him," the Sleep Master was saying, eyeing Tali so hard that Reen imagined he was fighting not to let his eyes slip to Reen.

"Do not be stupid," Tali shot back. "If he has other Cousins here, his sleep may be uncomfortable but not impossible. They slept last night, apparently. Oomal has learned many things in Michigan, Cousin. And one of them is how to do without the Community."

"A dangerous precedent," the Sleep Master agreed. "For without the Community, what are Cousins? And how chaotic may such lives become?"

Tali looked down at the presidential seal woven into the thick wool carpet. "The humans infect us. I believe it is time to cleanse this place. I will tell the Guardians to prepare the viruses."

Reen jumped to his feet. Only Thural's calm voice stopped him

from launching himself at his Brother. "You are not so much in the law as that, Cousin, to order such a thing. After all, you are no First. There are others, like me, who will refuse you."

"Back to the ship," Tali commanded.

"I think I will stay. You have a gift for avoiding witnesses, and you have too great a love of secrets. I wonder what you would talk about if I left the room. And I wonder where you went last night alone when the rest of the Cousins were settled into their niches."

Tali gasped. He whirled on Thural. "Back to the ship!"

Thural didn't move. It seemed to Reen that the Cousin was scarcely breathing.

"Didn't you hear me?" Tali screamed, the fury in his voice surprising even the Sleep Master, who stepped away from the pair.

"Kill me, then," Thural said quietly, "as you once led my Brother Jonis to slaughter. Kill me so that all the Community will know you are *tulmade,* and Oomal can take your place."

"Enough of this," the Sleep Master hissed from his refuge against the wall. "The sickness of disobedience has fevered us. You, Tali, must accept the charges of your Cousin, for he heard the wrong that the human Hopkins admitted to. And you, Thural, must forgive Tali."

Slowly, slowly, Thural turned to the Sleep Master. The light from the French doors glinted in his eyes, making them seem less flesh than obsidian. "Have someone with clean hands point the way, then. Give me a First I can follow, and I will study forgiveness. The mother that spewed forth these Brothers was cursed, and she laid the germs of her insanity in them. Two Brothers as murderers. Perhaps if we breed the female, we will find that our seed is not barren but warped, and we will father a generation of killers. Ask him yourself, Sleep Master. Ask why he left the Cousin Place last night alone with three Loving Helpers."

From Tali's throat came a snarl of rage. He seized a vase from an end table and, before the Sleep Master could stop him, hurled it at Thural's chest. The thin porcelain shattered with a bang. Amazement on his face, Thural staggered into a loveseat.

The Cousin in the secretary's office came rushing in to stare aghast at the shards of china that littered the floor.

"Are you all right?" the Sleep Master asked in a horrified voice.

Shakily, Thural grabbed the arm of the sofa and pulled himself upright. "Yes. I think so."

"It is best that you rest now," the Sleep Master suggested.

Thural gave a weak nod.

"When your rest is over, the world will look better."

Thural's expression suggested strongly that he doubted that. Tali's secretary backed cautiously from the room. After a pause to gather his composure, Thural left, too.

When they were gone, Tali said, "Thural goes too far."

"Silence," the Sleep Master said. "And watch yourself, Tali-ja. I back you because you know the law, but I begin to see that for you the law is a surface thing. Perhaps Thural is right. Perhaps there was something wrong with the eggs in your batch. I warn you now: Break the law again, and you will find yourself a ghost like your Brother."

Tali looked thoughtfully at the Sleep Master as the old Cousin stalked out. From the anteroom Reen heard the tap-tap of clumsy Cousin hands on a keyboard, the quiet murmur of voices.

"Have you ever stuck a stick into an ant bed, Cousin Brother?" Reen asked quietly.

Tali walked over to the French doors and pulled back the sheers.

"That is what you have done," Reen told his Brother's back.

Somewhere in a neighboring office a phone rang, and Reen heard the high, clear, enchanting sound of a human laugh.

"You are stirring the stick, Cousin Brother. Ants, when disturbed, will sting. I have a piece of advice for you: Learn to love chaos, for you will be surrounded by it now."

When Reen left a few minutes later, Tali was still staring wordlessly out at the Rose Garden.

30

Reen wandered the West Wing until he wearied of being ignored, then went down to the main building for lunch.

The pantry was a cozy, utilitarian room with an old kitchen table in the center and cabinets all around. As Reen walked in, he found the butler and Jeremy Holt having brunch. The burly black chief of the serving staff popped the last of his omelette into his mouth, swallowed, and asked Reen, "Lunch, sir?"

"Yes," Reen said, looking at the new President, who was toying with his coffee cup.

"Where do you want me to serve you, sir?"

The President spoke. From the broad Bostonian *a*'s Reen could hear that he was dealing with Kennedy and not the medium. "Serve him in here, ah, Kevin, if you will. It's always good to have a little company with lunch."

"Yes, sir. Yes, it sure is." The butler wiped his mouth with his napkin and rose, taking his empty plate with him to the kitchen.

In the ensuing and prickly silence, Reen sat.

Kennedy said, "Your, ah, Brother seems to have moved into the Oval Office. I take that as a sign you're out of favor. Am I right?"

"As I recall, that was one of your most annoying habits—always being right."

"There were a few glaring exceptions." Kennedy sliced the remains of his Denver omelette into fussy strips. "Anyway, I notice your Brother has taken over with a dexterity that must have come from careful planning. Always be cautious of people who are prepared, Reen," Kennedy lectured, one eyebrow cocked. "Beware of Boy Scouts."

"I thought you'd never want to talk to me again," Reen said.

Somehow Jeremy's mousy features arranged themselves into Kennedy's brilliant smile. "Oh, I learned a few things on the other side."

"Like forgiveness?"

Kennedy threw his head back and laughed. "No, no. I mean, I found out who to blame."

Fascinated, Reen asked, "Who? My Brother?"

A tired shake of his head. "No. J. Edgar. He suckered you, Reen. Hoover told you I tried to have you assassinated, didn't he?"

"Yes, that's why—"

"Don't apologize," Kennedy said curtly. "When I was President, you didn't understand humans very well. Or politics. I'm not angry with you for murdering me. Hoover was a master manipulator. But I wish you hadn't murdered my brother."

Brothers again, Reen thought as he watched Kennedy refill his cup from the silver pot. In the world of Brothers it was perfectly understandable that Jack would forgive Reen for killing him yet still resent his murdering Robert. In the world of Brothers, Oomal would protect Reen because he hated Tali more.

"So you're saying you *didn't* plan to assassinate me," Reen said.

"I don't know why you were so gullible as to think I'd try."

Gullible. Odd, Reen thought, how he believed in his own keen insight, and others thought him naive. "You plotted against Castro. Hoover told us that, and he had proof. He said you wanted to control everything: Cuba and Russia and the Cousins. He told us you wanted to get rid of Khrushchev and me, too. You were dangerous. At least

that's how Hoover explained it. Personally, I had no interest in killing your brother, but Hoover insisted on a trade."

It struck Reen that he knew where Tali had learned some of his trickery. Not from Hopkins. And not all from Hoover. Some of it came from Reen himself.

Kennedy seemed amused. "I told you Hoover played you for a sucker. Think about it. It made sense to assassinate Castro. Castro was a one-man band. Khrushchev, on the other hand, was an orchestra. Kill Khrushchev, and I'd have the whole politburo to deal with. And what sense would it have made to assassinate you? I'd stop the woodwinds, maybe, but the strings would only play louder. Action in politics has to make sense."

The butler came out of the kitchen with a plate of finger sandwiches and fresh fruit.

Reen speared a slice of melon, then put it down, uneaten.

"The Senate is up in arms," Kennedy said.

Reen gave him a questioning look.

"Womack had two more years to his term. That even makes the Democrats uncomfortable. In spite of my assurances, the Senate feels the country is adrift. Partially your fault, you know, for urging the passage of the unlimited term amendment. Fifty-one years of Womack. Fifty-one years. The people can't imagine another president. Ah, well. If you'll excuse me, I have a state funeral to arrange."

When Kennedy left, Reen took a couple of finger sandwiches and ate them as he made his way upstairs.

The maids had been in the oval study. The surface of Womack's scarred table was agleam with lemon oil. Fresh flowers had been set out: chrysanthemums and hothouse roses. Reen went into the next room.

The bed was rumpled, the floor cluttered. His uniform still lay on the bathroom floor. As he bent to pick it up, his claw clicked on something in the pocket.

Marian's tape.

He took the cassette out, went to the oval study again, and closed

the door to the hall. In the cabinet of the bar he found a tape recorder, the one Womack had been using to dictate the eighteenth volume of his autobiography. Popping the cassette out with his claw, Reen replaced Jeff's tape with Marian's.

He turned on the recorder. From the speaker came the squeak of a chair, the empty hiss of white noise. Then, "Do you know why the President has called the press conference?"

The words were distorted, but Reen recognized the voice. It was Tali.

A tap-tap-tap. Someone rapping out a rhythm on wood. A pen against a desktop?

"No idea."

Superstitious horror made Reen nearly drop the recorder: Hopkins's voice was so clear. The man must have been sitting much closer to the mike. "The Speaker says there's gossip that Womack will spring some surprise on Congress tomorrow. Doesn't know what it is yet, but he says not to worry. Platt's dense but malleable. I've told him to take care of it. He will. We hit Womack, anyway. You bring the Helpers in and put them on Security Chief Landis. It can't be one of my men. I want Landis to pull the trigger, you understand?"

"We do not need the Loving Helpers. It is dangerous to bring them into the building. I am afraid one of the other Cousins might see. Besides, the suggestion has already been implanted, and the man is under my control. I will say the word, and he will do anything I ask."

"Bring the Helpers," Hopkins said.

A sigh.

"So. It's all decided. And the kidnapping's set up. A few minutes from now my men will snatch Reen, take him out to Camp David, and bury him with Jonis." A pause. Then Hopkins said slyly, "That's what you want, isn't it?"

Tali made a small throaty sound. "It is not what I wish. It is simply what must happen. Reen-ja is wrong about many things. And he lacks the morality to lead. But this decision about Womack is

different. It is a human one. I have done as you requested. I have put Landis under control. I do not wish to know what you do with my Brother. And I do not wish to watch what happens to the President. These violent matters are disturbing to me. I will give the order, I promise you, but other than that . . ."

Hopkins's laugh was rich and careless and vibrant, nothing like the laugh of a dead man. "No. I want *you* to do it. I want you to bring the Helpers in, and I want you there when Landis blows Womack's brains out. Otherwise I'll see the Community gets all the evidence I have. They'd be shocked, don't you think, to learn how you traded Womack's assassination for the murder of your Brother?"

The angry squeal of a chair, a thump.

"Sit down. You're not going anywhere," Hopkins said calmly. "I have copies of that evidence salted all over Washington. And an interrogation session with the Helpers isn't going to help, so don't even think about it. Sit down. Sit down!"

The chair squeaked again. Tali's voice was plaintive, hurt. He hardly sounded like himself. "You told me J. Edgar Hoover was your hero. That's why I had Reen appoint you. That's why I trusted you enough not to use an implant. Hoover would never do such a thing to me."

"Tough shit." Then in a conversational tone Hopkins said, "Tomorrow."

"All right." Tali's voice seethed. It sounded like Tali again. "Tomorrow."

Reen started, hearing footsteps in the hall. Quickly he turned off the recorder and slipped it into his pocket. The footsteps continued down the hall to the elevator. Just the Secret Service. Or one of the staff.

Taking out the recorder, Reen held it in his hand. Marian was right. This was all the proof he needed. He would go to the Oval Office and confront Tali and the Sleep Master. The Sleep Master wouldn't listen to Reen, but he couldn't ignore the tape.

He hurried out of the oval study, ran down the steps and through

the colonnade. He passed a Cousin typing in the reception area and threw open the Oval Office doors.

The room was empty.

Reen whirled to the Cousin secretary, set the recorder on his desk. "Listen. I know you are not allowed to hear me, but listen." Reen punched the REWIND button, fumbled for the PLAY. From the speaker the squeak of a chair, a thump, Hopkins saying, "Sit down. You're not going anywhere . . ." And Tali's injured response.

The Cousin never paused in his typing.

"Listen to it!" Reen shouted.

REWIND. PLAY. Tali: ". . . put Landis under control. I do not wish to know what you do . . ."

Picking up a pile of papers, the Cousin walked from the office. He never looked back.

Reen sat on the edge of the desk, looked at the recorder, tapped a defeated, listless finger on the buttons, REWIND, PLAY. ". . . snatch Reen, take him out to Camp David . . ."

STOP.

Sighing, he looked through the open doors and saw that in the Oval Office the portrait of Millard Fillmore was crooked.

A quick three-step throb of his heart. Stuffing the recorder into his pocket, he walked into the office, pulled a chair up next to the fireplace, and checked behind the painting.

The manila envelope was still there. Reen, in his haste, had left the portrait awry.

As he pried the envelope from its hiding place, a slip of paper dropped from the open end. He picked it up: that nine-digit number.

What could it be? It was about the right length for a bank account but one number too short for Social Security.

7039713991.

703. The first three digits leaped from the page, and the picture fell into place. There were no dashes to indicate area code and exchange, but it was obviously a phone number. A phone number in Fairfax County, Virginia.

Reen walked to the telephone and dialed. There was a pause as the circuits clicked through, then a shadowy, faraway ring.

For some nonsensical reason he thought of the Old Ones. Oomal had said Jeff was setting up an AT&T long-distance line with the Old Ones. For an instant Reen had the absurd thought that the Old Ones had rented a house in Fairfax County, and Jeff had found out about it.

Ring.

A nice house. The Old Ones would rent a nice house. A traditional Fairfax County place with red brick and white trim and a pretty garden.

Another ring.

They'd have flowers, a few trees, and maybe a springer spaniel. Heritage would demand it.

Click. The sound of the receiver being picked up. "National Wildlife Federation," a female voice chirped.

Reen hung up. The National Wildlife Federation?

He left the Oval Office and went to the East Wing to find Oomal.

31

Oomal was in an office barking into a phone. He looked and sounded more like a leader than Reen or Tali ever had.

"Goddamn it!" his Brother was shouting. "I don't give a flying fuck *how* the bugs got into the macaroni! We have a warehouse full of weevils, and we're not feeding them to one-year-olds! You come—no, no, *you* come and take that macaroni out of our warehouse. You—I'm not finished. No, Cousins don't have some magic wand that makes weevils—no. Hey, but I have a team of lawyers with twelve-inch dicks. What? Watch me. I said *watch me!*"

Oomal slammed the phone down so hard that it gave a broken-piano complaint. "What do you want?" he snapped at Reen, who was standing, a penitent, in front of his desk, Womack's envelope in one hand and the recorder in the other.

The phone rang again.

"*What?*" Oomal screamed into the receiver. Abruptly his face and his tone softened. "Yeah, Jerry. Sorry, I . . . Right, uh huh. Burn the production records. Trust me. Just trust me on this. . . . No, nothing's going on. Just tell the reporters you don't have any comment other than what I said at the press conference. What? No, no. Of course I wasn't making it up. The birthrate's just going into a little dip.

It's nothing to worry about. . . . Come on, Jer. Have I ever lied to you? No. . . . No need to apologize. Just— Yeah. I appreciate this."

He hung up, this time softly, and sat staring into space.

The official photo of Jeff Womack, taken during his first term, smiled down impishly from its perch on the wall. Hurriedly, Reen slipped the recorder back into his pocket, hoping Oomal hadn't seen. He had been wrong to play the tape for Tali's secretary. The truth was a responsibility he now wished he didn't have.

Tali's treachery was merely his way of following in his big Brother's steps. Reen and Hoover taught him how to use assassination and deceit.

Oomal wiped his hands down his cheeks. "Well. Have you seen the front page of the *Post*?" He shoved the paper across the desk.

Reen glanced at the top half of the front page. More about Womack's suicide. A piece on the birthrate. He flipped the paper over and looked below the fold.

INDICTMENT SOUGHT IN KENNEDY ASSASSINATION

WASHINGTON, D.C.—The Justice Department is looking into allegations that the White House chief of staff may be implicated in the November 22, 1963, death of President John Fitzgerald Kennedy.

"We have talked to the President, and he is disinclined to pursue the matter," Ted Rice, Justice Department Special Prosecutor, said in an interview with the *Post* today. "But this is not a civil case, and there is no statute of limitations on murder. The Justice Department feels that there is cause to bring charges of criminal conspiracy before a grand jury."

President Kennedy/Holt could not be reached for comment.

"Murder?" Reen said in a weak voice. "I'm going to be accused of murder?"

"Not that story. Forget about that story. I'm talking about the

one that's not there. The Hopkins piece. He had a maid. Why didn't the maid report the body?"

Because that's where Tali went last night. He went to get Hopkins's evidence, didn't find it, and then hid Hopkins's body to buy himself more time.

Hopkins had been a good teacher.

Oomal sat back and linked his hands across his belly. "What's that you're carrying around?"

Reen stiffened, then realized his Brother wasn't asking about the recorder. "Oh. Jeff's envelope? I found the National Wildlife Federation's phone number in it."

Oomal sat forward. "Let me see," he said, taking the envelope from Reen. He thumbed through the pages, pausing momentarily to wince at the autopsy photo. Then: "This one? This 703 number?"

"Yes."

"I keep getting the feeling that the other shoe is about to drop. And I keep wondering why the humans who know about the sterilization haven't talked. Maybe this will give us a clue." Oomal pressed a button on his intercom. "Zoomer? Come see me." His face pensive, he asked Reen, "Where's Marian Cole gone off to, Brother?"

Reen stared at Oomal, Oomal the Conscience, Oomal who was burdened now with upholding the law. "I don't know."

"You have to know, Reen. I know you know."

Zoor's entrance saved Reen from answering.

"Zoomer," Oomal said, getting to his feet. "Round up two or three Helpers and meet us at the ship."

Reen's heart sank. He followed his Brother's quick stride from the East Wing and to one of the small Michigan commuter ships. "Why do you suspect Marian?" Reen asked.

"We did a fly-by of the entire border of China. There were no troops massed there. If there were no troops, Reen, and if Womack signed the tariff bill, what are those tanks doing still stationed in front of the White House?"

Reen looked at the fence. The soldiers were staring at them. The cannons of the tanks were pointed at the street, but they could just as easily be turned. They could . . .

"Just before Hopkins died," Oomal went on, "he was trying to tell us something. Something about Marian. And she got rid of her competition very conveniently, don't you think? We go to Camp David, and Kapavik's already dead. She tells you Hopkins is behind it all, and you kill Hopkins before he can tell his side."

Reen tore his anxious gaze from the tanks. "His side? We know Hopkins's side. He admitted it. You heard him. We all heard him."

The door of the ship spread open, and Oomal threw himself into the navigation seat, leaving Reen to crawl around him to the back. "I heard him admit to killing Womack and Jonis. That's all I heard. He never said he kidnapped the others. Besides, if Marian was so worried about what Hopkins was doing, why didn't she just come out and tell you earlier?"

"Maybe she was frightened," Reen said miserably as he watched Zoor herd three Loving Helpers out the door and across the lawn to the ship.

"That doesn't solve the problem of why the humans haven't talked. Or why the other Cousins were kidnapped. Come on, come on, Zoomer," Oomal said anxiously under his breath.

"Maybe Hopkins kidnapped the Cousins to put more pressure on Tali, Cousin Brother."

The Helpers began to file into the ship, taking their places behind Reen. When Zoor got into his seat, Oomal jerked the command ball upward, and the ship shot into the air.

"You don't believe that," Oomal replied.

No, Reen didn't believe that. But in the press of other dilemmas he had put the problem of the kidnappings out of his mind.

"It was a good thing that you saved Marian from Tali," Oomal went on. "If he killed her, we'd never learn the whole truth. But we'll have to talk to her sooner or later, and when that time comes, I want

you to tell me where I can find her. And don't lie to me, okay? You know that frequency like a human baby knows its mother's breast. And when I ask for it, I want you to give me that frequency, understand?"

Reen watched the noon traffic on Route 50. The spidery winter trees of the Virginia countryside flashed by. He had always said he would kill Marian if she proved too dangerous, but he had lied to the Community. He had lied to himself. "I took the transmitter out of her two years ago."

"What?" Oomal tore his eyes from the controls to glare at Reen. "You did what?"

Zoor flung himself across Oomal and righted the ship before it could dive.

"There was no sense in keeping it in her. Angela was a viable embryo."

"Goddamned Marian was the CIA director! You made her CIA director, Cousin Brother! And you thought it would be a nice idea to let her walk around unsupervised?"

"Watch where you're flying, Oomal," Zoor said quietly. "Can you just watch where you're flying?"

Oomal took back the controls and looked out the window. "We passed it. We're halfway to fucking West Virginia. Shit on a stick." He jerked the ship around so fast that the angle overrode the baffles. Reen was flung into a wall with a thump.

They flew to the National Wildlife Federation in silence and didn't speak as the ship settled into the parking lot beside the red-brick building.

The Cousins left the Helpers on board and went up the long sweeping concrete ramp to the entrance. In the huge lobby two receptionists sat behind a doughnut-shaped desk where two young raccoons were playing.

"May I help you?" one of the women asked while a raccoon went through her Rolodex with its quick, inquisitive fingers.

Reen found himself staring at the bandit eyes, the furry banded

tails. It looked as if the animals had been placed there as part of the Wildlife Federation decor.

"The director, please," Oomal told her in a no-nonsense tone.

Near the second receptionist, the second raccoon had managed to pull out a drawer and was trying to fit its body between the hanging files.

The first receptionist whispered into the phone, then turned brightly to Oomal. "He's on his way."

A thud from the drawer. The raccoon had apparently gained entrance. Neither receptionist paid any attention to the animals, as if the raccoons, like Reen himself, were sentenced to invisibility.

People sat on chairs lined up near the windows. A man who looked like a farmer waited next to a cardboard box that periodically made a mewling sound. A housewife sat holding a plaster cast of a hoof.

"Good afternoon!" a boisterous bass voice said. Making his way across the carpet, hand out, was a friendly looking bald man in a dark suit. "I'm Ralph Gunnerson. What can I do for you?"

Oomal stepped forward and shook the man's hand. "You can tell us why the National Wildlife Federation's number was found in papers that belonged to a murder victim."

Gunnerson's rosy skin went pale from cheek to scalp. "I think," he said, licking his lips nervously, "we'd better talk in private."

The Cousins followed the director through a room of secretaries. In the back of the building Gunnerson ushered them into a large paneled conference room and sank into a raspberry-colored velour chair. "First off," he said, "you have to guarantee all of us protection. All our wives, all our kids."

Reen kept silent. Across the table from him, Zoor sat mystified.

"Promise me," Gunnerson urged. "You have to promise."

Oomal nodded.

Gunnerson passed an unsteady hand over his forehead. "Look. We're dedicated to animals. Everyone here loves animals. It's a job requirement. I get choked up when I see a bald eagle. I've seen one

of our staff bawl when someone brought in a wounded deer." He stopped, as though either afraid or ashamed to go on.

Oomal said gently, "Continue, Mr. Gunnerson."

"It was the men." The director picked at a nail.

"What men?" Reen asked.

"I don't know. I don't know who they were. They wanted animals. You see how people bring in wild animals. They bring them in all the time. I don't know why. It's not like we're a zoo. But we never turn an animal away. We've had coyotes, rattlesnakes, you name it. If they're hurt, we patch them up. If they're sick, we tend to them until they're well. Then we take them back to the wild and let them go."

The director picked at the nail until he brought up a bead of crimson blood.

"The men," Oomal prompted.

Gunnerson's head bobbed. "They wanted wild animals. I told them no. I started getting phone calls late at night. Threatening calls. They harassed my wife at work. At the store. It got so she was afraid to go out. They followed my children. . . ." His lower lip trembled. Tears gathered in his eyes. "They . . ." His voice lowered. "They raped one of our assistants."

"You don't know who they were?" Reen asked after a decorous pause.

"No. But they came every day to see if we had animals. If we had any, they'd take them. I had to give up the animals. You can see that, can't you? I was responsible for my staff. I couldn't let anybody else be hurt. Then one day, about three years ago, the men stopped coming. About four months after the men left, I found a bug in my office. It was poorly hidden, so I'm sure I was supposed to find it. A reminder not to talk. When AT&T installed our new phone system last year, they said there were indications that someone was tapping our lines. I don't know what the men did with the animals, but I imagine . . ." His voice trailed off, and he swallowed hard.

Oomal asked, "When did these men start taking your animals?"

"Five—no, six years ago. It started six years ago."

"Do you have any idea who they are?"

Gunnerson let his breath out in a sigh. His body sagged. "You might ask the SPCA. One of our receptionists came from there, and after the men stopped coming to us, she said the SPCA started having problems with them, too."

32

AT THE FAIRFAX COUNTY SPCA A well-dressed woman filled out forms at a counter while on the other side stood a lanky young man with a beard and ponytail. The building stank of disinfectant. A cacophony of muffled yips and meows came from behind double doors.

Run, Reen thought suddenly. *We should run as far and as fast as we can. Because what we find out here won't be about Tali and Hopkins at all but about something else. Something I don't want to know.*

The two people looked up as the Cousins entered.

"The director, please," Oomal said.

The young man behind the counter indolently scratched his cheek. "You don't want to adopt, do you? I mean, I don't know that we could clear that."

The woman wore an expensive fake fur, and she was eyeing Reen analytically and somewhat contemptuously, as if Reen were a mangy prospective pet.

"We want to speak with the director." Oomal snapped his finger on his claw. "Now."

Suddenly the double doors burst open, and a petite young woman in an apron came through, holding the collar of a golden retriever.

When the dog saw the Cousins, he staggered back a few feet in astonishment and then, perhaps considering some aspect of canine integrity, lunged forward. The dog had a bark that made the walls tremble.

The girl held on. "Down!" she shouted. The dog paid her no heed.

Reen, the closest to the dog, shrank from the yellow snapping teeth, the frantic scrabbling of claws on linoleum, and the harsh panting as the animal strained against its collar.

"Harry," the girl said in exasperation.

Harry opened a swing latch in the counter and sauntered out to the dog.

"Door to the right," he said over his shoulder.

Oomal and Zoor fled through the steel doorway, Reen not far behind.

On a dusty cabinet in the main office of the SPCA a phone was ringing. The two typists in the room paid no attention to it.

"The director?" Oomal asked.

A typist looked up from her ancient Selectric, a myopic editor's frown on her face. "Go on back," she said, jerking her head in that direction.

The Cousins made their way past a mountain of dog food that sandbagged one side of the room. To the left of the Purina was an unassuming door, the kind that might lead to a bathroom or mop closet. Behind it was a scarred metal desk and a pile of manila folders paperweighted by a slumbering calico cat. And behind the folders was an impressive battleship of a woman, who said, "What the hell do you want?" in a voice not unlike the retriever's.

Awakened, the cat gave the Cousins a sleepy double take, then leaped off the folders, scattering the top two inches of the stack onto the threadbare carpet. The cat vanished, a streak of white, black, and russet, into a dark back room.

That's how I should run, Reen thought. *I should run as though all the nightmares humans ever dreamed were at my heels.*

Oomal took the only available chair, a cheap steel and plastic

thing. "Somebody's been threatening you. They've been taking animals."

The woman blinked. "Lots of animals. Hundreds of animals. You going to get the bastards?"

"Who are they?" Oomal asked.

"Russians," the woman said. She leaned back in her chair and laced her hands across a generous belly. "Germans. A few Latin Americans."

Reen asked, "How can you be so sure?"

She gave him a sour smile. "Got a master's in linguistics. They speak English well enough, but I can tag 'em. I can always tag 'em."

"They still come around?" Oomal asked.

"Not for a couple of days. So you know who they are?"

"Yes," he said quietly.

"They're doing experiments on the animals, aren't they?"

"I think so."

"Castration's too good," she said by way of suggestion.

The Cousins left. In the secretarial area the phone was still ringing, but the dog and the fake-furred woman had disappeared from the lobby. Under the stares of the girl and the ponytailed man, the Cousins exited and made their way to the ship.

"So you know who's been taking the animals?" Reen asked his Brother.

The ship's door spread open in welcome. Zoor took a wordless seat in the back. Reen sat next to Oomal.

"The CIA," Oomal said.

Apprehension crawled, dainty-footed and insectile, up Reen's spine. "How can you be sure?"

"Because," Oomal said as the ship lifted into clear, bright air, "when the consolidation hit, the CIA merged with the KGB, North Korean intelligence, and every thug in every crappy little police state south of the American border. I know who's been taking those animals because I know the FBI is xenophobic. The FBI has stayed as all-American as goddamned apple pie."

Reen remembered Hopkins's accusation of Marian at the last NSC meeting. *Start investigating at Langley*. Too bad that Reen had not believed him until it was too late.

Twenty-eight of the Community, both Loving Helpers and Cousins, had been kidnapped— and it all started the same time the confiscation of animals at the SPCA began.

33

CIA HEADQUARTERS, TUCKED BEtween parks on the west and the Potomac on the north, looked more imposing from the ground than from the air. In fact, flying in low from the northwest, Reen could hardly see the massive installation until the ship was nearly on top of it.

As they approached, Zoor said, "There's nobody in the guardhouse."

"I know." Oomal's voice was tense.

Reen studied the rolling tree-studded lawn of the complex. No one moved on the walkways. No one was outside to catch the last gleam of the Indian summer sun.

And the parking lot was empty.

Oomal settled the ship on the lawn. "Get the Loving Helpers, Zoomer."

The Cousins and Helpers climbed out and walked through the porte cochere to the huge brick building. The lobby was brightly lit. No guard sat at the station; no receptionist sat at the desk. The building was so silent that Reen could hear the whisper of air through heating ducts and the far, faint hum of a PC.

The corridor was a deserted river of beige carpet banded by sun slanting from western windows. Somewhere in the bowels of the

building a phone was ringing. Ringing. In the SPCA, the ringing had been part of the din. Here, it was a hammer tapping against brittle silence.

The three halted before a red EXIT sign. The phone rang again.

"Let's not get on the elevators. No telling what traps they've set up." Oomal opened the steel door, and they entered the stairwell.

As Reen mounted the first step, Oomal snagged his sleeve. Reen turned and saw a look of determined, fearful intensity, as though Oomal were an exorcist about to enter a haunted house. "Downstairs."

Oomal was right. Downstairs. When humans wanted to hide something, they went to basements. They went to ground.

No one spoke. The only sound in the stairwell was the slippery, soft steps of booted feet, the feathery echoes of breathing. At the bottom, in a pool of shadows, Zoor fumbled for the knob.

"Do you hear something?" Oomal asked, holding out his hand to stop them.

Reen froze. In the dim light he could see Zoor's eyes move back and forth as though searching by sight for the noise.

"No," Reen said at last. He grasped the knob and opened the door into fluorescent brilliance.

The fourth level of the basement was a rabbit warren of offices, all empty. A door to the right was open, and on its painted steel surface were the words CLEAN ROOM. Reen walked inside. The telexes were silent, their power lights off. On a small table sat a red phone, its receiver a foot or so away. A persistent waa-waa came from the speaker, the Chesapeake Bay Bell reminder that the phone was off the hook.

Reen heard Oomal's faint "Reen? Come here."

Someone had slipped a tumbler into a door marked RESTRICTED, and it was standing ajar. Past the security-card access was a long linoleum hall where Oomal stood. Reen made his way down the corridor to his Brother and looked at an office plaque. At first the name didn't register. Nothing registered. Not the implications of it,

not his Brother standing next to him. Then Reen's head started to pound.

DR. HOWARD FRANKLIN, PROJECT SUPERVISOR

"He was working for the CIA, too," Oomal said. "Working for them the whole time, and she never told you. Now you know who was important to her and why, Cousin Brother. Now you see—"

A muffled cry.

"Zoor?" Oomal called.

"Here, Cousin! Here! It's . . ."

Oomal hurried toward Zoor's voice, Reen lagging behind. The corridor led to a huge room that held the earthy stench of a zoo. Under the stench was a cloying odor, sweet and at the same time metallic.

This room, like the SPCA, must once have rung with barks and plaintive questioning meows. Now it was silent. Dead animals lay in their screen cages, forlorn bits of bloodied fluff. A thick crimson sea, just beginning to congeal to black, ran down the sloping floor to a center drain. The Helpers, oblivious, stood in the pool of blood, amidst the carnage. Zoor, his face anguished, was trying to call them to higher, cleaner ground.

"Why kill the animals?" Zoor asked. "They've been shot, all of them. Why do this? It doesn't make sense!"

Oomal rushed back to Howard's office, Reen at his heels, pleading silently for them to leave now.

Oomal rounded the doorway at a dead run and began frantically flipping through papers. He jerked open a credenza drawer, sending it tumbling, spilling accordianed computer printouts and staplers and rolls of masking tape. The heavy drawer hit the floor with a crash.

"You had to take her into your confidence, didn't you? Goddamn it, Reen." Oomal booted Howard's computer.

The expression in his eyes was wild, savage, nearly human. "It crashed! See? They left in a hurry, but Howard had time to run a viral program to wipe the hard drive clean! They knew we'd come."

"Oomal?" Zoor called. "I found something."

In the empty hall, sticky red footprints tracked messily on the shiny linoleum, across a threshold, and over the beige carpet in the next room. It might have been a conference room anywhere but for the crimson prints on its carpet, and Zoor and the Helpers standing there. Twelve plush aqua chairs were placed equidistantly on either side of an oak table. Charts and graphs lined the walls, and in one corner stood a television hooked to a VCR.

Oomal halted at Reen's shoulder. He was breathing hard. "Onset of Death," he read from the top of the nearest graph. "Goddamn her."

He lunged to the television, turned it on, and hit the VCR's PLAY.

Snow. A long minute of snow. Then on the screen Hans Krupner was peering directly at them, his face distorted by the fish-eye lens. His eyes too round, too wide, and his balding head Cousin-bulbous.

His voice was distorted, too, garbled by terror and by the echoes in the bare room. "Marian? Marian? I know you are angry with me, yes?"

What sort of room was it? Tiny, windowless, more like a closet. The walls were seamless gray metal. At the bottom of the television screen was a series of red numbers: 00:00:00.

Like a digital clock set to time a race.

Krupner turned. Two paces, and he was at the back wall. "*Gott,*" he whispered.

Two agitated steps. He was pleading into the camera again. "Please. What was so important about the fax, Marian? You are the one who told me to feed the German ministry information. You remember, yes? So they would not become suspicious I was a double agent? And I was fired! I could not help that I was fired! Sent back to Germany. And the ministry wanted something. A little something, Marian. It was just a small item I found. Something amusing. Nothing of importance. You were the one who said—"

A loud clang. At the left of the screen, a door opened. Two men with sticks herded a Loving Helper into the room.

"Zoor! Get the Helpers out of here!"

Oomal's curt order jerked Reen's attention from the TV.

"Take them down the hall. Quick!"

On the screen the abandoned Helper shrieked its loneliness. It charged the open door, the men. Its Brothers must have been just beyond, close enough to smell them. Nothing but longing could have made it that desperate.

A prod from a stick. A bacon-fat sizzle. A short-circuit *zzzt* as voltage hit flesh. The Helper squealed, staggered backward, turning in frantic circles to escape the pain.

Eyeing the Helper, the men backed out. The door closed with clanging finality. Krupner sat down in a corner, hugged his legs, and eyed the Helper, too.

Pain now forgotten, the Loving Helper stopped spinning. It faced the door expectantly, as if it were a compass needle and its unseen Brothers magnetic north.

00:00:01

The red numerals began clicking off tenths of seconds, time unrolling with dizzy speed.

00:02:39

Something was wrong with the Helper. It scratched urgently at its throat.

00:04:21

A spasm sent arms and legs flailing.

Krupner got to his feet, clamping hands over the bottom of his face. He was breathing in hard, jerky pants. Above the cage of his fingers, his eyes were demented, luminous, as if terror were burning him inside-out.

00:06:03

Blood leaked from the edges of the Helper's eyes. A mad chatter from the television speaker, the sound of the Helper's claws against the metal floor.

00:08:42

The Helper's mouth bubbled blood. The feet twitched, then were still.

00:10:31

And Krupner was alive. He was sitting in a corner, body tucked into a small ball.

Reen jumped at the abruptness of the white-noise hiss as the picture changed to snow.

With a blow of his fist Oomal turned off the television. "Goddamn her."

Reen caught his arm. "Let's go now, Oomal."

Oomal shook off the warning claw. Reen pursued him from the conference room, past a confused Zoor, past the animal cages. Oomal slipped on the bloody tiles and fell. He heaved himself upright, uniform wet, hands and cheeks a gelatinous crimson. One savage push on an adjoining olive-green door. It swung open.

And the Helpers with Zoor began to shriek.

"Come see, Cousin Brother," Oomal said. "Come see what Marian was up to."

An immaculate white room. White tile walls, white tile floor. At the center two steel tables. Krupner and the Helper lay on those cold hard beds, their skulls and their chests open.

For all its uncompromising neatness the room had a cluttered look, of things left in haste. A bone saw, still bloody, lay on a table next to Krupner. A scalpel sat forgotten atop the Helper's ruptured chest.

There was a humming in Reen's ears as he watched Oomal walk to a bank of steel cabinets. As he saw him slide open a drawer, saw him peer in.

It was a pleasant room, really. All steel-gray and white. The ordered squares of the tiles and the larger squares of the cabinets all fitted perfectly. Like fractals. Even the autopsy Ys and the clean-edged openings into the skulls had been done with a meticulous hand. Not at all like the ruin of Jeff Womack's head. Or Hopkins's.

Oomal drew back with a gasp, as though something in the drawer had bitten him. His bloody footprints disturbed the pattern of the floor. His bloody palm prints disturbed the pristine surface of the cabinets.

He began pulling out drawers, one after the other. "Damn her!" he shouted. "They're all in here! The room's full of dead Cousins and Helpers!"

The place was so quiet, so antiseptic that Oomal's loud carelessness annoyed Reen. He walked out, his boots making sucking noises in the animals' blood.

Oomal caught up with Reen in the hall near Howard's office.

"Where do you think you're going, Cousin Brother? Are you afraid to see what she's done?"

Reen looked away from the red on the linoleum. The wall was soothing and white, like blank beginnings. Like the potential of paper before it is written on. Like the untrampled snow of West Virginia.

A fierce tug on his arm. "Marian! Marian was the kidnapper!"

Reen's eyes shifted. Zoor was standing at the end of the corridor, the Loving Helpers around him.

"Oomal," Zoor said. "They're still nervous. Something down this way, I think. You'd better come see."

Oomal nearly pulled Reen off his feet. He dragged him, stumbling, behind.

Images in flashes. A door open to a littered office. A paper shredder adrift in a snowfall of confetti. A pressure door. A sign: WARNING—TOXIC GAS. A border of yellow and black stripes, pleasing, systematic stripes, but just the wrong colors.

And a smell, too. Stale sleep. Spice with a hint of decay.

Oomal spun Reen around to face a quiet blue room. Nest blue. In a padded corner two Loving Helpers and a Cousin lay tangled.

"That's how she kept them alive!"

Reen wanted to tell Oomal to shut up, that he would wake the sleepers. So serene, the Helpers and the Cousin, their arms around one another.

Zoor saying, "I left the Helpers by Howard's office. What was it? What made them nervous?"

The three lying so still. A broad dark stripe down the Cousin's

head. A splash of brown on the floor, like a check mark or a bird in flight.

"Something must have happened," Oomal was saying. "The agents dropped everything and got out quick. They couldn't take the Helpers and the Cousin, so they shot them, like they shot the animals."

A smudge on a wall like a flower, petals opening. Reen pulled his sleeve from Oomal's grasp and walked toward the exit sign.

"Brother!"

Reen's pace quickened. He started to trot. Wrenching open the door, he hurried up the stairs. By the second floor he was taking the steps two at a time, and when he reached the lobby, he was running.

"Reen!"

Panting, taking air in huge gulping whoops as he ran clumsily past the reception area, toward the sunlight. His legs knew no rhythm, only haste and direction. He burst through the glass and steel entrance and ran across the cement of the porte cochere. Thrashed through a border of flowers. Shouts of concern behind him.

The ship, round and cool and silent, waited on a grassy hummock. He stumbled, tripped, sprawled facedown in the smell of loam, fallen leaves, and the quiet natural death of autumn.

Boots stopped near him. "Brother?" Oomal whispered.

Reen didn't answer. And Oomal waited as blue shadows barred the lawn, as daylight faded to gray, as the first stars began to peer from the violet sky.

Finally Oomal said, "You trusted her too much."

Reen somehow managed to get back on his feet. He dusted his hands. "Don't you think I know?" he said.

34

"WE HAVE TO FIND HER," OOMAL SAID as they walked to the ship. "And we'll use the Loving Helpers this time. It looks as though the CIA perfected that toxin they were working on but didn't have the time to put it into production. Still, we have to make sure."

Reen kept pace with him, his eyes on the grass at his feet. "There's a farm in Virginia," he said. "Fly up Chain Bridge Road to Wolf Trap. I think I might be able to find it again."

In the smoky dusk, lights were going on in houses, and each looked as warm and friendly as home. Marian could have been hiding in any one of them.

The ship flew on in the cold, dim evening.

"Now where?" Oomal asked when they reached Wolf Trap.

"North, I think."

They circled the area for a long time, over dozens of dilapidated barns, hundreds of solitary farmhouses, but nothing looked familiar. They went to Camp Peary, but the CIA farm was deserted.

Oomal gave up around midnight and flew back to the White House. When they landed, he motioned Zoor and the Loving Helpers out, to sit alone in the ship with Reen.

"From the notes I found," Oomal said into the dark silence between them, "the wild animals were a dead end. That's when they started experimenting directly on Cousins. I don't know how this toxin works, Reen, but you saw that it's effective and fast. Tali wants to find Marian, and he's bound to search Langley. When he discovers what the CIA was working on, the Community will panic. They'll order the viruses used."

Ahead, the portico lights bathed a solitary marine guard.

After a moment, Reen reached into his pocket and took out the tape recorder. When Oomal saw the recorder, he cocked his head in mute question.

"Oomal?" Reen asked. "How much is Tali's life worth? Ten humans? A thousand? Thirty billion?"

"I don't understand."

Reen hit the REWIND button, then PLAY. He heard Oomal's gasp at Tali's voice, Oomal's low moan when he realized what Hopkins was saying.

"God, Reen," Oomal said when the tape was finished. "Poor Tali. Murder. Blackmail. I thought *I'd* become too human. I thought you had. But Tali . . . Christ. None of us is really a Cousin anymore."

"You'll be First."

"Tomorrow." Oomal, in his anger, sounded so much like Tali that it startled Reen. "Tomorrow I'll go to Andrews and present this to the Sleep Master."

The White House lawn was dark, with only the fountain lit. Reen could imagine the Old Ones walking there, searching, trying to find where Reen and his Brothers had so carelessly misplaced the Cousin legacy.

"If you know where Marian is, Reen, tell me."

"If I knew, I would."

Oomal climbed out of the ship, Reen following. At the top of the grand staircase, Reen paused.

"Aren't you coming to sleep?" Oomal asked.

"In a moment."

"About what we saw at Langley . . .you're not going to do anything stupid?"

Reen gave his Brother a lopsided smile. "Haven't I always?"

Oomal gazed longingly down the hall toward the promise of sleep. "Look, what happened wasn't your fault. You may have trusted Marian too much, but Tali also trusted Hopkins. It's hard for us to understand human deception. I see it all the time, and even I don't understand it. Suppliers and their lies about the freshness of their produce. Salesmen making overblown claims. They look you right in the eye and lie. It's not—"

"Go ahead and sleep, Oomal. I'll be there in a minute."

Reen watched his Brother turn and make his reluctant way to Jeff Womack's old bedroom. When Oomal was safely inside, Reen went downstairs.

In the pantry one of the staff was sleeping in a chair, his head on the table. At the entrance to the colonnade a dull-eyed Secret Serviceman sat at his desk, watching a bank of monitors.

The White House was as dead as Langley had been.

Reen paused at the entrance to the Green Room. In that plush, silent chamber someone was sitting in a chair by the fireplace, his back to Reen.

Reen entered. It was Jeremy Holt, staring into the cold hearth. The medium looked up. "Oh, hello."

"Who are you tonight?" Reen asked. "Kennedy? Van Cliburn? Rachmaninoff?"

"No," Jeremy said with a shy shrug, as if ducking a blow. "It's just me this time."

"Then why are you sitting in here?" It wasn't a place for the medium. It was Jeff's room. Jeff's chair.

"I got lost," the man said miserably.

Reen sighed and sat down.

"It's a big place, isn't it? The White House, I mean." Jeremy's glasses magnified his pond-brown eyes. "When President Kennedy's

here, he knows his way around, but he never bothers to tell me. Do you know where I'm supposed to sleep?"

"The Lincoln bedroom."

"Yes, I know that," he said, regarding a Remington oil without interest. "I know I'm supposed to sleep in the Lincoln bedroom. But I'm not in myself much anymore, and I forget where it is. I went to where I thought it was, but that was a big room with a piano in it."

"The East Room. You needed to go up a floor."

"Oh."

Jeremy was a small man, Reen realized with a stab of pity. A little soul who was easily misplaced. "I'm going upstairs. I'll show you where it is."

The man's face brightened. "Thanks. I'm very tired."

"Just don't come in this room again."

"Is it the laughter?" Jeremy asked.

Halfway to his feet, Reen froze.

"I hear laughter in here sometimes."

"Yes," Reen said. "It's because of the laughter."

They trudged up the steps in silence. At the door to the Lincoln bedroom, Reen said good night.

Jeff Womack's old bedroom smelled of sleep, and in the blue glow from the lamp Reen could see the pea-podded lumps of the Cousins. On the bed he found a sheet laid out for him, and he wrapped himself in it tightly. He fell asleep more easily than he thought possible.

He awoke before dawn and inched himself out of the sheet. Quietly, in order not to wake the others, he crept from the room and into the study next door.

The air was moist and cold on the Truman balcony. Across the Potomac the lights of Arlington shimmered. The sun, just below the eastern terminator, had turned the sky a bruised purple.

"Reen," a voice said.

He turned. The speaker was hidden in shadow, but he knew the voice.

"I was hoping you'd wake up," Marian said. "I kept thinking of you. Is that the way you used to wake me?"

Sunrise began to paint the tip of the Washington Monument lavender.

"I went to Langley," he said.

A yellow flame in a corner of the balcony. The gentle glow cupped Marian's cheek. She lit her cigarette and with a click extinguished the lighter.

That face. He had seen it softened in sleep, contorted with fear. He had seen it grow old. Forty-seven years, and he had never really known her.

"You planted the bomb at Dulles," he said.

She tilted her head and blew a thread of smoke at the ceiling. "Yes."

"You kidnapped Cousins and Helpers, and Howard experimented on them."

She pulled her leather jacket tighter against the moist dawn chill. "Yes."

Reen looked across the lawn. The tops of the tallest trees had netted the morning and were ablaze.

"You told me too much," she said quietly. "You handed me all that responsibility. What did you expect me to do? Did you think only Cousins loved their own? Did you think that just because we're not as good as you, you could destroy us and we wouldn't care?"

"No. No. I never thought that," he whispered.

"King Leopold in the Congo." Her voice was wry and amused. "That's how you acted. Sometimes you were such a condescending bastard, Reen. You had to love everybody, and I was only good at loving one thing." She looked out pensively at the tender apricot sunrise. "But it came down to genocide, didn't it? Secrets and genocide. If I wanted to live with myself, I had to stop you before the birthrate went any lower."

A promising ruddy sun peered over the horizon. "The birthrate doesn't matter, Marian. Your DNA is now infected with the same

flaw as ours is. Except that we produce Loving Helpers. Sometime in the next generation you'll begin to produce nothing. Your DNA will not replicate anymore."

A throaty sound of surprise. She got up and walked to the edge of the balcony, resting her elbows on the railing. The Potomac below was a dusky pink ribbon in the dawn.

He thought she would weep. It shocked him when she chuckled. "God help me. I've been a spook too long. If I were normal, I wouldn't find this funny. But I've never been normal, have I?"

A flick of her adroit human fingers. The cigarette arced toward the lawn, a ruddy falling star.

"You outfoxed me. That sweet innocent little face. That pint-sized childlike honor. I thought humans were better at deception, Reen. We were so good at it, I felt sorry for you. Oh, Jesus." She laughed. "You learned a lot from Jeff Womack. Political half-truths. You even hid things you shouldn't have. I didn't know you couldn't sleep without others around. When you told me that, you scared me to death. I thought I could always protect you."

"If you hadn't put the Cousins in with the Helpers, you would have found out that we die if left alone."

She turned to face him. Behind her, down the gentle bowl of the sky, the violet brightened to a rim of gold.

"Here," she said, taking a plastic bag from the pocket of her jacket.

He took it. Small pink squares at the bottom, like confetti.

"It's an antidote. Enough for you and Oomal and the Cousins from Gerber. It works like adrenaline. Under stress, your body produces an endorphin that shuts down your system."

Confetti. Like something from a child's birthday party. And pink, the color of dawn.

Her voice was hurried. "When everything starts, put one in your mouth. It's adhesive. There will be a burning sensation. Your pulse will race—"

"When what starts?"

"Stay in the White House. You'll be safe here. The troops will guard you. Vilishnikov promised me that."

"Marian!" he shouted, alarmed. "What's going to happen?"

"Vilishnikov put all military troops on alert two days ago. At nine o'clock Eastern Standard Time they'll attack the Cousin installations. Your defense can scramble electronics, but I know from what you've told me that you're not prepared for a sudden overwhelming attack. I don't want you to set foot outside the White House, Reen. I don't want you to try to stop it."

The plastic bag fell from his fingers.

"Pick it up!" Marian ordered angrily. "Damn you! Pick that up! Go in there and give it to the rest of those Cousins! At nine o'clock put one in your mouth. Make sure the others do, too."

A quick triple pump from his heart. His head swam, and he sat down hard on a lounge chair. The delicate light of morning flooded the Mall and the leafless cherry trees.

He checked his watch. Six A.M. Oomal was wrapped in slumber in the room next door. At Andrews the Community was tucked into niches. In West Virginia the children were still riding their dreams.

"Will it work on the children?"

"What?"

"Will it work on Angela? Marian, did you ever once think about your daughter?"

He could see the answer in her face.

"Get out," he told her.

She hesitated. "Promise me you'll use the antidote."

"Damn you. Goddamn you." Oomal's words, but his own hushed voice. "A house in the country. Me all to yourself. Marian, must you always get everything you want?"

Turning his back on her, he watched morning fill the streets. No cars moved on Constitution Avenue. The windows of the nearby buildings were dark. Saturday, he remembered.

It was Saturday, and the morning was so quiet, he could hear her every soft footstep as she left.

35

"GIVE ME YOUR GUN," REEN SAID.

The Secret Serviceman in the colonnade looked up in dazed and sleepy alarm. Reen recognized him: the same agent he had encountered on the stairway after Jeff Womack's assassination.

"Excuse me, sir?"

"I need a gun. Give me your gun."

Indecision. Then, "Sir, there *are* regulations. I can't give you mine, but . . ." The agent got up and walked with Reen to Landis's office. A jingling of keys as he opened a steel gun safe. "This is a nine-millimeter federal issue. Ever handle a gun before? No? Okay, this is the slide. Pull it back to chamber the first bullet. After that, well, it's an automatic, sir. It pretty much does the rest on its own. Here's the safety. Leave that on until you have to shoot. The magazine's loaded with Hydra-Shok hollowpoints. The gun's light. Should be light enough for you to use. But it's got plenty of stopping power."

Reen took the automatic. Heavy, not at all light. It looked very much like Hopkins's gun. His three-fingered hand and claw felt unwieldy on the grip.

The Secret Serviceman was young, earnest, and anxious. "About the assassination . . . are you worried we can't protect you? Or is

there something going on the Service should know about? I admired President Womack very much, sir. And I know he was fond of you. Both President Womack and President Kennedy left very specific instructions as to your safety. An agent hasn't been assigned to you, but that can be remedied. I can call—"

"Don't bother. It's nothing. I'm fine."

Reen took the gun and left. On the landing of the staircase he remembered to pull the slide to chamber the bullet. Then, despite what the agent had said, he flicked off the safety.

He took an old gym bag out of the desk drawer in Jeff Womack's study. Stuffing the gun into the tote, he walked into the bedroom and looked at the slumbering Cousins.

They seemed so peaceful, so innocent that some compassionate thing in Reen wanted to go away and leave them there.

"Oomal," he called.

In the dim blue light, one of the cocoons stirred.

Louder: "Oomal!"

Radalt pulled the sheet down from his face. Next to Radalt, Oomal grunted and shrugged himself out of his bonds.

"Get up. All of you need to get up. Don't bother bathing."

"Are you okay, Cousin?" Zoor asked, crawling out from his sheet. "You sound—"

"In three hours the army will attack. We have to get the recombinants off Earth."

Oomal's fingers slowly unhinged, and his sheet fluttered to the floor. "Get the Gerber commuter," he told his staff. "Fly up to one of the main ships to get more runners. There are twenty-one recombinant centers. I want them all cleared in two hours and those children up in space where they'll be safe."

Sakan made a graceless, overwrought gesture. "But what about the payroll? What are the workers going to do if we're not there to sign the checks?"

"It's all right," Oomal said. "Everything will be all right. Go on."

With troubled backward looks the Gerber execs left the room.

"She was here, wasn't she? Marian was here," Oomal said when they were alone.

"I want to go to West Virginia."

"Yes, that's fine, Reen. But I have a responsibility. The Community—"

"Oomal, think! Humans and Cousins are becoming extinct. If there is to be any future, we *must* save the children."

The truth hit Oomal like a blow. He looked around the room, bewildered, then shook his head to clear it. "The Community ship's over by the West Wing. We'll take that."

He hurried from the room, Reen after him. At their passage the maids looked up from their cleaning; the Secret Service agent in the colonnade glanced up from his daily report. The ship was parked on the lawn, Thural standing by it. His sleep must have been thin for him to awaken so early.

Thural's gaze flicked to Reen and then settled on Oomal.

"Get on the ship's net. Alert the Community at Andrews. Tell them to send the word out," Oomal called. "The humans are planning an attack."

Thural tipped his head as though he thought Oomal was making a poor joke.

"Do it now, Thural," Oomal said as he bounded onto the ramp, Reen at his heels. "And take us to West Virginia."

Thural followed them. "But I am under rebuke, Cousin."

"Just *do* it!"

"They will not believe me."

Oomal turned, his face contorted. "Goddamn it to hell, just *do* it!"

Stunned, Thural walked down the short hall to the navigation room.

When the ship lifted, Reen said, "I want you to take the children to Mars station."

Oomal stared out the window.

"Did you hear me?"

"Yes."

"I want you to keep them away from the rest of the Community. Promise me that."

Reen saw the glimmering string of lights along the George Washington Parkway blink out. For a moment he feared that it had something to do with the coming attack, then realized that it was only the automatic timer kicking in.

Time had come for the Cousins. Past time. In his mind he saw lights going out all over the universe.

"When you're safe," Reen said, "I'll go back to help the Community."

After a silence Oomal asked, "What do you have in that bag?"

"A gun."

"For Christ's sake. A gun?" Oomal's voice wavered between amusement and grief.

Reen looked out the window at the gold dawn streaking the sky. "Oomal, I shouldn't have trusted Marian."

Oomal hooked the side of Reen's tunic and drew him near. "Listen to me." His Brother was so close that Reen could smell the spice of sleep on him. "I loved my human employees. And in a few hours the whole truth will be out. They'll be wondering why I lied to them. They'll wonder how I could have eaten dinner in their homes and gone to Little League baseball games, all the while doing my best to make their race extinct. You don't have a corner on the guilt market."

They stood like that, perilously close, closer than Communal Law allowed, and together they watched the ship leave the lights of Fairfax County behind.

Reen put his finger to the emblem on his Brother's chest, thrilling at the contact of childhood Mind.

Oomal didn't move but looked at Reen in query.

"Intelligence," Reen whispered.

"Yes?"

"Both of us. We should have been more intelligent than to love the thing we were destroying."

It had snowed in the West Virginia mountains, and the trees were thick with white.

"You know?" Oomal said wistfully. "In Michigan we used to go sledding with the human kids. I'll miss the snow."

The snow. The trees. Oomal's humor. Angela's beautiful hands.

Reen and Oomal made their way from the ship. At the door they met Thural.

"Did you call ahead to warn them?" Oomal asked.

"I warned them, but I do not know if they believed me."

Oomal nodded. "You've done all you can. Go round up the West Virginia Cousins and get them on the main transport."

The children's house smelled of blueberry muffins. In the dining room the recombinants were having breakfast. As Reen and Oomal entered, Angela jumped up from the table and ran over to hug Reen's waist. His hand dropped to cradle the warm bulge of her cranium, the wisps of blond hair.

Quen came around the table, his expression furious. "You bring him here?"

"Get the children together, Quen," Oomal said. "Get them on board the transport. We're going to Mars station."

"Mars station is deserted!"

"Now, Quen." Oomal's face was strangely impassive. Shock? Reen wondered. Or an effort not to alarm the children?

Mrs. Gonzales emerged from the kitchen, a spatula in her hand.

"The army plans to attack the Cousins," Reen told her. "Stay here if you like. It will be safe enough for a while. We must take the children."

After a long, steady look at Reen, the caregiver bent down to Angela. "Come on, sweetie, let's get your clothes. We're all going for a ride together."

She ushered the children from the table and into the dormitories.

Quickly, without looking back, Reen hurried outside. Thural was

still standing by the commuter, pretending not to have noticed Reen's exit. Behind him the West Virginia Cousins were packing the transport to leave.

Stepping off the porch onto the snow, Reen went around to the side of the house, Jeff's gym bag bouncing at his side.

Tali had spies, Reen knew. Hopkins had been a teacher of deception, Tali a good student. The spy from West Virginia would have been told to keep an eye on Reen. Whoever the spy was, he would follow.

He heard the door of the house open. Heard footsteps crunch in the snow. He paused and looked over his shoulder. Quen was walking behind him, and Thural was a few paces back.

Seeing him stop, they stopped, too, and peered at the snowbound trees in a parody of innocence.

"Go back to the ship," Reen said.

Neither Cousin moved. Thural was engrossed in a tiny black-green pine, Quen in the eaves of the roof.

"Go back," Reen said. "Please." *Please, not Thural.*

Thural finally turned and made his way slowly to the other ship, his boots leaving blue-pooled indentations in the white.

Reen turned and kept walking, hearing the squeak of his own steps, of Quen's. Around a corner, in the center of a winter-blasted garden, he stopped and looked back. Quen was standing against the wall, beyond a row of spindly fig-tree corpses and the stick grave markers of withered tomato plants.

Reen unzipped the bag, took out the gun.

"Quen," he said.

The Cousin didn't look up.

It took both hands to lift the automatic. Reen sighted to the center of Quen's chest, just to the left of the lightning bolt.

"Quen," he said in low apology and pulled the trigger.

A sky-splitting crack. Reen's arms were jerked up over his head. Quen was flung backward. Blood sprayed the white wall, the snow.

On the ground Quen made a little sound, like someone surprised by bad news. He put his hand to his chest and then stared idiotically at the brown covering his palm.

Reen approached, and Quen finally looked up, looked right at him despite Communal law. His eyes were terrified.

It would take only a few minutes; Cousins never took long to die. But Reen couldn't walk away and leave him. He lifted the gun again. Quen raised his hand as though to ward off the bullet.

The explosion made Reen's ears ring. Quen's hand dropped. Without a single tremor, without another breath, he lay still.

Reen slipped the gun back into the bag. When he walked around to the front of the house, he saw Oomal and Thural by the door of the transport. The children were boarding.

There was horror in Oomal's face. "Reen? My God. I thought I heard—"

"No one will report back to Tali now. You're safe enough. I'll go to Anacostia and try to warn the Cousins."

Angela stood in the line of children at the ship, making a snowball. When she saw Reen, she stopped her play and ran over, flailing in the ankle-deep snow. He sank to one knee and gathered his daughter to him.

Too bad, oh, too bad. If only he had broad shoulders and a wide strong back, he wouldn't have failed her. He could have kept the world at bay.

"Go for a ride, Daddy," she said.

"Yes," he whispered into her hair.

The human need for embraces, it must have something to do with never wanting to let go. Angela against him, stomach to stomach, chest to chest, furnished him with a sort of magic. A daughter-shaped impression that, if his mind ever failed to remember, his body would never forget.

"Reen. It's getting late." Oomal took Angela by the shoulders and gently pulled her from her father.

Reen couldn't get up. The cold snow had soaked his uniform so

that he couldn't feel his legs. Angela, standing next to Oomal, was looking at him as gravely as any Cousin. Her thumb was in her mouth. Then Oomal turned her around and walked her inside. Kneeling there, Reen watched his whole world rise, round and silver, into the robin's-egg-blue day.

36

The house was empty, but not in the way Langley had been. It was as if the house had simply taken a breath and in a moment the children would return, carried on the warm, muffin-scented wind, to pick up the doll left on the chair, the mittens forgotten on the floor.

Reen slid his finger down one side of the long breakfast-strewn table and thought he could feel in the wood the vibration of high piping voices, of laughter, of small running feet.

The house remembered. It would remember for a long, long time.

Finally, hefting the tote, he walked out to the small runner they had left him. A glance at his watch. He was surprised to see it was only twenty minutes to eight, time enough to finish his duty.

All duties finished sometime, he thought as he lifted the ship into the clear morning air. All projects, all lives had an end. If he could, he would go to Mars when he was done. There he would spin out the remainder of his days, watching his daughter grow up and his own race die.

In a few centuries the Cousins would fade in the new race's memory like photographs in a family album. But the children wouldn't completely forget.

Here's my grandfather. He had a farm in Ohio.

Reen remembered looking at the family album Jeff had once placed in his lap.

And my grandfather on my father's side. Here. Here's a picture of him in Poland.

Perhaps Angela's children would inherit from the humans that specific love of family rather than the Cousins' generic love of race. If they did, Reen would grow old and sweet and distant, as Jeff's round-faced grandfather in Poland or the laughing Ohio farmer with his arm around his pudgy wife.

Below Reen, a few early risers in Falls Church were going outside to pick their papers from the lawn. Cars drove in a leisurely Saturday morning pace to the store or a weekend shift of work. It all looked very peaceful.

He took a moment to fly past the White House one more time, and even that huge building seemed sleepy. Angling southeast, he sailed over the poor neighborhoods of Washington and the boats bobbing on the sparkling Potomac. A few minutes later he lowered the ship on the flat center of hard white spume that was the Cousin complex in Anacostia.

The bag over his shoulder, he strode past the parked ships to the nearest door. A Cousin in the hall, apparently recognizing Reen, hurriedly turned his face away.

Reen said, "I know you're not supposed to hear me, but I came to bring you news, and you must listen. The humans will attack in an hour. Call everyone together and get them to safety."

The Cousin walked down the hall, and Reen couldn't be sure he was going to warn the others. He headed to one of the communication centers and on the way passed a Brother.

"Kredin?" he asked.

Kredin's eyes immediately sought sanctuary on the floor. Reen put out a claw to stop him, but Kredin changed course slightly to avoid the touch.

"The humans will attack in a little while," Reen said to the retreating back. "Get everyone together and into the ships." He watched

his Brother disappear around a curve in the corridor. Kredin did not quicken his stride.

As Reen walked toward the communication modules, he lifted his arm to look at the Rolex and stopped mid-stride. The time.

Time had run out.

It was nine o'clock. When he had looked at the watch before, it was twenty to nine, not twenty to eight. He had never learned to read anything but a digital.

He ran headlong down the corridor. Ahead stood three Cousins in a gossipy knot.

"Get out!" Reen screamed as he raced toward them, the wet soles of his boots beating a frantic slap-slap on the soft shiny floor.

They turned in tandem, curiosity and disgust in their eyes. And in tandem they looked away.

Reen ran. His breath came in hard painful gulps. The gun bumped crazily at his side. At the first communications module, his feet nearly slid out from under him, and he grabbed a doorjamb to stay his fall.

In the room a Cousin sat before a screen, calmly talking to another Cousin in another communications room. He looked up, then jerked his head away.

"Who are you talking to?"

The Cousin didn't answer. He continued his calm conversation.

Reen pushed him out of the chair and shouted into the terminal. "Tell everyone! The humans are attacking!"

The distant Cousin on the screen stood and walked away. The Cousin on the floor got to his feet and brushed at his uniform.

"Go to the ships and lift off! Lift off!" Reen shrieked into the terminal. He punched the controls. "Get to the ships and lift off!"

The floor slipped a little beneath him. He staggered. The Cousin on the floor uttered an astonished cry, and the building moved again.

Reen pounded the controls so hard, his hand went numb. "Get to the ships!"

The walls and floor shook. With a wail of terror, the Cousin ran to the hall.

The next explosion was more than motion; it was sound, too. A bass rumble, and tenor Cousin shrieks. Somewhere in the complex a wall had been breached.

Reen ran into the hall, pulling the gun from the bag. Ahead of him Cousins were standing stock-still, watching smoke pour down the corridor.

"Run!" he shouted. But they didn't run. They couldn't. Cousins were genetically incapable of either fight or flight.

Suddenly soldiers, too, were running in the corridor. Reen watched as a man ran a tiny Cousin down and crushed his head against the wall.

Reen lifted the gun and fired. The man reeled back a couple of steps, then tried to rush Reen, but his legs weren't working well and he toppled.

The humans looked up from their murder like lions disturbed from a kill. Their arms were brown to the elbow with blood, and their eyes were wild with strange excitement.

They blocked the only exit Reen knew. He didn't know how to get out. Far to the back of the building he could hear the high, thin cries of the dying.

The closest soldier lifted his rifle and aimed it at Reen. Cousins didn't understand battle, they didn't understand killing, but what they knew was quickness. Precision. The automatic in Reen's hand barked once, and the man fell. The other soldiers retreated.

No one had told them a Cousin would fight back, Reen thought as he fled down a right-hand hall. Marian must have promised it would be easy.

A Cousin hunkered in a corner, babbling. Reen tried to grab him, but the Cousin pulled away.

"Come with me!" Reen urged.

The Cousin's small body shook. He had wrapped his arms around his knees, as if to make himself a smaller target. His mouth kept moving.

Reen left him.

The smoke was so thick that Reen wasn't sure in which direction he was going. Around a bend, the peppery sweet smell of blood hit him, and he saw that the corridor was littered with black-uniformed bodies. A section of the ceiling had fallen, exposing the building to a flood of sunlight. At his feet a severed Cousin head lay like a gray basketball.

Reen ran down another hall. Near the end were two doors. He blundered through the one on the right, into blue. The blue of nests. The blue of sleep. It was silent, everything in order. The meditation room was cool and serene in the manner of Cousins.

He lowered the gun and noticed that his arms were aching. The room greeted him with its distant welcome, as it might have greeted anyone. A smell in it of calm, and the light, heady spice of rest.

Looking down, he saw that his uniform and his boots were filthy. How tired he suddenly was. The gun dropped from his fingers and hit the floor with a clank.

He gasped, realizing he had very nearly dozed off. Not sleep. No, not at all. The little death.

Panicky, he bent and grabbed the gun. The little death tugging at him, he whirled to the door. It opened, and he was facing a human.

The man was in camouflage. His helmet was off, his uniform blouse askew. His eyes widened at Reen's unexpected appearance. His right hand came up, lifting a pistol.

There was no hatred in the man's face, only mild surprise, as though he had met someone he recognized at a party. *Oh, hello,* he might have said, *and how are you?* Instead, he fired.

Reen heard the boom, saw the flame from the muzzle, felt hot gunpowder stipple his cheek. Before the soldier could pull the trigger again, Reen fired. The man crumpled.

Reen squeezed himself through the left door the moment it started opening. Outside, the air was cold, the wind rank with oily smoke. Ahead of him the Cousin ships sat untenanted on their pads. He ran to the nearest and threw himself into the seat. As the ship lifted, he looked down.

All of Anacostia was burning, and the ruins of the Cousin center squatted in that inferno, one entire side of it open to the smoky sky.

Reen clipped the control ball southeast, and the ship hurled itself over Suitland Parkway toward Andrews. Tanks were moving on the Beltway, and fighter planes sailed the bright air.

As he passed over Andrews, what he saw made him weak. Loving Helpers were stacked at the fences, thousands and thousands of Loving Helpers, eight and ten deep.

At the Cousin Place he settled the ship onto the tarmac. Cousins were moving back and forth from the building to the largest ships, carrying boxes. Reen trotted past them to the door where Tali and the Sleep Master were standing.

"Forget the supplies and records," Reen told them. "Just get on the ship. Anacostia's on fire."

Tali looked away, but the Sleep Master didn't. He stared hard into Reen's eyes.

"The Helpers won't stop them!" Reen's voice rose in frustration. "Listen to me. They have guns! They have a new toxin. They— The Helpers won't get close enough to them to matter!"

The Sleep Master looked at Reen with contempt. "Leave. Go where you wish. You are not wanted here."

Perhaps because the Sleep Master had spoken, Tali at last found the courage to turn around. "It is your fault. All of it. Your fault. Go to your humans. See if they love you now."

Reen could hear the faraway rattle of machine-gun fire and the first reedy screams of the Helpers.

A bomber flew low, thunder in its wake. The ground shook. The Cousins carrying boxes ducked. And the entire western perimeter of Andrews went up in black smoke and red flame. It was as though the sky let go a cloudburst of fire.

From the throats of the few surviving Helpers came a shrill lamentation. Tali clapped his hands over his ears.

The Sleep Master's face changed. "Quick," he said to Tali. "Get the Cousins on board."

Tali hesitated. His hands dropped. "The Helpers . . ."

"Gone. All that are not gone are insane. Get the Cousins now."

Reen saw small bodies dancing in the hellish flames, saw demented Helpers, their mouths wide, running in panicked circles.

"Leave here," the Sleep Master told Reen.

"Yes," Reen said, nodding. "Yes."

He walked wearily to the nearest runner but halted when he saw the huge shape emerging from the building. Large as a room, slow and ponderous as a cloud. Sunlight turned the female's skin pearlescent.

Tali was barking orders, and the Cousins attending the female were trying to avoid her tail. She flowed over the tarmac, her body rippling.

Reen called to the Sleep Master, "This is wrong! The female never leaves the chamber! Let her die!"

The Sleep Master's eyes were as dark and expressionless as berries.

"You can't take a full-grown female on the ship! The attraction of the Communal Mind will be too strong! The Cousins can't fight it! She'll kill someone! You know that!"

The Sleep Master turned away.

The Cousins were trying to nudge the creature up the ramp, but she was balking. Terrified of approaching too close, they were prodding her with sticks, with raised voices.

She wasn't moving. And Reen knew that Tali wouldn't let the ships leave without her.

Without stopping to consider the enormity of it, Reen put his hand into the bag and brought out the gun. Tali saw him first. His mouth dropped. He held up his hand like a policeman ordering traffic to stop.

Around him Cousins were shouting, shouting at the stubborn female, shouting at Reen. Their voices were all but drowned out by the screeches of the Loving Helpers.

With shaking hands, Reen aimed. In front of him, Cousins scattered. Even Tali stepped away. The female inched around as though she was planning a return to the building.

Something hit Reen in the back. He staggered, fought to keep himself upright. But lethargy sucked him down. Over his shoulder he caught a glimpse of the Sleep Master's face.

The gun dropped from Reen's hand and clattered to the asphalt. He felt a claw rake his side only to be stopped by something hard in his pocket. Remotely he felt the Sleep Master's question the instant before they were both claimed by the murk of Communal Mind.

"The tape," he whispered.

37

Blue. An eerie and empty nest blue. A sensation of heaviness and a vague ache in his chest. Reen hung in sleep like a sodden log below a river's surface.

He drifted, wanted to sink further, but there was no drag of Communal Mind to pull him down. Unable to sink, he tried to rise but was swept by a current of exhaustion. In a timeless eddy he waited until, with a groan, he forced himself to sit up.

He was in a nest; the niches around him were vacant, haunted not by Communal Mind but by stale and long-abandoned spice. He swung his legs out and tried to stand, but his rubbery knees nearly gave out on him. Another smell overlaid the sleep: a fetid smell of human decay. He looked down at himself and saw that his uniform was stiff with dried blood.

Holding on to a wall for balance, he walked the empty tomb of the nest. Was this Andrews? And if so, where were the Cousins? Had they left him to face the humans alone?

He paused at the entrance to a hall. Ceiling lights sensed his presence and lit up in welcoming sequence. At the end of the hall was a door. He walked to it and found that it was locked. He rested there a while, leaning against the wall, letting his body, then his mind, gather the energy for the long trek to the baths.

The baths were neat and vacant. When he stripped off his uniform, he noticed the tape recorder was gone. Just below the center of his chest was a perfectly round bruise with an angry brown dot at its center. When he lowered himself into the water, he saw that his arms and legs were trembling, as if he had slept three hundred years and awakened palsied with age.

When he had finished bathing, he limped up the steps of the pool, found a uniform in a nearby closet, and put it on. Then he walked aimlessly through the strange silence of the abandoned nest, feeling a loneliness so keen that he wished he could end it by crawling into a niche and pulling oblivion in after him.

Where were they? Where were the Cousins? Why had they left him alone? He remembered the video of the Helper, how, without sight but with unerring precision, it had sensed the location of its Brothers.

Circling past the hall again, he stopped. The lights were blazing, and at the end near the door, Tali and the Sleep Master waited.

"The little death clings to you, Reen," the Sleep Master said. "You slept, and I thought you would die from it."

With that, he turned. The door opened for him, and he and Tali walked through.

Reen followed. The neighboring room was pale gray. Against a curved wall on the left was a row of chairs, where Tali seated himself. To the right, a single window looked out on a barren plain above which hung a slice of turquoise Earth.

Reen walked to the window and looked across the moon's dry sea. To either side of him the huge Cousin complex rose in stately billows that made Reen feel light-headed and small, like a bird lost among clouds.

His eyes rose to the white-whorled Earth. Over the eastern Pacific was a storm, dazzling as new-fallen snow. Reen wondered how they would live with the news, this fecund race gone barren. He wondered with what savage grief they would cling to the last of their children.

He took a breath. "How long have I been asleep?"

"Two weeks," the Sleep Master said. "I came every day to see if you were breathing. To touch you and feel your thoughts."

Reen pictured the old Cousin's hand on him, examining him for life as Reen had once examined Tali. He remembered feeling the darkness in his Brother and wondered if what the Sleep Master felt had been sadness. "There was a recorder in my pocket. It's not there now."

The Sleep Master said, "I have it."

"And?"

"I will keep it." The Sleep Master walked to Reen, stopped just at his shoulder, and looked out the window. "The Community is nearly gone."

Reen put a steadying hand to the wall. "How many were saved?"

"Forty-three."

Forty-three out of more than three thousand. The humans had nearly destroyed the Community.

"Never before have we waged war, Reen, and for good reason. The Cousins cannot sleep with visions of blood and death in their minds."

Of course the Cousins couldn't sleep. The butchery was over, but chaos possessed the collective Mind. As Reen himself had learned with the murders of Hopkins and Quen, killing was best done at a distance.

Kill but do not look, his ancestors might have said. *If you look, you will see brain on the floor. If you look, you will see your victim beg for mercy. If you dare look, you will see a beloved world die.*

History was supposed to be instructive, but Reen had ignored its lessons. He had wanted to know Angela's other parent, that hot-blooded human half, and had ended up with his Brothers' blood on his hands.

Three thousand Cousins. And how many humans? One last short generation, and he would kill them all.

He looked up. The Sleep Master was regarding him thoughtfully. "Tali cannot lead," he said.

Hope stirred in Reen's chest.

"So you must abdicate."

With a final exhausted twitch, hope died. "If you want me to leave . . ."

"There are those who would leave with you. Who are still loyal. It would deplete the Community even further. Tali needs you to acknowledge him as First, and that is what I am asking."

Reen shot an angry look at Tali. "He is no innocent. The tape . . ."

Tali jumped to his feet. "You are the one who brought this destruction on our heads, not me. You are the one who trusted humans too much, who—"

The Sleep Master whirled to Tali. "Silence!" he roared. "You will be silent! And take your seat! Remember, Tali-ja, that Reen is your Brother!"

Tali quickly sat.

"You can't do this," Reen argued. "Even under rebuke you can't let him be First. If you have heard what the tape says, then you know Tali has no heart for rule."

The Sleep Master took his eyes from Reen and let them rest on the star-strung space in the window. "I know he has no heart, and I know now where your heart belongs. But what matters is that the Community find its way out of turmoil. Tali was always the more ordered, the more disciplined Brother, so it is Tali we need. But Tali knows that should he seek revenge on the humans, I will use the tape against him." The old Cousin's expression softened. "Reen, I will hold your wishes dear, as though they were my own."

The Sleep Master was asking him to die. Reen opened his mouth, found himself saying, "How?"

Would they give him back the gun and leave him alone in the room, as courteous humans used to do with even more courteous traitors? Or would they open the door to the vacuum and expect him to walk outside?

"The sleep is thin, and only one thing can make it better. You have been tested and found viable. Go meditate your decision now,

as custom dictates. Remember, not for Tali's goals but for simple, full sleep this is what we must do."

Simple, full sleep. Reen's exhaustion was back. His head was heavy, his arms and legs felt weighted, and he fought to swim against the current of the old Cousin's words. Somewhere in that cold numbing deluge was meaning, but Reen was too tired to find it.

"I have chosen you to be consort," the Sleep Master said.

38

Reen wandered the echoing halls that once had teemed with Cousins. He had brought extinction on his Community too quickly, too soon. He thought he could avoid the unavoidable with Angela. Fifty years of dreams.

He wanted to see her grow up. Wanted to know and love her children. He should have gone with Oomal while he had the chance. Even now he could escape to Mars, where Thural and Oomal and Angela waited.

Guilt stopped him; remorse brought him back. Angela was only his hope. Cousins, no matter how doomed, were his future.

When he returned to the room, he found three Cousins waiting. Two were standing together at the window. The third rose at his approach.

That Cousin. That unfamiliar Cousin.

"He has come a long way to see you," the Sleep Master said, turning.

Beside the Sleep Master, Thural turned, too. One final betrayal: Thural had left the children. Reen's pulse slowed as if it were coming to a stop.

"Reen," Thural said, hands fluttering. "Oomal didn't go to Mars. He went home."

Bewildered, Reen tipped his head to one side.

"Home," Thural explained. "He went through the Window to Setis. The home place."

Setis. The planet with a sky as blue as Earth's. Reen remembered the vast buildings riding the red oceans of its grass.

Oomal had taken Angela home.

The Sleep Master pointed nervously to the solemn wordless Cousin. "Mito-ja. Cousin First Brother of home place."

Beside the fretful Sleep Master and the embarrassed Thural, Mito stood as Reen himself must have once stood, as they all must have stood before being tainted by human impatience. With slow inevitability, Mito turned to regard Thural and the Sleep Master.

He did not order them away. He did not speak at all. But after a hesitant moment, the pair left.

The hush in Mito's eyes was spellbinding. *How beautiful he is,* Reen thought. And how alien. Reen had become accustomed to fleeting human expressions. Had become inured to faces in which fear, bemusement, and irritation chased and tumbled after each other like puppies.

Mito was an elegant still life.

"I come," Mito-ja finally said, "for Brother's love for Brother."

Reen felt the habit-formed human urge to ask Mito to sit down. He restrained himself and stood, feeling awkward.

"Oomal sends his message." Mito's words were eerily deliberate. If a mountain could speak, it would speak like this.

"The message is that he has done as he saw best, to seek my protection."

Reen looked at the floor and was silent so long that he thought Mito would leave. A human, an Earth Cousin, would have. But when Reen finally looked up, Mito was watching him, the universe in his eyes.

Reen shuddered. The Cousin First Brother of home was no ordinary Cousin sheltered from alien contact. No. Mito was a completely unfamiliar thing.

The First Brother of Setis was so still that for a moment Reen wondered if he was conversing with a ghost. Then Mito said, "Oomal wishes you to know that the children are welcome."

"Will they live with you?"

With stately grace Mito raised his hands. "We tunnel," he said.

"I don't understand."

"We tunnel. The aboveground no longer interests us."

We tunnel. Perhaps that was the solution every Cousin should have sought. Mito seemed larger, taller than other Cousins, and Reen wondered if it was poise alone that lent him height.

"Will Oomal live with you?" Would Oomal succumb to Mito's tranquility—that heady, abbreviated end to Cousin evolution?

Mito made a regal gesture with one arm, as though he were sweeping away thirty million years of history. "Oomal is *nadiye*. He is other." He gazed at Reen—sadly, it seemed, if the sea, the sky, could be thought sad. "You are, all of you, *nadiye*."

Without another word he left the room.

Reen watched the door close and fought the urge to run after. There was so much he longed to ask.

Did I fail, then? was the obvious question.

From that long black tunnel which led to extinction, Reen had plucked the closest and easiest answer. Mito had chosen the hard way: reaching farther than an arm's length.

Do I disappoint you?

The answer was plain. Mito had taken the Community in his keeping to where life was as ordered as crystalline structure. And in that unemotional order there was no place for disappointment. No room for heartache.

The door opened. The Sleep Master walked in and stood by the door as motionless as Mito, but stiffly. "I did not think to give you food. You might be hungry."

"No."

"So. Will you come?"

Before he lost his courage, Reen straightened his tunic. Taking a deep breath, he walked through the doorway.

He followed the Sleep Master down the hall to the right, down the next gray, sloping passageway. Down and down. In front of the female's chamber was a wall painted pale yellow in warning. There a knot of Cousins waited.

Reen came to a halt and stared at Tali, the Brother who had seemed most ordered until Mito came to show them the true pattern. If Reen had been wrong to cheat destiny for Cousin survival, Tali, so loyal to the old laws, had been wrong, too.

Reen's eyes must have contained something of his contempt because Tali quickly looked away.

"You do this willingly?" the Sleep Master asked.

Reen regarded the gathered Cousins one by one. No matter how much he loved Angela's new race, no matter how much he loved the humans, the Community always came first.

He caught Thural's eye. His aide would not have been able to live comfortably among the too-human Michigan Cousins, but he was too corrupted by alien contact for Mito to take in. Thural, in sympathy, Reen supposed, was trembling.

Reen walked on. As he neared the yellow wall, it opened. Inside was another wall, the next-to-last barrier, paler than the first.

DANGER, DANGER, the color said.

When Reen's people first left their nests in the earth and sought food and room above, the gleam of the yellow sun meant death. From its radiance fanged predators swooped. After thirty million years all that remained of those deadly hunters was the color from which they had come. Everything ended. Everything.

Turning aside to the antechamber, Reen pulled off his uniform and, for the second time that day, slipped into the bath. The ocher water was acidic and soothing. He washed until he was free of all human smells.

Nude, dripping, he walked up the steps to the second yellow wall and saw the Sleep Master standing there. They didn't speak. Dipping

his head slightly, the old Cousin gathered Reen's uniform from the table where he had left it. Then he retreated to safety, where he would stand at the window and watch Reen die.

Reen stood, water droplets from his body making dark pimples on the floor. Suddenly he realized that he had gone through the ritual without having answered the Sleep Master's question.

He wanted to blunder back through the safe wall and shout "Yes! Yes!" to the Cousins waiting there.

But willingly? Die willingly? All the other decisions he had made had hurt those around him. And how could he watch as the rest of Earth Community declined?

We tunnel, Mito had said. All intelligent creatures tunneled. The burrowing itself should have been enough. It was for Mito. But Reen, digging for truth, had unearthed spurious and faulty answers.

His body had always been the ordered part of him, had always done the correct thing. Now, like a law-abiding good citizen, it moved him toward the second door. Beyond that would be the third door. The last. Between the two he would pause for a while, and gather his courage.

The door opened to cloudy light, and as he stepped through, it shut fast. The air was heavy with spice and with the narcotic torpor of Communal Mind. He halted in confusion. Instead of the final yellow wall there was a vast dim chamber where a huge shape moved.

High-voltage terror. Reen's heart raced into a frantic beat. He had made a terrible mistake. In those few paces from the second door he had somehow got lost and missed the meditation room.

Mito's stoicism now failed him, as did the Cousin instinct to stand and die. Reen whirled to the door and was dumbfounded that it didn't open.

He pounded his fists against the yellow wall even as he realized that it wasn't meant to open. No consort was that willing, not at the end. And that was the reason behind the final trick for the condemned: that missing meditation room.

A Cousin was watching him from the chamber's small window. Not the Sleep Master.

"Tali!"

Reen ran to the window and slapped his hands to either side of his Brother's face. His claws screeched against the glass.

"Tali, please!"

In his Brother's eyes was an expression so unexpected that Reen barely recognized him; for shame came naturally to Cousins, but repentance had to be taught. Tali lifted his fists to the glass as though he wanted to batter down the wall between them.

Too late. There was a slap on Reen's leg. His skin flamed from ankle to hip as the thick burr of the female's stingers pulled away. He howled and leaped to the side. His leg crumpled. He hit the wall with a thump and lay there, dazed.

"Tali?" he whispered. "I changed my mind, Tali."

A curious nudge at his hip brought him instantly alert. It was the female. Reen limped to the far side of the chamber. She was watching him, her eyes bright, not with intelligence but with something like cunning.

The huge body shifted.

The burning sensation was gone. Now tendrils of ice sprouted from his knee. He took another step, realized too late that his leg was numb, and toppled, his fingers splayed on the soft floor.

Something touched his arm.

"Tali!" he shouted and snapped his head around.

Pigeons on the south lawn. Pigeons, the feathers at their necks gleaming rainbow shades of emerald and lavender-pink.

"Pigeons," Marian said. "I like pigeons. They graze just like cattle, don't they?"

Reen looked at the fat compact bodies dotting the grass.

"A whole herd of pigeons." Marian laughed. "Must be forty head of pigeons."

And, just then, one took to the air. Reen's eyes followed it. Against his face it seemed he could feel the dry flutter of its wings.

Marian put her hand on his shoulder, and love rose in him like baking bread, a love so different, so alien, that it took his breath away.

He grasped her hand and held it, as though afraid that she, too, would take flight. He held her so hard that his claw must have dug into her flesh. He held her. He held Marian. And she didn't pull away.

The pigeons were gone, and the opalescent skin of the female was right against Reen's face. He tried to rise and failed. The vaginal tube detached from the base of the female's tail and wavered, as if trying to catch his scent.

Run, he told himself, just as he had shouted to the doomed Anacostia Cousins. Run.

He tried to pick himself up but fell, burdened by drowsy spice, by the stupor of Communal Mind. Numb, he tried to think. Something was happening. Something . . . Then he remembered he was dying.

Reen watched the tube approach. It was fluted, the outside pearl, the inside a rich golden brown.

The air was thick with the waxy smell of crayons. Kevin, large gray head down, was coloring a kitten. Beside Reen, Angela was working to fill in the stark, simple lines of a horse. Her small hands held the crayon in a stranglehold, and she sighed in disappointment when the brown strayed outside the lines.

Don't try so hard, he wanted to tell her, but then Angela had something of the Cousin drive for perfection. Warning would do no good.

She colored, she colored, her expression as intent as that of an engineer working on the blueprint of a bridge, or of a physicist laboring over an equation.

"I love you," he told her, swelling with so much affection that it seemed his chest might rupture.

She stopped coloring to look up. Kevin looked up, too. And at the end of the table Mrs. Gonzales paused in tutoring a clumsy Michelle to look at Reen in wonder.

"I love you," he told his daughter.

Angela went back to her coloring book. "I love you, too," she said.

An ache. Disoriented, Reen looked down at his chest. The female had already pushed his plates apart and had burrowed inside. He gasped as he felt the first sucking theft of sperm.

Run, he told himself. But he couldn't.

Desire blossomed from her touch, desire as quick and disabling as the ice of her drugs. He groaned and shoved the tough muscle of her deeper. His greedy hands reached out to the iridescent flesh, his claws digging, pulling her closer.

His body shuddered as lust gave way to satiation. His insides loosened. There was a gout of pain as his lungs tore free.

Oomal was handing him a box all wrapped in colored paper while humans gathered around the birth, their eyes as wide as Cousins' and black and deep as night.

"Open it, First Brother," Oomal said with shy, fierce pride. "Open it for Angela."

Reen ripped the paper. It bled and shrieked. And from Reen's hands blue worlds spilled out like doves.

When the planets had spun away, Oomal spread his arms. Reen had forgotten how warm, how soft his Brother's body could be.

Love, that never-ending thing. If only Marian had seen their daughter grow from a single cell, maybe then she would roll her name around in her mouth like candy.

Angela, small as a mustard seed, tiny as faith.

Angela, large as an arm's span.

In a wash of pewter light from the window Jeff Womack sat rocking, a gun stoppering his mouth. His silent eyes met Reen's, and there was something like ecstasy in them.

Oh, how strange, Reen thought. The Old Ones loomed in the chamber like mountains, while in front of him, under a female, a Cousin lay motionless and nearly consumed.

I must be dreaming.

Reen was a tiny creature, growing smaller, a being on the intoxicating edge of disappearance. He clutched at the rim of oblivion until he realized that there was nothing to hold on to, and no reason to be afraid of the fall.

Yes, the Old Ones breathed. *You are.*